CLASSICAL PRESENCES

General Editors
Lorna Hardwick   James I. Porter

CLASSICAL PRESENCES

Attempts to receive the texts, images, and material culture of ancient Greece and Rome inevitably run the risk of appropriating the past in order to authenticate the present. Exploring the ways in which the classical past has been mapped over the centuries allows us to trace the avowal and disavowal of values and identities, old and new. Classical Presences brings the latest scholarship to bear on the contexts, theory, and practice of such use, and abuse, of the classical past.

Remembering Parthenope

*The Reception of Classical Naples
from Antiquity to the Present*

Edited by
JESSICA HUGHES
AND CLAUDIO BUONGIOVANNI

OXFORD
UNIVERSITY PRESS

OXFORD
UNIVERSITY PRESS

Great Clarendon Street, Oxford, OX2 6DP,
United Kingdom

Oxford University Press is a department of the University of Oxford.
It furthers the University's objective of excellence in research, scholarship,
and education by publishing worldwide. Oxford is a registered trade mark of
Oxford University Press in the UK and in certain other countries

© Oxford University Press 2015

The moral rights of the authors have been asserted

First Edition published in 2015

Impression: 1

Published in the United States of America by Oxford University Press
198 Madison Avenue, New York, NY 10016, United States of America

British Library Cataloguing in Publication Data
Data available

Library of Congress Control Number: 2014946088

ISBN 978–0–19–967393–3

Printed and bound by
CPI Group (UK) Ltd, Croydon, CR0 4YY

Acknowledgements

In putting this book together we have incurred several debts. Firstly, we are extremely grateful to the *Classical Presences* series editors, Lorna Hardwick and James I. Porter, for encouraging this project, and to Hilary O'Shea and Annie Rose at OUP for their patience and enthusiasm. We also thank our anonymous OUP reviewers for giving us some crucial advice both in the early stages of preparation and after the initial submission of the manuscript. Other people who offered us help of different sorts include Vaishnavi Ananthasubramanyam, Rowena Anketell, Joanna Brown, Adriana Buongiovanni, Benedetto De Martino, Bruno De Martino, Alida Ferrara, Helen Hughes, Linda Hughes, Janet Huskinson, Dunstan Lowe, Clelia Riccardi, Antonia Ruppel, Julia Spain, and Sue Zacharias. Finally, we are grateful to our colleagues of the Dipartimento di Studi Umanistici at the University of Naples Federico II and the Department of Classical Studies at The Open University.

C.B. and J.H.

Contents

List of Figures   ix
List of Contributors   xiii

1. Introduction: Entering the Siren's City
   Claudio Buongiovanni and Jessica Hughes   1

PART I. CLASSICAL NAPLES IN ANTIQUITY

2. Setting the Agenda: The Image of Classical Naples in
   Strabo's *Geography* and Other Ancient Literary Sources   19
   Lorenzo Miletti

3. The Temple of the Dioscuri and the Mythic Origins
   of Neapolis   39
   Rabun Taylor

4. Colonizing the Past: Cultural Memory and Civic Identity
   in Hellenistic and Roman Naples   64
   Kathryn Lomas

5. Greek Magistrates in Roman Naples? Law and Memory
   from the Fourth Century BC to the Fourth Century AD   85
   Mauro De Nardis

6. Between Classical and Modern Naples: 'Cultural Forgetting'
   at the Time of the Gothic War   105
   Giovanni Polara

PART II. CLASSICAL NAPLES AFTER ANTIQUITY

7. *Marmora Romana* in Medieval Naples: Architectural
   Spolia from the Fourth to the Fifteenth Centuries AD   121
   Angela Palmentieri

8. *Virgiliana Neapolis Urbs*: Receptions of Classical Naples
   in the Swabian and Early Angevin Ages   152
   Fulvio Delle Donne

9. Naples—A Poets' City: Attitudes towards Statius and
   Virgil in the Fifteenth Century   170
   Giancarlo Abbamonte

10. Memories from the Subsoil: Discovering Antiquities
    in Fifteenth-Century Naples and Campania   189
    Bianca de Divitiis

11. City Branding and the Antique: Naples in Early
    Modern City Guides   217
    Harald Hendrix

12. *Ex dirutis marmoribus*: The Theatines and the Columns
    of the Temple of the Dioscuri in Naples   242
    Fulvio Lenzo

13. Reshaping the Past, Shaping the Present: Andrea de Jorio
    and Naples' Classical Heritage   266
    Annalisa Marzano

14. 'No Retreat, Even When Broken': Classical Ruins
    in the *Presepe Napoletano*   284
    Jessica Hughes

AFTERWORDS

15. Neapolis and the Future of Naples' Museums   311
    Stefano De Caro

16. Parthenope on the Metro: or, Links with the Past,
    on the Journey into the Future   317
    Luigi Spina

Bibliography   323
Index   367

List of Figures

1.1 The 'Corpo di Napoli' sculpture, Piazzetta Nilo, Naples   2

3.1 Naples, facade of the church of S. Paolo Maggiore with standing remains of the temple of the Dioscuri   40

3.2 Detail of an ink drawing of the pediment at S. Paolo Maggiore   41

3.3 Anonymous sketch of the facade of S. Paolo Maggiore   43

3.4 Didrachm of Neapolis, c.300–275 BC   44

3.5 Reconstruction of the pedimental sculpture of the temple of Via S. Gregorio, Rome, c.150 BC   50

3.6 Copies of sculptures of two members of the Julio-Claudian dynasty found in situ at the macellum in Pompeii   51

3.7 Statues of the two Dioscuri from the vicinity of the temple   54

3.8 Model of the temple of the Dioscuri on display at Complesso Monumentale S. Lorenzo Maggiore, Naples   55

3.9 Terracotta pedimental figures of the 'Grande Tempio' at Luni, second century BC   56

4.1 Naples: street plan and limits of the Graeco-Roman city   68

4.2 Naples: major Roman buildings. 1: S. Paolo Maggiore (temple of the Dioscuri); 2: S. Lorenzo Maggiore (macellum); 3: theatre and odeion; 4: Carminello ai Mannesi (insula and baths); 5: S. Gregorio Armeno (insula); 6: Donnaregina Nuova (baths); 7: Archivio di Banco di Napoli (houses); 8: Duomo (Greek and Roman buildings); 9: Palazzo Corigliano (Roman houses); 10: Piazza Nicola Amore (portico and temple of imperial cult; possible site of gymnasium)   68

7.1 Plan of Naples marked with locations of reused material. 1: Pietrasanta complex; 2: S. Paolo Maggiore—(temple of the Dioscuri); 3: S. Lorenzo Maggiore; 4: S. Restituta, Duomo, and Stefania; 5: Carminello ai Mannesi; 6: S. Giorgio Maggiore; 7: S. Agostino alla Zecca; 8: Piazza Nicola Amore (temple of imperial cult; agonistic inscriptions; gymnasium); 9: S. Giovanni a Mare (the 'Capa di Napoli'); 10: S. Eligio Maggiore; 11: S. Agata degli Orefici; 12: Palazzo of Diomede Carafa; 13: Palazzo of Carlo Carafa; 14: Piazzetta Nilo (the 'Corpo di Napoli'); 15: S. Maria della Rotonda; 16: Pappacoda chapel; 17: S. Giovanni Maggiore; 18: Piazza Giovanni Bovio (marble arch); 19: S. Chiara; 20: S. Antoniello a Port'Alba   122

7.2 The church of S. Restituta in Naples, detail of interior   124

7.3 Portico of the Stefania basilica, Naples   125

7.4 Excavations at S. Maria della Rotonda, Naples   127

7.5 Detail of *spolia* in the church of S. Giorgio Maggiore, Naples   129

7.6 Pilaster decorated with vegetal and animal motifs, from the church of S. Giovanni Maggiore, Naples   132

7.7 Detail of Fig 7.6   133

7.8 The Pietrasanta bell tower, Naples   134

7.9 Detail of the interior of the church of S. Giovanni a Mare, Naples   139

7.10 Detail of the interior of the church of S. Lorenzo Maggiore, Naples   141

7.11 Portico of the church of the Incoronata, Naples   144

7.12 The Pappacoda chapel, Naples   145

7.13 Detail of the Pappacoda chapel, Naples   146

7.14 View of the clock tower of the church of S. Eligio Maggiore, Naples   148

7.15 Portrait of Vespasian, reused in the palazzo of Diomede Carafa, Naples   149

7.16 The 'Capa di Napoli' ('head of Naples')   150

10.1 Inscription from the foundations of the palazzo of Diomede Carafa in Naples   191

10.2 Relief of Mithras killing the bull from the Crypta Neapolitana   193

10.3 View of the palazzo of Carlo Carafa in Naples   194

10.4 Channels of the aqueduct in Naples   196

10.5 Sincero meets the nymph of the stream who leads him underground back to Naples   203

10.6 Francesco di Giorgio, topographical sketch of the 'Lago Chumano'   206

10.7 View of the entrance of the Crypta Neapolitana   208

10.8 Girolamo Mocetto and Ambrogio Leone, *Detail representing Naples with the Crypta Neapolitana (bottom) from the map of the* Ager Nolanus *in Leone,* De Nola (1514), engraving   209

10.9 View of the catacombs of S. Gennaro extra Moenia   213

10.10 View of the chapel of the Succorpo in the Cathedral of Naples   214

10.11 Giovanni da Nola, *Presepe*, church of S. Maria del
Parto in Naples   215

11.1 Virgil's grave at the Piedigrotta entrance of the Posillipo
tunnel   220

11.2 Sannazaro's grave and sepulchral monument, S. Maria
del Parto   224

11.3 G.A., *Il vero disegnio in sul propio luogho ritratto del infelice
paese di Posuolo* (Naples, 1540)   227

11.4 Joris Hoefnagel, 'Neapolis et Vesuvii montis prospectus', in
Georg Braun and Franz Hogenberg, *Theatrum orbis terrarum*
(Cologne, 1578)   228

11.5 Benedetto di Falco, *Descrittione dei luoghi antichi di Napoli*
(Naples, [1548]), title page   230

11.6 Antoine Lafréry and Étienne du Pérac, *Quale e di quanta
importanza e bellezza sia la nobile Cita di Napole* (Rome, 1566)   235

11.7 Commemorative plaque (dated 1544) near the alleged grave of
Virgil, Naples, with graffiti by Stanislaus Cencovius (1589)
and other visitors   241

12.1 Domenico Gagini, *The Triumph of King Alfonso*, formerly in
the Sala dei Baroni of Castelnuovo, Naples. The temple of the
Dioscuri and the Roman theatre are depicted in the background 248

12.2 Agustinus Prygl Tyfernus, facade of S. Paolo Maggiore
in Naples   249

12.3 Massimo Stanzione, *St Peter Makes the Pagan Statues of Castor
and Pollux Fall*, fresco (1642), formerly on the ceiling of
S. Paolo Maggiore (destroyed 1943)   252

12.4 Frontispiece from the *Chroniche de la inclyta città de Napole
emendatissime. Con li bagni de Puzolo et Ischia. Novamente
ristampate, stampate in la inclita città de Neapole, per m.
Evangelista di Presenzani de Pavia*, adi xxvii de Aprile 1526   254

12.5 The pronaos of the temple of the Dioscuri converted into the
porch of S. Paolo Maggiore and the new staircase built by
the Theatines.   257

12.6 Engraving after a drawing of Arcangelo Guglielmelli,
S. Paolo Maggiore before and after the earthquake of 1688   263

12.7 S. Paolo Maggiore, Naples. Columns of the temple of the
Dioscuri and statue of St Paul   265

14.1 Dominique Vivant Denon, family group. The inscription reads
'Preso dal presepio de S.i Terres compost da Francesco
Viva Napoli nel mese d'Aprile del anno 1785'   288

14.2 The *presepe Cuciniello*   290

14.3 *Presepe di sughero* (cork Nativity), exterior   291

14.4 *Presepe di sughero* (cork Nativity), interior   292

14.5 View of *presepe* merchandise on sale in Via S. Gregorio Armeno,
       including figurines of Pulcinella and S. Gennaro   294

14.6 View of *presepe* merchandise on sale in Via S. Gregorio Armeno,
       including figurines of Totò and Eduardo De Filippo, the singers
       Adriano Celentano and Vasco Rossi, the footballer Edinson
       Cavani, and Marilyn Monroe   295

14.7 Mechanized figurine of a *figuraro* (*presepe* maker), bought in
       S. Gregorio Armeno, Christmas 2011   296

14.8 *The Vision of the Emperor Augustus and the Ruins of the
       Temple of Peace*, c.1400, tempera   298

14.9 The *presepe per L'Aquila*, 2009, Ferrigno workshop, Naples   306

List of Contributors

Giancarlo Abbamonte is Professor of Classical Scholarship in the Department of Humanities at the University of Naples Federico II. His PhD was on the Aristotelian tradition in the Greek and Latin imperial and Middle Ages at the Universities of Salerno and Copenhagen, with a particular focus on Alexander of Aphrodisias' commentary on Aristotle's *Topics* and its reception. Subsequently he was a member of the international team that published the critical edition of the work written by the Italian humanist Niccolò Perotti (1430–80) entitled *Cornu copiae*. He is interested in the reception of classical works (Virgil and his commentator, Servius Honoratus, and Statius' *Silvae*) in Italian humanism of the fifteenth century. He has recently published a book on lexicographical and Virgilian studies in fifteenth-century Rome (*Diligentissimi uocabulorum perscrutatores*, Pisa, 2012).

giancarlo.abbamonte@gmail.com

Claudio Buongiovanni is a Research Fellow in Latin Language and Literature in the Department of Humanities at the University of Naples Federico II. His research focuses on Latin literature from the late Republic to the second century AD, and he has particular interests in historiography (especially Sallust and Tacitus), Flavian poetry (especially Martial), political vocabulary, and the reception of classical authors from antiquity to the modern age. He has published several articles and two monographs, *Sei studi su Tacito* (Naples, 2005) and *Gli* epigrammata longa *del decimo libro di Marziale. Introduzione, testo, traduzione e commento* (Pisa, 2012).

claudio.buongiovanni@unina.it

Stefano De Caro, archaeologist, is the Director General of ICCROM, the International Centre for the Study of the Preservation and Restoration of Cultural Property, in Rome. Previously, he served as Superintendent for the Antiquities of the provinces of Naples and Caserta, Regional Director for the Heritage of Campania, and Director General for the Antiquities of Italy. His academic work has been devoted to the topography and history of ancient Campania, while his heritage work has included the reorganization of the

Archaeological Museum of Naples and the creation of many new museums in Campania.

sdc@iccrom.org

Bianca de Divitiis is Associate Professor in the History of Art at the University of Naples Federico II and Principal Investigator of the ERC project *Historical Memory, Antiquarian Culture, Artistic Patronage: Social Identities of the Centres of Southern Italy between the Middle Ages and the Early Modern Period* (2011–2016). She studied for her PhD in the History of Architecture at the School of Advanced Studies in Venice and has since been awarded post-doctoral fellowships from the IUAV University in Venice, The Warburg Institute, Villa I Tatti, The Mellon Centre for Studies in British Art and Architecture, and the Francis Haskell Memorial Fund. Her main research fields are eighteenth- and nineteenth-century British architecture and art, and patronage and antiquarian culture in the Kingdom of Naples between the fifteenth and sixteenth centuries. She has published several articles in international journals and a book on the architectural patronage of the Carafa family in fifteenth-century Naples (2007).

Fulvio Delle Donne teaches Medieval Latin Literature and Medieval History at the University of Basilicata. His research ranges from the early middle ages to humanism, and combines philological and historical methods. Recent book publications include *Dall'*Ars dictaminis *al Preumanesimo? Per un profilo letterario del XIII secolo* (Florence, 2013), *Federico II: la condanna della memoria. Metamorfosi di un mito* (Rome, 2012), *Le scritture della storia* (Rome, 2012), and critical editions of Gaspar Pelegrí's *Historiarum Alphonsi regis libri X* (Rome 2012) and *Annales Cavenses* (Rome, 2011).

fulvio.delledonne@unibas.it

Mauro De Nardis is a Senior Research Fellow in the Department of Humanities at the University of Naples Federico II. His published work focuses primarily on the social and cultural history of the Roman world, and in particular on land use and surveying in Roman times, as well as on the interaction between ancient history and geographical knowledge.

maur.denard@libero.it

Harald Hendrix is Director of the Royal Netherlands Institute in Rome and Full Professor of Italian Studies at Utrecht University. With a background in Cultural History, Comparative Literature, and Italian Studies, he has published widely on the European reception of Italian Renaissance and Baroque culture, on the early-modern aesthetics of the non-beautiful, as well as on the intersections of literary culture, memory, and tourism. Recent book publications include *Writers' Houses and the Making of Memory* (New York, 2012), *Dynamic Translations in the European Renaissance* (Rome, 2011), *The Turn of the Soul: Representations of Religious Conversion in Early Modern Art and Literature* (Leiden and Boston, 2012), *The History of Futurism: Precursors, Protagonists, Legacies* (Lanham, MD, 2012), and *Cyprus and the Renaissance, 1450–1650* (Turnhout, 2013).

haraldhendrix@knir.it

Jessica Hughes is a Lecturer in Classical Studies at The Open University. Her research focuses on Greek and Roman material culture and its reception in later periods, and she has particular interests in material religion, memory studies, the body, and the cultural history of Naples and Campania. Her publications include articles on anatomical votives, human–animal hybrids, restorations of ancient sculpture, and viewer responses to Roman imperial monuments. Her monograph on votive body parts dedicated in ancient sanctuaries (*The Anatomy of Ritual*) is forthcoming. She also edits the journal *Practitioners' Voices in Classical Reception Studies*.

jessica.hughes@open.ac.uk

Fulvio Lenzo is a Postdoctoral Fellow in the History of Architecture on the HistAntArtSI Project, at the University of Naples Federico II (<http://www.histantartsi.eu>). His research focuses on the Italian Renaissance and early eighteenth-century architecture (in Naples in particular). He has published the Italian edition of Antony Blunt's *Neapolitan Baroque and Rococo Architecture* (Milan, 2006), and a monograph entitled *Architettura e antichità a Napoli dal XV al XVIII secolo: Le colonne del tempio dei Dioscuri e la chiesa di San Paolo Maggiore* (Rome, 2011).

fulviolenzo@gmail.com

Kathryn Lomas is Honorary Senior Research Associate at University College London, and researches on the history and archaeology of

Italy and the western Mediterranean, ethnic and cultural identities, and early literacy. Her publications include *Rome and the Western Greeks* and *Roman Italy, 338 BC–AD 200*, several volumes of collected papers, and numerous articles.

k.lomas@ucl.ac.uk

Annalisa Marzano is Professor of Ancient History at the University of Reading. Her areas of research are the economy of the Roman world, Roman social history, and Roman archaeology. Publications include *Roman Villas in Central Italy: A Social and Economic History* (Brill, 2007); *Harvesting the Sea: The Exploitation of Marine Resources in the Roman Mediterranean* (OUP, 2013); 'Capital Investment and Agriculture: Multi-Press Facilities from Gaul, Iberian Peninsula and the Black Sea Region', in A. K. Bowman and A. I. Wilson (eds.), *The Roman Agricultural Economy: Organisation, Investment and Production* (OUP, 2013); 'L'antichità attraverso l'Italia', in M. Wallace and M. Kemp (eds.), *La Cultura Italiana: L'arte e il visuale* (UTET, 2010); 'Le ville marittime tra *amoenitas* e *fructus*', *Amoenitas: Rivista di Studi Miscellanei sulla Villa Romana* 1 (2010); 'Trajanic Building Projects on Base-Metal Denominations and Audience Targeting', *PBSR* 77 (2009).

a.marzano@reading.ac.uk

Lorenzo Miletti has a PhD in Classical Philology and is currently a postdoctoral fellow on the ERC Project HistAntArtSI at the University of Naples Federico II. His main areas of research are classical rhetoric, Greek historiography and biography, and manuscript traditions and classicism in the Renaissance. His publications include a book on language and linguistic terminology in Herodotus (*Linguaggio e metalinguaggio in Erodoto*, Pisa and Rome, 2008) and an edition of Aelius Aristides' *Or. 28 K* with Italian translation and commentary (*L'arte dell'autoelogio: Studio sull'orazione 28 K di Elio Aristide, con testo, traduzione e commento*, Pisa, 2011).

lorenzomiletti@hotmail.com

Angela Palmentieri is Assistant Professor of Classics at the University of Naples Federico II. Her research focuses on the Roman archaeology and history of Campania; she has particular interests in Roman funerary monuments, the medieval reuse of Roman sculpture, and technical innovation in Heritage Studies. She has published several articles and notes on these topics, including, most recently, 'Testimonianze romane nel centro di Sant'Agata dei Goti e i loro reimpieghi', in *Napoli Nobilissima* (2013) and 'Addenda ai sarcofagi romani della prima età imperiale: Nuovi dati dall'area campana', in *Römische Mitteilungen* (2013). Her monograph on the reuse of Roman marble in Salerno is currently in press.

palmenti@inwind.it

Giovanni Polara is Full Professor of Latin Language and Literature in the Department of Humanities at the University of Naples Federico II. His research mainly focuses on late antique and early medieval Latin texts, to which he has devoted critical editions, numerous books, and articles; he has also written on classical authors. His publications include *Potere e contropotere nell'antica Roma: Bande armate, terrorismo e intellettuali* (Rome, 1986), *Letteratura latina tardoantica e altomedievale* (Rome, 1987), *Guida alla traduzione dal latino* (Turin, 1998), and *Ricerche sulla tarda antichità* (Naples, 2001).

giovanni.polara@unina.it

Luigi Spina was (until 2009) Full Professor of Classical Philology at the University of Naples Federico II. In 2009 he held a Gutenberg Chair at the University of Strasbourg. His research interests include the reception of the ancient world in modern cultures, in particular the reception of rhetorical forms and the relationship between cinema and the ancient world. He is the associate editor of the journal *Rhetorica* and secretary of the *Associazione Antropologia e Mondo Antico*. His most recent publications include *Il mito delle Sirene: Immagini e racconti dalla Grecia a oggi* (Turin, 2007), which he wrote together with Maurizio Bettini.

luigi.spina@unina.it

Rabun Taylor is Associate Professor of Classics at the University of Texas at Austin. His most recent books are *Roman Builders: A Study of Architectural Process* (Cambridge, 2003) and *The Moral Mirror of Roman Art* (Cambridge, 2008). He is working on two collaborative books on urban history in Italy: *Ancient Naples: A Documentary History*, with Joseph Alchermes; and *Rome: An Urban History*, with Katherine Rinne.

rmtaylor@austin.utexas.edu

1

Introduction

Entering the Siren's City

Claudio Buongiovanni and Jessica Hughes

'You're all disgusting! Look at what you've reduced me to!'[1] So proclaimed a sign that hung around the neck of the ancient marble river god in Naples' Piazzetta Nilo in the summer of 2009, when many of the city's streets were 'decorated' with bags of uncollected rubbish. Through its annotation by protestors, this Roman sculpture, which has been widely known since the Renaissance as the 'Corpo di Napoli' (Fig. 1.1), was drawn into a political debate about the future of the city it personified, and made to accuse passers-by of failing to look after Naples' glorious ancient heritage. This dynamic appropriation of the Corpo di Napoli (which only a few months earlier had worn a sign reading 'Free Palestine') stands at the end of many centuries of interactions with Naples' classical past: already in antiquity, the accounts of the city's foundation and early history were being drawn into the service of later agendas and ideologies; over the centuries that followed, the Greek and Roman past of the city played a vital role in the construction of civic identity, and in debates about what it meant to be Neapolitan.

This volume presents an initial exploration of the history of classical reception in Naples, focusing on a series of case studies which range from Roman literary and visual representations of the city's Greek foundation myths through to the fierce contemporary debates about the preservation and presentation of its archaeological heritage.

---

[1] 'Fate schifo! Vedete in quale stato mi avete ridotto!'

Fig. 1.1. The 'Corpo di Napoli' sculpture, Piazzetta Nilo, Naples.
Source: Photograph: Angela Palmentieri.

One of the factors that motivated the editors to put this book together was an awareness of an imbalance in existing literature—an imbalance, that is, between a veritable industry of locally produced books and articles on Naples, and a surprising lack of engagement with this rich material on the part of international scholars, who have tended to sideline the urban centre of Naples at the expense of other sites on the Bay. It is true that recent years have seen the beginnings of an increase in scholarship on Naples in the English language.[2] However, the dynamics of classical reception in the city still remain unexplored—and this is particularly noticeable when compared with the wealth of exciting work on the reception of the nearby sites of Pompeii and Herculaneum (which are deliberately and

---

[2] Cf. Astarita (2013); Calaresu and Hills (2013), whose introduction discusses and challenges the 'tired paradigms' which have previously characterized scholarship on Naples, and which have led to the depiction of southern Italy as a 'poor, crude subaltern sister' (p. 2) to the North (see Annalisa Marzano, Chapter 13 in this volume, for further discussion of this issue). For a documentary history of ancient Naples see Taylor and Alchermes (forthcoming). For introductory overviews of Neapolitan history in English aimed at a more general readership see Lancaster (2009) and Robb (2011).

almost provocatively put aside here in order to 'make room' for their glorious older metropolis).[3]

In fact, the urban centre of Naples offers us a unique resource for studying the reception of antiquity: it is one of the oldest continuously inhabited cities in the Western world, and has been a centre of cultural contact ever since its foundation in the seventh century BC. Periods of Greek, Roman, Gothic, Byzantine, Norman, Angevin, Aragonese, Spanish, and Bourbon occupation—together with significant encounters with other foreign peoples, including the Arabs—have all left their mark on the city, which continues to be a hub of commercial exchange with other sites around the Mediterranean basin and beyond. Traces of the classical past remain in the city's institutions, traditions, cults, language, toponymy, art, and architecture—but it is the combination of this tangible classical heritage with later multicultural influences that makes Naples such a rich site for studying *Classical Presences*. This volume, then, aims to help redress the balance in the literature about Naples, by making some of the Italian scholarship and Neapolitan source material accessible to an anglophone audience, and by sketching the outlines of the city's classical reception history. It also aims to bring this material into a productive dialogue with more recent theories and ideas about processes of reception, cultural memory, and urban identity construction.

Ultimately, this book offers a diachronic exploration of how and why the image of classical Naples has been created, enhanced, and modelled over the centuries, according to the agendas, preoccupations, and tastes of different recipients.[4] As the chapters' authors will collectively demonstrate, this inheritance is constantly being re-evaluated, with effects that are sometimes unexpected, and which can challenge our modern and contemporary certainties. One of the most striking examples concerns the *auctoritas* of Virgil at Naples University—which is, we might note, the institutional home of several authors contributing to this volume. Today, we place an enormous value on 'our' treasured Latin poet, but—as Fulvio Delle Donne shows in Chapter 8—this has certainly not always been the case. During the

---

[3] On Pompeii and classical reception see Cremante et al. (2008); Hales and Paul (2011); Mattusch (2013); Heringman (2013).

[4] The book takes particular inspiration from the Jaussian notions of 'actualizing reception' and 'heritage appropriation' (see the list of works by Jauss in the Bibliography).

thirteenth and fourteenth centuries, Virgil's literary output was considered far less interesting and useful than that of other classical and medieval authors, whose work was thus far more frequently appropriated. In fact, in this period Virgil was famous not only as a poet, but also as a thaumaturge with magical healing powers, a creator of talismanic animals, and the builder of the miraculous tunnels that still form the backbone of the modern city.

ORGANIZATION OF THE BOOK

The main section of the volume is divided into two parts, the first of which takes us from the foundation of the city into late antiquity, and the second from the Middle Ages to the present day. The chapters in Part I (2–6) demonstrate how the image of ancient Neapolis began to be constructed and reconstructed in antiquity itself, focusing primarily on texts and monuments of the Hellenistic and Roman periods (we should note here that the names Naples and Neapolis are used interchangeably in this volume, in order to prevent excessive repetition). This part of the book looks particularly closely at the city's foundation narratives and their representation and reuse in later periods of antiquity, as well as the question of continuity between the early Greek and later Roman imperial periods. Meanwhile, the chapters in Part II (7–14) explore aspects of the reception of the classical past from the medieval period up to the present day. The volume concludes with two afterwords written by an archaeologist and a classical philologist, who offer their more informal reflections on the city's current condition, as well as on the future of its artistic and cultural heritage.

The material drawn on in the volume is extremely wide-ranging; it includes Greek and Roman literature, popular medieval legends, architectural *spolia*, underground tunnels, and studies of body language. The volume also covers a vast chronological scope, which inevitably means that the identity of the city being 'remembered' as we move through the book is constantly shifting. In Hellenistic and Roman times, 'antiquity' was equated with the earliest periods in the city's history: that is, the foundation of the first settlement, Parthenope (later known as Palaepolis) in the seventh century BC, the subsequent move to Neapolis in the fifth century, and the nebulous first stages of that city's life. In later periods, while the Greek roots of

Parthenope (which became a poetic denomination of Neapolis in Roman times) would continue to be central to Neapolitan civic identity, they came to be overshadowed by the Roman elements of the city's heritage. The physical *lieux de mémoire* celebrated by Renaissance humanists are virtually all Roman: the temple of the Dioscuri, the 'Crypta Neapolitana' (the tunnel excavated through the hill at Posillipo, which in the Middle Ages was believed to have been created in a single night by Virgil's magic powers), the 'Grotta di Seiano', the villa of Lucullus on the island of Megaride, and of course the grave of Virgil. Meanwhile, the dominance of the Roman past in medieval accounts of Neapolitan antiquity is exemplified by the *Cronaca di Partenope,* that influential fourteenth-century history of Naples attributed to a lay Neapolitan patrician named Bartolomeo Caracciolo-Carafa, which will reappear several times in the pages of this volume. Of the thirty-two chapters of the *Cronaca* that deal with the pagan antiquity of Naples, half (nos. 16–32) are given over to a discussion of Virgil and the miraculous works that he created for the good of the city. The preceding chapters describe the foundation and early history of the city, but here the narrative is also dominated by a Roman—this time, the figure of Tiberius Julius Tarsos, the Roman whose name was preserved on the inscription of the temple of the Dioscuri, and who was credited in the *Cronaca* as being the founder of Neapolis.[5]

Many of the protagonists who appear in this volume come from the elite, intellectual classes—kings, cardinals, writers, and their aristocratic patrons—but we have also tried to include, where possible, more popular receptions of antiquity in Naples, accessed indirectly from sources such as the widely circulated medieval legends about Virgil and the inexpensive, mass-produced models of ancient ruins

---

[5] For the *Cronaca* see the recent edition by Samantha Kelly (2011), which includes a detailed commentary in English. As Kelly explains (p. 55), the *Cronaca* can be divided fairly neatly into three chronological sections: chapters 1–32 treat pagan antiquity (although chapters 38 and 39 also belong to this section, since they concern the Cumaean sibyl); the second section treats the early Christian and early medieval history, which Kelly terms the 'sacred era' (chapters 33–55); while the third section deals principally with reigns of the rulers of southern Italy from the Normans to the accession of Joanna 1 (chapters 56 to the end). The earliest chapters of the book treat the foundation of Cumae and then Parthenope (1–5), the foundation of Neapolis by Tiberius Julius Tarsos (6–7), and the early encounters with the Romans (8–15). Virgil is the subject of chapters 16–32. On the sources for the section on pagan antiquity, see Kelly (2011), 56–67.

that can be found on sale in the city today. We also deliberately chose
to focus on Neapolitan rather than 'outsider' or 'tourist' responses to
the city's heritage, in an attempt to redress the dominant trend in
anglophone scholarship whereby Naples is seen from the perspective
of visitors (with the city and its residents often thereby characterized
as foreign, exotic, and anomalous). In this sense, while the contributors to this book all adopt subtly different approaches to reception
and have different ways of conceiving the relationship between past
and present, we felt justified in alluding in the book's title to the
related field of Memory Studies, which shares with Reception Studies
the basic theoretical premise that the past is reshaped in the process of
receiving/remembering, but which brings with it the idea of a common, *shared* past, which is used to construct and reinforce group (in
this case civic) identity.[6]

The early stages of this ongoing process of civic identity construction are partially accessible through the ancient literary sources,
which are set out and reappraised in Chapter 2 by Lorenzo Miletti.
Miletti reads Strabo's famous description of Neapolis, which appears
in the context of a longer description of the Campanian coastal area,
in the light of modern knowledge about the city's foundation and
early history. He demonstrates how this first-century AD text—which
might itself be seen as a work of reception which drew on other texts
from previous centuries—crystallizes some of the themes that would
be important in the subsequent reception history of the city. Much of
Miletti's discussion focuses on the rather complex story of the city's
foundation, which Strabo and other ancient authors describe as
happening in two stages—firstly with the foundation of Parthenope
on the rocky promontory of Pizzofalcone, and secondly with the
'refounding' of that city at a nearby site which was subsequently
known as Neapolis. The variants and alternative traditions surrounding these events suggest that already in Roman times the ancient past
was being drawn into the service of different ideologies and debates
about civic identity. Like other authors in this first part of the volume,

---

[6] The interdisciplinary field of Memory Studies, like that of Classical Reception
Studies, is vast and ever-expanding. The monographs by Cubitt (2007) and Erll (2011)
are recommended entry points into the debates and bibliography. A sense of the
breadth of work in the field can be gained by looking at the journal *Memory Studies*
and the monograph series *Palgrave Macmillan Memory Studies*. For memory in the
Roman world see the collection edited by Galinsky (2014), which shows how much of
the modern scholarship might be used to illuminate ancient material.

Miletti is interested in how the surviving sources present the relationship between Parthenope and Neapolis—and while he gives several examples of features that were shared by both cities, he also reminds us that the very name Neapolis emphasizes the novelty and discontinuity of this 'New City'—while also implicitly ensuring that the distant memory of another, older city was preserved for future generations.

In Chapter 3 by Rabun Taylor we have our first encounter with the temple of the Dioscuri—a first-century AD monument in the heart of ancient Neapolis that was built by a wealthy freedman of Tiberius (see the map at Fig. 7.1, no. 2). Most of this temple's architecture no longer survives, although some Corinthian columns are still visible in the facade of the church of S. Paolo Maggiore, and fragments of the sculpted decoration can be seen in the National Archaeological Museum. Using both ancient and later antiquarian sources, Taylor works to reconstruct the temple's now-lost pediment; in the process, he offers a hitherto-unrecognized example of how the ancient past of the city was pressed into the service of the (Roman) present. In particular, Taylor argues that the pediment may have represented certain events from the foundation narratives that we met in Chapter 2 by Lorenzo Miletti: these include the city's 'parent' god Apollo, Diotimos (the Athenian general who established the Sebasta games and 'the first historically verifiable figure in the chronicles of Naples'), and personifications of the river Sebethos, Neapolis, and perhaps even Parthenope. The visual emphasis on Neapolis in the centre of the pediment would accord with the dedication of the temple to the Dioscuri *and* the *polis*; meanwhile, the representation of both Parthenope and Neapolis would provide a visual nod to the 'two-stage' foundation which was being worked out in the literary sources. Particularly important in Taylor's reconstruction is the proposed presence of Diotimos, since many scholars believe that the games he founded were the direct ancestors of the *Italika Rhomaia Sebasta Isolympia* held in honour of Augustus. In this way, Taylor suggests that the pediment, through its representation of the 'origins' of the Sebasta games, may have emphasized the city's Roman imperial links and reminded viewers of its status as a place favoured by the Julio-Claudian emperors.

In fact, the games appear again in both Chapters 4 and 5, each of which explore different aspects of the Greek past in Naples as the city developed under Roman rule. Chapter 4 by Kathryn Lomas gives a broad overview of the physical and cultural backdrop of Roman

Neapolis, and reappraises this evidence using the theoretical tools of cultural memory, in particular the work of Maurice Halbwachs and Paul Connerton. Lomas looks for Roman examples of continuity with the city's past, and finds plenty of evidence in the city's unusually high proportion of Greek-language inscriptions, as well as the Greek magisterial offices, ancient civic institutions like the phratries (kinship-based groups with social and religious responsibilities), and Greek cults and festivals. However, rather than automatically taking these surviving Hellenic forms as evidence for a deliberate and meaningful evocation of the city's past, she shows how in many cases the evidence is more ambiguous than it might first appear. The example of the Sebasta games is a case in point, for the putative links between this festival and the older games held for Parthenope need to be balanced by the realization that the Sebasta were nevertheless configured according to a new Roman imperial matrix. Ultimately, she shows that while Naples was undoubtedly perceived as having a vibrant Greek heritage, many of the city's ancestral elements were overhauled in the early Roman Empire, and drawn into the service of new agendas, including that of philhellenism.

Chapter 5 by Mauro De Nardis begins by laying out the facts of the evolving relationship between Neapolis and Rome, from the siege of Neapolis in 327/6 BC to its passing under the control of *correctores* and *consulares* in late antiquity. He then returns to the Neapolitan constitution and magistracies, and the question of continuity with earlier periods. For while the Greek names of these magistracies have been taken both in antiquity and later times as providing evidence of the city's Hellenism, De Nardis shows that the evidence is really too fragmentary and problematic to support this picture of simple continuity between the Greek and Roman periods of the city's history. While Strabo presents the demarchs in terms of a 'preservation' of the Greek past, De Nardis argues that the other magistracies might be seen more in terms of dynamic remodelling: the enigmatic magistrature of the *laukelarchos*, for instance, may have been revived or even invented at the time of the institution of the Sebasta games, and as such suggests a conscious programme of 'heritage management' on the part of those who sponsored the festival. Certainly, it is possible to imagine how this emphasis on the Hellenic character of the festival would have worked in the favour of the emperors in whose honour they were held: for one thing, it may have mitigated the more exotic 'imperial cult' elements of the ceremony, and also allowed Augustus and his successors to tap into the broader discourse of Roman philhellenism that Kathryn Lomas described at the end of Chapter 4.

The final chapter in Part I takes us out of the imperial era and into the world of late antiquity. Some time around the close of the fifth century AD, the last emperor of Rome, Romulus Augustulus, drew his last breath on the island of Megaride—the very spot where the Siren Parthenope is said to have arrived so many centuries earlier. In the following century, the emperor Justinian sought to recover and restore the western half of the Empire, which had been overrun by Goths. In Chapter 6, Giovanni Polara paints a portrait of the city during the so-called Gothic War (AD 535–53), when Justinian's general Belisarius led a twenty-day siege of the city before finally entering via a disused Roman aqueduct.[7] The brutal damage subsequently inflicted on the ancient city was mirrored, in a sense, by an obliteration (or at least temporary 'forgetting') of classical Naples; in the Greek and Latin sources on which Polara draws—Procopius of Caesarea, Sidonius Apollinaris, Cassiodorus, Jordanes, and Boethius— the Edenic image of classical Naples (the *dulcis Parthenope* of Virgil) that would be so important in the Renaissance and beyond is replaced, temporarily, by the image of a city ravaged by a terrible war, natural disasters, famine, and pestilence. By drawing attention to these sources and their non-traditional images of the city, Polara's chapter effectively problematizes the notion of a simple continuity between classical and 'neoclassical' Naples. In turn, it implicitly draws attention to the 'cultural forgetfulness' that would prevail in later periods, in which the troubled era of late antiquity would all but disappear from the Neapolitan historical consciousness.[8]

If Chapter 6 is about a process of 'undoing', Chapter 7 instead addresses a sort of 'remaking' of the city from the remnants of ancient Greek and Roman buildings. Angela Palmentieri discusses the use of architectural *spolia* in later structures—both sacred sites like churches and, at a later point, private palazzi of the elite. This story looks at Neapolitan *spolia* over the *longue durée* from late antiquity to the

---

[7] For an account of Naples in this period see Arthur (2002).

[8] On cultural forgetting see Connerton (2008); Assman (2008). Assman argues that 'the continuous process of forgetting is part of social normality', and goes on to distinguish between active forms of forgetting (e.g. material destruction, taboo and censorship) and passive forms (e.g. neglect and disregard). See Hughes (2014) for a Roman case study of cultural memory and forgetting.

Renaissance, highlighting, in the process, the sheer abundance of ancient fragments in the fabric of the modern city. The chapter focuses on the identification of the types of *spolia* in a series of monuments and the investigation of their provenances. In Naples, as in Rome, most spoliated marbles are architectural fragments—columns and capitals—although figurative sculptures became increasingly popular in later periods. And although it is often hard to specify the exact provenance of the reused material, it does seem that in late antiquity and the early medieval period most of the *spolia* seem to have come from buildings within the city, while later cases involved *spolia* from the Campanian countryside and the rest of the Phlegraean area. Palmentieri also identifies two specific symbolic meanings of the *spolia* in their new contexts: firstly, the use of fragmentary remains of antiquity to signal the rebirth of Naples as a Christian city, and secondly, the appropriation of antiquity for the purposes of Renaissance self-fashioning. Both of these themes will resurface and be explored in more detail in later chapters of this volume.

After this panoramic view of a whole millennium of reuse, Fulvio Delle Donne's Chapter 8 takes us to the Angevin age, when Naples became the capital of southern Italy and one of the most important cities in the Mediterranean. He starts by introducing us to a document of 1259, in which Manfred of Swabia describes Naples as a 'Virgilian city' brimming with poetry and knowledge. As Manfred's words suggest, inhabitants of Naples in this period were keenly aware of their city's ancient heritage, which was embodied above all in the figures of classical authors. However, Delle Donne argues that we are looking here at a peculiarly 'non-literary' type of reception, in the sense that contemporary Neapolitans often found the ancient texts themselves less interesting and useful than the biographies of the men who wrote them. Virgil is the obvious example here, since his fame in this period clearly depended primarily on his powers as a magician, rather than on his poetic output; however, Delle Donne also shows how other classical authors seem to have taken on new identities that were independent of the texts they had written. These texts were frequently 'cut up' into citable portions for reuse in a wide range of new contexts, and here Delle Donne introduces a contrast between what he calls 'real' and 'ideal' reuse. While the former would signify a direct engagement with an ancient text, and a genuine attempt to understand and reflect that text's original meaning, the latter type of reuse reduces the ancient text to a mere (visual or verbal) cipher, which is fleetingly evoked in order to embellish a work or to give it extra authority. This chapter also highlights the role of Neapolitan sovereigns in transmitting classical texts and translations to other places in Europe, and considers how the city's classical heritage may have contributed to its rise to the intellectual capital of the Kingdom and home of the first state university in Europe.

The next four chapters focus on the reception of the Neapolitan past in the fifteenth and sixteenth centuries, when the city was home to some of Italy's most prominent humanists. The protagonists of this section of the volume include the neo-Latin poets Antonio Beccadelli—also known as 'il Panormita'—Giovanni Pontano, and Jacopo Sannazaro, who operated within the learned atmosphere of the Aragonese court. Chapter 9 by Giancarlo Abbamonte looks at how these poets represented their relationship with two of their ancient forebears, Virgil and Statius. Virgil's influence in this period is well known, and will be the topic of further exploration in Chapter 11. Here, however, Abbamonte adds a new perspective by arguing that over the course of the 1470s we see Neapolitan intellectuals attempting to place Virgil and Statius side by side—and even to substitute Virgil with Statius as the representative of Neapolitan poetry. This 'rejigging' of the classical canon was motivated in part by the rediscovery of Statius' Neapolitan origins, as well as of his major poetic work the *Silvae*—a collection of verses containing numerous references to Naples as the author's city of origin. This new knowledge inevitably made Statius and his writings an appealing ancestor for Neapolitan poets, whose work became infused with Statian vocabulary and ideas.

Bianca de Divitiis adds yet another new dimension to our understanding of Neapolitan humanism in Chapter 10 by highlighting the role played by ancient material culture in this period. She begins by drawing attention to the many artefacts that were emerging from the subsoil in and around Naples, which included marble statues, architectural elements, and a wealth of Latin inscriptions. These objects, which were either chance finds made during building works or the result of specially commissioned archaeological excavations, were soon absorbed into the collections of the city's elite, or—as already documented in Chapter 7 by Angela Palmentieri—built into the structures of their private residences. The chapter then moves on to explore the ancient network of aqueducts, catacombs, and other structures underneath the city, arguing that these served as a source of inspiration for the humanists' antiquarian and literary work, as well as their own building projects. De Divitiis shows how recognizing the humanists' archaeological activities can heighten our understanding of their literary works; her analysis of Jacopo Sannazaro's famous classicizing work *Arcadia*, for instance, demonstrates how the poet's description of his protagonist's subterranean journey not only draws on ancient written texts, but also more than likely reflects the writer's personal experience of exploring the channels of the Bolla and Serino aqueducts. Ultimately, we discover in this chapter that the Neapolitan humanists were profoundly interested in the wider historiographical problems concerning the subsoil of Naples and the wider Campanian area, and found as much inspiration in the city's underground network of tunnels as in any academic meeting-place or library.

Chapter 11 by Harald Hendrix begins by picking up on an activity mentioned briefly by de Divitiis in Chapter 10—that is, the attempts made by Renaissance intellectuals to associate archaeological sites in and around Naples with people and places mentioned in classical texts. Hendrix traces this literary perspective back to Petrarch, whose interest in identifying Virgilian sites occasionally overcame his critical ability to take the physical evidence on its own terms. The chapter then moves forward in time to consider how representations of the ancient city evolved over the course of the sixteenth and seventeenth centuries, drawing on chorographic descriptions in city eulogies and guides, as well as visual representations of the city's topography. Hendrix identifies some elements of continuity with earlier humanist representations of Naples, in particular the centrality of Virgil's tomb and the villa of Sannazaro. However, he also highlights some important changes over time—for instance, we find an increasing reliance on 'eyewitness' antiquarian investigations as opposed to the literary projections favoured by the humanists, as well as a growing interest in other aspects of the urban landscape, including Christian monuments and the more recent urban projects instigated by the viceroy Toledo. The chapter also addresses the impact that the growing presence of visitors in the city had on urban identity, pointing out that, while visitors to Naples in this period were attracted by the city's illustrious classical heritage, their perspective on this past was more distant and neutral than that of the Neapolitan intellectuals of earlier generations, who had used the past predominantly for purposes of self-fashioning and identity construction. The fact that these 'outsider' perspectives appear to have then influenced 'indigenous' Neapolitan representations of their city reminds us of the complex interplay between inside and outside—an interplay which would become ever more important in the following century as the Grand Tour got into full swing.

Fulvio Lenzo's Chapter 12 also presents evidence for a shift in attitudes to classical antiquity over time, here focusing on the case study of the church of S. Paolo Maggiore and its changing fortunes over the course of the sixteenth century. This church was built on the site of the Roman temple of the Dioscuri, discussed by Rabun Taylor in Chapter 3 of this volume. Lenzo focuses his investigation on two episodes in the building's post-antique history: the acquisition of the site by the Theatine Order of monks in 1538, and the rebuilding of the front steps in 1576. In the first instance, Lenzo argues that the acquisition of this site by Cardinal Gian Pietro Carafa (whose grandfather Diomede Carafa and uncle Oliviero Carafa appear in earlier chapters as prominent 'receivers' of antiquity) was driven by an awareness of the importance of the ancient temple; this betrays an ecclesiastic vision of pagan antiquity that, while never wholly unambiguous, was relatively positive when compared with that of later decades. For by the time the staircase was rebuilt in 1576, it was felt necessary to reassure visitors that the ancient stones used in the staircase were now consecrated to the triumphant Christian saints rather than to the 'false gods' of pagan antiquity. Lenzo explains this apparent shift from a positive to a negative attitude towards classical antiquity with reference to the unease following the Protestant Reformation; at the same time, though, he also introduces other sources which show the continued positive valency of the temple and its ancient inscription, which were reproduced throughout this period by Neapolitans and foreigners alike, in a variety of new media.

Chapter 13 by Annalisa Marzano focuses on Andrea de Jorio's 1832 treatise *La mimica degli antichi investigata nel gestire napoletano*, a text devoted to the exegesis of gestures depicted in Roman and Greek art and literature through a comparison with gestures still in use in nineteenth-century Naples. Marzano introduces the methodology and aims of this influential semiotic treatise and situates it in

relation to a series of intellectual, cultural, and political developments
taking place across the rest of Italy and Europe. De Jorio's project was
based on the conviction that the culture and body language of the
ancients were preserved in the modern populace of Naples; notably,
in contrast to the receptions studied in the other chapters of this part
of the volume, the 'antiquity' that was privileged here was the city's
Greek past—and Marzano suggests that this reflects the growing
influence of Winckelmann, who visited the museum where de Jorio
worked and whose writings asserted the superiority of Greek art and
culture over all other traditions. At any rate, by emphasizing continuity between past and present, de Jorio was able to respond to
contemporary invective generated by northern Europeans, who often
denigrated the modern populace of Naples as poor and lazy, and as
ultimately *dis*connected from the noble ancient cultures that once
inhabited the same region. Marzano also demonstrates the relevance
of de Jorio's treatise to the debates about the North–South divide
within Italy—debates which permeated the rhetoric of the Risorgimento and which are still very much alive today.

The final chapter of this volume, Chapter 14, brings our journey
through Neapolitan receptions of the classical past right up to the
present day, by looking at the small-scale models of classical ruins
that are sold by vendors in Via S. Gregorio Armeno in the historic
centre of the city for display within Neapolitan *presepi* (Nativity
scenes). As background to these modern examples, Jessica Hughes
introduces the evidence for the inclusion of ruins in Neapolitan
Nativity scenes from the seventeenth century onwards, showing
how this fashion intensified around the time of the rediscovery of
Pompeii and Herculaneum. Much of the discussion of this chapter is
centred on uncovering the different meanings attributed to these ruin
models over time—meanings which are accessed primarily through
written sources, but also visual analysis of individual *presepi*. The
chapter shows that there has always been a widespread awareness that
the ruins in the *presepe* (like those in other representations of the
Nativity from elsewhere in Italy) symbolize the death of paganism
and the triumph of Christianity: in this sense, the *presepe* fits neatly
alongside other Catholic appropriations of ancient material culture,
including examples discussed earlier in the volume by Palmentieri
and Lenzo. At the same time, the ruins are shown to have additional
meanings in the context of the *presepe*, where they form part of a

dominant aesthetic of anachronism and multi-temporality, as well as often serving to physically transplant the Nativity to Campania through visual evocation of particular monuments. The examination of particular case studies of *presepi* on display in S. Gregorio Armeno over the past few years also shows how these traditional elements of *presepe* imagery are often appropriated by individual craftsmen for their own unique purposes, from the desire to make a subversive political comment on the decline and fall of a nation, to the injection of pathos—as well as hope—in the representation of a natural disaster.

The volume closes with two short afterwords which address 'the future of the city's past', first from a museological and then from a wider cultural and philosophical perspective. Both take inspiration from the recent work on the city's underground Metro system, which has uncovered a wealth of new archaeological material. In Chapter 15 Stefano De Caro presents a brief history of Neapolitan antiquities collections, before considering how best to conserve and communicate the city's precious archaeological heritage. Luigi Spina then uses the metaphor of hybridity in Chapter 16 to explore the question of how best to reconcile the 'two cities' above and below the ground level. The questions raised in these afterwords are becoming ever more urgent and pressing: just a few weeks before the final submission of this book, the European Commission approved an investment of €75 million from the European Regional Development Fund to restore the historical centre of Naples.[9] At the time of writing, we do not know exactly how and where the money will be spent, but it is clear that the next months and years will furnish us with many new case studies of 'cultural memory in action', involving processes of selection and valorization that will impact on all future generations. For now, though, we leave the reader of this book in the company of the ancient city's foundress and namesake, the Siren Parthenope, who reappears throughout these pages in different places and guises: whether lying in her tomb on the shore beneath the ancient citadel, presiding over the Roman games from her temple, sprinkling water from her breasts over fifteenth-century diners in the gardens of the Castel Capuano, or boarding the Metro in search of new adventures in this vibrant and beautiful city.

---

[9] Futher details at: <http://ec.europa.eu/regional_policy/upload/documents/Com missioner/IT-2013-09-26-restore-Naples-historic-centre.pdf> (European Commission press release of 26 September 2013, accessed 24 March 2014).

Part I

Classical Naples in Antiquity

2

Setting the Agenda

The Image of Classical Naples in Strabo's Geography *and Other Ancient Literary Sources*

Lorenzo Miletti

This chapter aims to define how the city of Neapolis was represented in ancient literary sources, and to show how Greek and Roman authors transfigured, reused, and interpreted historical information in their descriptions of the city. In turn, it also aims to identify how these literary descriptions contributed to the construction of Naples' identity in later periods of the city's history. Two immediate challenges face the historian embarking on such a project. The first relates to the fact that the Greek sources for the earliest phases of Naples' history are now lost. It is true that they sometimes survive 'hidden' behind later Latin works, but these works generally manipulate the material to such an extent that they cannot be taken as unproblematic evidence for a 'Greek point of view'. The second problem is that both the Greek and Latin texts that survive are generally late: most of the Hellenistic historiography dealing specifically with Magna Graecia is lost, and can only be reconstructed by reading between the lines of later authors like Diodorus, Dionysius of Halicarnassus, Livy, and Pliny. In the case of Neapolis, we have lost not only the works of local (and rather obscure) Hellenistic

The research leading to these results has received funding from the European Research Council under the European Community's Seventh Framework Programme (FP7/2007-2013)/ERC Grant agreement n° 263549; ERC-HistAntArtSI project, Università degli Studi di Napoli Federico II, Principal Investigator Bianca de Divitiis.

historians such as the Cumaean Hyperochus and the Neapolitan
Eumachus, but also those of more famous authors such as Timaeus
of Tauromenium and Antiochus of Syracuse, both of whom were
sources for several Greek and Roman writers dealing with Magna
Graecia's history.[1]

The historian's lifeline in this wreckage of sources is the work of the
Greek geographer Strabo, and this chapter will focus primarily on
how Strabo's famous description of Neapolis both incorporated *and*
influenced other textual representations of the city and its classical
heritage. Strabo's description of Neapolis comes directly after his
treatment of Puteoli (Dicaearchia):

> After Dicaearchia comes Neapolis, a city of the Cumaeans. At a later time
> it was re-colonized by Chalcidians, and also by some Pithecussans and
> Athenians, and hence, for this reason, was called Neapolis. A monument
> of Parthenope, one of the Sirens, is pointed out in Neapolis, and in
> accordance with an oracle a gymnastic contest is celebrated there. But
> at a still later time, as the result of a dissension, they admitted some of the
> Campani as fellow-inhabitants, and thus they were forced to treat their
> worst enemies as their best friends, now that they had alienated their
> proper friends. This is disclosed by the names of their demarchs, for the
> earliest names are Greek only, whereas the later are Greek mixed with
> Campanian. And very many traces of Greek culture are preserved
> there—gymnasia, ephebeia, phratriae, and Greek names of things,
> although the people are Romans. And at the present time a sacred
> contest is celebrated among them every four years, in music as well as
> gymnastics; it lasts for several days, and vies with the most famous of
> those celebrated in Greece. Here, too, there is a tunnel—the mountain
> between Dicaearchia and Neapolis having been tunneled like the one
> leading to Cumae, and a road having been opened up for a distance of
> many stadia that is wide enough to allow teams going in opposite
> directions to pass each other. And windows have been cut out at
> many places, and thus the light of day is brought down from the surface
> of the mountain along shafts that are of considerable depth. Further-
> more, Neapolis has springs of hot water and bathing-establishments
> that are not inferior to those at Baiae, although it is far short of Baiae in
> the number of people, for at Baiae, where palace on palace has been

---

[1] On Hyperochus see Athenaeus 12.528 d–e, who calls him the 'author of Ky-
maika', and Pausanias 10.12.4, who stresses his origins from Cumae. The fragments
are collected in *FGrHist* 576. On Eumachus (*FGrHist* 178) see Athenaeus 13.541 a–b,
although it is unclear if his birthplace is the Italian Neapolis or another homonymous
town.

built, one after another, a new city has arisen, not inferior to Dicaearchia. And greater vogue is given to the Greek mode of life at
Neapolis by the people who withdraw thither from Rome for the sake
of rest—I mean the class who have made their livelihood by training the
young, or still others who, because of old age or infirmity, long to live in
relaxation; and some of the Romans, too, taking delight in this way of
living and observing the great number of men of the same culture as
themselves sojourning there, gladly fall in love with the place and make
it their permanent abode. (trans. H. L. Jones)[2]

According to a scheme followed throughout the *Geography*, Strabo's
description of Neapolis re-elaborates earlier sources relating to the
city, and can thus be seen as a reception of earlier literary and
historiographical traditions, which can help us to fill the lacunae of
the pre-Strabonian documentation. At the same time, the passage can
itself be seen as an important source for later receptions, insofar as it
contains several of the features and themes that would become central
to the construction of Naples' identity in later periods. Specifically,
these are (1) the 'double' origin of the city, together with the story of
the Siren Parthenope; (2) its ethnic composition and cultural 'Greekness', which endured despite the Romanization of the territory;
(3) the peculiarity of its landscape, which was characterized on the
one hand by the gulf and on the other hand by the volcanic morphology;

---

[2] Strabo 5.4.7: Μετὰ δὲ Δικαιάρχειάν ἐστι Νεάπολις Κυμαίων· ὕστερον δὲ καὶ
Χαλκιδεῖς ἐπῴκησαν καὶ Πιθηκουσαίων τινὲς καὶ Ἀθηναίων, ὥστε καὶ Νεάπολις
ἐκλήθη διὰ τοῦτο. ὅπου δείκνυται μνῆμα τῶν Σειρήνων μιᾶς Παρθενόπης, καὶ ἀγὼν
συντελεῖται γυμνικὸς κατὰ μαντείαν. ὕστερον δὲ Καμπανῶν τινας ἐδέξαντο συνοίκους
διχοστατήσαντες, καὶ ἠναγκάσθησαν τοῖς ἐχθίστοις ὡς οἰκειοτάτοις χρήσασθαι, ἐπειδὴ
τοὺς οἰκείους ἀλλοτρίους ἔσχον. μηνύει δὲ τὰ τῶν δημάρχων ὀνόματα τὰ μὲν πρῶτα
Ἑλληνικὰ ὄντα, τὰ δ᾽ ὕστερα τοῖς Ἑλληνικοῖς ἀναμὶξ τὰ Καμπανικά. πλεῖστα δ᾽ ἴχνη
τῆς Ἑλληνικῆς ἀγωγῆς ἐνταῦθα σώζεται, γυμνάσιά τε καὶ ἐφηβεῖα καὶ φρατρίαι καὶ
ὀνόματα Ἑλληνικὰ καίπερ ὄντων Ῥωμαίων. νυνὶ δὲ πεντετηρικὸς ἱερὸς ἀγὼν
συντελεῖται παρ᾽ αὐτοῖς μουσικός τε καὶ γυμνικὸς ἐπὶ πλείους ἡμέρας, ἐνάμιλλος τοῖς
ἐπιφανεστάτοις τῶν κατὰ τὴν Ἑλλάδα. ἔστι δὲ καὶ ἐνθάδε διῶρυξ κρυπτή, τοῦ μεταξὺ
ὄρους τῆς τε Δικαιαρχείας καὶ τῆς Νεαπόλεως ὑπεργασθέντος ὁμοίως ὥσπερ ἐπὶ τὴν
Κύμην, ὁδοῦ τε ἀνοιχθείσης ἐναντίοις ζεύγεσι πορευτῆς ἐπὶ πολλοὺς σταδίους· τὰ δὲ
φῶτα ἐκ τῆς ἐπιφανείας τοῦ ὄρους, πολλαχόθεν ἐκκοπεισῶν θυρίδων, διὰ βάθους
πολλοῦ κατάγεται. ἔχει δὲ καὶ ἡ Νεάπολις θερμῶν ὑδάτων ἐκβολὰς καὶ κατασκευὰς
λουτρῶν οὐ χείρους τῶν ἐν Βαίαις, πολὺ δὲ τῷ πλήθει λειπομένας· ἐκεῖ γὰρ ἄλλη πόλις
γεγένηται, συνῳκοδομημένων βασιλείων ἄλλων ἐπ᾽ ἄλλοις, οὐκ ἐλάττων τῆς
Δικαιαρχείας. ἐπιτείνουσι δὲ τὴν ἐν Νεαπόλει διαγωγὴν τὴν Ἑλληνικὴν οἱ ἐκ τῆς
Ῥώμης ἀναχωροῦντες δεῦρο ἡσυχίας χάριν τῶν ἀπὸ παιδείας ἐργασαμένων ἢ καὶ
ἄλλων διὰ γῆρας ἢ ἀσθένειαν ποθούντων ἐν ἀνέσει ζῆν· καὶ τῶν Ῥωμαίων δ᾽ ἔνιοι
χαίροντες τῷ βίῳ τούτῳ, θεωροῦντες τὸ πλῆθος τῶν ἀπὸ τῆς αὐτῆς ἀγωγῆς
ἐπιδημούντων ἀνδρῶν, ἄσμενοι φιλοχωροῦσι καὶ ζῶσιν αὐτόθι.

(4) the wealthy and sophisticated lifestyle enjoyed by the city's inhabitants, and the attraction it held for Romans. Each of these points will be developed in detail in the following pages.

ORIGINS

Since the complicated issue of the city's origins will recur throughout this chapter and the whole volume, it is worth providing a brief outline here of the current state of knowledge about Neapolis' foundation.[3] Neapolis, whose orthogonal urban grid has developed into the modern city centre of Naples, was founded by colonists from the city of Cumae in Campania, itself a colony founded by the Euboeans from Chalcis in the eighth century BC. The foundation of Neapolis constituted the second phase of a Cumaean colonizing project on the coastline of the Gulf of Naples.[4] In the seventh century they founded the city of Parthenope on the hill known today as Pizzofalcone, close to the site on which Neapolis would later be built.[5] Parthenope apparently went into a decline during the last decades of the sixth century BC, at the same time as the new city appears to have been founded.[6] The foundation seems to have been accomplished by aristocratic families, who may have been forced to abandon the city of Cumae following the rise of the local tyrant Aristodemus.

---

[3] In addition to the classic work of Beloch (1890), see the following (necessarily limited) selection from the impressive bibliography on Neapolis (in more than one of the following items the city is analysed in connection with the whole Campanian area): *La Parola del Passato* (1952) (a special issue dedicated to Naples); Napoli (1959); Lepore (1967a); Lepore (1967b); D'Arms (1970); Frederiksen (1984); *Napoli antica* (1985); *Neapolis* (1986); Greco (1987); Valenza Mele (1993, with extensive bibliography updated to 1990); Leiwo (1994); Raviola (1995); Stärk (1995); Giampaola and d'Agostino (2005); Mele (2009); Spina (2010b). The Greek and Latin literary and epigraphic sources are collected by Buchner, Morelli, and Nenci (1952), and by Valenza Mele (1993).

[4] Cumae's influence on the whole Gulf of Naples was profound: Strabo says that Eratosthenes called it the 'Cumaean gulf', although Cumae is not in fact located there (Strabo 1.2.13: ἐν τούτῳ τῷ κόλπῳ τῷ ὑπὸ Ἐρατοσθένους λεχθέντι Κυμαίῳ).

[5] It is still unclear if Parthenope began life as a Rhodian centre or *emporium*, which pre-existed both of the Cumaean foundations (this issue will be discussed further below).

[6] Giampaola and d'Agostino (2005); Mele (2009).

Significantly, the foundation of Neapolis implied both a continuity and a discontinuity with the older city of Parthenope. The very name 'New City' clearly emphasized novelty, innovation, and hence discontinuity—by stressing what was 'new', however, the founders indirectly commemorated the existence of something 'old', which *ipso facto* escaped oblivion. At the same time, the citizens of Neapolis aimed to reaffirm the maritime-oriented policy which had previously been pursued by the Parthenopeans. For instance, Neapolis may have played a role in the naval combat in which the Syracusans, with the support of the Cumaeans (who controlled Cumae and the other cities of the Tyrrhenian coast), defeated the Etruscans in 474 BC. After this battle, the Syracusans occupied Pithecussae (modern Ischia), thereby taking control of the whole Tyrrhenian Sea from the coasts of Campania down to Cape Pelorus. This hegemony was, however, short-lived: in *c.*466 BC the Syracusans abandoned Pithecussae, which was immediately occupied by the Neapolitans. Some years later, Neapolis occupied Capri too, thereby taking control of both entrances to the gulf.

Returning to the text of Strabo, we find some confirmation of this modern reconstruction of the city's origins. However, there are also some notable peculiarities. Strabo seems to be aware of the two phases of the colonization, but he presents these phases in a rather obscure way.[7] For instance, he underlines, at a general level, the Cumaean identity of Neapolis (Νεάπολις Κυμαίων, 'Neapolis, a city of the Cumaeans'), presenting the second foundation (i.e. the 'real' foundation of Neapolis) as an ἀποικία ('colony') established directly by 'Chalcidians' together with 'some Pithecussans and Athenians'. It is noteworthy that Strabo does not mention the name of Parthenope in relation to the first foundation, nor does he present the Cumaeans as the authors of the second foundation. This suggests that he was drawing on sources which denied or minimized Cumae's involvement in the second phase, and which ascribed this element of the foundation to other Hellenic groups.[8]

---

[7] This data is not to be taken for granted, since other sources refer to Neapolis simply as a Cumaean foundation, without highlighting the two phases. Cf. Ps.-Scymnus, 251–2 and Velleius 1.4.2.

[8] It is possible that Strabo was also influenced by the new Augustan propaganda, which tended to underplay the significance of the ancestral 'Parthenopean' element. See Raviola (1995), 53–5 and Federico (2010), 282 for the Augustan 'deal' that

It has recently been proposed that the main source of Strabo's account of Neapolis was the historian Ephorus of Cyme, who embraced the Cumaeans' point of view and stressed the Chalcidian and Athenian element in the reconstruction of events.[9] As far as Strabo's use of the term 'Chalcidians' is concerned, it is possible that some colonists from Euboea were 'invited' to contribute to the new city's foundation, but it is more probable that here Strabo (or, presumably, his source) is reflecting a strand of ideological propaganda about Neapolis' foundation that underlined the Chalcidian element of the city's identity. Other authors (who may have been influenced by the same sources) also refer to Neapolis as a Chalcidian city while making no mention of the Cumaeans.[10] It is likely that the Neapolitans, who had received several Cumaean refugees after Cumae had been occupied by the Samnites of Capua in 421 BC, had inherited the status of main Chalcidian city of the area. Strabo's mention of the Pithecussans should probably also be seen as a reference to the Chalcidian origins of Cumae, rather than as a direct reference to the island, which was occupied by Syracuse at the time when Neapolis was founded; according to Livy, Cumae was founded by the Chalcidians, whose earliest settlement was that of Pithecussae.[11]

As for Strabo's reference to the Athenians, their contribution to the political life of the newborn Neapolis is well attested, albeit in periods subsequent to the foundation.[12] The historian Timaeus recalls a visit to Neapolis made by the Athenian general Diotimus (*c.*452 BC), who is said to have sacrificed to Parthenope and instituted a torch race (*lampadophoria*) in her honour.[13] Another well-known tradition gives Neapolis the Attic name of Phaleron, while the presence of a cult of Demeter Eleusinia also suggests an Athenian influence that

---

motivated the diffusion of a version according to which Parthenope was named Neapolis under this *princeps* (Solinus 2.9: *Parthenope a Parthenopae Sirenis sepulcro, quam Augustus postea Neapolim esse maluit*; see also Isidore of Seville, who 'Christianizes' his source Solinus by making Parthenope a simple maiden and not a Siren: *Parthenope a Parthenope quadam virgine illic sepulta Parthenope appellata; quod oppidum postea Augustus Neapolim esse maluit* (15.1.60).

[9] Mele (2009), 195.

[10] Cf. Pliny the Elder, *Natural History* 3.62; Statius, *Silvae* 5.3.109–11.

[11] Livy 8.22.5.

[12] On the relationship between Athens and Neapolis see Maurizi (1993–5) and Mele (2007). See also Taylor, Ch. 3 in this volume.

[13] Timaeus, *FGrHist* 566 F 98 (= Scholia in Lycophr. *Alexandra* 732). For the chronology of Diotimus' visit see Mele (2007) and Maddoli (2010).

finds further confirmation in the presence of Athenian coins among the numismatic evidence relating to the early phases of Neapolis' history.[14]

Another passage of Strabo contains hints of a foundation account according to which Parthenope would have been a Rhodian (and thus ethnically Dorian) centre, pre-dating the 'first' Cumaean foundation. In book 14 of the *Geography*, Strabo notes how, even before the institution of the Olympic games in 776 BC, the Rhodians sailed far and wide across the Mediterranean Sea and founded several colonies in the West, one of which was Neapolis 'among the Opicians', i.e. in Magna Graecia.[15] It is likely that here Strabo was using Rhodian sources, which he may not have been acquainted with when he wrote his description of Neapolis in book 5.[16] As far as the historical 'truth' of this account is concerned, it has been pointed out that the cult of the Sirens is consistent with what we know about Rhodian culture.[17] Interestingly, however, even if this account of Neapolis' Rhodian identity is historically accurate, it has notably failed to become incorporated into the city's cultural memory.[18]

An alternative account of Parthenope/Neapolis' history is found in a fragment of the second-century BC Roman historian Lutatius, which mentions a rivalry between Parthenope and the Cumaeans who had founded the city:

---

[14] The Neapolitan coinage is described by Rutter (1979), 142–58; Rutter (1980). For the name Phaleron see Lycophron, *Alexandra* 717 and scholia; Stephanus of Byzantium s.v. Φάληρον. On Demeter Eleusinia see Statius, *Silvae* 4.8.50–1.

[15] Strabo 14.2.10: 'It is related of the Rhodians that their maritime affairs were in a flourishing state, not only from the time of the foundation of the present city, but that many years before the institution of the Olympic festival, they sailed to a great distance from their own country for the protection of sailors. They sailed as far as Spain, and there founded Rhodus, which the people of Marseilles afterwards occupied; they founded Parthenope among the Opici, and Elpiae in Daunia, with the assistance of Coans' (trans. H. C. Hamilton) ('Ἱστοροῦσι δὲ καὶ ταῦτα περὶ τῶν Ῥοδίων, ὅτι οὐ μόνον ἀφ᾽ οὗ χρόνου συνῴκισαν τὴν νῦν πόλιν εὐτύχουν κατὰ θάλατταν, ἀλλὰ καὶ πρὸ τῆς Ὀλυμπικῆς θέσεως συχνοῖς ἔτεσιν ἔπλεον πόρρω τῆς οἰκείας ἐπὶ σωτηρίᾳ τῶν ἀνθρώπων· ἀφ᾽ οὗ καὶ μέχρι Ἰβηρίας ἔπλευσαν, κἀκεῖ μὲν τὴν Ῥόδην ἔκτισαν ἣν ὕστερον Μασσαλιῶται κατέσχον, ἐν δὲ τοῖς Ὀπικοῖς τὴν Παρθενόπην, ἐν δὲ Δαυνίοις μετὰ Κῴων Ἐλπίας. A later source that confirms this hypothesis, Stephanus of Byzantium (s.v. Παρθενόπη), is probably to be interpreted as dependent on Strabo; see Càssola (1986), 42.

[16] Càssola (1986), 42.

[17] Peterson (1919), 14, 174–81; Pugliese Carratelli (1952b).

[18] Others have argued that this account is isolated and unconvincing: for a full discussion see Mele (2009), 186–7.

Parthenope. Lutatius in Book Four reports that Cumaean inhabitants
left their fathers and founded the city of Parthenope, from the name of
the siren Parthenope, whose body is buried there. After the city got
more and more crowded thanks to the wealth and the beauty of the site,
the Cumaeans, concerned by the eventuality that Cumae would be
totally abandoned, planned to destroy Parthenope. But later, afflicted
by a pestilence, according to an oracle they restored the city and
celebrated the cult of Parthenope with great piousness, and then gave
the city the name of Neapolis because of the new foundation.[19]

The reference to Parthenope's 'wealth and beauty' is worth highlighting, albeit *en passant*, since *amoenitas* ('beauty') would become a
central topos of descriptions of Naples in later centuries. As for
Neapolis' foundation, several features of Lutatius' description are
significant. For instance, he does not say that the Cumaeans destroyed
the city, but only that they planned to do so (Parthenope does,
however, seem to have been damaged, since the Cumaeans were
later punished with a plague and forced to 'refound' Parthenope
and re-establish the cult of the Siren). Like Strabo, Lutatius is aware
of the two phases of colonization, and he too regards Neapolis as a
refoundation of Parthenope; unlike the Greek geographer, however,
he considers this to have been achieved by the Cumaeans alone,
without any help from allies. The foundation of Parthenope is presented by Lutatius as the decision of some of Cumae's citizens
(*Cumanos incolas a parentibus digressos Parthenopen urbem constituisse*); his account thus contains the seeds of the later rivalry.[20]
Meanwhile, the foundation of Neapolis is presented here as a form
of 'compensation' for the destructive policies of the motherland.

---

[19] Quintus Lutatius Catulus, *Communes historiae*, 4, fr. 7 Peter = 7 Chassignet
(Scholia Vaticana to Virgil, *Georgics* 4.563): *Parthenope. Lutatius libro iv. dicit Cumanos incolas a parentibus digressos Parthenopen urbem constituisse, dictam a Parthenope sirena, cuius corpus etiam <illic sepultum sit.> postquam ob locorum ubertatem
amoenitatemque magis coepta sit frequentari, veritos (Cumanos), ne Cumae omnino
desererentur, inisse consilium Parthenopen diruendi. Postea tamen pestilentia affectos
ex responso oraculi urbem restituisse sacraque Parthenopes cum magna religione
suscepisse, nomen autem Neapoli ob recentem institutionem imposuisse.* The question
of whether this historian is to be identified with Quintus Lutatius Catulus or Lutatius
Daphnis (both writers of the second century BC) is disputed; *status quaestionis* in
Chassignet (2004), 21.

[20] A parallel analysis of Strabo and Lutatius can be found in Mele (2009).

The first settlement, Parthenope, was later called Palaepolis (the 'Old City') in order to distinguish it from Neapolis (the 'New City').[21] It is unclear what status Parthenope had after the foundation of Neapolis. Livy's account of the war over Neapolis (*c.*328–326 BC) does imply that Palaepolis played a leading role, as though it were still the political centre of the area:

> There was a city called Palaepolis, not far from the spot where Neapolis is now, and the two cities were inhabited by one people. Cumae was their mother city, and the Cumani derive their origin from Chalcis in Euboea. (trans. B. O. Foster)[22]

As if to prove the close links between the two cities, Livy states that the Roman consul Publilius Philo put his camp at the midpoint between the two settlements, thereby preventing them from organizing a common defensive line against the siege.[23] At the same time, Livy seems to be aware of a certain inconsistency in his sources when he notes that the treaty made by the Romans after the surrender of Palaepolis was called the *foedus Neapolitanum*, rather than *foedus Palaepolitanum*. Neapolis may have become the main centre after the cities were brought under Roman control (and indeed, Livy's subsequent words suggest as much).[24] The name Palaepolis, however, did appear in official documents at Rome, with the form *Palaeopolitaneis* figuring in the *Fasti Triumphales*.[25] In that period, Palaepolis/Neapolis was under the political influence of the Samnites who, from the beginning of the fourth century BC, had controlled the whole of Campania (as well as being partially integrated in the Neapolitan citizenry, as seen above in Strabo's account). The Roman war against Neapolis was in fact part of a broader conflict with the Samnites, and

---

[21] The original name of this first city could not, of course, have been Palaepolis. It is noteworthy that Strabo does not specify the city's name. Other sources do, however, call it Parthenope (as we will see throughout this chapter), and modern scholars agree that there is no reason for calling this denomination into question.

[22] Livy 8.22.5: *Palaepolis fuit haud procul inde ubi nunc Neapolis sita est; duabus urbibus populus idem habitabat. Cumis erant oriundi; Cumani Chalcide Euboica originem trahunt.*

[23] Livy 8.23.10.

[24] Livy 8.26.3: *foedus Neapolitanum—eo enim deinde summa rei Graecorum uenit.*

[25] *Fasti Triumphales Capitolini, Inscr. Ital.* xiii.1, 70–1 (362 BC = a.U.c. 428): *Q. Publilius Q. f. Q. n. Philo II primus pro co(n)s(ule) de Samnitibus, Palaeopolitaneis k. Mai ann. CDXXVII.*

Livy may be drawing on Neapolitan sources that were hostile to the
Italic invaders and consistent with Strabo's statement about the
forced coexistence of Greeks and Samnites in Neapolis. The population increase that resulted from the arrival of Samnite groups in
Naples may have led to a rearrangement of the fortified area of the
acropolis of Parthenope, which was now called Palaepolis in order to
distinguish it from the newer city. The fact that the *Fasti* and Livy
refer to Rome's enemies as the 'Palaepolitans' may be understood as a
'diplomatic success' for Neapolis, insofar as the post-war city does not
appear to be hostile to Rome; meanwhile, the new treaty with the
Romans is said to have been signed by the Neapolitans.[26]

No source other than Livy, however, mentions the contemporary
existence of two distinct cities, Palaepolis and Neapolis.[27] It may be
that authors like Strabo and Lutatius were influenced by local traditions that placed more emphasis on the 'continuum' pattern of the
refoundation than on the 'discontinuity' pattern of two coexisting
cities that were, to use Livy's words, 'inhabited by the same people'.
The most evident testimony of this trend is the use of the name
Parthenope, which became a denomination for Neapolis.[28] In his
discussion of the origins of this name, Strabo mentions the Siren
Parthenope, although (unlike most of the other surviving sources) he
does not use her name in connection with the earlier foundation.
Here as elsewhere in his work, however, Strabo underlines the presence of Parthenope's μνῆμα (a monumental 'sepulchre') in the city,
and the fact that the inhabitants celebrated games 'in accordance with
an oracle'.[29] These games are to be identified with the torch race
mentioned above, while the presence of Parthenope's tomb is confirmed by several other authors.[30]

It is not possible to cite here all the sources which report or discuss
the myth of the Siren Parthenope, nor to reopen the *vexata quaestio*

---

[26] Similar conclusions in Mele (2009), 192–3. For an analysis of Livy's account see
also Frederiksen (1984), 207–10.

[27] See e.g. the extant fragments of the *Antiquitates Romanae* by Dionysius of
Halicarnassus (15.5–8) where no mention is made of Palaepolis; it should be noted,
though, that the fragmentary nature of the text does not allow an exhaustive analysis.

[28] Cf. Silius Italicus 12.27–39; Pliny, *Natural History* 3.62: *Neapolis Chalcidensium
et ipsa, Parthenope a tumulo Sirenis appellata.*

[29] Strabo 1.2.13.

[30] Lycophron, *Alexandra* 717–72; Suetonius fr. 203 Reifferscheid; Dionysius Periegetes, 357–9 (and its Latin trans. by Priscianus, 351–3); Suda, s.v. Νεάπολις, 115
Adler.

of where the Sirens were thought to have been located in antiquity. The myth is attested in numerous sources, in which the Siren Parthenope is frequently associated with places on the Gulf of Naples. While Cape Athenaion (modern Punta della Campanella, near Sorrento) and the Sirenussae islands (three rocks emerging from the sea near Cape Athenaion, now known as Li Galli) are said to be places where the Sirens stayed, Neapolis is the place where the body of Parthenope was found after her *katapontismos* ('death by plunging into the sea'). Capri is also considered a place of Sirens, albeit in later sources.[31] Each of these versions may reflect different traditions and ideologies, which depended to some extent on which powers dominated the gulf at the time of writing.[32] Most relevant here, though, is the fact that these mythical traditions about Parthenope can be seen as evidence of Parthenope/Neapolis' influence over the whole gulf area.[33] In fact, the Neapolitans dominated the gulf in the fifth century BC, and it seems clear that from shortly after its foundation, the identity of Naples was tightly interwoven with that of the whole gulf—a phenomenon that again would characterize perceptions of the city throughout the centuries.

To sum up this discussion of the origins of Naples, the surviving sources are often inconsistent, above all in their treatment of the difficult relationship between Parthenope/Neapolis and Cumae. It is clear that the sources reflect two distinct perspectives on this issue.[34]

---

[31] For an up-to-date study of the myth of the Sirens see Spina (2007).

[32] Full discussion in Mele (2009), 188–92; Federico (2010). See also Pugliese Carratelli (1952b); Breglia Pulci Doria (1987); Spina (2007), 112–24.

[33] Such a conclusion seems to be confirmed by Lycophron's *Alexandra* 717–21, which connects the Neapolitan area with the Siren Parthenope: 'One of them washed ashore the tower of Phalerus shall receive, and Glanis wetting the earth with its streams. There the inhabitants shall build a tomb for the maiden and with libations and sacrifice of oxen shall yearly honour the bird goddess Parthenope' (trans. A. W. Mair and G. R. Mair) (τὴν μὲν Φαλήρου τύρσις ἐκβεβρασμένην | Γλάνις τε ῥείθροις δέξεται τέγγων χθόνα. | οὗ σῆμα δωμήσαντες ἔγχωροι κόρης | λοιβαῖσι καὶ θύσθλοισι Παρθενόπην βοῶν | ἔτεια κυδανοῦσιν οἰωνὸν θεάν). Lycophron refers to Neapolis as 'the tower of Phalerus' and cites the Clanius, or Glanis, river as a geographical identifier. This river, which flowed into the modern Lago di Patria, was quite far from the city, closer to Cumae, and it flowed through territories that were not under Neapolis' control. Peterson (1919: 174–81) suggests that Lycophron may have confused it with the Sebethos; alternatively, he may have mentioned it in order to flaunt his own topographic erudition about Campania. Be that as it may, it is possible to read this citation as a clue that Neapolis could 'absorb' the identity of inner areas.

[34] Cf. the discussion in Mele (2009).

The first emphasizes the Cumaean origin of the city: this is the view held by Strabo, which can probably be traced back to Ephorus. The second perspective, which is offered by Lutatius and by his sources, stresses the autonomy of Neapolis, and depicts Cumae as jealous of and ungenerous towards its colony. Meanwhile, the myth of Parthenope both reflected and constructed the identity of Neapolis, stressing the city's close links with the sea and its 'osmotic' relationship with the coastal area surrounding it. The cult of the Siren was one of several features that the new city of Neapolis inherited from the old city of Parthenope—her enduring use as the city's symbol thereby provided a mnemonic link back to the 'deep past' and the earliest moments of Naples' long history.

NAPLES AS 'GREEK CITY'

Strabo's description of Neapolis draws attention to the city's vibrant ethnic composition, both in the early phase of the two foundations (Cumaeans, Chalcidians, Pithecussans, Athenians) and in later times as well. After Strabo has referred to the monument of the Siren Parthenope, he marks a chronological shift using a laconic and generic 'later' ($\H{v}\sigma\tau\epsilon\rho o\nu$). He then introduces the reader to the mention of an internal struggle which led to the Neapolitans granting citizenship to the Campanians, i.e. the Samnites who ruled Capua and the inland area surrounding Neapolis. Strabo's source text appears to have been severe with the Neapolitans, judging from the words used by the geographer: 'and thus they were forced to treat their worst enemies as their best friends, now that they had alienated their proper friends' ($\kappa\alpha\grave{\iota}\ \mathring{\eta}\nu\alpha\gamma\kappa\acute{\alpha}\sigma\theta\eta\sigma\alpha\nu\ldots\check{\epsilon}\sigma\chi o\nu$).[35] The 'proper friends' to whom Strabo alludes are the Cumaeans, who presumably had not been rescued by the Neapolitans when they were attacked by the Samnites. From that time onwards, Campanians as well as Greeks could be citizens and even city officials: ultimately, the presence of

---

[35] Breglia Pulci Doria convincingly concludes that these words are drawn from Ephorus' work, and are modelled on a passage of Isocrates' *Panegyric* (111) (1996), 53. Isocrates, as is well known, was Ephorus' teacher of rhetoric.

Samnites from Capua within the city walls implied, for Strabo, a fusion of the two peoples.[36]

While the ethnicity of Neapolis was mixed, however, the city continued to boast a strong Greek identity, and Strabo comments that several strong traces of the city's Greek past survived in the (Roman) city of his own time.[37] The Augustalia (Σεβαστά) games (whose name is not given by Strabo) are mentioned immediately after as an example of Neapolis' 'Hellenism' (as further discussed in Chapter 4 of this volume by Kathryn Lomas). These games were extremely popular in the early imperial age, and attracted competitors from across the Mediterranean world, as we know from some recently discovered inscriptions.[38] Although devoted to Augustus and thus deeply 'Romanized' (cf. the argument of Mauro De Nardis in Chapter 5 of this volume), the Sebasta games used Greek as the official language, were Greek in form and organization, and included rhetorical and poetical performances in Greek.

Strabo explicitly underlines the persistent Greek identity of the city, while, in general, our other Greek sources seem to take it for granted, and refer to Neapolis *sic et simpliciter* as a Greek city. The case of the historian and rhetorician Dionysius of Halicarnassus, a contemporary of Strabo, is particularly striking. When Dionysius describes the beginning of the war between Rome and the Neapolitans, he notes that both the Romans and the Samnites sent embassies to the Neapolitans in order to obtain their alliance. Both the embassies attempted to persuade their hosts by arguing that the Neapolitans should act in a way 'worthy of Greek people' (5.1: μήτ᾽ αὐτοὺς ἔργα πράττοντας, ἃ μὴ προσήκει Ἕλλησι; 5.2: ὡς προσῆκεν Ἕλλησι), implying that the population was (or claimed to

---

[36] As mentioned above, the Samnites from Capua became very influential throughout the whole region of Campania before the Romans took control at the end of the fourth century BC. Strabo's statement about the forced 'cohabitation' of Greeks and Samnites echoes Livy's comments about the Roman siege of Palaepolis: since the Palaepolitans could not bear the arrogant presence of the Samnites, they chose to deliver the city to the Romans, who were considered the lesser of two evils (Livy 8.25.5–26.7).

[37] A hint of this attitude is found in the well-attested Neapolitan habit of granting citizenship to Greek intellectuals and poets; see Deniaux (1981) and Leiwo (1989).

[38] The institution of the Augustalia games is mentioned by Dio Cassius 55.10 (cf. also Velleius 2.123). For the recently discovered epigraphic evidence, see Miranda (2007) and Di Nanni (2007–8).

be) Greek. Frederiksen argues that Dionysius' source for this passage must date back to a period in which Neapolis had a largely Greek population.[39] Be that as it may, we cannot necessarily infer that the arguments used by the embassies were also present in Dionysius' source; instead, they may have been projected back onto the past by the later author. It is nevertheless clear that such a portrayal of Neapolis as a Greek city was apparently unproblematic when the *Antiquitates* were written, around the middle of the Augustan age.

Significantly, it is in the Latin context that we find more explicit references to Neapolis' Greekness. Cicero, for example, stresses the city's Hellenic cultural identity alongside that of three other Greek cities in Magna Graecia, namely Locris, Tarentum, and Rhegion.[40] The philhellenic *princeps* Nero is said by Suetonius to have addressed the Neapolitans with a speech in Greek, apparently assuming a Greek-speaking audience.[41] In a passage from Tacitus' *Annals* it is affirmed that Nero 'chose Neapolis because it was a Greek city' (*Neapolim quasi Graecam urbem delegit*).[42] In a poem dedicated to his wife, Statius (who was born in Neapolis and was acquainted with the local mythical Greek traditions) praised the Neapolitan way of life, which he described as mixing Roman respectability (*Romanus honos*) with the Greek love for pleasures (*Graia licentia*).[43] In another passage, the same author celebrates the Euboean origins of Neapolis by evoking the myth of Eumelus, who came to Magna Graecia under Apollo's protection, following a dove.[44] Several other passages from the *Silvae* also contain examples of Statius' representation of Neapolis as a Greek city (see the discussion by Giancarlo Abbamonte, Chapter 9 of this volume).

Neapolis' status as *Graeca urbs* is central to the depiction of the city given in Philostratus the Elder's second-century AD work, the *Imagines*. In this text, the author—a Greek sophist—describes a series of sixty-five paintings using a virtuoso ecphrastic technique. The prologue informs the reader that these descriptions were originally 'performed' by the author on site in a private art gallery in Neapolis; his audience was a group of young men drawn from the leading families of the city.

---

[39] Frederiksen (1984), 211.
[40] Cicero, *Pro Archia* 3.
[41] Suetonius, *Nero* 20.2.
[42] Tacitus, *Annals* 15.33.
[43] Statius, *Silvae* 3.5.94.
[44] *Silvae* 4.8.47–9.

The occasion of these discourses of mine was as follows: it was the time of the public games at Neapolis, a city in Italy settled by men of the Greek race and people of culture, and therefore Greek in their enthusiasm for discussion. And as I did not wish to deliver my addresses in public, the young men kept coming to the house of my host and importuning me. I was lodging outside the walls in a suburb facing the sea, where there was a portico built on four, I think, or possibly five terraces, open to the west wind and looking out on the Tyrrhenian sea. It was resplendent with all the marbles favoured by luxury, but it was particularly splendid by reason of the panel-paintings set in the walls, paintings which I thought had been collected with real judgment, for they exhibited the skill of very many painters. (trans. A. Fairbank)[45]

Philostratus explains here that he had come to Neapolis for the Augustalia games (ὁ παρὰ τοῖς Νεαπολίταις ἀγών). The city is described as thoroughly Greek, just like its citizens' interest in λόγοι (speeches), and more specifically μελέται (public declamations). The reader is also given a description of the building within which the performance took place: a grand portico (στοά) composed of four or five levels, which was located outside the city walls overlooking the gulf. Neapolis is represented in the text as a cultivated city (see the term ἀστικοί, i.e. *urbani*), whose local elite was eager both to collect pictures of mythological subjects and to entrust their progeny to a successful Greek-speaking rhetorician. Since Philostratus gives no hint of any linguistic gap between the author and his young public, one must assume that these Neapolitans were also Greek speakers. And although the situation described in the text is a fictitious creation, it can nevertheless be taken as reliable evidence that Neapolis was still perceived as a Greek city in the second century AD.

---

[45] Philostratus the Elder, *Imagines* Prologue, 4: ἀφορμαὶ δέ μοι τουτωνὶ τῶν λόγων αἵδε ἐγένοντο· ἦν μὲν ὁ παρὰ τοῖς Νεαπολίταις ἀγών – ἡ δὲ πόλις ἐν Ἰταλίᾳ ᾤκισται γένος Ἕλληνες καὶ ἀστικοί, ὅθεν καὶ τὰς σπουδὰς τῶν λόγων Ἑλληνικοί εἰσι – βουλομένῳ δέ μοι τὰς μελέτας μὴ ἐν τῷ φανερῷ ποιεῖσθαι παρεῖχεν ὄχλον τὰ μειράκια φοιτῶντα ἐπὶ τὴν οἰκίαν τοῦ ξένου. κατέλυον δὲ ἔξω τοῦ τείχους ἐν προαστείῳ τετραμμένῳ ἐς θάλασσαν, ἐν ᾧ στοά τις ἐξῳκοδόμητο κατὰ ζέφυρον ἄνεμον ἐπὶ τεττάρων οἶμαι ἢ καὶ πέντε ὀροφῶν ἀφορῶσα ἐς τὸ Τυρρηνικὸν πέλαγος. ἤστραπτε μὲν οὖν καὶ λίθοις, ὁπόσους ἐπαινεῖ τρυφή, μάλιστα δὲ ἤνθει γραφαῖς ἐνηρμοσμένων αὐτῇ πινάκων, οὓς ἐμοὶ δοκεῖν οὐκ ἀμαθῶς τις συνελέξατο· σοφία γὰρ ἐν αὐτοῖς ἐδηλοῦτο πλειόνων ζωγράφων.

MORPHOLOGY AND POROSITY

Following a historiographical tradition dating back to Herodotus, Strabo then moves on to describe Neapolis' *mirabilia*, starting with a tunnel to be identified with the famous 'Crypta Neapolitana', or else with the so-called 'Grotta di Seiano'. Strabo himself mentions with admiration the windows which brought light and air into the tunnel, and the considerable width of the path, which allowed two chariots going in opposite directions to comfortably pass each other by. He also mentions the thermal virtues of Neapolis' soil, which was apparently as good as that of Baiae.

In highlighting these particular features of the Neapolitan landscape, Strabo was unwittingly preparing the ground for the development of an enduring tradition, which saw Neapolis (and later Naples) as a city characterized by its subsoil.[46] Over the subsequent centuries, the yellow tufa underneath the city would be shaped by its inhabitants into a system of caves and tunnels, which facilitated the circulation of water, as well as people and goods. The morphological 'porosity' of the soil would later be central to Walter Benjamin's famous definition of Naples as a 'porous city', which mapped the physical qualities of the subsoil onto a socio-anthropological structure.[47] It is important to underline, however, that porosity is a feature shared by the whole volcanic area of the Phlegraean Fields, not only Neapolis. In fact, the tunnel was just one of a series of monumental excavations carried out by the Romans between the late Republican and the early imperial periods across the whole Phlegraean area. Strabo himself also mentions the so-called 'crypt of Cocceius', a tunnel connecting Lake Avernus with Cumae. In Strabo's opinion, Cocceius Auctus, the Augustan architect to whom both the tunnel and crypt are ascribed, is likely to have been inspired by a legend recounted in the work of the historian Ephorus of Cyme. According to this legend, Lake Avernus (traditionally considered to be one of the entrances to Hades) was inhabited by the mythological people of the Cimmerii, who lived in an underground network of tunnels that they had made in the area surrounding the lake.[48]

---

[46] The humanists' interest in the Neapolitan subsoil is discussed by Bianca de Divitiis in Chapter 10 of this volume.

[47] Benjamin (2007).   [48] Strabo 5.4.5.

In this way, both the porosity and the thermal properties of the soil constituted themes that linked Neapolis to the surrounding Phlegraean cities, in particular Cumae, Baiae, and Puteoli/Dicaearchia. The theme of porosity thus helped to create a shared 'Phlegraean' identity, which was independent from that of Neapolis. Similar comments might also be made of the representation of Vesuvius, which was treated by ancient authors as an organic part of the broader volcanic landscape of southern Italy (rather than being linked exclusively to Naples, as is often the case in modern times). Strabo himself mentions a Greek tradition dating back to Pindar, which considered all the volcanoes on the Tyrrhenian side of Magna Graecia, from the Phlegraean Fields to Mount Etna, as manifestations of the same underground volcanic activity.[49] Here again we can see a certain degree of 'osmotic' interaction between the identities of Neapolis and the gulf—as well as between Neapolis and the wider Phlegraean area.

A third way in which there was a blurring of boundaries between Neapolis and its wider region involved the assimilation of the Neapolitans with other inland populations. In this respect, the case of Nola is noteworthy: this city was founded in the hinterland by the Italic people that the Greek sources called Ausoni, before the Greeks themselves started colonizing southern Italy. From the fifth century BC onwards, Nola developed such a close relationship with Neapolis that both Pompeius Trogus/Justin and Silius Italicus dubbed it a 'Chalcidian city', i.e. Cumaean or Neapolitan.[50] The same Chalcidian origin is ascribed by Justin to Abella, nowadays Avella, which was located close to Nola. This 'cultural penetration' of Neapolitans into the hinterland is also entrenched in the mythological traditions about the area. Virgil, for instance, records a tradition according to which the hero Oebalus—who was said to have controlled the Sarno river plain and the city of Abellae—was the son of Telon, king of Capri, and the nymph

---

[49] Strabo 5.4.9, where we find a quote from Pindar, *Pythicae* 1.18–20. It seems clear that Pindar's perspective reflects Hiero of Syracuse's aim to control the whole of Tyrrhenian southern Italy.

[50] Silius Italicus 12.161–6: *hinc ad Chalcidicam transfert citus agmina Nolam*; Justin 20.1.6–13: *Denique multae urbes adhuc post tantam vetustatem vestigia Graeci moris ostentant.* [. . .] *Iam Falisci, Nolani, Abellani nonne Chalcidensium coloni sunt?*

Sebethis.[51] Sebethis can be viewed as a sort of personification of Neapolis, since the Sebethos was the city's main river. As others have already pointed out, this myth is clearly of Neapolitan origin, and reflects the hegemonic role played by the city in some parts of the inland area in the fifth century.[52] An indirect testimony of Nola's eagerness to be considered Greek is offered by the passage of Dionysius of Halicarnassus mentioned above, in which it is said that a Nolan embassy came to Neapolis in order to persuade the citizens to avoid any alliance with Rome, and that the Nolans 'greatly loved the Greeks' (Νωλάνων... σφόδρα τοὺς Ἕλληνας ἀσπαζομένων).[53]

In Magna Graecia, non-Greek communities often absorbed aspects of the identity of the main Greek city in their area; in other words, these Greek cities could influence minor centres (which were open to ethnic 'fusion' and cultural innovation) to such an extent that this caused a sort of 'identity transfer'.[54]

GOOD FOR A REST, GOOD FOR PHILOSOPHY

In the concluding lines of his description, Strabo mentions that many Romans in his own time moved to Neapolis in order to find a place of *otium* and quiet. Neapolis' 'Greekness'—which was perhaps embodied above all in the Epicurean school directed by Siro on the hill of Pausilypon—together with the remarkable natural beauty of the gulf, contributed to making Neapolis the perfect environment for

---

[51] Virgil, *Aeneid* 8.733–43.   [52] Mele (2009), 197–8.

[53] Dionysius of Halicarnassus, *Antiquitates Romanae* 15.5.2: 'Others also had come, sent by the Nolans, who were their neighbours and greatly admired the Greeks, to ask the Neapolitans on the contrary neither to make an agreement with the Romans or their subjects nor to give up their friendship with the Samnites' (trans. E. Cary) (καὶ ἕτεροι ὑπὸ Νωλάνων ὁμόρων ὄντων καὶ σφόδρα τοὺς Ἕλληνας ἀσπαζομένων, τἀναντία τοὺς Νεαπολίτας ἀξιώσοντες μήτε σύμβολα ποιεῖσθαι πρὸς τοὺς Ῥωμαίους ἢ τοὺς ὑπηκόους αὐτῶν μήτε διαλύεσθαι τὴν πρὸς Σαυνίτας φιλίαν).

[54] A similar process happened to the Nolans in connection with the Etruscan hegemony in the area. Cato and Velleius (who is our source for Cato) both explicitly mention an Etruscan foundation of Nola (Cato, *Origines* fr. 69; Peter = III 1 Chassignet; Velleius 1.7.2), which in reality was more a conquest or an occupation. See Solinus 2.16, who speaks about Nola founded *a Tyriis*, an odd statement which should probably be amended to *a Tyrrhenis* or similar.

Roman notables and intellectuals.[55] This image of Naples is recorded almost exclusively in Latin sources, and it is immortalized in the famous autobiographical verses of Virgil, which are strategically located at the end of the *Georgics* (*Illo Vergilium me tempore dulcis alebat | Parthenope studiis florentem ignobilis oti*); echoes of these lines are perceptible in Ovid's phrase *in otia natam | Parthenopen*, as well as in several passages of Statius which concern Neapolis.[56] In fact, the final section of Strabo's chapter is the sole Greek attestation of this phenomenon, and we might thus hypothesize that it is based on the author's personal experience.

A passage from a letter of Pliny the Younger allows us to appreciate how profound was the 'philoneapolitan' and 'philhellenic' attitude of many Romans who visited Neapolis or made their homes there. Pliny's letter contains an obituary of the Latin poet Silius Italicus, who is said to have adored the city and the whole of Campania:

> News has just come that Silius Italicus has starved himself to death at his villa near Naples. [. . .] At last he retired from the city, prompted thereto by his great age, and settled in Campania, nor did he stir from the spot, even at the accession of the new Emperor. A Caesar deserves great credit for allowing a subject such liberty, and Italicus deserves the same for venturing to avail himself of it. He was such a keen virtuoso that he got the reputation of always itching to buy new things. He owned a number of villas in the same neighbourhood, and used to neglect his old ones through his passion for his recent purchases. In each he had any quantity of books, statues and busts, which he not only kept by him but even treated with a sort of veneration, especially the busts of Virgil, whose birthday he kept up far more scrupulously than he did his own, principally at Naples, where he used to approach the poet's monument as though it were a temple. (trans. B. Radice)[57]

---

[55] On Siro and his connection with Philodemus and Virgil see Gigante (1990) and Gigante (1991). On the Roman villas of Neapolis and the rest of the gulf area see D'Arms (1970).

[56] Virgil, *Georgics* 4.563–4; Ovid, *Metamorphoses* 15.711. For a discussion of the Latin sources dealing with the amazing landscape of Neapolis and the gulf see Leiwo (1994), 33–41 and Stärk (1995), esp. ch. 2 (*Crater ille delicatus*, 99–219).

[57] Pliny the Younger, *Epistles* 3.7.1–8: *Modo nuntiatus est Silius Italicus in Neapolitano suo inedia finisse vitam.* [. . .] 6. *Novissime ita suadentibus annis ab urbe secessit, seque in Campania tenuit, ac ne adventu quidem novi principis inde commotus est:* 7. *magna Caesaris laus sub quo hoc liberum fuit, magna illius qui hac libertate ausus est uti.* 8. *Erat "philokalos" usque ad emacitatis reprehensionem. Plures isdem in locis villas possidebat, adamatisque novis priores neglegebat. Multum ubique librorum, multum statuarum, multum imaginum, quas non habebat modo, verum etiam*

According to Pliny, who provides a lively biographical sketch of the poet, Silius owned several villas in Campania and in Neapolis, which he filled with books and works of art. He especially venerated Virgil's *imago* (presumably a portrait bust), since he fervently worshipped this poet, 'whose birth date he celebrated more than his own' (*cuius natalem religiosius quam suum celebrabat*). Silius frequently went to visit Virgil's tomb in Naples: these visits constituted a sort of pilgrimage, since the funeral monument was considered a temple by Silius (*ubi monimentum eius adire ut templum solebat*). We might conclude, then, by noting that in Pliny's words we find a first attestation of the 'cult' of Virgil in Naples, a feature that would—as we shall see in later chapters of this volume—help to characterize the Neapolis of subsequent centuries as a city sacred to poets.

venerabatur, Vergili ante omnes, cuius natalem religiosius quam suum celebrabat, Neapoli maxime, ubi monimentum eius adire ut templum solebat.

3

The Temple of the Dioscuri and the Mythic Origins of Neapolis

Rabun Taylor

Naples is a city of few ruins. Even its best-preserved ancient temple, dedicated to the Dioscuri and the *polis*, hides in plain sight, its two surviving Corinthian columns projecting incongruously from the baroque facade of the church of S. Paolo Maggiore, the most recent of a sequence of buildings on the site dedicated to St Paul (Fig. 3.1).[1] Yet the Roman temple stood relatively undisturbed until its rededication in the late eighth century, and even thereafter the whole facade of the temple survived in place with only minor losses until several earthquakes in the 1680s brought down the pediment and most of the columns. The two surviving outer columns stood directly behind the hexastyle facade, of which only two bases survive. The temple stood on an exceptionally high podium faced in *opus reticulatum*; the core of an older temple may lie within it.[2] After the collapse many of the fallen elements were displayed in the piazza below, but except for a small fragment of the inscription they are lost today.[3] The full dedicatory inscription, preserved in full on the building's white marble architrave until the collapse, read:

ΤΙΒΕΡΙΟΣ ΙΟΥΛΙΟΣ ΤΑΡΣΟΣ ΔΙΟΣΚΟΥΡΟΙΣ ΚΑΙ ΤΗΙ ΠΟΛΕΙ
ΤΟΝ ΝΑΟΝ ΚΑΙ ΤΑ ΕΝ ΤΩΙ ΝΑΩΙ / ΠΕΛΑΓΩΝ ΣΕΒΑΣΤΟΥ ΑΠΕ-
ΛΕΥΘΕΡΟΣ ΚΑΙ ΕΠΙΤΡΟΠΟΣ ΣΥΝΤΕΛΕΣΑΣ ΕΚ ΤΩΝ ΙΔΙΩΝ
ΚΑΘΙΕΡΩΣΕΝ[4]

---

[1] Adamo Muscettola (1985), 196–9; Lenzo (2011).   [2] Carafa (2008), 44–8.
[3] Correra (1905), 220–1; Campana (1973–4); Solin (2004); Lenzo (2011), 40–2, 45.
[4] *CIG* 3.5791; *IG* 14.714; Miranda (1990), 11–13.

Fig. 3.1. Naples, facade of the church of S. Paolo Maggiore with standing remains of the temple of the Dioscuri.
Source: Photograph: R. Taylor.

> Tiberius Julius Tarsos [dedicated] this temple and everything in it to the Dioscuri and the City. Pelagon, freedman and procurator of the emperor, completed it with his own money and consecrated it.

Tarsos and Pelagon are identified as Asian-born freedmen of Tiberius (AD 14–37).[5] This emperor's devotion to the Dioscuri was famously

---

[5] Adamo Muscettola (1985), 200–1.

Fig. 3.2. Detail of an ink drawing of the pediment at S. Paolo Maggiore. Fo. 45v from the manuscript of *Os desenhos das antiqualhas* by Francisco d'Ollanda.

Source: Real Biblioteca del Monasterio de El Escorial. © Patrimonio Nacional.

manifested in the great temple on the Roman Forum, dedicated in AD 6. Commonly known to Romans as the Castors, the brother horsemen had enjoyed a cult in Rome at least since the late fifth century BC. Rome, like other cities, venerated them as deified saviour-heroes who had intervened in a crucial conflict—in this case, the Battle of Lake Regillus in the 490s—to defeat a powerful foe.

Despite the survival of several drawings and written descriptions of the pediment both before and after the collapse, the sculptural programme, which lacked its central figures even in the Renaissance, eludes easy interpretation. A fine drawing from 1540 by Francisco D'Ollanda seems the most reliable of those that survive (Fig. 3.2). It shows a large gap in the centre of the pediment with seven complete or almost complete figures around it. The sculpture was rendered in high relief, not as free-standing statuary.[6] Three standing figures survive: two males to the left of the gap, and a female to the right. On each side a reclining figure, legs outward, accompanies a smaller Triton or Tritoness in the corner who gestures attentively towards the figure. These hybrid mermaids and mermen are said to be blowing trumpets.[7] Denoting Poseidon's power over the

---

[6] Richard Symonds, in a sketch of *c*.1651, calls it a 'bassorilievo' (Oxford, Bodleian Library, Rawlinson D.121, fo. 23): see Lenzo (2011), fig. 39. Palladio, Summonte, and Celano—likewise eyewitnesses of the pediment (the latter after its collapse)—refer to its sculpture as relief. Finally, certain details of the drawing confirm this testimony; see Bernabò Brea (1935), 71–2.

[7] Capaccio (1607), 219 (*buccinas concinentes*); accepted by Capasso (1905), 80; Correra (1905), 226–7; and most subsequent scholars. Yet in 1547 Jean Matal,

seas, semi-recumbent Tritons had been appearing in pediment corners since the Archaic period, as on the early temples of the Athenian Acropolis. Even their association with the Dioscuri has a precedent: on a fifth-century BC temple at Locri Epizefiri, thought to commemorate the brothers' intervention in the Battle of Sagra in the sixth century BC, Tritons bear their horses providentially over the waves.[8] By the Roman imperial period, they had long been generic symbols of the sea.

The reclining figures beside each Triton fit a Julio-Claudian tendency to represent place allegories in meaningful pairs in the pediments of temples.[9] But what do they represent in particular? On the right is a semi-nude male water deity, mature and bearded. His shoulders, lap, and legs are draped, his torso bare; his right elbow rests on an overturned urn; he seems to wear a crown of vegetation. The female figure reclining symmetrically on the left side is similarly semi-nude; she may wear a crown (of grain?) on her head, barely suggested by Francisco's pen strokes. In the crook of her right elbow is a cornucopia, a feature confirmed in numerous texts and an anonymous illustration in Paris made shortly before the collapse (Fig. 3.3). She rests against a triple-hooped *modius*, or grain basket, a common attribute of allegories of abundance.[10]

The reclining male figure is indisputably a water god; but who in particular? Sceptical that Neapolis' puny rivers would have merited inclusion in this grand pediment, Duhn and Adamo Muscettola identify him as Oceanus, mirroring the equally generic figure of Gaia/Tellus.[11] In fact, the eyewitness testimonies of Pighius and Summonte seriously undermine this attribution, for they indicate that he held a freshwater reed (the *canna palustre*) in one hand.[12]

working from an illustration of the pediment, confessed *nescio quid* in relation to the attributes that they were holding. Lenzo (2011), figs. 35, 36.

[8] Costabile (1995).

[9] Wiseman (1995), 146–50; Bell (2009).

[10] Capaccio (1607), 219 says *Tellus ad dexteram copiae cornu tenet* ('Tellus on the right holds a cornucopia'). Jean Matal's 1547 description also mentions this feature; see Lenzo (2011), figs. 35, 36. Pighius (1587), 456 seems to confuse the figure's right and left hand, but is otherwise lucid; Summonte (1601), 1.86–7 misinterprets the *modius* as 'una picciola torre sovrapposta a un Monticello' ('a small tower placed on a hillock'). Lenzo (2011), fig. 40.

[11] Duhn (1910), 10–11; Adamo Muscettola (1985), 203–4.

[12] Pighius (1587), 456; Summonte (1601), 1.86; Bernabò Brea (1935), 71; Hommel (1954), 53.

Fig. 3.3. Anonymous sketch of the facade of S. Paolo Maggiore.

Source: Cabinet des Estampes VB 132 (L, 1) Fo. P 64623. Courtesy of the Bibliothèque Nationale de France.

The river identification may have another point in its favour. The figure seems to wear a chaplet of vegetation; but below it, a few ambiguous pen strokes seem to suggest two projections, highlighted in white, that break the normal contours of the forehead. They project slightly forward, like vestigial horns.[13] If horns are intended—and we may postulate that by the sixteenth century these were nothing more than the stumps of the originals—then we are certainly dealing with a river god in the manner of Acheloos. From Archaic times to the

---

[13] They seem too broad to be identified as the stumps of crab legs or claws, common hornlike features on the head of Oceanus; see Cahn (1997).

Fig. 3.4. Didrachm of Neapolis, *c*.300–275 BC.
Source: Ex-Paul Mathey Collection. Courtesy of the Classical Numismatic Group.

Hellenistic period this god, along with his many iconographic filiations in Magna Graecia and Sicily, took several hybrid forms merging features of a man and a bull: most commonly, either the body of a bull with the head of a bearded and horned male, or a youth with the horns of a bull.[14] By the early imperial period, however, this tradition of representing rivers had dissipated almost entirely in favour of the reclining humanoid lacking theriomorphic features.[15] Why, then, would it have appeared here?

The answer, I suggest, is tied to Roman Neapolis' unique identity, which it preserved through scrupulous attention to its Hellenic origins. Most Greek cities in Italy had developed foundation myths which we may occasionally glimpse in literary references, public sculpture, and coins. Neapolis' own coinage, though long out of circulation by the Julio-Claudian age, contributed a local iconographic convention that probably continued in other media. As such, it offers a clue to understanding the nature and identity of the male reclining figure on the pediment. The most common reverse type on Neapolitan silver coinage was the man-headed bull striding in profile, his head turned frontally (Fig. 3.4). Often a winged Nike hovered above him, her outstretched hand bearing a victor's crown (*stephanos*) intended for his head. On the pediment, I believe, the reclining figure's attendant sea creature is replicating this very gesture, not sounding a trumpet. Older pediments tend to present Tritons as bearded males, but Francisco's drawing renders the bearer

---

[14] Imhoof-Blumer (1923); Isler (1970); Isler (1981); Weiss (1988); Taylor (2009).
[15] Ostrowski (1991).

of the diadem as a Tritoness with ample breasts, perhaps to strengthen the associations with Nike. Precisely what she holds, however, remains a mystery. This is not a coronation, for the god is already crowned; instead, the object seems to decant a liquid, visible in cascading strokes of ink and white, onto his shoulder. The trope is unusual, but in effect it resembles a coronation: it is an anointing of sorts, symbolic at one remove of the hydrologic cycle (which Greeks understood reasonably well) but at another remove, of tribute to Neapolis and her territory from the sea.

Elsewhere I have supported the traditional identification of the bull-man on the local coinage as the Sebethos, a now-defunct local river of uncertain location.[16] Though always small and unnavigable, symbolically it prevailed as the river by which Neapolis identified itself. In fact, a Neapolitan silver obol of about 400–380 BC depicts on its obverse the bull-horned head of a youth surrounded by the legend *Sepeithos*.[17] A local cult of this river god was still active in the Roman imperial era.[18] So one might reasonably follow Summonte and his successors who identify the pedimental figure as a Romanized embodiment of the river. On the whole, he fits a standard Roman type; but his bovine horns, if horns they are, evoke Neapolis' atavistic iconographic tradition.

On the obverse, the striding Sebethos coinage featured a female bust in profile universally acknowledged by scholars (though never overtly identified by inscription) as that of Parthenope, the doomed Siren whose body was washed ashore at this site on the Bay.[19] The early Euboean colony took her name, and when a new colony was founded nearby it was named Neapolis ('New City') to distinguish it from the first. Parthenope was evidently on the rocky headland of Pizzofalcone, where a Greek cemetery dating back at least to the early seventh century BC has been discovered.[20] The pairing of these two figures on the obverse and reverse of Classical and Hellenistic Neapolitan coinage was so common that it suggests a close bond. Consequently the reclining female figure on the left side of the pediment could be interpreted as Parthenope herself—in her toponymic guise,

---

[16] Taylor (2009).
[17] Sambon (1903), 181; Imhoof-Blumer (1923), 175–6; Cantilena (1985), 361, no. 110; Rutter (1979), 43–4; Taylor (2009), 26–7.
[18] *CIL* 10.1480.   [19] Lycophron, *Alexandra* 712–38.
[20] De Caro (1974); Giampaola and D'Agostino (2005).

representing the original settlement on the rocky promontory of Pizzofalcone. In their traditional manifestation, Sirens were depicted either as sea birds with the heads of women or naked women with the legs of birds.[21] As with the Sebethos river, which may or may not have had visible horns, the older therianthropic dualism was minimized— hardly an unexpected development in Julio-Claudian pedimental schemata, which favour simple humanoid forms to represent geographic features in the corners of pediments. Having no birdlike features, this figure could have been understood as Parthenope the *place*, but not Parthenope the *Siren*.

That said, I resist particularizing the reclining figures' identities. Neither bears a specific, localized attribute; to the contrary, they are both generic, one representing fresh flowing water, the other earthly abundance. Geographically, the cornucopia and the grain *modius* have no direct association with Parthenope itself, which was (and remains) a rocky outcropping without agriculture; rather, it symbolizes the bounty of the town's productive hinterland.[22] The reclining female figure on the left of the pediment, then, might simply embody the bounty of the region, or even be generalized into Campania at large, as others have suggested.[23] Meanwhile, the river god on the right perhaps embodies the well-watered nature of the landscape without referencing any river in particular.

The manner of the Triton's interaction with the reclining female on the left is uncertain. If we follow the most conventional interpretation, he was sounding a seashell trumpet, most of which had broken away before the drawings were made. But the trumpet would have to pass in front of the dense mass of fruit atop the cornucopia, cluttering a composition that in all other respects seems to have exemplified figural and gestural clarity. Both Francisco's drawing and the anonymous Paris sketch allow for another interpretation: he slyly picks at the fruit while the cornucopia's bearer is distracted (see Figs. 3.2 and 3.3). This kind of gentle subversion answered to contemporary tastes.[24] The trend effloresced in the Julio-Claudian period, especially with

---

[21] Hofstetter (1997).

[22] In the same manner, Dionysios Periegetes, writing sometime in the second or third century AD, refers to 'Parthenope, heavy under the weight of grain sheaves' (358).

[23] Capasso (1905), 80; Trendelenburg (1911); Bernabò Brea (1935), 75–6; Peterson (1919), 190.

[24] The sophisticated irony and even subversiveness of late Republican and Augustan lyric poetry, for example, are well known; see Lyne (2007).

the interjection of genre scenes into more solemn contexts. A famous example of this phenomenon is the Algiers Relief, believed to be a reasonably accurate reproduction of the group of cult statues in Augustus' temple of Mars Ultor at Rome. On it, a mischievous Cupid, having pinched the war god's sword, slips it to his mother Venus.[25]

An anointing Tritoness and a harvesting Triton: they evoke respectively tribute and consumption by sea. The tribute may symbolize Neapolis' maritime glory days, when for a century after the fall of Cumae in 421 it exercised dominion over Tyrrhenian sea lanes.[26] In 327/6, Neapolis ceded its control of the region to Rome but remained Rome's faithful ally thereafter, providing a friendly harbour and tactical naval support.[27] Provision and consumption by sea remained a constant part of Neapolitan civic identity. From Neapolis' harbour the bounty of Campania flowed. Into it, and through it, were funnelled the goods and peoples of the world. The lively commercial traffic at Neapolis in the Hellenistic and Roman periods has grown more evident with the excavation of a mass of ceramics from the harbour.

The emperors continued to maintain a navy but the theme of marine conflict, everywhere evident in the public discourse of Augustus, was losing its rhetorical immediacy under Tiberius. The symbolic aspect of marine creatures and demigods softened perceptibly over time as the martial tone of Julio-Claudian sea imagery reverted to a generic, mythologized language of Mediterranean dominion. Likewise, the Dioscuri themselves evolved from warrior-saviours to the patrons of many marine pursuits, including sea transport.

The pediment corners provide the symbolic and geographic setting for the actions taking place in the centre. Unfortunately, the uncertain identity of some of the remaining figures and the complete loss of the central one(s) renders any iconographic analysis of the whole a hazardous game of conjecture made worse by the fact that we know very little about the history of Parthenope/Neapolis and even less about the Neapolitans' proprietary foundation myths. As Lorenzo Miletti has already mentioned in Chapter 2 of this volume, most scholars

---

[25] Zanker (1988), 196–7. On the Hellenistic taste for the 'burlesque' see Fowler (1989), 44–65.

[26] Lepore (1967a).　　[27] Lepore (1967b); Frederiksen (1984), 221–37.

agree that Parthenope was founded by the Euboean colony of Cumae.[28]
The Siren's tomb was central to the city's identity even in the Roman
imperial age, and a cult in her honour probably still existed at this
time.[29] According to the Hellenistic poet Lycophron, all three Sirens,
when foiled by Odysseus, dashed themselves to death into the sea and
were drawn by the 'bitter thread spun by the Fates' to far-flung
locations along the shore of Italy. Parthenope's body floated to the
vicinity of the Glanis river (probably the northern boundary
of Neapolitan territory), where the 'Tower of Phaleros' received it.
Statius adds the detail that Apollo, following the flight of Aphrodite's
dove, guided the body of Parthenope to the site.[30]

The drawings of the pediment bear no hint of an episode resembling these events. But enough remains of the intermediate figures to
indicate the unfolding of a dramatic event (a theophany?) in the lost
centre. All the standing and reclining figures seem to turn their heads
or their bodies inward, their attention drawn to the compositional
core. Standing next to the river god on the right is a headless female
figure usually and correctly identified as Artemis/Diana. She wears a
tunic in the accustomed manner of the hunter-goddess, double-belted
and drawn up to the knees.[31] In her lowered left hand is a slender
object that is best identified as a bow.

Artemis' presence here leads Correra and Adamo Muscettola,
eccentrically, to identify her symmetrical counterpart—the smaller
male figure on the left, whose arm is raised in a standard gesture of
surprise or revelation—as Artemis' brother Apollo. Pighius, Capaccio, and Summonte, all eyewitnesses, identified a tripod between the
two standing male figures to the left of the gap, and this has been
taken to corroborate an Apollonian connection; but sensibly, they

---

[28] Lepore (1967a); Frederiksen (1984), 85–95, 104–7; Mele (1985); Càssola (1986);
Raviola (1995), 151–207.

[29] Strabo 5.4.7; Pliny, *Natural History* 3.62; Scholia Bernensia and Philargyrius,
scholium of Virgil, *Georgics* 4.564; Tzetzes, scholium of Lycophron, *Alexandra* 732.

[30] *Silvae* 3.5.78–80.

[31] Bernabò Brea (1935), 74–5; Hommel (1954), 53; Adamo Muscettola (1985),
203–4. Summonte (1601), 86 had difficulty identifying this figure because of its
headless and battered state. Surprisingly, he settled on Mercury, 'poichè se gli scorge
presso i piedi il caduceo con i serpenti'. He says nothing about the figure itself, which
Francisco and the Paris sketch render in the manner of Artemis/Diana. Nor does he
explain how the serpents of a caduceus, which are always at the top of the staff, should
have been down around the figure's feet.

understood Apollo to be the larger, more godlike figure to the right.[32] To be sure, between both figures there appears the front leg of what must have been a three-legged object. But this is no tripod. Typologically, the leg belongs to a standard three-legged *trapezophoros*. This would be a muscular feline leg with a paw at the bottom and an animal or humanoid head emerging near the top.[33] The tabletop is visible, indicating that the ensemble terminates at thigh level. A tripod usually reaches a height anywhere from the hip to the head, always with much slimmer legs.[34]

The figure to the left of the table cannot possibly be Apollo. He is dressed like a mortal in formal garb, the excess fabric of his voluminous himation draped heavily over his left arm, evidently broken off just below the elbow, while his right chest and right arm are bare. At least in late Hellenistic and Roman contexts, male gods are not clothed this way. If they are not nude outright, their drapery is lighter or hangs around the hips (as on the next figure to the right). Apollo appeared in well-defined types, none resembling this figure.[35] And it is particularly inapposite that one of the 'parent gods' of Neapolis should be caught in a posture of alarm. After all, Apollo is par excellence the god who sees the truth over time and distance; he was the source of the oracles by which most colonization in the Greek West was rationalized. Like his sister, he would have assumed the dignified pose of a knowing witness or agent of world events, not a startled and awestruck bystander. To a Roman sensibility, at least, the heaviness of the drapery denotes the old-fashioned toga worn by sacrificants, and a table would serve not as the locus of a burnt offering, but as a support for the implements of sacrifice. Also, encoded in monumental Roman art was the presupposition that a sacrificant usually stands to the left of the furniture—be it altar, tripod, or table. The rule breaks down in smaller objects such as gems and coins, but it runs so deep in public sculpture, where spatial relationships convey greater narrative complexity, that the ratio of left to right is more biased than that of right- to left-handedness in

---

[32] Pighius (1587), 456; Summonte (1601), 86; Capaccio (1607), 219; Correra (1905), 227; Duhn (1910), 12; Adamo Muscettola (1985), 203–4.

[33] Moss (1988), 37–43, cat. C1–118.

[34] For tripods of varying heights, see Simon (1984), nos. 54l, 61k, 200, 263, 330, 332, 359, 375a, 404, 409, 410, 482, 519, 596, etc. No. 330, on a pediment, is especially apposite; see also Hommel (1954), 55–7.

[35] Simon (1984).

Fig. 3.5. Reconstruction of the pedimental sculpture of the temple of Via S. Gregorio, Rome, *c.*150 BC.

Source: From Ferrea (2002). Courtesy of Arnoldo Mondadori Editore.

human populations.[36] The god or gods receiving his attention, if they are present, are at liberty to appear anywhere to its right. Setting aside momentarily the sacrificant's distinctive gesture of surprise that so obviously marks an interruption in the proceedings, we may recognize here a long-established theme in public reliefs, a human sacrifice in the presence of gods. Similarly, the second-century BC terracotta pediment of the Via S. Gregorio in Rome includes both gods and a heavily togate figure with a similar table for sacrificial implements (Fig. 3.5).[37] One final detail removes all doubt that this was a sacrifice: the head of the sacrificial bull, its face and upturned horns clearly visible between the sacrificant and the figure to its right.

So who stands to the right of the table? This figure engages with the central event, his hips in contrapposto, torso flexed attentively towards the action; but the arms, by far the most important vehicles of affect in Roman art, are indistinct; the left one, at least, seems to have broken off below the elbow.[38] His shin-length tunic drooping loosely off the hips (*Hüftmantel*) belongs to the rarefied world of gods and heroes, and sets him in stark contrast to the mortal sacrificant. By the Julio-Claudian period this particular signifier extended to a penumbral zone where mortal meets divine: a hero of myth, either

[36] However, when the narrative flows from right to left, as on the south and west sides of the Ara Pacis enclosure, the sacrificant may stand to the altar's right. In the rare occasions, as on the *Alimenta* relief of the Arch of Trajan at Benevento, when a static scene features the sacrificant on the right, most of the scene opens out to the left.

[37] Ferrea (2002). The scale of figures on Roman pediments is elastic and does not strictly correlate to rank or status. See Hommel (1954), 55–63, pls. 12–14; Wiseman (1995), 146–50.

[38] Summonte's (1601) amateurish and unreliable rendering shows the arm on this figure raised and bent—in essence, reversing the gestures of Francisco's pair.

Fig. 3.6. Copies of sculptures of two members of the Julio-Claudian dynasty found *in situ* at the *macellum* in Pompeii.

Source: Originals are at the Museo Archeologico Nazionale, Naples. Photograph: R. Taylor.

before or after apotheosis; or a great man of history deified by posterity. Beginning with images of Caesar, Julio-Claudian art in particular emphasized the latter kind of persona by appropriating the lowered tunic, its surplus fabric twisted around the hips and draped over the relaxed left arm, as the sole habiliments of a deified dynast. The famous Julio-Claudian reliefs of Algiers and Ravenna instantiate this type, as does a statue in the *macellum* of Pompeii (Fig. 3.6). But despite the superficial similarity, nothing would indicate that such a personage appeared on this pediment.

It is often presumed that the Dioscuri themselves must have been present. But the contention that this figure represents one of them, and that his brother stood nearby in the pediment's lacuna, is unsupportable.[39] By this time, and even much earlier, the brothers conformed to a rigid, and completely distinct, iconographic tradition. In large formats they were accompanied by their horses and were habitually either nude, wearing only the chlamys pinned at one shoulder,

---

[39] Capasso (1905), 80; Correra (1905), 226; Adamo Muscettola (1985), 203–5.

or in full armour with the chlamys, and in either case equipped with swords or spears.[40] Nothing suggests such figures inhabited this pediment. We will return later to the problem—if a problem it is— of the brothers' evident absence here.

An identification advanced as early as Pighius may very well be the right one—that *this* is Apollo.[41] Unfortunately, none of Apollo's usual diagnostic features are visible. Long tresses cascading down the shoulders are virtually obligatory, and the vast majority of Apollos include at least one of the following features: a quiver with its diagonal baldric, a chlamys, or a cithara—the last, if present, usually held in his left hand, so possibly obliterated on the Naples pediment. Nothing rules Apollo out either, least of all the appropriately lithe physique. Our draughtsmen were observing the monument from below, and written testimony confirms its battered state.

At least implicitly, this god plays the largest role in the early history of Neapolis apart from Parthenope. As we have seen already, he guided the Siren's body to her future colony. This act suited his status as one of Neapolis' parent gods (*di patrii*) alongside Demeter and the Dioscuri.[42] But several sources also assert that two important events in Neapolis' history *after* the foundation of Parthenope were under- taken because of an oracle: the Cumaean refounding of the colony as Neapolis with the revival of its cult of Parthenope, and the establish- ment of torch races there in the Siren's honour.[43] Apollo was the implicit source of the oracles, as he was for most vatic consultations involving Greek foundation rituals.[44] The Cumaeans in particular would have favoured their tutelary god for this purpose.[45] Crucially, in all three of these events—be they myth or fact—Apollo behaves as an intermediary between the Cumaeans and their goddess of place, Parthenope. In his accustomed role as a guarantor of successful new beginnings by mediating local cults, Apollo is thus properly positioned on this pediment, and appropriately scaled at intermediate

---

[40] Bernabò Brea (1935), 75; Gury (1986). Given the battered state of the head, we cannot expect the obligatory conical cap (*pilos*) to be visible here.

[41] Pighius (1587), 456.   [42] Statius, *Silvae* 4.8.45–54.

[43] Foundation of Neapolis: Pseudo-Skymnos, *Periegesis* 252–3; Philargyrius, scho- lium on Virgil's *Georgics* 4.564; torch races and subsequent games: Lycophron, *Alexandra* 732–5; Tzetzes, scholium of Lycophron, *Alexandra* 732; Strabo 5.4.7.

[44] Dougherty (1993), 31–44; Dougherty (1998).

[45] On the Cumaean Sibyl and the possibility of her early existence see Squarciapino (1941–2); Heurgon (1987); Parke (1988), 71–99. The Delphic, not the Cumaean, Apollo was the oracle of usual recourse in the matter of founding or rectifying cities.

size, between the sacrificant and the now missing central god to whom both direct their attention. I will return to that god's identity in a moment.

Adamo Muscettola's interpretation of the pediment leaves no space for the expression of local identity at all. Hers is a cosmic reading in which the Dioscuri, who according to one strand of their mythology traded places among the living and dead on a daily basis, appeared as guarantors of harmony and fertility. According to this reading, the Tritons conveyed generic connotations of Octavian's naval victory at Actium. It is a reading immersed in suppositions about Augustan ideology and strangely divorced from the world of the Neapolitans themselves. But most significantly, her argument seems to be driven by the conviction that the Dioscuri must have appeared on the pediment of their own temple. Roman pedimental themes do often have some connection to the dedicatee god(s) within, but the tendency is not universal. I believe the connection exists, but in a hitherto unexamined manner.

Sculpted images of the Dioscuri were indeed present at this temple, but *not on the pediment*. A matched pair of headless white marble statues of the brothers survive, composed in mirror image—their identities unmistakable despite their fragmentary form, since both chlamydes are visible (Fig. 3.7). Known since at least the sixteenth century, and even then attested on the church's premises, they bid fair to have belonged in some fashion to the preceding temple.[46] Of a size to fit the centre of the pediment, they were long identified as the figures missing from Francisco's drawing. But Bernabò Brea, by demonstrating that the pediment sculpture was in relief, not in the round, put that error to rest long ago; and Adamo Muscettola has observed indications that they were accompanied by their customary steeds, which the pediment could not possibly have accommodated.[47] These free-standing Dioscuri appeared prominently somewhere on the temple, or in front of it, perhaps in dialogue with the pedimental sculpture. Where did they stand?

Certainly they were not acroteria. To be sure, three pedestals for acroterial statues surmounting the pediment are visible in the drawings. But the roof is no place for the principal dedicatees of a temple; and stone statues, because of their weight and low tensile strength,

[46] Correra (1905), 224–6; Adamo Muscettola (1985), 205.
[47] Bernabò Brea (1935), 71–2; Adamo Muscettola (1985), 202, 205–6.

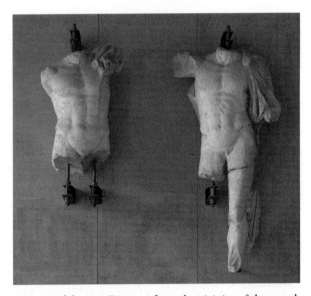

Fig. 3.7. Statues of the two Dioscuri from the vicinity of the temple.

Source: Museo Archeologico Nazionale di Napoli. Photo: R. Taylor. By permission of the Ministero per i Beni e le Attività Culturali–Soprintendenza Speciale per i Beni Archeologici di Napoli e Pompei.

are ill-suited to such high, windblown places anyway. Instead, this pair was probably positioned symmetrically out in front of the temple or on its porch. At least two major temples in Rome, including the one *in Circo Flaminio* dedicated to the Dioscuri themselves, displayed statues in the round of each brother with his horse on a pair of prominent external architectural features—in the case of the temple *in Circo,* probably the pedestals flanking the grand stairway. These are the pairs standing today in the Piazza del Quirinale and the Piazza del Campidoglio.[48] The temple at Neapolis had an unusually high podium and its stairway would probably have been protected by pedestals at either side (see the model at Fig. 3.8). We can plausibly situate the Neapolitan Dioscuri upon them or on prominent bases nearby.

[48] De' Spagnolis (1984); Richardson (1992), 75–6; Taylor (2004). A third, the famous temple of the Castors on the Forum rebuilt by Tiberius, stood directly beside the Lacus Iuturnae, which also prominently displayed statues of the Dioscuri with their horses; see Harri (1989), 177–98.

Fig. 3.8. Model of the temple of the Dioscuri on display at Complesso Monumentale S. Lorenzo Maggiore, Naples.

Source: Photograph: R. Taylor.

There is no reason whatsoever to expect these divine brothers, already so prominent below, to be duplicated on the pediment. Nor should we suppose that the pedimental scene was steeped in the static, oblique symbolism of Augustan ideology, a tendency that was already receding when this temple was built. Instead we should look for a visual programme of distinctly local significance. A crucial part of the dedicatory inscription bears considering. This temple was dedicated not only to the Dioscuri, but also *to the City (tēi Polēi)*—i.e. an allegorical goddess in the manner of Roma and the innumerable Tychai who served for tutelary deities of cities around the Hellenized world.

Fig. 3.9. Terracotta pedimental figures of the 'Grande Tempio' at Luni, second century BC.

Source: Museo Archeologico Nazionale di Firenze. By permission of the Ministero per i Beni e le Attività Culturali–Soprintendenza Speciale per i Beni Archeologici della Toscana.

Surrounded, then, by a cast of characters both human and divine, but all in a passive or quasi-passive stance of witness, the centre of the pediment probably displayed a theophany—not of the Dioscuri, who stood heroically below, but of Neapolis herself, inextricably entwined in the identity of Parthenope.[49] She may have appeared in a static, hieratic fashion like the Tyche of Antioch, who is often shown enthroned on the back of a swimming youth, the allegory of the Orontes river, or Diana/Luna, who appears at the centre of the second-century BC pediment on the 'Grande Tempio' at Luni flanked by Apollo Citharoedus and Dionysus or Honos, and then by two female figures of uncertain identity (Fig. 3.9).[50] Or she might have taken a stance more like that on the pediment of the temple of the late Antonine Genius of Oea (modern Tripoli), whose embodiment stands

[49] Hommel (1954), 52. He mistakenly supposes that the Dioscuri flanked her.
[50] La Rocca and Parisi Presicce (2010), 154–5, 246. For Antioch see Balty (1981).

frontally in the centre.[51] But in keeping with the dramatic tension of the staffage elsewhere on the Naples pediment, she may have struck a more dynamic pose, like the windblown allegory of Aphrodisias on the Julio-Claudian Sebasteion and other reliefs of that city.[52]

There was no widespread tradition of displaying city Tychai in the Greek West. Cities in the region usually represented themselves by their rivers, local nymphs, or eponymous heroes or demigods. But a harbour city with many eastern connections would reasonably prove an exception, and a pediment, with its strong proclivity for personifications, was the likeliest place for them to appear. The artists may have been aware of the Classical temple at Locri, on whose pediment a central Nike-like figure seems to have appeared, along with the Dioscuri in each corner—or similar pediments now lost.[53] As owners of the most famous Italian myth involving the Dioscuri—their miraculous intervention in the Battle of Sagra—the Locrians naturally chose to represent the battle itself. As far as we know, Neapolis had no similar moment of crisis in its mythic history, and the rise of the new Julio-Claudian aesthetic made it easy to choose a more abstract, but far from static, schema.

Neapolis was unique in many ways. Most importantly, it had enjoyed a cosmopolitan identity founded on maritime trade between East and West. As the principal port on Italy's Tyrrhenian coast from the fifth century BC until the rise of Puteoli in the first century BC, it had been a major Mediterranean entrepôt, funnelling massive quantities of Attic ceramics and a wide variety of other wares into Italy during the Classical period and later developing the black-gloss tableware called Campana A, around which developed one of the most voluminous ceramic export industries in the ancient world.[54] In the Julio-Claudian period, as the axis between Egypt and Italy developed into a lifeline of food and other imports for Rome, Alexandrian merchants would have developed a strong presence at Neapolis and Puteoli.[55] The cult of the Dioscuri was familiar to them;

[51] Hommel (1954), 52, 55–7; Simon (1984), no. 330.
[52] Erim (1984), 1. On a bas-relief of the imperial period, she is identified specifically as the *Polis*.
[53] Costabile (1995).
[54] Attic ceramics: Vallet (1967), 225–7; Lepore (1967a), 187–90, 321; Càssola (1986), 62–3. Campana A: Morel (1981); Morel (1985).
[55] On the prominence of Alexandrians on the Bay of Naples see Acts 27–8; Suetonius, *Augustus* 98 and *Nero* 20.

even the Alexandrian ship carrying St Paul from Malta to Puteoli was sailing under their sign.[56]

That Neapolis as an allegorical entity should have stood entirely apart from Parthenope is unlikely. Even in Roman imperial times the 'new city' continued to carry the poetic name Parthenope and the cult of the Siren was still active. Numerous sources referring to the foundation of Neapolis, although differing in the particulars, uniformly recognize the centrality of the Siren's cult there.[57] Yet they also indicate that the settlement's historical identity suffered a traumatic rupture that necessitated a refounding; and it is on the fulcrum of that event that the pediment's meaning turns. Citing the history of Lutatius Catulus, Philargyrius provides a sketchy account of the surrounding events:

> [Some] inhabitants of Cumae, leaving behind their ancestors, founded the city of Parthenope—called Parthenope from the Siren, whose body also [is buried there]. Later, on account of the fertility and pleasantness of the precinct, it began to be more heavily populated. Fearing that Cumaean territory would be deserted, [the Cumaeans] contrived to destroy Parthenope; but later, beset by a pestilence, on the strength of an oracle they restored the city and took up the rites of Parthenope with great religious vigour.[58]

This passage has been variously interpreted (see, for instance, Lorenzo Miletti's discussion in Chapter 2 of this volume), but it must now be read with an eye to recent archaeological discoveries. It was long believed that the walled city of Neapolis was founded after the Battle of Cumae in 474 BC, but refinements in ceramic analysis now suggest an approximate date of 490, give or take a decade. This places the refoundation squarely within the chronological sphere of the tyranny of Aristodemos at Cumae (*c.*505–485 BC).[59] The events surrounding the tyranny are murky and controversial; here it is enough to make a few salient points. Aristodemus' rise and fall were embodiments of a bitter class division at Cumae, pitting his ruthless populism against a

---

[56] Acts 28:11.

[57] Lycophron, *Alexandra* 712–38; Tzetzes, scholium of Lycophron, *Alexandra* 732; Pseudo-Skymnos, *Periegesis* 252–3; Strabo 5.4.7; Pliny the Elder, *Natural History* 3.62; Scholia Bernensia, on Virgil's *Georgics* 4.564; Philargyrius, scholium on Virgil's *Georgics* 4.564.

[58] Philargyrius, scholium on Virgil's *Georgics* 4.564.

[59] Giampaola and D'Agostino (2005).

party of oligarchs with strong family networks.[60] As a Cumaean colony with an excellent harbour situated only 18 kilometres from the mother city, Parthenope would inevitably have been drawn into this conflict. So it is naïve of Lutatius to interpret the population drain from Cumae to its colony as a mere competition in living standards. Parthenope must have been not only a refuge for the exiles (as we know that Capua was too), but also a staging post for their revanchist ambitions. That must be why Cumae (i.e. Aristodemus) contemplated wiping out the town; but in the event, it seems that a plague accomplished that objective.[61] This plague may also have contributed to Aristodemus' downfall around 485, after which the old order was more or less restored at Cumae. Thus arose a golden opportunity to refound Parthenope on contemporary urbanistic principles, with a street grid, a central agora, and sanctuaries all encompassed within a defensive circuit.

Lutatius emphasizes two religious components of the refounding: an oracle that dictated it, and a religious cult ('the rites of Parthenope') to expiate it. An oracular consultation with Apollo was the usual way to justify a colonization, and the consequences often included elaborate refashionings of ancestral and local mythologies.[62] The conventions of colonization also required sacrifices—to atone for any crimes or impieties in the colonists' past, to remedy the disruptions in local life and religion caused by the incursion, and to ensure success for the venture.

If our pediment marks the moment at which the New City arrived into the world, then the sacrifice scene on its left side is best interpreted as the moment when the Cumaeans 'restored the city and took up the rites of Parthenope with great religious vigour'. Since we know nothing more about this event, we cannot identify the sacrificant. However, the moment of foundation may be conflated with another episode in the early history of Neapolis, also centred upon an act of piety towards Parthenope. It is recorded in a reference by a scholiast of Lycophron to an account of this event in the lost history of Timaios of Tauromenion (*c.*345–250 BC), the most authoritative ancient source for this period in Magna Graecia:

---

[60] Dionysius of Halicarnassus 7.6–11.

[61] This may have been the same plague that is said to have beset the Volscians just after Aristodemus' death; see Dionysius of Halicarnassus 7.12.4–5.

[62] Dougherty (1993); Dougherty (1998).

Lycophron [in the voice of Cassandra, forecasting the future of Greek peoples]: There one day shall the foremost of the whole naval command of Mopsops [i.e. Athens] dedicate a torch race for his sailors to the first of the sisters [i.e. Parthenope], which, in time, the Neapolitan people shall augment.[63]

Tzetzes: Timaios says that Diotimos, admiral of the Athenians, came to Neapolis; and, according to an oracle, he sacrificed to Parthenope and founded a torch race; wherefore even up to [Timaios'] own time, a torch race was taking place among the Neapolitans.[64]

Diotimos is the first historically verifiable figure in the chronicles of Naples. Yet his intervention would have occurred well after the refoundation; scholars place his embassy to Neapolis somewhere between 454/3 and 440/39.[65] His authority and prominence, alongside his role in consulting and honouring the oracle, would make him an appropriate candidate for the sacrificant beside Apollo on the pediment.

Writing in the mid-third century BC, Lycophron indicates that the Neapolitans expanded the torch races on their own. These were augmented again centuries later as the Sebasta, quadrennial games hosted at Neapolis in honour of Augustus.[66] The event continued to enjoy direct imperial patronage at least through the Flavian period.[67] Naples reciprocated by maintaining a robust imperial cult, including a *Kaisareion*, or temple of Augustus.[68] The wealthy freedmen of Tiberius who sponsored the temple of the Castors may have wished to emphasize the city's close relationship to the imperial house by representing the Athenian Diotimos' sacrifice to Parthenope. The proximity of Apollo seals his role as a 'parent god' not just of Neapolis but also of one or both oracles chronicled in the city's surviving history—those dictating the foundation of the New City and of its games.

Apart from Neapolis/Parthenope in the centre, we are left with one other missing figure in between the city personification and Artemis

[63] Lycophron, *Alexandra* 732–5.

[64] Tzetzes, scholium of Lycophron, *Alexandra* 732.

[65] Lepore (1967a), 172–9; Frederiksen (1984), 104–6; Càssola (1986), 63–4; Raviola (1993); Raviola (1995), 67–73, 87–91.

[66] Sbordone (1967b); Miranda (1982); Miranda (1985a); Miranda (1990), 1.75–114; Beloch (1989 [1890]), 73–6; Napoli (1997² [1959]), 193–6; Miranda de Martino (2007).

[67] Robert (1939), 242–3; Miranda (1988a); Miranda (1990), 1.35–9; Miranda de Martino (2007), 211–12. See Suetonius, *Claudius* 11.2; Dio Cassius 60.6.1–2.

[68] On the possible discovery of the *Kaisareion* see Bragantini (2010), 609–12.

on her right. The prime candidate would be Demeter/Ceres, Neapolis' other 'parent god' alongside Apollo and the Dioscuri.[69] She too had an intimate association with the refoundation, since a sanctuary at Caponapoli, enclosed within the walls on the city's north side at this time, was almost certainly dedicated to her.[70] The sanctuary's beginnings seem to date to the end of the sixth century, coinciding with the founding of the New City. Her dominant local role, along with the reclining female allegory of abundance on the pediment, intersect with Neapolis' important role in the movement of Campanian grain and other foodstuffs through the region.

If Demeter was a natural choice, her neighbour is harder to place. Artemis/Diana is so ubiquitous in Helleno-Roman culture, especially in Apollo's company and especially in early Julio-Claudian art and literature, that it hardly seems necessary to interrogate her presence here. But in fact her cult was not prominent in Neapolis; surviving inscriptions barely manifest its presence at all, although one of the Roman city's numerous phratries, or brotherhoods, was called the Artemisioi.[71] Why then did she have such a prominent place here?

As usual, we are hamstrung by the poverty of our sources. But if we follow the strand of the region's earlier maritime history into the Roman era, we perceive that Neapolis inevitably played an important strategic and commercial role. The city was an unwavering ally of Rome from the time of the Second Samnite War; having the best and most developed harbour in the region at the time, it would have been heavily involved in naval operations in the Second Punic War. The defection of Capua to Hannibal in 216 BC and the consequent loss of the *ager Campanus* and its agricultural bounty was catastrophic for the Roman alliance. A symbolic calamity ensued when Hannibal chose nearby Monte Tifata for his new base of operations. This hill harboured Campania's most important sanctuary, that of Diana Tifatina.[72] A significant part of the allied war effort in the ensuing years centred on retaking Capua and its territory. It was probably shortly after this happened in 211 that Neapolis issued three new bronze coin

---

[69] Statius, *Silvae* 4.8.45–54.
[70] D'Onofrio and D'Agostino (1987); Carafa (2008), 48–52; see also Cicero, *Pro Balbo* 55.
[71] Peterson (1919), 170–2; Ferone (1988); Fishwick (1989).
[72] Frederiksen (1984), 238–65.

types. On one group appears Apollo, his cithara and omphalos on the reverse. The second group features a male bust with a star behind his neck and a horseman on the reverse: the Dioscuri. The third represents a bust of Artemis/Diana on the obverse, a cornucopia on the reverse.[73] The first two coin types need no explanation; they simply confirmed pre-existing Neapolitan cultic identity. The Diana-cornucopia type, however, anchors the whole group of coins in contemporary history by merging the two dominant signifiers of Capua and its territory: the fertile fields of the *ager Campanus* and the famous sanctuary of Diana. The recapturing of these assets was a turning point in the war. From that time onwards the *ager Campanus*, because of its fundamental importance to Rome, was owned and leased by the Roman treasury. Thus did Neapolis, ever the faithful ally of Rome, present itself as a custodian and representative of all Campania. We cannot know its specific role in the events, but the city's agency in their unfolding would have been at least matched by its gratitude for regaining a commercial advantage in the regional economy.

Several of the Julio-Claudian emperors had close ties to Neapolis. It is striking to contemplate that Tiberius, who famously retreated to Capri in his later years, would by this very fact have been steeped in Neapolitan culture and lore; for the island had long been in Neapolis' possession before Augustus absorbed it into imperial property, and Capri's inhabitants continued to participate in the customary local traditions.[74] It made sense that he or his surrogates should have sanctioned the construction of a temple that promoted a version of history the Neapolitans themselves relished. But the scene we have envisioned on the pediment would also have suited the emperor ideologically. First of all, this temple responded to Tiberius' sumptuous restoration of the Temple of the Castors (i.e. the Dioscuri) on the Forum in Rome some years earlier. It was clearly amplifying a cult the emperor was already known to favour. Second, since Augustus' time, the Tychai of cities had close ties to the imperial cult.[75] The temple's oblique references to Campanian bounty and Campanian cult, now controlled by Rome, would also have pleased him. And so would its appeal to an old brand of Greek politics favouring an aristocratic,

[73] Taliercio (1986), 247, 332–3, 351–3.
[74] Capri's acquisition: Strabo 5.4.9; Suetonius, *Augustus* 92, 98; Dio Cassius 52.43.2. See Federico and Miranda (1998), 375–415.
[75] Fischer (1996).

quasi-dynastic bouleutic system that actively resisted a tyranny—
something approaching the republic that Augustus claimed to have
restored.[76] And it did so in a way that Augustus and Tiberius themselves had promoted at Rome—by reviving neglected cults and re-
establishing the proper piety due to the gods of the place.

[76] Aristodemus had allegedly backed Tarquinius, the deposed final king of Rome,
against the Roman Republic. After his death, perhaps in solidarity with the anti-
Aristodemus party, various Tyrrhenian cities sent food aid to Rome, which was
suffering from a plague; Neapolis may have been among them. See Dionysius of
Halicarnassus 7.12.1–3.

4

Colonizing the Past

Cultural Memory and Civic Identity in Hellenistic and Roman Naples

Kathryn Lomas

The development of cultural identities, and the intricate relationship between Greek and Roman cultures in the late Republic and early Empire, have been intensively studied, but much of the research on this important topic has focused principally on Greece and the eastern Mediterranean. Naples, however, provides a fascinating example of the ways in which cultural memory, especially that of the Greek past, played a complex role in the development of civic and regional identities even in the western Mediterranean.

Although Naples was, in origin, a Greek colony, by the Roman period it was a mixed ethnic and cultural community. Even before it formed an alliance with Rome in 327 BC, it had a substantial minority of Oscan inhabitants as well as Etruscan settlers.[1] By the time it was absorbed into the Roman state in 90 BC, it had long since ceased to be a purely Greek community. Despite this, however, it retained a strong Greek identity until well into the second century AD—long after other Greek colonies in Italy had lost most of their Greek identity. Tacitus was plausibly able to refer to it as *quasi Graecam urbem*.[2] This statement raises some important questions about the civic culture of

---

[1] Strabo 5.4.7; Livy 8.22.7–29.5; Diodorus 12.31.1; Dionysius of Halicarnassus 15.5.1–9.2; Frederiksen (1984), 134–57.

[2] Tacitus, *Annals* 15.33.

Naples in the early Roman Empire. Tacitus pointedly says that Naples was like a Greek city, not that it still was a Greek city, although the importance of Hellenism in its civic culture—and the attractions of this for the Roman elite—is well documented.[3] This may be simply because, like all Italian cities, it had Roman citizenship and was legally and administratively part of Rome. However, it raises some interesting questions about identity in Naples and how we should best interpret it. The Greek heritage of the city—exemplified by the continuation of Greek magistracies and constitutional practices, the Greek language, and Greek games and festivals—formed an important element of the civic culture of Naples until well into the Roman Empire, and was actively fostered by the Neapolitans, suggesting that cultural memory of the Greek past was influential in the development of the Roman city. In other respects, however, Naples adopted many features of other Roman *municipia* in Italy, and by the early Empire it was an ethnically and culturally mixed community with complex and multi-layered identities.[4] This raises some interesting questions about how far, and in what respects, cultural memory of the Greek city shaped the culture of Roman Naples, and whether there were aspects of active reimagining and reworking of Hellenism to create a new Greek identity. Explaining these cultural developments and analysing them poses some significant challenges, not least because Naples is better documented for the period after the Roman conquest than for its independent existence.

Cultural memory, which is sometimes defined as the operation of the past in the present and/or the present in the past, is an essential element in the creation and maintenance of group identities, whether of states or of subgroups within them.[5] There is, however, considerable debate about what constitutes social or cultural memory, how it

[3] Tacitus' point is that Nero used Naples to test out his musical performances before performing in Greece itself. On Hellenism at Naples, and its attractions for Romans, see D'Arms (1970); Hardie (1983); Lomas (1997), 124–7. Dio Cassius (55.10.5–6) describes the Neapolitans as zealous about this Greek culture. Strabo (5.4.7) implies that the atmosphere of Hellenism was an attraction for Romans and others who retired to the city, and also to teachers and intellectuals who were attracted by its Greek history.

[4] On the changing ethnicity of Naples and on language and ethnic identity, see Leiwo (1994).

[5] For this definition see Alcock (2001), 323–5; Alcock and Van Dyke (2003), 3–7. On various other definitions of social or cultural memory, see Connerton (1989); Halbwachs (1992); Fentress and Wickham (1992); Assmann (2006).

is transmitted, and how it differs from similar concepts such as tradition. It is, by definition, a collective rather than an individual memory, which can encompass various registers such as perpetuation of myths and associated rituals about the distant past, selective commemoration of more recent significant events, or even the creation of entirely fictive traditions.[6] Cultural memory can be transmitted by various means. Halbwachs saw it as a phenomenon with an essential spatial component, in which significant monuments and places in the landscape acted as repositories of cultural memory, an approach which has been highly influential in archaeology.[7] Others, in contrast, have argued that it can be just as effectively embodied and transmitted through means such as rituals and other regular events, written documents, or even ritualized forms of personal behaviour, gesture, and dress.[8]

One of the important factors in cultural memory, however, is that it is invariably selective, and entails choice about which aspects of a community's past should be preserved, and conversely, which should be downgraded or suppressed.[9] This makes it particularly significant in situations of conquest and empire, in which there are unequal power relations and in which subordinate groups need to negotiate identities and roles in relation to dominant groups.[10] Although cultural memory is always a collective memory, it is also fluid and can change over time, or vary between different groups and memory communities.[11] Given the prominence of the Greek past in the culture of Roman Naples, examination of this as a case study in cultural memory may be a useful way to understand the development of Naples in the Roman Empire.

---

[6] Halbwachs (1992); Connerton (1989), 20–2. On the definitions of collective memory and how or if different types can, or should, be distinguished, see Assmann (2006), 5–29.

[7] Halbwachs (1992); Alcock and Van Dyke (2003), 3–4; Ashmore and Knapp (1999).

[8] Connerton (1989), 39–40, 72–4; Alcock and Van Dyke (2003), 4–6. As Alcock and Van Dyke note, these are not mutually exclusive, as many archaeological artefacts such as burials and votives are the material evidence of rituals and ceremonies, from which we can deduce something about embodied memories. Cf. also Rowlands (1993).

[9] Connerton (1989), 20–2.

[10] Connerton (1989), 14–21; Alcock (2001), 323–5.

[11] Connerton (1989), 35–8; Assmann (2006), 1–9; Alcock and Van Dyke (2003), 2–3.

MEMORY AND SPACE: THE CULTURAL GEOGRAPHY
OF EARLY IMPERIAL NAPLES

Many studies of cultural memory—both theoretical studies and archaeological case studies—approach the question from the standpoint
of topography.[12] The difficulty is that the archaeology of Naples, like
that of all Italian cities which have been continuously occupied since
antiquity, is imperfectly preserved, so we cannot be sure what the city
looked like and any conclusions must come with the obvious caveat
that they are based on incomplete evidence.[13] Some structures are
known only from ancient descriptions and are not archaeologically
attested.[14] Topographically, the transition from pre-Roman to
Roman Naples is particularly difficult to trace, as pre-Roman Naples
is not as well documented as the Roman city. The Greek street plan
was based on the Hippodamian model of two intersecting main
thoroughfares and a grid of long narrow blocks of housing, and a
sixteenth-century description by Fabio Giordano locates the agora,
and later the forum, in an area bounded on one side by the Via del
Duomo and transected by the Via dei Tribunali (Figs. 4.1 and 4.2).[15]

From the late first century BC there seems to have been an increasing amount of building in a Roman style. Much of this was private
housing, such as the *insula* of Carminiello ai Mannesi, another
example near the church of S. Gregorio Armeno, or the area of
Roman housing near the Palazzo Corigliano.[16] However, a number
of public buildings have been excavated in the area around the
churches of S. Paolo Maggiore and S. Lorenzo Maggiore, the location
of the forum (Fig. 4.2). The four principal structures are the theatre,
an *odeion*, the temple of the Dioscuri (the subject of Chapter 3 in this
volume, by Rabun Taylor), and a large and complex structure beneath
the church of S. Lorenzo, all dating to the first century AD. The

---

[12] Halbwachs (1992); Connerton (1989); Assmann (2006), 5–29.

[13] Written sources are also partial, since many of them focus almost exclusively on
Greek monuments, to the exclusion of other aspects of Roman Naples.

[14] According to Strabo (5.4.7), for instance, there was a monument to the Siren
Parthenope, but he gives no indication of what this was or where it was located.

[15] Napoli (1959); Greco (1986), 199–211; Greco (1985a), 132–9; Baldassarre
(1986), 227–8. Greco identifies the area around the church of S. Lorenzo as Giordano's commercial forum and the area between the theatre and the temple of the
Dioscuri as the forum/agora proper.

[16] Arthur (1994); Pozzi (1988); Bragantini (1991); Zevi (2003), 910–21; Nava and
Salvatore (2009), 707–13.

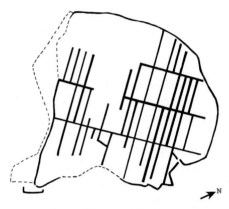

Fig. 4.1. Naples: street plan and limits of the Graeco-Roman city.
Source: After Napoli (1959).

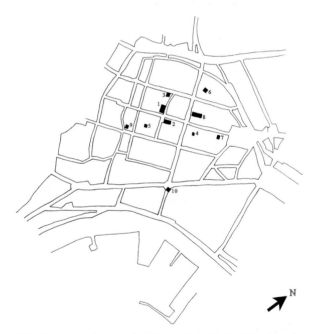

Fig. 4.2. Naples: major Roman buildings. 1: S. Paolo Maggiore (temple of the Dioscuri); 2: S. Lorenzo Maggiore (*macellum*); 3: theatre and *odeion*; 4: Carminello ai Mannesi (*insula* and baths); 5: S. Gregorio Armeno (*insula*); 6: Donnaregina Nuova (baths); 7: Archivio di Banco di Napoli (houses); 8: Duomo (Greek and Roman buildings); 9: Palazzo Corigliano (Roman houses); 10: Piazza Nicola Amore (portico and temple of imperial cult; possible site of gymnasium).
Source: Lomas, after Leiwo (1994).

monumental centre of the city seems to have undergone two principal phases of reconstruction, under Augustus and Tiberius and under the Flavians. It involved construction (or substantial remodelling) of the theatre and *odeion* and addition of at least one temple. Both the chronology, and the building types and styles, are typical of wider patterns of public building in Italy at this date.[17] The urban development of Naples in this respect seems to be consistent with that of the rest of Roman Italy.

The building beneath S. Lorenzo was probably the *macellum* of the city. It was a rectangular structure built on a terrace with a large cryptoporticus and was similar in form to the *macellum* of Pompeii, with *tabernae* lining the inner walls and an open central area containing a circular *tholos*.[18] Two theatres were located on the northeast corner of the forum/agora area. The extant remains are entirely Roman, although both were probably rebuildings of Greek originals. The larger theatre is a semicircular structure in *opus reticulatum* and dates to the Augustan period, although it was extensively remodelled in the late first century AD, with the addition of a portico, and construction of a bath building behind the *cavea*.[19] The smaller theatre was an *odeion*, and is badly preserved. It was a square structure decorated with pilasters and stucco facing, located on the east side of the theatre and of similar date. Like the theatre, it also has parallels from early imperial Campania.[20]

The temple of the Dioscuri was incorporated into the church of S. Paolo and the facade is recorded in numerous drawings (cf. Figs. 3.2, 3.3, 12.2, and 12.4–6 in this book). It was largely destroyed in an earthquake in 1688, but drawings and prints show it as a Roman-style temple *in antis* set on a podium, with a facade of six Corinthian columns. It was built and dedicated by Tiberius Julius Tarsus, a freedman of Tiberius.[21] Despite the Roman structure and decoration

---

[17] Jouffroy (1986), 319–29; Lomas (2002), 28–45.

[18] De Simone (1985), 185–95.

[19] The theatre is similar in style, construction technique, and date to other theatres in Campania, such as those of Nuceria and Beneventum. Johannowsky (1976).

[20] Johannowsky (1976).

[21] There is a more general Tiberian connection with the cult of the Dioscuri, as Tiberius himself rebuilt a temple of Castor and Pollux at Rome in honour of his dead brother Drusus (Suetonius, *Tiberius* 8.20; Dio Cassius 55.27.4; Ovid, *Fasti* 1.707–8). On the cult and temple of the Dioscuri, see Rabun Taylor, Chapter 3 in this volume.

of the temple, the dedicatory inscription is in Greek.[22] If the drawings of it are accurate, it was—despite its Greek dedication—a building redolent of Roman style and Augustan iconography, with references to the Tellus panel of the Ara Pacis, the cult of Apollo, and the use of Tritons and Oceanus to symbolize the victory of Actium.[23]

Construction work on the Naples Metro has unearthed an important complex of buildings near Piazza Nicola Amore, between the ancient city walls and the harbour (Fig. 4.2, no. 10).[24] This included the podium and columns of a temple dating to the early first century AD and a second-century AD portico with a paved area between them. The site matches Dio Chrysostom's description of the gymnasium, which locates it near the harbour.[25] The excavation has also yielded a life-size marble statue of Nike, a Julio-Claudian marble head, possibly of one of Augustus' family, and many fragmentary inscriptions.[26] These inscriptions appear to have come from marble slabs, at least 2 metres high, which lined the inner wall of the portico, and which were inscribed with the names of the victors of the games. These victory lists are highly suggestive, and it seems very likely that this was the site of the gymnasium, while the temple has been identified as a temple of the imperial cult.[27] The programme of the games implies that there was also a stadium and hippodrome.

Some structures have been excavated outside the monumental centre of the city, mostly of typically Roman type. Numerous baths examples have been found within the city or attached to suburban villas. Some appear to have belonged to private houses rather than being public baths. Roman structures beneath the Archivio di Banco di Napoli on Via Tribunali include a late Republican phase of a

---

[22] Miranda (1990); Adamo Muscettola (1985), 200–1; *IG* 14.714: 'Ti. Julius Tarsus (dedicated) the temple and the things which are in the temple to the Dioscuri and the city. Pelagon, freedman and procurator of the emperor, completed this dedication at his own expense.'

[23] Adamo Muscettola (1985), 204–5; Zanker (1988); Taylor, Chapter 3 in this volume.

[24] Strabo 5.4.7. On the gymnasium, cf. also *IvO* 56.13–17; Suetonius, *Nero* 40.1; Miranda (2007).

[25] Dio Chrysostom, *Orations* 28.1. He describes the athletes as running on a track outside the gymnasium, and it has been suggested that the paved area between the temple and portico may be identified as this track.

[26] The fragments recovered all date to the Flavian period. Miranda (2007), 311–12; Miranda (2010).

[27] *IvO* 56.45–50 mentions a procession to the *Kaisareion*, the temple of the imperial cult, to offer sacrifices at the opening of the games.

probable bath building decorated with monochrome mosaics and third-style wall painting, and a second phase in *opus reticulatum*, of early imperial date. Part of a *caldarium* of the second–third century AD has been unearthed beneath the church of Donnaregina Nuova.[28] Houses of the Roman period have also come to light. The most fully excavated example is that of Carminiello ai Mannesi, an *insula* block lying close to the Via Tribunali. This included, amongst other things, a bath complex and courtyard, and dates to the late first century BC–late first century AD.[29] Further Roman houses have been found near the church of S. Gregorio Armeno and the Palazzo Corigliano, and the excavations for the new Naples Metro have brought to light many other structures, notably the remains of a suburban villa and its bathhouse near Piazza Municipio.[30]

Cultural memory does not seem to be expressed directly in the urban landscape of Naples as far as it has been preserved. This is an important contrast between Naples and the cities of Greece and the eastern Empire. Athens, for instance, reorganized the Agora and surrounding area to emphasize the Classical past of the city, creating what Alcock has termed a 'theatre of memory' in which buildings and monuments served to remind both the Athenians and visitors of this distinguished past.[31] At Naples, in contrast, most of the civic buildings of the first and second centuries AD are Roman constructions, built in contemporary Roman style. Greek identity was not expressed through topographical features or through the built environment, at least in the most central public spaces such as the areas round the forum/agora and the gymnasium.[32] Even locations which had close associations with the Greek past of the city—such as the agora, theatre, or gymnasium—were refashioned in Roman style and many of the prominent public buildings were ambiguous. The theatre, for instance, may symbolize cultural memories of Naples' rich dramatic and artistic heritage, but theatres were a popular building type in Augustan Italy and often had specific Augustan resonances.[33] The

---

[28] Via Tribunali: Pozzi (1986); Pozzi (1987); Donnaregia Nuova: Pozzi (1988).

[29] Arthur (1994).

[30] Arthur (1994); Pozzi (1988); Bragantini (1991); Zevi (2003), 910–21; Nava and Salvatore (2009), 707–13.

[31] Alcock (2001), 325–35.   [32] Lomas (1997), 120–4.

[33] The *Lex Julia Theatralis* lays out a systematic view of Augustan society, physically mapped out by virtue of regulating theatre seating arrangements. Jouffroy (1986), 96–101; Rawson (1987), 83–114; Bejor (1979), 126–38.

main temple in the forum, that of the Dioscuri, was dedicated to a
Greek cult with a long history at Naples, but it was built in Roman
style and its iconography, according to some readings, may have
made specific reference to the Augustan regime. The newly discovered gymnasium also seems to have been at least partially rebuilt
in the same period and in contemporary Roman style. This must
inevitably pose some important questions about how far these buildings acted as a repository of cultural memories of Greek Naples.
Although they were all connected with the Greek past, they were
very much in a contemporary Roman manner. This was, of course,
greatly influenced by Greek style at this date, to the point where
Wallace-Hadrill has argued that some aspects of the culture of
Roman Italy had simply absorbed and internalized some elements
of the Greek.[34] In a city like Naples, however, which made considerable cultural capital out of its Greek heritage, it cannot be assumed
that the aspects of Greek culture which survived were a matter of
internalization or cultural hybridity.[35] The keen engagement with the
city's past suggests that the process involved a much more deliberate
selection of which aspects of the past to preserve and which to
suppress.

One important caveat is that there may have been many locations
which did act as repositories of cultural memory which have not
survived. The monument to Parthenope mentioned by Strabo was
clearly an important location and one which—given the centrality of
Parthenope to the foundation myths of Naples—is likely to have been
an important reminder of the city's Greek past. Its ongoing importance is underlined by the athletic contest associated with it, which
Strabo implies was still current in his own day. Unfortunately, he
gives no clue to the location or appearance of this shrine, but the
presence of an active cult of Parthenope suggests that there were
locations within the city which served as repositories of cultural
memory. However, the evidence currently available suggests that
the most important civic spaces and structures, such as the forum,
theatres, and gymnasium, were reconstructed in the early Empire in a
much more Romanized style. Cultural memory in the urban landscape of Naples seems to have been largely filtered through a contemporary Roman sensibility.

---

[34] Wallace-Hadrill (2008), 73–102.   [35] Wallace-Hadrill (2008), 73–103.

LANGUAGE AND MEMORY: WRITTEN
AND SPOKEN GREEK

One aspect of the urban landscape which may have acted as a powerful form of cultural memory is the presence of Greek inscriptions.[36] Naples was almost unique in Italy in using Greek as a written language—even for forms of public epigraphy for which Latin was almost universal elsewhere in Italy—until well into the second century AD.[37] Greek inscriptions account for approximately 25 per cent of the body of epigraphic evidence from the city, which is an unusually high ratio of Greek to Latin by the standards of southern Italy.[38] The use of Greek is not universal, however, which suggests that it was chosen for specific purposes to make a specific point. More significantly, Greek was used in contexts such as civic decrees or other public and official documents, which are precisely those in which Latin was adopted as the preferred language elsewhere in Italy. Many funerary inscriptions from Naples are, in contrast, written in Latin. The use of Greek seems, therefore, to be closely connected with civic activity rather than with private commemoration, and to be closely linked with the activities of the city's elite.

This is significant, because the use of Latin as a formal written language, particularly in inscriptions and even more so in inscriptions of a public or official nature, is an important marker of Roman culture.[39] In many other areas of Italy, the adoption of Latin for inscriptions such as civic decrees, building dedications, and others set up by the elite is a demonstration of the use of Roman cultural forms as means of demonstrating status, either by individuals or groups. Non-Latin languages, where they persist, are more often found in inscriptions of a more private nature, such as those of ownership and graffiti on objects.[40] In Naples, however, Greek persists as an epigraphic

---

[36] Quite literally an example of Connerton's inscribed memory. Connerton (1989), 74–9.

[37] Greek inscriptions are found in some other areas of Magna Graecia in the first century AD, notably at Rhegium and Velia, but in much smaller quantities; moreover, the use of Greek in these places dies out significantly earlier than at Naples. Lomas (1993), 149–60, 172–87; Vecchio (2005), 386–96.

[38] Miranda (1990); Miranda (1995). For discussion, Lomas (1993), 161–87; Leiwo (1994), 133–56.

[39] Woolf (1996). [40] Häussler (2002).

language until well into the second century AD, and this raises some important questions about Neapolitan culture in the early Empire.

Writing is a powerful means of transmitting cultural memory, not just in the content and meaning of a text, but also by its appearance.[41] In societies such as that of Naples, in which a significant section of the population would have had no literacy, or only a limited ability to read, the visual appearance of a text can be as important as the content, if not more so.[42] The continued use of the Greek language and alphabet, particularly for prominent official inscriptions such as decrees of the *boule*, dedicatory inscriptions on buildings, and the victory records of the games, would have had an immediate visual impact, reminding the viewer of Naples' Greek past. For those who could read, whether Neapolitans or visitors, it firmly underlined the difference between Naples and even its near neighbours, drawing attention to both the Greek past and the continuing Hellenism of the present. Even for those who could not read an inscription, the use of a different alphabet and the visual difference between Greek and Roman inscriptions might have acted as a reminder of Naples' difference and drawn attention to its past history. Greek was, of course, widely spoken by the Roman and Italian elites, and its high status as a language was undoubtedly a factor in its survival in Naples.[43] Its use as a written language for certain types of public document, however, seems to represent a deliberate choice designed to emphasis Greek aspects of civic culture. The continued use of Greek as an epigraphic language for public inscriptions would have operated on two levels—as a source of cultural memory for the Neapolitans, and as a way of gaining civic prestige by reminding visitors of the city's Greek heritage.

GREEK INSTITUTIONS AND GREEK GAMES

Other civic institutions also emphasize the Greek heritage of Naples. Decrees were issued in the name of the *boule* and magistrates were

---

[41] On writing and cultural memory see Connerton (1989), 74–7.

[42] Harris (1989), 3–24; cf. Horsfall (1991); Hopkins (1991) for the debate about levels and dissemination of literacy.

[43] Adams (2003), 9–18; Leiwo (1994), 49–58, 165–72; Swain (1996), 69–100.

known by Greek titles: *demarchos, archon, laukelarchos,* and *gymna-siarchos.*[44] Phratries, which probably originated as a kinship-based element of pre-Roman civic organization, also remained an import-ant part of civic life until well into the Empire.[45] Twelve of these are known—the Aristaioi, Artemisioi, Euboiai, Euereidai, Eumeleidai, Eunostidai, Hermaioi, Kretondai, Kymaioi, Pankleidai, Theotadai, and one other whose name is unclear.[46] Their Archaic names, which reference the origins of the city, gods, heroes, or ancient families, suggest an ancient origin.[47] They are documented by a series of inscriptions, mostly written in Greek and in some cases quite lengthy and detailed. Although they may have started out as subdiv-isions of the citizen body of Naples, by the imperial period mem-bership includes Roman notables as well as Neapolitans, suggesting that the link between membership and citizenship had been eroded. Phratry members or patrons include the consulars L. Cresperius Proculus and L. Claudius Arrianus, and an imperial freedman and his sons, none of whom appear to have been of Neapolitan origin.[48] Inscriptions reveal that each phratry had its own cults and meeting house, held regular meetings, and elected officers.[49] One of their functions seems to have been to channel high-level patronage and benefactions from members of both local and Roman elites. Gifts and donations offered to phratries were frequently valuable, ran-ging from new buildings to smaller gifts such as statues, cups, and

[44] Miranda (1990), nos. 30–41. The office of *laukelarchos* is unique to Naples and its function is unknown. Pinsent (1969); Girone (1994); Dubois (1994); Mauro De Nardis (Chapter 5 in this volume). It seems more likely that it was a civic magistracy than a priesthood, as it occurs most frequently in cursus inscriptions.

[45] Strabo 5.4.7. Suetonius, *Claudius* 11.2; Varro, *On the Latin Language* 5.85; *CIL* 6.1.1851, 12.3232; *IG* 14.721, 722, 742, 743, 744, 748; Miranda (1990), 61–74; Polito (2000). The latest phratry inscription dates to the late second/early third century AD. *IG* 13.742; Miranda (1990), no. 42.

[46] It is unclear whether the Antinoitoi was a new phratry created in the Hadrianic period, or was a Hadrianic renaming of an existing phratry in honour of Antinous. Hadrian was honoured by being named honorary *demarchos* of Naples (SHA, *Hadrian* 19.1), suggesting that he had a close connection with the city. His noted philhellenic sympathies would make both of these gestures highly appropriate as ways of honouring him in the hope of gaining imperial favour.

[47] Suetonius, *Claudius* 11.2; Varro, *On the Latin Language* 5.85; Strabo 5.4.7; Napoli (1959); Guarducci (1936); Lomas (1993), 166–7; Leiwo (1994), 150–6.

[48] *IG* 14.721, 743, and 744; Miranda (1990), nos. 9, 31, and 32; Leiwo (1994), 150–6. Leiwo conjectures that both consuls may have been from Asia Minor.

[49] Guarducci (1936); Lomas (1993), 166–8; Girone (1994); Polito 2000.

candelabra of precious metal.[50] For example, the phratry of the
Artemisioi conferred honours on Munatius Hilarianus, a benefactor
of the phratry and the city, and on Hilarianus' deceased son, mark-
ing the event by dedicating a shrine and setting up a statue.[51]
Meetings and social events organized by phratries also facilitated
contact between members and provided a forum in which Neapolitans and Romans could mingle.

One of the most important events in Neapolitan cultural life was
the Greek games, the *Italika Rhomaia Sebasta Isolympia*, which were
related to the torch race instituted by Diotimos (see Rabun Taylor,
Chapter 3 in this volume) but augmented in 2 BC in honour of the
emperor Augustus.[52] It was a Panhellenic festival, celebrated every
four years, and the rules and events were directly modelled on those
of the Olympic games, with events for both adults and boys, and also
some for women and girls.[53] Participants were required to report to
the gymnasium and register thirty days before the games began. They
were paid a daily allowance but prizes were crowns of wheat, rather
than money.[54] Athletic events were based around the Olympic programme of foot races, combat sports (boxing, wrestling, and *pankra-
tion*), and equestrian events, including horse races and chariot races.
Musical and artistic events followed, and unlike the athletes, the
victors were rewarded with cash prizes.[55] The prestige of this festival
attracted many athletes and performers, particularly in the first century AD when it seems to have been ranked between fifth and eighth in

[50] *IG* 14.715, 721–2, 728, 742, 748; *CIL* 10.1491, *SEG* 19.622; Maiuri (1913).

[51] Munatius Hilarianus paid for the restoration and adornment of the phratry's
buildings, including gilding the roof, and the construction of a magnificent new
dining room and shrine to Artemis, in return for which the phratry offered him
fulsome thanks, four statues and *imagines clipeatae* in honour of himself and his son,
and 50 *chorai*, the exact meaning of which is unknown. Maiuri (1913); Fishwick
(1989); Miranda (1990), 66–72; Polito (2000).

[52] Dio Cassius 55.10.5–6, Suetonius, *Augustus* 98.5; Strabo 5.4.7; Geer (1935);
Merkelbach (1974); Crowther (1989); Miranda (1982); Miranda (1985b), 390.

[53] *IvO* 56. Despite the prestige of the games, Geer suggests that the term *isolympica*
refers to parity with the Olympics in terms of events and eligibility for entry to
competitions, not status. Geer (1935), 209; Miranda (1982), 181.

[54] *IG* 14.748; Geer (1935), 210–11 argues that events for boys were limited to
citizens, noting that in other areas of the Greek world, participation in the boys' events
at games was part of ephebic training, and since Strabo (5.4.7) mentions the survival
of the ephebeia at Naples, this may well be the case here. Only the adult events were
open to participants from the wider Greek world.

[55] *IvO* 56; Lucian, *Of Dancing* 32.

the order of international games.[56] The names of over 170 competitors have been recovered thanks to the recently discovered inscriptions, and these were drawn from all over the Greek world.[57] The close connection between the games and the imperial family is evident in the Olympia inscription setting out the programme and rules, which specify that the games were preceded by a procession to the *Kaisareion* and sacrifices in honour of the imperial family. Some emperors competed in the games: Claudius entered a play in honour of his brother Germanicus in the dramatic competition and Domitian is named in the victory lists as winner of a chariot race. They were also honoured in other ways. Many victors in the competition for composition and delivery of panegyrics chose to eulogize the emperor or his family.[58] The role of *agonothetes*, the official who presided over the games, was held several times by emperors. Titus was *agonothetes* at least three times, in AD 70, 74, and 78, holding the office as an honorary one, *in absentia*, on at least one occasion. Numerous consuls and senators also held this office.[59]

Whether the games were an entirely new event or a reorganization of an existing one is unclear, despite plentiful evidence of a long tradition of both agonistic and artistic contests at Naples.[60] A festival in honour of the Siren Parthenope, a central figure in the foundation

[56] Suetonius, *Augustus* 98; Velleius Paterculus 2.123; Strabo 5.4.7; Dio Cassius 55.10.9, 56.29; Statius, *Silvae* 3.5.91–2. On the international character of the festival, see Miranda (1982), 165–81; Miranda (1985b), 390–2; and Hardie (1983), 2–14. It is possible that the Greek games were most prominent in the first century AD, although they continued to be held long after this. Games elsewhere in the West, in the form of the Capitolia at Rome (AD 86) and Eusebeia at Puteoli (AD 138), eroded the prestige of the Neapolitan games (Geer (1935), 213–14) but they continued to be celebrated throughout the second century AD. The latest known reference to them dates to the third century AD (*IG* 3.129). Miranda (1982); Miranda (2007).

[57] Miranda (2007); Miranda (2010). Cf. also commemorations of, and honours offered to, other competitors: *IG* 14.737, 738, 739, 746, 747, 748, 754, 755; Miranda (1990), 47–80.

[58] Miranda (2010), 419–20.

[59] *IG* 14.729 (= *CIL* 10.1481); Miranda (1988a). Titus was in Judaea during the games of AD 70. There is no evidence on whether he presided in person or not on the other occasions.

[60] Naples was one of the cities frequented by Cicero's client Archias as he attempted to build his literary reputation in Italy and it had a well-established guild of Dionysos. Cicero, *Archias* 10; Plutarch, *Life of Brutus* 21. Cf. also Seneca (*Epistles* 76.4), who makes reference to the keen interest in actors and musicians at Naples. There may also have been an association of actors at Naples, although the evidence dates to the imperial period. *IG* 14.737; *IG* 14.2495 (= *CIL* 12.3232); Jory (1970), 247–9.

myths of the city, whose cult dates to the earliest phase of settlement at Naples, was established in the fifth century BC. It is said to have been instituted by the Athenian general Diotimos during his visit to Naples, in response to an oracle, and to have been celebrated annually. It included a torch race, although it is unclear what precisely this consisted of and whether it was, strictly speaking, an athletic event or part of a ritual.[61] Strabo mentions the festival in honour of Parthenope quite separately from his description of the Augustan games, and seems to imply that they were both still celebrated.[62] There may also have been contests in honour of Aphrodite and possibly Demeter, which may or may not have been part of the same festival as those in honour of Parthenope.[63] The inscriptions from the imperial temple throw some light on this matter, as one of the events listed is a *lampas* (torch) dedicated to Augustus, implying that a torch contest or race was part of the new games. It is possible that the Sebasta developed from an annual festival based around a torch race in honour of Parthenope but the character of the new games was very different and subsumed local characteristics. Its name makes no reference to any antecedents, but underlines its Italian, imperial, and Olympic credentials. The games were explicitly Panhellenic and also very closely linked with the imperial cult, the imperial family, and the Roman elite. If the Sebasta was a reorganization of an earlier Greek festival, it largely subsumed the identity of this into something very different.

HELLENISM AND NAPLES: CULTURAL MEMORY OR CULTURAL APPROPRIATION?

The identity of Naples in the early Empire was undoubtedly complex. The physical appearance of the city, and the way it developed in this period, seems to be influenced most strongly by contemporary Roman architectural styles and ideas about urban development.

---

[61] Timaeus fr. 566 F 98 Jacoby; Lycophron, *Alexandra* 732–7; Strabo 5.4.7. Timaeus, quoted in Tzetzes' scholia on Lycophron, describes the festival as a torch race and contest, while Lycophron himself merely mentions a torch race established in honour of Parthenope in response to an oracle. On the arguments for and against continuity, see Miranda (1985a); Miranda (1985b), 390.

[62] Strabo, 5.4.7; Geer (1935), 217–19; Miranda (1985b), 390.

[63] Beloch (1989 [1890]), 51–60; *IG* 14.745; Miranda (1990), no. 33.

Structures with strong links to the city's Greek past clearly did survive, but possibly not in a form which provided immediate reminders of the city's past. Instead, they reference the contemporary culture of the Augustan and Julio-Claudian age. The theatre and *odeion*, for instance, are rebuilt in a typically Augustan style, and the buildings under Piazza Nicola Amore seem to have undergone a similar process.[64] Cultural memory of the type proposed by Halbwachs, which was sustained and transmitted by visual reminders in the urban landscape, is difficult to identify archaeologically. At best, we could read these as an example of indirect cultural memory, or possibly even one which appropriated aspects of the Greek past and subsumed it into a more Roman present. The associations between buildings such as the theatre, *odeion*, and gymnasium and the city's Greek heritage may have served as visible reminders of Hellenism and of Naples' intellectual, artistic, and athletic culture, but they did not specifically reference the past. Instead, they presented Hellenism as part of contemporary Graeco-Roman culture rather than linking it overtly to cultural memories of the past.

Other aspects of Greek civic culture also demonstrate ambiguities. The continued use of Greek titles and terminology for magistrates, council, and assembly, and the issue of Greek decrees would have acted as a powerful reminder of the Greek past of the city, particularly the persistence of the enigmatic office of *laukelarchos*, which was unique to Naples.[65] There must be some possibility that these coexisted with at least some elements of a Roman municipal administration, but if so, the continued use of Greek terminology seems a powerful way of maintaining cultural memories.[66] The survival of social institutions such as the phratries or the ephebeia was also a way of keeping cultural memory alive and linking the people of Roman Naples with their past.[67] They may have been particularly powerful as they were not static symbols to be viewed but were participatory, requiring an active engagement with and participation in social activities which were redolent of Naples' past history. As the membership of some phratries demonstrates, however, Hellenism was not

---

[64] There was a great increase in construction of the types of building found at Naples in the early Empire, and many cities reconstructed their public spaces to reflect the ideology of Augustus. Jouffroy (1986); Zanker (1988).

[65] On the Greek decrees see Lomas (1993), 148–52, 177–81.

[66] Lomas (1993), 148–52.   [67] Connerton (1989), 62–3.

just a matter of cultural memory, but could also be used to attract patronage from powerful Romans with an interest in Greek culture.

The Sebasta games, in contrast, are a more complex case. Superficially, they seem a very powerful vehicle for promoting cultural memory, showcasing the Greek heritage of Naples for an international audience, and drawing spectators and competitors from across the Mediterranean. Their regular recurrence served to reinforce this and give the impression of cultural continuity, thanks to their fixed framework of rules, events, and rituals.[68] The gymnasium and its associated buildings, with its inscribed victory lists, also emphasizes this continuity and displays it between games. Despite this appearance of cultural continuity, however, they were, in fact, a new innovation. Even if they were based on games with a longer history, the dedication to Augustus, the new name and the new rules and programme of events, and the self-conscious remodelling on the Olympic games all signal a break with tradition. Even the structures excavated in Piazza Nicola Amore, and believed to be part of the gymnasium complex, date to the first century AD, suggesting that the gymnasium was extended or rebuilt at the same time as, or shortly after, the establishment of the Sebasta. They are, therefore, very ambiguous. On the one hand, they were a reminder of Naples' cultural traditions, but on the other hand they were a new departure, launched in honour of the emperor, modelled on the contemporary Olympics rather than on local Neapolitan traditions, and patronized by people from outside the city. They were certainly effective as a way of promoting the civic status of Naples, and used its Greek heritage very effectively to engage with the Roman elite, but it is questionable whether they promoted cultural memory at any level other than a general consciousness of Hellenism. Roman Naples was clearly something of a hybrid, which combined many aspects of a Roman *municipium* with Greek survivals and also with newly created Greek institutions. It raises many questions about why some Greek institutions and cultural practices survived and others did not, who selected what to encourage or suppress, and what motivations underlay this process.

Preservation of cultural memory—or, conversely, suppression of it—is a selective process. The Greek aspects of Naples' civic culture are not simply the afterlife of a Greek community that took longer to

---

[68] Connerton (1989), 63–5.

adopt Roman civic culture than the rest of Italy but the result of cultural choices, and an active and ongoing reinvention of the past. However, this raises many questions: Which aspects of culture are omitted and why? Who decides which aspects are worth preserving or reinventing and whose agenda does this serve? How do we interpret cultural memory in areas where the cultural and ethnic history of the community is so mixed? It is very apparent that the past culture which survived and was promoted at Naples, particularly in the context of 'official' civic culture, was Greek. The Oscan and Campanian cultures which became part of Naples in the late fifth century vanish almost entirely from the record. This is not because people of Campanian descent vanished, or became invisible. They remain visible in the epigraphic record because of the persistence of Campanian names such as those found in some of the Via Foria and Via Cristallini tombs, or in the names of eminent citizens such as the poet Statius.[69] The coexistence of Greek and Oscan names within the same families and the expression of Oscan names in Greek form suggests both intermarriage and some degree of adaptation to Greek onomastic forms, but also demonstrates the ongoing presence of people of Oscan descent in Naples, who maintained a recognizably non-Greek family identity. Cultural memory is invariably selective, as a memory community opts to promote particular aspects of the past but to suppress others, and in the case of Naples, the Campanian aspects of the city's past do not feature much in the Roman period. The retention of Oscan names suggests that the Campanian aspects of the past may have formed part of the cultural memory of particular subgroups, but were not part of the civic culture of Naples.[70]

The reason behind this is not difficult to fathom. From the second century BC onwards, many members of the Roman elite developed a strong—if ambivalent—interest in Greek culture. Greek language and culture formed an important element in the education of upper-class Romans, and aspects of Hellenism became increasingly embedded in

---

[69] Campanian names of Oscan origin, such as Bibios (Vibius), Trebios (Trebius), Pakea (Pakkia), Statia, and Mamarchos (Mamercus), are not uncommon in the funerary inscriptions of Naples, although they are often lightly Hellenized and given in Greek onomastic form, e.g. Bibios, Pakea, and Trebios Epilytou (Levi (1926); Leiwo (1994), 61–5); Statia Mamarchou (Leiwo (1994), 82–4); Strabo 5.4.7; Statius, *Silvae* 5.3.103–94.

[70] Cultural memory is a collective but also a variable concept, and may vary between different groups within a society (Alcock and Van Dyke (2003), 2–3).

Roman culture.[71] Naples and its surrounding area became very popular with the Roman elite from the second century BC onwards. The notoriously philhellene Scipio Africanus owned a villa at Liternum, on the north side of the Bay of Naples, and many wealthy Romans followed suit. By the early Empire, many eminent families owned villas on the Bay of Naples, and a complex of imperial villas had grown up at Baiae, on the far side of the Bay.[72] The Greek culture of this part of Campania was one of its attractions. Naples, in particular, had the reputation of a cultured backwater, a centre of *otium* remote from the sordidness of political life in Rome and an appropriate place for a Roman to go to sample Greek culture and learning.[73] Its Greek festivals and games, and other ongoing Greek survivals, attracted rich Romans and secured it the patronage of philhellene emperors such as Nero, Domitian, and Hadrian. Naples was also still a point of contact between the Greek world and Italy, and attracted Greek visitors to its games.[74] It was also used as a handy stepping stone by some Greeks who aimed at a career in Rome, such as the poets Archias and Statius.[75] These were not trivial considerations. Greek culture conferred prestige, and after Hadrian's creation of the Panhellenion, a league of Greek cities which enjoyed significant privileges, it also conferred serious benefits and enhanced civic status on a community.[76] By showcasing elements of Greek heritage, Naples was well placed to take advantage of this phenomenon, and before that, to benefit from the long-standing Roman admiration of Greek culture which gave rise to it. It is not surprising that the Neapolitan elite was keen to promote its Greek heritage for the benefit of the city, given the civic prestige which could accrue from it.

How far this reflects cultural memory of the Greek past is another matter. Institutions such as the phratries, and Greek cults and festivals—particularly those such as the festival in honour of Parthenope which

---

[71] Woolf (1994); Swain (1996), 69–100; Adams (2003), 9–18; Wallace-Hadrill (2008), 73–103.

[72] D'Arms (1970).

[73] Statius, *Silvae* 3.5.85–8; Seneca, *Epistles* 68.5; Strabo 5.4.7. D'Arms (1970), 48–55; Hardie (1983), 2–14. Much the same sort of topos is applied by Strabo (4.1.5) to Massilia in a very similar context, with a stress on the combination of Hellenism and a role as a centre of learning and Greek culture.

[74] Strabo 5.4.7; Dio Cassius 55.10.5.

[75] Cicero, *Archias* 5–6; Statius, *Silvae* 5.3.103–94.

[76] Spawforth and Walker (1985); Swain (1996).

were connected with the foundation myths of the city—were all repositories of cultural memory, which served to link the people to their Greek past and integrate it into their present. Greek titles for magistrates may have served the same purpose, and Greek inscriptions may have acted as visual cues to remind the citizens of their connections to the past. If examined closely, however, many of these features of Roman Naples are somewhat ambiguous. Greek inscriptions may have acted as a constant visual reminder of the city's Greek heritage, to both Neapolitans and visitors, but some of them seem to be little more than Greek translations of Roman-style cursus inscriptions.[77] The games were closely modelled on contemporary Panhellenic games, not on earlier Neapolitan games, and were comprehensively linked with the imperial cult and symbolism connected with the imperial family. Many of the most significant buildings and locations connected with Greek culture by writers such as Strabo, such as the theatre and the portico and temple which may have been part of the gymnasium, were rebuilt in the early Empire in contemporary Roman style, and, in some cases, heavily imbued with Augustan symbolism. Paradoxically, the areas of the city, and some aspects of its culture, which were most closely associated with its past were comprehensively overhauled and revised in the early Empire in ways which reduced their value as vehicles for cultural memory. Instead, they took on a more contemporary Greek flavour, or adopted the Graeco-Roman norms of Augustan Italy.

Naples' Greek identity in the early Empire was multi-layered, and can best be understood as a series of nested identities. In order to benefit from Roman interest in Greek culture, the city had to present a form of that culture which was comprehensible and unthreatening, couched in terms of contemporary Hellenism rather than local tradition. Selective cultural memory was used to suppress the less prestigious Campanian elements of Naples' culture and past at a civic level, although families with Campanian names still lived there. The Greek culture of the city was, however, not just about preserving cultural memories of the city's Greek past. Instead, the most high-profile elements of it, and the ones for which the city was most noted, were reconfigured in terms of contemporary Hellenism and to incorporate Roman features, the better to appeal to the Roman elite. Greek

---

[77] Girone (1994), 84 points out that much information about magistracies comes from inscriptions which—although written in Greek—are in fact standard Roman cursus inscriptions in form.

institutions, cults, rituals, and language may have served as triggers for cultural memories which helped to maintain Greek identity and a sense of difference from neighbouring cities, but the Greek culture and institutions also contained many new elements, which referenced different—and non-local—forms of Greek culture, and in particular used Greek culture as a vehicle for honouring emperors and their families. Greek culture in Roman Naples was not just a case of cultural memory but also involved appropriation of some aspects of the Greek culture of the city as a form of dialogue with Roman power.

5

Greek Magistrates in Roman Naples?

Law and Memory from the Fourth Century
BC to the Fourth Century AD

Mauro De Nardis

Some of the most challenging questions about the evolution of the municipal system and the development of Roman administrative structures in Italian communities after the beginning of the first century BC concern the peculiar political structure of ancient Neapolis, as it seems to emerge from the surviving body of evidence, in particular for the period before and after the Social War (90–88 BC). Most previous studies—driven by assumptions about Naples' identity as a 'Greek city'—have stressed the conservative nature of the city's constitution in Roman times, as well as its continuity with earlier Greek institutions. These seemingly sound assumptions have often taken on a life of their own within the scholarly debate. Nevertheless, a partially different picture seems to emerge when we approach the ancient source material in a new and possibly provocative way, drawing on some of the theories and methodologies of reception studies.

In this chapter I will examine the possibility that the institution of the Sebasta games in AD 2 led to a 'hybridized' reinvention of the former local Greek-styled magisterial outfit. The reversion to an earlier pattern of Greek city offices (now apparently centred upon

I am immensely grateful to Jessica Hughes for reading through several drafts of this paper and greatly improving it by her many constructive suggestions and comments. I also owe huge thanks to Claudio Buongiovanni for his perceptive criticism and advice. Any mistakes that remain are my own.

an eponymous chief magistrate *demarchos* and an *agonothetes*, whose job it was to deal directly with the organization of the new games) was deeply significant for a city of Greek tradition like Naples. It may be linked to a political intervention in the local civic constitution which aimed to give an appropriate administrative apparatus to a *polis* that became the first centre in Italy where Isolympic games were held. If the suggestion I offer here is sound, it follows that the survival of the city's Greek culture and constitutional framework well into the Empire did not depend only on its Greek urban history and identity, but also on a politico-cultural 'revival' connected to the cultural traditions of the Hellenistic East, and in particular with the Olympic games.

This chapter will present and discuss the main literary and epigraphic evidence for the Neapolitan constitution and magistrates (in particular the offices of *demarchos*, *archon*, and *laukelarchos*), in order to single out uncontroversial points, with an emphasis on Naples' constitutional transformations in the shift from the Greek federate city to the enfranchised *municipium*. It will then move on to reconsider the traditional interpretations of this evidence, showing that some of the Greek magistracies in Naples were in fact substantially 'reinvented' at the time of the institution of the Sebasta games. It goes without saying that this new interpretation has significant consequences for our understanding of the interaction of Roman Naples' institutions and social life with the city's Greek past, allowing for a better assessment of the interplay of Roman and Greek elements in the civic elite culture of both Naples and imperial Italy.

HISTORY AND LAW IN NEAPOLIS—AN INTRODUCTION TO THE EVIDENCE

General historical accounts of Rome's first contact with Naples are given by Livy and Dionysius of Halicarnassus: these writers describe how Naples, which was allied with Nola and the Samnite League, was besieged by Roman troops in 327/6 BC after having raided the territory of Romans settlers in the *ager Campanus* and *ager Falernus*.[1] Since an

---

[1] Livy 8.23.3; Dionysius of Halicarnassus, *Roman Antiquities* 15.6.5ff. On both sources see Oakley (1998), 629–46.

early surrender was arranged by the Roman consul Q. Publilius Philo and two of the Neapolitan leaders, this city received a very favourable alliance with Rome and became a *civitas foederata*. According to the traditional view, this treaty was so generous that more than 200 years after the end (in 89 BC) of the Social War between Rome and her Italian allies—which ended largely thanks to the granting of citizenship by the Romans—most of the inhabitants of Naples did not initially want Roman citizenship at all, preferring 'the freedom enjoyed under their own treaty'.[2] In fact, since the actual degree of freedom of Naples as a federate city theoretically implied no major change in either its constitutional status or the structure of its magistracies, such a vast public hesitation before accepting Roman citizenship is rather difficult to understand.

At a later stage, Naples was granted the status of colony—either under Titus, or in the late Antonine age, or under Caracalla.[3] Since the evidence for the administrative restructuring of Campania in late antiquity is regrettably fragmentary (it consists primarily of occasional references to individual office holders), any reconstruction has been correspondingly tentative. Latin inscriptions from both Latium and Campania attest that between the last decades of the third and the first quarter of the fourth century AD Campania, like the rest of the new Italic districts, was put under the control of new officials, *correctores*, who were succeeded by *consulares*. Neapolis was part of this province, although Capua became the most important town in late antique Campania.[4] Research into the evolving status of Neapolis and the political implications of the introduction of the municipal constitution by Rome is somewhat hindered by the significant gap in evidence for the period between the 326 BC treaty with Rome and the years after the granting of Roman citizenship to the Italians (in 90–88 BC). Beyond the references in ancient Greek and Roman literary sources, the main bulk of evidence for local practices and administrative structures in this earlier period comes from the surviving Greek and Latin inscriptions, most of which post-date 90 BC.[5]

---

[2] Cicero, *Balbus* 8.21 (trans. after R. Gardner, Loeb Classical Library 1958).

[3] See *ILS* 6458 (dating to the first year of the reign of Alexander Severus, AD 222): *Colonia Aurelia Augusta Antonina Felix Neapolis*. For the dating to the reign of Titus see Beloch (1989 [1890]), 40.

[4] See Savino (2005), 18–26.

[5] A rich collection of both literary and epigraphic evidence on Naples is provided by Morelli and Nenci (1952), 371–413. A comprehensive, commented collection of

Significantly, in terms of the theme of this volume, much modern discussion of the supposed adjustments and changes in Neapolis' constitution and administrative system after the Social War is dominated by presuppositions about the enduring Greek culture and heritage of this city. Both Mommsen and Kaibel insist on the pre-Roman roots of Neapolitan magistracies and Greek institutions, and attempt to connect the local magistrates and Roman municipal offices by assimilating the archons or the demarchs and the *agoranomoi* with the typical supreme magistracy of a *municipium*, namely the *quattuorviri iure dicundo* and *quattuorviri aediles*.[6] Beloch, starting from the same assumption about the roots of Neapolitan magistrates in the Roman Empire, also underlines the fact that the archons were much the same as the Roman *quattuorvirate*, but points out that the demarchy had instead lost its importance in the political life of the city by the Antonine age, when it (like that of *laukelarchos*) had only religious functions.[7] De Martino, on the other hand, states that after the 326 BC treaty with Rome and before it became a *municipium*, Neapolis underwent some constitutional changes (with the office of demarch being superseded by the new role of the archon), but even after 90–89 BC it retained the typical administrative structure of a Greek city.[8] Sartori argues that such a change seems to be attested epigraphically by the end of the first century AD: accordingly, two archons (as *duoviri quinquennales*) and two *agoranomoi* became the main executive office-holders of Neapolis, thus matching the typical supreme magistracy of a standard *municipium*, namely the board of *quattuorviri*.[9] Costabile asserts instead that, notwithstanding our scanty evidence, a gap in the constitutional history of Neapolis seems to occur during the first century BC, which must coincide with the introduction of a new administration based on the Roman

Naples' Greek inscriptions is found in Miranda (1990) and Miranda (1995). As for local Latin records, in addition to *CIL* 10.1 (1852) and its supplement in *Ephemeris Epigraphica* (1899), see Beloch (1989 [1890]), 26–88, and Leiwo (1994), *passim*.

[6] Mommsen (1883), 171–2; Kaibel (1890), 191.

[7] Cf. Beloch (1989 [1890]), 48; Beloch (1926), 506–8. For the role of the Greek heritage of Naples in the early Empire, see D'Arms (1970), 142–52; Lepore (1985), 121–2. On the readings of Mommsen, Kaibel, and Beloch, see the discussion in Pinsent (1969), 368–70. According to Tutini (1644), 241–5, the Neapolitan 'tribuno popolare' of the early Middle Ages had some kind of close historical and constitutional ties with the demarchs of Graeco-Roman Neapolis.

[8] De Martino (1952 [1979]), 328–38, esp. 334.

[9] Sartori (1953), 45–53.

pattern of municipal government (meanwhile, he argues that the explicit Greek survival of the pre-Social War constitution should be limited to the office of demarch).[10] Furthermore, Lepore argues that the 'institutional decline' ('parabola istituzionale') of Naples began soon after Sulla's time, when the archons and *agoranomoi* were replaced by the *quattuorviri*.[11]

In general, then, previous interpretations stress continuity between Greek and Roman forms of city administration, and emphasize how the Greek offices were preserved within the citizen *municipium*. Less emphasis is placed on how these offices may have been received and transformed into hybridized forms to fit the new political needs of a changing social and cultural environment, from the first century BC onwards. In the light of such extensive historical debate, another general reconsideration of the nature of the administrative structure of Neapolis after the Social War and under the Empire may seem unnecessary, particularly given the partial and problematic nature of the evidence. However, a new consideration of these issues starting from a much more careful analysis of the existing evidence may be illuminating, as the following example illustrates.

According to current academic opinion, it is believed that a lost fragmentary inscription from Naples (*IG* 14.745 = Miranda 1990, no. 33 = Leiwo 1994, no. 119), known to us through a seventeenth-century report, has to be regarded as the principal document testifying to the existence of the quattuorvirate after Neapolis became a citizen *municipium*. The text of this inscription tells us that it was set up by the inhabitants (*polítai*) of Naples in honour (so it seems) of a certain 'Seleukos son of Seleukos', who is said to have held a number of important posts in this city—two of which seem to have been municipal offices or functions. According to the career recounted in this inscription, Seleukos had been a gymnasiarch and 'one of the college of four officials' (a college that has been identified with the Roman quattuorvirate), had held the otherwise unattested function of *laukelarchos*, and, finally, was also in charge of what has been interpreted as a quinquennial censor-like office (namely, either *duovir* or

[10] Costabile (1984), 126–8 (he speaks of a 'costituzione mista' in Naples, unilaterally bestowed by Rome).

[11] Lepore (1985), 121. A similar view is found in Miranda (1985b), 386; Lomas (1993), 156.

quattuorvir quinquennalis).[12] Now, it is theoretically possible that Seleukos was either a transmarine Greek or an Oriental magnate who, after being incorporated as a townsman of Naples, was granted citizen status after the Social War (90–88 BC). But in this case it seems quite odd that Seleukos, who as a municipal magistrate was entitled to hold at different times two (different) high offices of a citizen *municipium*, is nevertheless recorded in what seems to be a publicly inscribed document using only his individual name and his patronymic, and not by any other nomenclature which may indicate that he had become a Roman citizen. Instead, another (this time funerary) inscription from Naples, possibly dating to the second century BC (*IG* 14.780 = Miranda 1995, no. 118), clearly indicates the enfranchisement of the (deceased) honorand along with his full nomenclature: *Gaius Herennius, son of Gaius, Rhomaios*—that is, a Roman citizen.[13] It may well be that Seleukos was allowed, as a resident Greek extern but not yet an ordinary Roman citizen, to take part in Naples' social life, fulfilling some of the functions that fell to the local magistrates of the *municipium*, such as looking after games and ceremonies. Nevertheless, the case of Cicero's associate L. Manlius Sosis of Catina (modern Catania) shows that this latter individual started his participation in civic life, becoming a member of the local council (*decurio*) of Naples, right *after* he was granted Roman citizenship by the *Lex Julia* (90 BC), even though he already was *ascriptus* in his adoptive *patria*—that is, a citizen and a resident of Neapolis.[14] Even the second-century BC Greek inscriptions of the banker Philostratus of

---

[12] On Seleukos' inscription see De Martino (1952 [1979]), 332; Sartori (1953), 49 (for Seleukos as a 'magistrate' appointed to preside over the quinquennial games in honour of Aphrodite); Miranda (1990), 50–1; Leiwo (1994), 145–6. Pinsent (1969), 371 thinks that the 'conventional' formula of this honorary inscription is 'an alternative for' *agoranomēsanta*, that is, 'having held the function of a *agoranomos*', basically the equivalent of a Roman *aedilis*.

[13] Miranda (1995), 47, rightly points out that *Rhomaios* is a specific addition which seems reasonable only if we date this text to the years before Naples became a Roman *municipium* (90 BC).

[14] Cicero, *Letters to Friends* 13.30 (46–45 BC): 'Manlius Sosis was of Catania, but became a Roman citizen along with the other inhabitants of Naples, and a city councillor (*decurio*) in this city. For he was ascripted to that municipality before the citizenship was given to the allies and Latins.' On the *decuriones* and their role and offices in Roman imperial cities, see *Digest* L, 2. On L. Manlius Sosis, see Deniaux (1993), 325–6. On the procedure for gaining Roman citizenship through the *Lex Julia* and *Lex Plautia Papiria*, as well as on the case of Sosis, see Sherwin-White (1973), 150–5.

Ascalon and his son Theophilus erected in Delos record that they both were citizens of Neapolis (and, naturally, of Ascalon) and do not hint at any public office they might have held in this city.[15] Thus we are constrained to admit that the career of an individual like Seleukos is too poorly documented to prove either his precise legal condition or his role within the political life of the *municipium*. Conversely, if we tentatively suppose that the offices held by Seleukos—who does not seem to have been an enfranchised resident—were exclusively euergetic, it follows that his inscription cannot be taken to illustrate the official administrative structure of enfranchised Naples immediately after the Social War.[16]

The available evidence for Naples' administrative structure has the potential to contribute to the debate about the development of the civic offices which 'survived' from Greek times into the Roman imperial period; nevertheless, the discussion of Seleukos' career here has shown that, at least in this case, inscriptions are of limited use in understanding whether and how chief Greek magistracies were preserved or transformed during the introduction of the municipal constitution by Rome in the period after the Social War. The starting point of any further consideration of these issues must be the analysis set out here of the literary and epigraphic evidence dealing with Naples' main city offices.

DEMARCHS, ARCHONS, LAUKELARCHS

In his famous excursus on Neapolis (on which see Lorenzo Miletti, Chapter 2 of this volume), Strabo emphasizes that the earliest names of their demarchs 'are Greek only, whereas the later are Greek mixed with Campanian. And very many traces of Greek culture are preserved there—gymnasia, ephebeia, phratriae, and Greek names [. . .], although the people are Romans'.[17] It is worth noting that Strabo clearly recognizes as the most distinctive Greek features of Neapolis

---

[15] See Leiwo (1989), 575–84.

[16] The *nomen* Seleukos/Seleucus in Naples is unattested: see Leiwo (1994), 145. His Greek name leads us to wonder whether this Seleukos might have been either an athlete or an illustrious member of a community from the Greek East, settled in Naples as a foreign resident.

[17] Strabo 5.4.7 (trans. after H. L. Jones, Loeb Classical Library 1923).

Mauro De Nardis

its gymnasia, its clubs of ephebes (young men), and its phratries: apart from the demarchs, there is no reference to any other Greek civic magistrature or office in this passage. Moreover, according to Strabo, besides Neapolis only Tarentum and Rhegium survived a complete 'barbarization'.[18] Guy Bradley has rightly pointed out that 'these are surprising choices to pick as standard-bearers of Greek culture in Italy, since Tarentum had received a Roman colony in the late second century and Rhegium was not only seized by the Roman legion which had been sent to garrison it in the early second century (and which killed most of the population in the process, according to Strabo) but had also been colonised by veterans in the late Republic'.[19] Strabo is one of the most significant of all our sources and his description of Neapolis has generated the idea that this city was a distinguished but fairly typical example of 'Greek tradition' in Italy, whose Greek language, culture, and institutions resembled those of other Greek democratic communities (a city council, an assembly of citizens, and elected chief magistrates, of whom one or more held the eponymous supreme annual magistracy, so that each year could be named after its chief magistrate in office).[20] Instead, such a peculiar articulation of Roman Neapolis' political structure may well be seen as a reflection of what Kathryn Lomas has appropriately called 'the revival of Hellenism' during the first and early second centuries AD, that is, 'a cultural construct, not something which is consequent on ethnicity'.[21] It is therefore worth considering whether we should interpret Neapolis' municipal structures in the first and second centuries AD in terms of a deliberate 'revival of Hellenism' through a process of manipulation of Greek heritage by the local elite, fostered by the central government. But first a word of warning, in general,

---

[18] Strabo 6.1.2.

[19] Bradley (2006), 177. As for southern Italy's 'specifically Greek identity until the second century AD', cf. Lomas (1995), 114 ff.

[20] For Neapolis as a city of recognizably Greek culture, see e.g. Cicero, *Archias* 3.5; Strabo 5.7 (C 247); Statius, *Silvae* 3.5.85–104; Dio Cassius 60.6.1–2; for explicit reference to Neapolis as a 'Greek city' in Nero's times see Tacitus, *Annals* 15.33. For discussion of this commonplace, see Leiwo (1994), 42–5, and my own conclusions below.

[21] See Lomas (1993), 181. According to Lomas, this kind of Hellenism 'was largely an elite construct since it appears primarily in the inscriptions of the urban elite'; 'such an emphasis on Hellenism in civic life in cities which were not predominantly Greek in population and were certainly Romanised in their municipal structures lies in the prevailing philhellenism of the Roman elite'.

about the fact that we have to work with a fairly small and very particular selection of documents, which create difficulty in assessing sound and univocal interpretations.

The passage of Strabo cited above suggests that, at some point before the city became a *municipium*, the annual lists of Neapolis' chief eponymous magistrates were made up of, or must have included, demarchs. As for their function, since Neapolitan demarchs 'cannot have anything to do with demarchs as they are known in Athens and Cos', Frederiksen suggests that 'perhaps their functions were to preside over and answer to the popular assembly'.[22] Sherk, on the other hand, suggests that 'the demarchs were actually eponymous in the Roman era', that is, until the end of the second century AD Naples possessed the (nominal) privilege of naming the year after its Greek-style higher magistrates, the demarchs, as we may infer from an inscription of AD 71 as well as from an honorary decree of AD 194.[23] According to the epigraphic evidence, the office of demarch still seems to be referred to as a magistracy of the civic political cursus even after Neapolis was given the status of a colony, that is, during the second or third centuries AD or later, as corroborated by the inscription of Munatius Concessianus, a prominent local figure.[24] Nevertheless, both from an administrative and a political point of view, it seems very unlikely that this office's role and powers remained unchanged in the transition from the Greek constitution to Roman types of municipal and, later, colonial government.

As far as the role and functions of the archons are concerned, the arguments advanced within the scholarly discourse have often been very general. To contribute to the debate, it is therefore worth taking

---

[22] Frederiksen (1984), 92. Liebenam (1900), 292 thinks that in Naples they were 'einst die erste Obrigkeit, jetzt noch eine hohe Ehrenstellung'. Both Liebenam (1900) and D'Arms ((1970), 151, 162–3) underline that even a pantomimist, P. Aelius Antigenides, became *demarchos* in Naples during the Antonine age. On Antigenides' honorary inscription, see Miranda (1990), no. 47.

[23] Sherk (1993), 274. For both these inscriptions, see Miranda (1990), nos. 84 and 44.

[24] See *CIL* 10.1492 / *ILS* 6459, from Naples. This honorary inscription praises L. Munatius Concessianus, *patronus coloniae* and *vir perfectissimus*, for his benefactions and outstanding munificence, especially when his son held *demarchia*. Since Neapolis seems to be referred to here as *colonia*, it follows that this text cannot be earlier than the Severan age, after Neapolis was promoted in status from citizen *municipium* to Roman colony. According to Leiwo (1994), 156, this inscription indicates that the office of *demarchos* 'was kept up until the late empire'.

another, closer look at individual sources. By putting together the
evidence from Dionysius of Halicarnassus (15.6.1–3) and an inscription of the second half of the third century BC from Cos, modern
scholars have argued that the town council, the primary assembly,
and supreme magistrates called *archontes* were working in Naples from
at least the middle of the fourth century BC onwards. Nevertheless, it is
worth noting that the formula used in the aforementioned decree from
Cos in relation to a resolution of the Neapolitan '*archontes*, Council
and People' is very generic, and cannot be used to determine the
political structure of Neapolis in the third century BC. Such epigraphic
formality was a typical feature of inscriptions dealing with the formal,
diplomatic, military, and financial relationship between Greek cities,
Hellenistic kings, and, later, Rome; they served to name and specify all
the standard offices and governmental functions of a city or community, and examples of such usage are attested well into the Roman
Empire.[25] It is worth noting that only Neapolitan inscriptions, two
decrees of the early first century AD, make reference to the posts of
archon and *antarchon* (deputy archon).[26] There is in fact no epigraphic
evidence for the office of archon before the early Empire: therefore, it
remains wholly unclear whether its functions in Greek times differed
from those kept up well into the imperial period. As far as one can say
from the existing evidence, one might simply argue that in imperial
Naples *archontes*, rather than a specific municipal magistracy, were
subsidiary officials whose role seems to be that of overseeing the town
council, when summoned to make decrees.[27]

---

[25] For the Coan decree (recording that special agents called *theoroi* had been
dispatched from Cos to Naples, to win from this city public recognition of the
inviolability of the Asclepius sanctuary in Cos) and its address formulae, see *SEG*
12.378. Other examples of such conventional formulae are given, e.g., by the letter of
Q. Oppius to Aphrodisias' *archontes*, *boule*, and *demos* (Reynolds (1982), doc. 3: 88
BC), by Antoninus Pius' letters to Ephesians (Abbott and Johnson (1968), nos. 100–1:
between AD 140 and 145) as well as by the letter from AD 174 written by the Tyrian
stationarii at *Puteoli* and addressed to the *archontes*, *boule*, and *demos* of their
mother-city, the colony of Tyre (*IGR* 1.421). On this major subject, Jones's synthetic
view of 'the Greek City' remains essential (Jones (1940), 46–7, 174–8).

[26] For the Neapolitan inscriptions recording the post of *archon*, see Miranda
(1990), nos. 82, l. 7 and 85, l. 13. For the *antarchon*, cf. Miranda (1990), nos. 84, l. 8
and 85, ll. 6 and 18. On *archontikos*, see Miranda (1990), no. 34, ll. 5 and 9.

[27] It is worth noting that analogous lesser officials presided over the Attic Panhellenion, a congress of the Greek city and federal states, founded by Hadrian for
religious, political, and cultural purposes: the archon (appointed by the emperor)
was assisted by an *antarchon*. See Boatwright (2000), 144–9.

As for the *laukelarchoi*, many attempts have been made to determine their origin and functions (whether these were religious or political), but the role of this office within the civic life of Neapolis remains unknown. It is, however, significant that a Neapolitan Greek inscription of imperial times which deals with the procedure for appointing a new member into a council (*boule*) of former laukelarchs probably refers to a sacred rather than a civil board.[28]

So far, we have seen that any attempt to reconstruct the administrative structures of Roman Neapolis generally involves an attempt to trace them back to the early Greek city's constitution. According to such an interpretation, Neapolis' original Greek magistracies continued to exist well into the Empire, 'fused' (or confused) in a complex manner with the new institutions of the Roman *colonia*. As a long-lasting symbol of the city's identity, these offices became 'complementary' to the essential core of the career system of Roman administration; we may be inclined to think that under the Empire the *demarchos* and the other main Neapolitan magistrates 'ceased to have any real political or administrative significance' and that their functions became simply honorific.[29] My approach to these issues, as noted above, consciously diverges from the prevailing fashion, which is to treat such historical developments as little more than a model for constructing the cultural identity and political institutions of Naples under the Empire. In what follows, I want to suggest that it is crucial instead to focus on the institution of the new games in Naples, the Sebasta, and to evaluate the impact that these games had on both the administrative pattern and urban social life of Naples under the Principate.

---

[28] See Miranda (1990), no. 4, dated to the second–third centuries AD, and (on their function) Miranda (1990), 18 (who rightly points out that the office of *laukelarchoi* could be different from that of the *laukelarchesantes*, namely former *laukelarchoi*). This office is attested in both Greek (see Miranda 1990, nos. 3, 4, 30, 33, 40) and Latin inscriptions (*ILS* 6455), but, contrary to the *demarchos*, *laukelarchos* is never displayed as an eponymous magistrate. Full discussion in Miranda (1990), 17–18; Girone (1994), 81–7; Dubois (1994), 157–62. Frederiksen (1984), 92 rightly observes that, in addition to *laukelarchoi*, the powers and titles of the military and naval offices of ancient Neapolis are also unknown.

[29] Thus Lomas (1993), 151. As for the (seemingly) honorary demarchate given to the emperor Hadrian, see SHA, *Hadrian* 19.1. According to the conjectural restorations of the editors of a local Greek inscription, Titus also held the post of *demarchos* in Naples: see *IG* 14.729 = Miranda (1990), no. 20.

THE IMPERIAL REGIME, HELLENISM,
AND THE SEBASTA GAMES

After a general introduction to the urban magistrates' duties in arranging civic feasts and games and, in particular, to euergetism and donations of games and festivals of the Neapolitan elite, I would like to argue here that a substantial and decisive change in both the cultural history and the structure of political and public life in Naples was brought to bear by the establishment of the Sebasta games in AD 2, and that some of the Greek-style offices or functionaries attested in local inscriptions (most of which date from the early Empire) may have been instituted in connection with this important new festival.

First, some general background to the Roman magistracies' care of festivals and games. The epigraphic evidence clearly attests that, from an early date, new supreme magistrates and decurions of the Roman and Greek cities of the Empire, as well as the holders of civic priest-hoods and gymnasiarchs, were expected to contribute a variable sum of money to the municipal life of their home towns. This money, together with other donations from eminent local individuals and families, was primarily used to finance major urban building pro-grammes. In addition, local magistrates and leading families also sometimes sponsored the distribution of money, food, or oil for the gymnasia, as well as costly public displays, competitions, perform-ances, and games, which were held either in connection with religious rites and festivals or as part of some important public event.[30]

As for acts of public munificence in Roman Naples, Pliny the Elder informs us that the emperor Claudius appointed both Stertinius Xenophon (a famous physician) and his brother at 500,000 sesterces

---

[30] On *honores* and *munera* undertaken by the magistrates of Greek and Roman cities, see the full discussion in Abbott and Johnson (1968), 84–116; Langhammer (1973), 161–88, 219–62. On elite politics of munificence and civic euergetism in early imperial Italy, see Lomas (2003a), esp. 38–9. As for the main areas of civic euergetism of local magistrates in Latium and Campania, cf. Cébeillac Gervasoni (1998), ch. 4. According to the very important imperial dossier recently found at Alexandria Troas (north-western Turkey), which consists of three letters from the emperor Hadrian dating from the year AD 134 (replying to the requests made by the associations of theatrical performers and their members which met in Naples at the Sebasta of the same year), it is expressly stated that a city cannot 'apply to other expenditures the revenues of a contest that are managed according to law or decree or contractual agreement': on this document (and its English translation) see Slater (2008), 610–20; *AÉ* 2006.1403 a–c, with a French trans. of the Greek text.

a year: after this, in spite of large sums that they had spent 'by beautifying Naples with buildings, [they] left to the heir thirty millions'.[31] If we look at those Neapolitan inscriptions that relate to civic munificence, we find that the texts connected to acts of euergetism are relatively rare: in addition to the fragmentary inscription commemorating Titus' restoration of the city (probably after the earthquake of AD 62[32]), we have only two other badly damaged texts recording similar undertakings.[33] Despite this scarce evidence, it is clear that the local civic elite displayed their generosity by helping to embellish and restore Naples' buildings and infrastructures, possibly because the civic government was (especially after some serious events such as earthquakes) structurally unable to finance both the urban infrastructure and amenities from public revenues. But the really surprising thing about epigraphic evidence from Naples concerning euergetic expenditure on games or arrangements for the celebration of the civic festivals and rites either by local benefactors or by Naples' chief magistrates is actually the absence of data from inscriptions. Even the twelve attested Neapolitan phratries (the exclusively local permanent foundations dealing with their own cults and meetings) do not seem to have provided any income for the public feasts of the city.[34] This makes it rather difficult to reconstruct the ceremonial life of Naples both before and at the same time as the establishment of the Sebasta games for Augustus. All that is clear is that the torch race—an event connected with the festival of the eponymous goddess Parthenope which seems to have played an important religious and cultural role in Naples since the last decades of the fifth century BC—was still being held in Roman times.[35] Since two Neapolitan inscriptions can be connected with the worship of Leucathea and Athena Sikele, and two other local fragmentary texts (both now lost) seem to allude to a civic, sacred 'quinquennial contest', we may presume that a series of prominent Greek-style festivals were periodically held in Naples

---

[31] Pliny, *Natural History* 29.8 (trans. after W. H. S. Jones, Loeb Classical Library 1951).
[32] See Miranda (1990), no. 20.   [33] Miranda (1990), nos. 36, 39.
[34] See Miranda (1990), nos. 42–6.
[35] For the introduction (in about 430–420 BC) of the torch race within the festival of Parthenope, see discussion in Peterson (1919), 176–81, who thinks that even later 'the race with lighted torches would remain the central feature of the celebration'. According to Statius (*Silvae* 4.8.50–1), torches were also connected with the current ritual practice of the local cult of Actaea Ceres.

during the Republic and the Empire, although no reliable literary or
epigraphic evidence which might help us to reconstruct their institution and/or management has survived.[36] The lack of literary and
epigraphic evidence alluding to local elite benefactors honoured for
their public munificence or engagement in civic religious cults, festivals, and ceremonies makes it tempting to suppose that, at least
during the Julio-Claudian period, the popularity of these festivals
was challenged by a new opportunity for both the reinforcement of
the civic unity and for the persistence of its cultural identity: the
Sebasta games (in full *Italika Rhomaia Sebasta Isolympia*).[37]

As F. Millar has emphasized, 'the sudden outburst of the celebration of Octavian/Augustus was a new phenomenon' from 30/29 BC
onwards, which started from the provinces of Asia and Bithynia, by
formal permission of Octavian.[38] As clearly expressed by him, such a
turn of events 'was new first in its wide diffusion at the city level and
above all in the creation [. . .] of provincial cults, with common
temples of Roma and Augustus, common annual games associated
with them, and annual high priesthoods'.[39] In a passage that
undoubtedly reflects the reality of the 20s BC too, Dio Cassius writes
about the Roman emperors' commitment to avoid any overt sign of
an institutionalized imperial city cult in Italy: 'For in the capital itself

[36] For Leucathea and Athena Sikele see, respectively, Miranda (1995) nos. 94 and
112, which can be dated between the first century BC and first century AD; Miranda
(1998), 231 ff. For the 'quinquennial contest' see Miranda (1990), nos. 30 and 33
(possibly late Republican). For the religious functions of one of the offices there listed,
see Sartori (1953), 52–3.

[37] Cf. Miranda (1990), no. 52; Beloch (1989 [1890]), 51. Geer disagrees with
Beloch, and also objects to other modern attempts to connect Neapolitan sacred
contests held in honour of Parthenope with the more comprehensive Sebasta: Geer
(1935), 216–18. Strabo (5.4.7) still refers to 'a gymnastic contest' (set up at the
suggestion of an oracle, which seems to have been celebrated at the grave of Parthenope), which points to a reduced importance of this sacred festival, as suggested by
Cavallaro (1984), 179–80. A set of inscriptions relating to the Neapolitan Sebasta,
written in Greek and broken into more than 1,000 pieces after having fallen from the
wall of the gymnasium portico where they were located, were discovered in 2004 at
the Duomo Metro station in Piazza Nicola Amore in Naples. They have been dated to
the late first century AD on both historical and prosopographical grounds; the slabs
that have been joined together and published so far record lists of victors, events, and
features of this festival. One of the most revealing is the fragment referring to a *lampas*
(torch) 'for Augustus'; this is probably the same torch race that is mentioned in
Strabo's account, and thus seems to confirm that the Sebasta did include a torch race.
On these new documents see Miranda (2007), 203–10; Miranda (2010), 417–20.

[38] See Dio Cassius 51.20.6–9.   [39] See Millar (2002), 308.

and in Italy generally no emperor, however of renown he has been, dared to do this [namely, to allow precincts or temples consecrated to himself], still, even there various divine honours are bestowed after their death upon such emperors as have ruled uprightly, and, in fact, shrines are built to them.'[40] At the same time, Cavallaro has drawn attention to another passage of Dio (55.10.9) in which he explains why Naples was the only city in Italy allowed to establish penteteric Greek games in honour of Augustus, that is, 'nominally because he [Augustus] had restored it [Naples] when it was prostrated by earthquake and fire, but in reality because its inhabitants, alone of the Campanians, tried in a manner to imitate the customs of the Greeks'.[41] Since these were the first games of their kind to be instituted on Italian soil until the Neronia (and, later the Capitoline Agon) were founded in the capital city of the Empire, Cavallaro considers that a sacred festival in Augustus' honour called the Sebasta (the Greek equivalent to 'Augustan') was held in Neapolis, by means of a decree of the Roman Senate from 2 BC, because a celebration of this kind could be justified only if firstly established into 'Greek' Italy.[42] Now, if this assumption is accepted, it follows that the three-year interval between the date of the formal senatorial decree authorizing the Sebasta and the actual year of their first celebration (from 2 BC to AD 2) was necessary not simply to coordinate new *Italika Rhomaia Sebasta Isolympia* games with the 195th Olympic games. In fact, as Swan suggests, such an interval between the 'constitution' and celebration of the Sebasta is 'unremarkable', 'given the pre-eminence of the figure to be honoured, the need to construct or refurbish facilities, and time required for publicizing and organizing a new ecumenical event'.[43]

---

[40] Dio Cassius 51.20.8 (trans. after E. Cary, Loeb Classical Library 1914–27).

[41] On Dio's passage, in addition to Cavallaro (1984), 176–9, see Swan (2004), 101. It is worth bearing in mind that—as Geer rightly notes—up to the end of the first century AD the Neapolitan Sebasta were 'the most important games of the Greek type to be celebrated in the western half of the Roman Empire'. Geer (1935), 208.

[42] According to Cavallaro, the 2 BC senatorial decree was followed by an analogous local decision that Velleius 2.123 seems to be referring to: 'An athletic contest which the Neapolitans had established in his [namely, Augustus'] honour [. . .]' (trans. after F. W. Shipley, Loeb Classical Library 1924). Cavallaro (1984), 177. On formal public spectacles as a fundamental feature of the ideology of the Augustan regime, see e.g. Beacham (2005), 160–73.

[43] Cf. Swan (2004), 102–3. He further argues that the Roman Actian games in Augustus' honour, 'first celebrated 28 BC [. . .], had been voted two or three years earlier': cf. Dio Cassius 53.1.4–5 and 51.19.2.

In consequence, it does not seem excessively adventurous to assume that the institution of the Sebasta in 2 BC and their first celebration in AD 2 constituted a real turning point in Naples' public life.[44] Strabo clearly underlines that 'at the present time' these sacred games, which consisted of gymnastic contests and (possibly at a later stage) musical competitions, celebrated at Naples every four years and lasting several days, vied 'with the most famous of those celebrated in Greece'.[45] The extraordinary importance of the *Italika Rhomaia Sebasta Isolympia* games is not only confirmed by the fact that this festival was to be used as the basis of a new chronology, 'the new era to be reckoned by Italids instead of Olympiads', but 'is further indicated by the attention paid to them by various emperors' of the first two centuries.[46] As is well known, some days before his death in AD 14 Augustus decided to attend 'an athletic contest', that is the Sebasta, 'although he had already experienced [...] a change of his health for the worse'.[47] According to Dio Cassius, Claudius in Neapolis 'lived altogether like an ordinary citizen; for both he and his associates adopted the Greek manner of life in all respects, wearing a cloak and high boots, for example, at the musical exhibitions, and a purple mantle and golden crown at the gymnastic contests', a description that forcefully reminds us of the *agonothete* garments.[48] 'In memory of his brother [Germanicus], whom he took every opportunity of honouring, he brought out a Greek comedy [by his brother Germanicus] in the contest at Naples, and awarded it the crown in accordance with the decision of the judges'.[49] Even Nero, whose main interest was involving Roman citizens in Greek-style games within the very bounds of Rome by instituting a public quinquennial festival,

---

[44] For the institution year of these games, for the first year in which they were actually held and for their performance events, as well as for possible political and cultural explanations, see the exhaustive discussion in Cavallaro (1984), 176–9.

[45] Strabo 5.6.7 (trans. after H. L. Jones, Loeb Classical Library 1923).

[46] Quotations from, respectively, Ringwood Arnold (1960), 246–7; Geer (1935), 214–15. For *Italis* (the four-year period running from one celebration of the Sebasta to the next) in an agonistic inscription from Naples, see Miranda (1990), no. 52.

[47] Velleius 2.123.1 (trans. after F. W. Shipley, Loeb Classical Library 1924).

[48] Cf. e.g. Robert (1970), 7 nn. 4 and 5.

[49] Thus, rightly, Cavallaro (1984), 174 n. 72. *Contra*: Geer (1935), 214. In Geer's view, Claudius' presidency over these games in AD 42 is certain, but only probable according to Cavallaro (1984), 174 n. 72. The two passages cited above are, respectively, from Dio Cassius 60.6.1–2 (trans. after E. Cary, Loeb Classical Library 1914–27) and from Suetonius, *Claudius* 11.2 (trans. after J. C. Rolfe, Loeb Classical Library 1913–14).

the Neronia, displayed his lyric talents for the first time on the public stage at Naples in AD 64, which 'he fixed upon [. . .] as a Greek city'.[50] Whereas Nero, as far as one can say, did not preside over or take part in the Sebasta games, imperial interest in this festival was renewed in the time of the Flavians. Both Titus and Domitian served as *agonothetes* for the Sebasta three times: the former between AD 70 and 80–1; the latter presumably in AD 82, 86, and 90.[51] At the same festival, in August/September of AD 134, perhaps at the time when he was awarded an honorary demarchate,[52] Hadrian met with the representatives of the guilds of the athletes and the Dionysiac artists, together with delegates from many of the major cities of the East, in order to discuss important issues such as the (re)ordering of festivals and the related financial aspects and game regulations.[53] Consequently, since Naples owed a special position to the institution of the new Isolympic games and could be seen by both the Italian cities and the provinces as being a real Greek *polis*, it seems only right to assume that it was precisely because of this peculiar condition that Naples was given the privilege of an 'abnormal' internal constitution. In sum, in our present state of knowledge there is no good reason to exclude the possibility that, by the institution of the Sebasta, it was the eponymous *demarchos* that was retained at Naples as the most significant and eminent office of the earlier Greek city. Since it is this very office that was conferred on to the emperors, the suspicion is that in the Augustan period it was reinvented, by the first celebration of the Sebasta, within a 'hybridized' Roman pattern of municipal government.[54] Consequently, we may suppose that the colourless

---

[50] Tacitus, *Annals* 15.33 (trans. after J. Jackson, Loeb Classical Library 1937). On the Greek-styled festivals instituted by Nero in Rome, cf. Morford (1985), 2018–21.

[51] According to Geer, Titus presided at the Sebasta in AD 74 and 78, and at 'some special games at the time of the dedication in 80 AD or 81 AD': Geer (1935), 215. Miranda ((1990), 36–7, no. 19) suggests that only the *agonothesia* of AD 70 and 74 are certain, whereas the third is not datable. On Domitian's *agonothesia*, as well as those held by some prominent figures of the Roman elite in the late first century AD, and for the Neapolitan Sebasta in the light of the new information discovered in the 2004 excavations in Piazza Nicola Amore, see Miranda (2010), 417–20.

[52] SHA Hadrianus 19.1.

[53] See *AE* 2006: 1403 b, line 5. Unless one is inclined to think that this honorary office was given to Hadrian during his Campanian excursion in AD 119 or 120. For imperial involvement in building activity and imperial contributions to the cities of Campania up to the fourth–fifth century AD, see D'Arms (1970), ch. 4, and Savino (2005), *passim*.

[54] In the Antonine age this office was even given to non-Neapolitans, as in the case of the *pantomimis* P. Aelius Antigenidas (see Miranda 1990, no. 47), 'striking testimony to the local importance attached to such performances': D'Arms (1970), 151.

title of demark, which over time was increasingly overshadowed by the typical supreme magistracies of the *municipium*, was officially used again to designate the year (as Greek-style eponymous magistrates) when quinquennial Sebasta games were celebrated. No wonder that *demarchoi* also appeared in official documents, alongside the name of the consuls, as a sort of double dating by eponyms.[55]

CONCLUSIONS

It is noteworthy that, according to Dio Cassius, one of the alleged justifications for allowing the celebration of a quinquennial sacred Greek-styled festival in Italy in honour of Augustus was that it was to be held in the most thoroughly Greek of the Italian cities: Naples.[56] We might remember that Strabo's description of Naples identified the demarchs, its gymnasia, its associations of ephebes, and its phratries as the most distinctive Greek features of this city: these elements seem to have been sufficient to allow Naples to represent itself as a real Greek *polis* well into the Principate. It seems reasonable to assume that both the organization and management of the *Italika Rhomaia Sebasta Isolympia* games (which must also have been recognized in the Greek world as worthy of sacred rank) were modelled upon an old Greek festival. Epigraphic evidence explicitly suggests that the Sebasta were entrusted to *agonothetai*, at least in the early Principate.[57] Most

---

[55] See e.g. Miranda (1990), nos. 44, 55, and 84; Miranda (2010), 418, for the only (fragmentary) Neapolitan inscription containing the current date according to the names of the year's *agonothetes*, of the demarch, and of the consuls. By means of the existing epigraphic evidence, it is impossible to say whether a single demarch or a board of demarchs was elected every five years, so that its members served one year each in rotation, or whether the term of office was normally a single one of five years, in order to correspond with the quinquennial Sebasta festival.

[56] Or according to Dio Cassius' source, as suggested by Cavallaro (1984), 177–8. As for whether a city cult and a sacrifice directed at Augustus were introduced as part of the celebration into the series of the events in the Neapolitan Sebasta before or after his death, see Geer (1935), 220–1; Miranda (1998), 236–8.

[57] *IvO* 56 (ll. 23 and 34) refers to *agonothetai* (therefore, two or more) and their organizational duties in these games. This has been considered a document of the Neapolitan council defining the 'regulations' of the Sebasta, to be advertised 'to the crowds that gathered at the Olympian festival': Geer (1935), 209–10. On the *agonothesia*, its double character of liturgy and office, and its formal duties, according to the epigraphic evidence, see Liebenam (1900), 373–4.

of this burden was organizational rather than financial, since the funding for both the prizes and the infrastructure of the shows was contributed by either emperors or prominent members of the Roman elite (or both), who also served as *agonothetes* of these games. It is therefore reasonable to argue (although it cannot be proved on the basis of the existing evidence) that in addition to gymnasiarchs, presiding *agonothetes* were assisted in Naples by a body of new regular subsidiary functionaries and attendants whose job it was to serve at the Sebasta, and that the less prominent *laukelarchoi* were possibly also part of this staff.[58] It is impossible to know whether this office was originally a religious one, or whether it developed into a liturgical function connected with the Sebasta, so that it grew in prominence at the expense of traditional local priesthoods. It is worth noting that the only record that testifies to the celebration of a 'quinquennial contest in honour of the gods' (which is obviously different from the Sebasta games) is an honorary inscription set up by an unknown phratry to L. Herennius Ariston as benefactor.[59] Unfortunately, it is impossible to establish whether he performed this ceremony as *demarchos* or *laukelarchos* (the posts he held in Naples, in addition to *grammateus*, according to this inscription) or as a private individual. What we may infer is that such a Neapolitan '(sacred) contest in honour of the gods' is probably the procession to the *Kaisareion* to sacrifice to the gods of the city and to Augustus, a ritual act mentioned in the Olympia inscription (lines 49–50): that is, a definitive, central event of the Sebasta programme that was not entrusted to the presiding *agonothetes*.[60] And this in turn indicates that further study of the function of Neapolitan magistrates—both within the local administrative structure and in relation to the celebration of the Sebasta—may shed further light on their duties and the nature of their power.

[58] At the very damaged end of the Olympia inscription about the Sebasta we find the names of *agonothetes'* traditional attendants: *mastigophoroi* (whipbearers) and a *xystarches* (generally a prominent athlete that emperors appointed to control the activities of the associations in his home town): cf. *IvO*: n. 56 (l. 51).

[59] The inscription referring to this phratry, one out of twelve (or thirteen) Neapolitan 'social groups' concerned with the organization of local cyclic religious feasting and meetings, is now lost and only known in a seventeenth-century report. It supposedly dates to the second half of the first century BC: see Miranda (1990), no. 30.

[60] For the *Kaisareion* (that is, the temple devoted to the worship of the emperor) see Miranda (2007), 207–8.

At present, these conclusions can be only tentative, in part because concrete evidence relating to this issue is scarce. Nevertheless, as a working hypothesis it may be quite useful insofar as it provides a plausible solution to some puzzling aspects of the relationship between Naples' Greek administrative structures and the constitution of the Roman citizen *municipium*. Needless to say, this model is still provisional, and its central assumptions still remain to some extent hypothetical. Hopefully, though, it is now clear that any further investigation into city magistrates holding offices at Neapolis between the Social War and late antiquity has to start not from the over-simplistic concept that Neapolis was a 'Greek city' but rather from an examination of the hitherto untapped evidence of the Latin inscriptions from Naples that relate or allude to local municipal offices (included in *CIL* 10.1), in order to define their uncertain history or to determine their original archaeological context.[61] Only after such careful investigation may we begin to conjecture why substantial traces of Roman municipal offices have not been preserved in local epigraphic records written in Latin, and understand the complex processes of cultural memory and reception of the past that were at work in the Roman city.

---

[61] Even Rome is labelled a 'Greek city' by Juvenal (3.60), whereas the identity of the unnamed coastal Campanian 'Greek city' where the *Cena* in Petronius' *Satyricon* (81) is held is still disputed.

6

Between Classical and Modern Naples

'Cultural Forgetting' at the Time of the Gothic War

Giovanni Polara

This chapter provides a snapshot of Naples at a pivotal moment in her millennia-long history—a moment that was significant for the rest of Italy too, and which in hindsight marks an important watershed between the classical world and the Middle Ages. In many ways, this chapter is more about cultural forgetting of the past than cultural memory, for although we often assume that there has been a long-standing and enduring continuum in the transmission of Naples' classical heritage (according to which Virgil has always been 'our' Virgil, the Colosseum has always been 'our' Colosseum, and so on), the situation is far more nuanced than this picture of stasis might suggest. Past centuries had their own unique images of, and relationships with, the ancient world which were always conditioned by the historical and cultural context in which they were formed. In fact, in the period under discussion here (AD 535–53), Naples experienced a terrible war, which changed the classical landscape of the *locus amoenus* into a *locus horribilis*, erasing most traces of the classical *dulcis Parthenope* that would be so important to later writers. The image of Naples as a serene place of *otium* may well have been temporarily forgotten by the Neapolitan people, who were engaged in a daily struggle for survival, and who were facing an enemy determined to conquer the city. This period constitutes an important moment in the reception history of ancient Naples, not least because it represents a caesura between classical and modern times—a historical gap across which classical antiquity could be more easily perceived and defined as different to the present. This chapter will examine sixth-century Naples through the lens of one of the most important authors of the period, Procopius of Caesarea. Procopius' image of the city at the time of the Gothic War has been almost entirely neglected by modern scholars, despite his text's wide circulation and influence in the period between the Renaissance and the early modern era.

At the time of Theodoric (454–526), Naples became the principal town in Campania, sharing with Cumae the role of the strongest and best-defended city of the region. This era also saw a dramatic population increase, following the influx into the city of those escaping from the extreme danger posed by the Vandal invasions in the surrounding countryside.[1] The dire situation became known even in the furthest-flung parts of the old Empire: in his panegyric to the emperor Majorian, which describes the region's condition at the end of 458 and which was read out in Gaul on the occasion of the new emperor's journey there, Sidonius Apollinaris spoke of Campania in the following way:

> Under southerly breezes he [Majorian] invaded the Campanian soil and with his Moorish soldiery attacked the husbandmen when they dreamed not of danger; the fleshy Vandal sat on the thwarts waiting for the spoil, which he had bidden his captives to capture and bring thither.[2]

The devastation of the countryside around Naples in those years left a long imprint on the city's cultural memory. Three centuries later Paul the Deacon was still writing of the damages suffered by Capua and Nola, as well as the impoverishment of Naples, which had nevertheless resisted assaults thanks to its city walls.[3]

One of the most prominent characteristics of Naples in this period was its dynamic multiculturalism. In addition to the great numbers of new inhabitants who had poured into the city from the nearby rural

---

[1] Lepore (1967a), 139–371; ch. 3 deals with 'La "piccola città" tardo-antica': see esp. Lepore (1967a), 330–6 and 369–71.

[2] Sidonius Apollinaris, *Poems*, 5.388–92: *Campanam flantibus austris | ingrediens terram, securum milite Mauro | agricolam aggreditur; pinguis per transtra sedebat | Vandalus opperiens praedam, quam iusserat illuc | captivo capiente trahi.* Trans. from Loeb Classical Library.

[3] Paul the Deacon, *Roman History* 16.16.

territories at the beginning of the fifth century, Naples also had a strong Jewish community, which had initially settled in Pozzuoli when that port was enjoying greater prosperity. Many of these Jewish inhabitants were merchants who became very influential in the governing of the city; they were relied on above all for their close relations with the Germans, who—like them—practised a different religion from the rest of the Italic population. Naples also provided a home for a large number of refugees from North Africa, who had escaped the Vandal invasions and then been brought to Naples by Quodvultdeus, the bishop of Carthage.[4] Quodvultdeus was a pupil of Augustine who in AD 439 had overloaded his ramshackle ships with a *maxima turba clericorum* ('a great horde of clergymen') and a *senatorum atque honoratorum multitudo* ('a multitude of senators and honourable men') who had been converted to the faith and were prepared for every kind of deprivation and sacrifice. Quodvultdeus entrusted himself and his hapless companions to divine providence, and arrived at his destination after a dramatic crossing which prefigured many future navigations across the Mediterranean.

Unlike the majority of cities in the south of Italy, Naples had a sizeable Gothic military garrison, which necessitated the presence of a *comes* (an imperial official) tasked with military command and control of the port, as well as with the administration of justice. This *comes* needed to negotiate a relationship with the *consularis Campaniae*, who may have transferred his residence from Capua to the new, safer capital after the heavy damages suffered at the hands of the Visigoths and Vandals between AD 410 and 456, and whose office was as important as it always had been.[5] Other citizen magistracies were held by members of the different communities that had moved to the city over the course of the previous decades. We know from the importance of the port in this period, and from the accounts of

---

[4] Victor Vitensis 1.5. A. V. Nazzaro has published a translation with commentary of Quodvultdeus, *Liber promissionum et praedictorum Dei* ('God's Promises and Predictions'). See Nazzaro (1989), which also contains a good introduction to the character of Quodvultdeus and his works.

[5] von Falkenhausen (1992), 7–35 (esp. 7), with the mention of John, who was already the addressee of two of Cassiodorus' letters (*Variae* 3.27 and 4.10), dated to between AD 507 and 511. John was praetorian prefect and father of a senator, Reparato (who was destined to meet a tragic end during the Gothic War), as well as of a pope, Virgilius, who played a significant role in the last years of the same war. For the damage caused by the Goths and Visigoths see Savino (2005), 213.

Cassiodorus and Procopius, that traders from other parts of the Mediterranean often settled in Naples. This further diversified the multi-ethnic Parthenopean society, and represents an important strand of continuity with the Classical period that is still seen in the present day.

For the period immediately preceding the Gothic War, our main sources are three letters by the Roman writer and statesman Cassiodorus (*c*.485–585) which contain the *formulae* (the 'rules') for the office of *comes*.[6] These letters have a strange position within the text of the *Variae*, insofar as they appear—together with the *formula* for the *comes* of Syracuse, the capital of Sicily—in the sixth book, where we find reviews of the most prestigious offices of state, from the consul and Praetorian prefect to the prefect of the city. All of the other *comitivae*, including those of Rome and of Ravenna, are in the seventh book, along with more modest offices and laws, such as the *Formula qua census relevetur ei, qui unam casam possidet praegravatam*.

With their placement at the end of the book and their individual mentions of the *comitiva Neapolitana*, these three letters seem to give greater importance to the Gothic presence in the city than to the city itself. This is a very different treatment to the one Cassiodorus gives to his beloved Squillace (Scylletium) in Calabria, but it is analogous with his treatment of Syracuse. In contrast to earlier and later images of Naples, such as those discussed by Lorenzo Miletti and Fulvio Delle Donne (Chapters 2 and 8 in this volume), here we find no excursus on the quality of the environment or the prestige of its ancient history—rather, the letters focus on the jobs entrusted to the *comes* and the respect that the citizens of Naples owed to those holding this office.

Meanwhile, although Cassiodorus claims that Vesuvius was the only negative aspect of life in Naples, even the most affluent citizens in this period faced numerous hardships.[7] In his *Consolation of Philosophy* (*c*.524), Boethius documents the severe famine that struck Campania in the first decades of the sixth century. Boethius' account may have been influenced by a series of events that had begun in AD

---

[6] Cassiodorus, *Variae* ('Letters') 6.23–5. Andrea Giardina's edition of this text (which includes an Italian translation and commentary) is in press.

[7] Cassiodorus, *Variae* 6.24.1. On Vesuvius as the sole Neapolitan evil, see Cassiodorus *Variae* 4.50.3: *Laborat enim hoc uno malo terris deflorata provincia, quae ne perfecta beatitudine frueretur, huius timoris frequenter acerbitate concutitur.*

523 with the discovery of letters sent between Albino and Giustino (Boethius had defended Albino, who was accused of betrayal, but then was himself swiftly prosecuted, sentenced, detained, and finally executed at the end of 524). Boethius' conscious decision to end his life's work with a text on philosophy might have been made to suggest that his account of events was reliable and uninfluenced by any 'treacherous' thoughts. After mentioning a series of cases in which he had opposed other influential figures in the court of Theodoric, causing the king to intervene and stop these men from perpetrating crimes against wealthy but weak citizens who were intimidated by false accusations, Boethius says:

> Again, in a time of severe famine, a grievous, intolerable sale by compulsion was decreed in Campania, and devastation threatened that province. Then I undertook for the sake of the common welfare a struggle against the commander of the Imperial guard; though the king was aware of it, I fought against the enforcement of the sale, and fought successfully.[8]

Eruptions, famines, plagues, harassment by Goths and Romans as well as the usual, everyday hardships: these are all reasons why many fortunes dissolved and many rich Neapolitan families fell into poverty at this time. In one of his two letters to the *consularis Campaniae*, Cassiodorus explains how usurers were making their own unique contribution to the decline of Neapolitan fortunes.[9] This was a situation that needed to be tackled, since it not only caused problems for the community, but also led to multiple legal cases (whose numbers Theodoric and Cassiodorus were wisely trying to reduce) and potential violence on the part of the exasperated victims of these 'loan sharks', whose activities weakened the local economy and led to widespread disillusionment. All this led to acts of plunder, which was far from what the local governors wanted in their already troubled territory.[10]

---

[8] Boethius, *Consolation of Philosophy* 1.4.38: *Cum acerbae famis tempore gravis atque inexplicabilis indicta coemptio profligatura inopia Campaniam provinciam videretur, certamen adversum praefectum praetorii communis commodi ratione suscepi, rege cognoscente contendi et, ne coemptio exigeretur, evici.* Eng. trans. W. V. Cooper.

[9] Cassiodorus, *Variae* 4.10.

[10] Cf. Cassiodorus, *Variae* 4.10.1: *provincialium igitur Campaniae atque Samnii suggestione comperimus nonnullos neglecta temporum disciplina ad pignorandi se studia transtulisse et quasi edicto misso per vulgus licentiam crevisse vitiorum.*

This was the state of affairs when, a decade after Theodoric's death, Justinian and his troops disembarked in Sicily. Belisarius, who had already defeated the Vandals and occupied the island that the Goths had abandoned, made preparations to go up the peninsula towards Rome and Ravenna with a small army of 8,000 soldiers.[11] Meanwhile, Constantian and his troops conquered Dalmatia and occupied Salona (modern Split), threatening to enter Italy from the north, either crossing the Alps or entering Ravenna from the sea. For the Byzantines, the war was justified by the murder of Theodoric's daughter Amalasuntha by her cousin and second husband Theodahad (the son of Theodoric's sister, Amalafrida, from her first marriage, before her second marriage to the vandal Thrasamundus). Amalasuntha had brought Theodahad to the throne after the death of her child by her first husband, Athalaric, son of Eutharicus Cillica, who was consul in AD 519 and leader of the pro-Roman faction, praised by Cassiodorus in the *Chronica* and who died prematurely in 523, three years before Theodoric. This uxoricide enabled the Empire to intervene as avenger of the descendant of the last great king Amalus, and to pit itself against a violent, untrustworthy, and ungrateful usurper. In his *Gothic War*, Procopius records the official version given by Constantinople, representing the patrician Peter (Justinian's ambassador at the court of Theodahad) as a polite and intelligent diplomat who tried in vain to rescue Amalasuntha after she was jailed by Theodahad and then abandoned to the Goths, who needed to 'settle some accounts' with her. However, in the *Secret History* he gives a completely different version of events, claiming that it was fear of the empress Theodora that had initially motivated him to lie.[12] This time, he accuses Theodora of having planned to use Peter to kill Amalasuntha, thereby ruling out the possibility that Amalasuntha—who was bright, erudite, and capable—might arrive as an exile at the court of Constantinople and cast a shadow over Theodora's power and position.

Amalasuntha died in AD 535, and the war started in 536, but Naples had in fact already seen warning signs of conflict while Belisarius' troops were still busy fighting the Vandals in Africa. At that time, ten

[11] Procopius, *Gothic War* 1.5. Catania and Syracuse immediately went over to the imperial troops; Palermo, which had Gothic walls and a garrison, tried to withstand them, but the fortifications were very poor, because they were lower than the Byzantine warships' masts. Since the Byzantines on the ships could fight from above, the Goths were terrified and surrendered immediately.

[12] Procopius, *Secret History* 16.

Hunnish deserters had sought asylum in the town, where they were welcomed by the Gothic *comes* Uliari, with the approval of Amalasuntha, who did not want to appear too close to Byzantium, so as to preserve the Goths' autonomy in the foreign politics of the Empire. Her support for Belisarius' troops gained her some bases in Sicily and a considerable number of horses to use for military action. This small Hunnish community further diversified Naples' ethnic composition and increased the number and complexity of potential alliances in the case of war.

In AD 536 Belisarius arrived in Naples, empowered by the victories in Sicily and the swift surrender of Ebrimut (or Evermund), Theodahad's son-in-law, who had been sent by the king to Reggio along with his troops in order to prevent the rulers disembarking on the peninsula.[13] Having noted the difficult situation in the field, Ebrimut had immediately surrendered to the enemy and had then been sent to Constantinople along with a number of Gothic nobles who had been fighting alongside him. In this way, he had escaped from danger and ensured himself a *buen retiro* for the forthcoming years, while simultaneously putting an end to Theodahad's government, since an act of betrayal on the part of the king's son-in-law (the king who had caused the war in the first place) was a disgraceful deed that could not but provoke a serious response. 'He, with few and loyal conscious servants, went over to the winner, spontaneously throwing himself at Belisarius' feet; he chooses to serve the Roman princes.'[14] These are the words of the scandalized Jordanes, who was also fighting amongst the Goths in their assault on the Empire. The replacement of Theodahad by Witiges and his subsequent murder were brought forward by Jordanes in his narrative to demonstrate the Goths' swift reaction to villainous treachery, while Procopius and others locate these events later in their narratives, coincident with the fall of Naples.

Upon the arrival of the troops, the Neapolitans closed themselves within the city walls (which were fortunately much higher than the ones that had betrayed the poor Palermitans), and left the rest to Belisarius; he—knowing the city well, as Procopius reports—took

---

[13] Procopius, *Gothic War*, 1.8; Jordanes, *On the Origin and Deeds of the Getae (Getica)* 308–12.

[14] Jordanes, *Getica* 309: *Ad partes victoris cum paucis ac fidelissimis famulis consciis movit, ultroque se Belisarii pedibus advolvens, Romani regni optat servire principibus.*

over the port, which was far enough away from the town to be beyond the range of any weapons, and put his ships there in safety. He then took over the *castrum Lucullanum* so as to prevent attacks from that side, and set up camp near the town, preparing himself for a long siege, since 'Naples [was] strong because of the nature of the site and because of the many Goths on garrison duty'. Negotiations then took place with the dual aim of avoiding massacres (of the Neapolitans) and of saving time (for the Byzantines). Procopius, who was perhaps not unbiased, states that it was the Neapolitans who asked for a meeting, and that Justinian's general agreed to address a delegation of local *optimates* (nobles), who would be informed of his proposals, and would then communicate them to the rest of their community. The Neapolitan delegation was led by a certain Stephen, whose speech was extremely clear and full of skilful rhetoric:

'We are Roman, and therefore we are not enemies of the empire; the town is now under the control of the Gothic garrison, and we cannot rebel because they are powerful. But you should put yourselves in their shoes. They are not from here, they do not live in a city, but they have come to Naples on duty, leaving their families in the hands of the Goths in Rome and Ravenna. How can they give you a hand without putting their families at risk? And anyway, what do you need Naples for? Even if you manage to conquer it, you must eventually defeat Rome—so why do you not go straight there? If you win against the Romans, there's no doubt that Naples will then surrender immediately, but if Rome manages to resist, you will have to go and live much further south than Naples. Basically, this siege of Naples is a waste of time, and you'd be better off moving on.'

However, Stephen was talking to a Byzantium fed on 'bread and speeches', and their answer was immediate and clear:

'An imperial general does not come to Naples to learn strategy! You Neapolitans now have a chance to free yourselves from the Goths and the submission that you complain about—and you have the chance to do this without taking any risks or facing a war, because all you need to do is to open the gates. But if you decide to side with the Goths instead, if you lose you will have an unenviable fate, since you will be treated as enemies, and if you win, you will simply have strengthened the chains of your slavery. We have something to tell the Goths too: if they want, they can come over to our side, as Ebrimut and those from Sicily have done already; if they prefer, they can leave peacefully and go further north to

join the other Goths. You ought to be convinced by the fact that the
Sicilians are more than happy with their choice, and regret nothing.'

This was the 'official' part of the speech—the part that was delivered
in public, in front of the army and the citizens. But Procopius, who
knew the world and how these things worked, added the following
comment: 'These were the things that Belisarius told Stephen to
communicate to his people; privately, however, he promised him
great rewards, if he incited the Neapolitans to support the emperor.'

Stephen played his part and reported Belisarius' speech to the
inhabitants of the city, who had gathered to find out how the negotiations had gone—adding, finally, that it would be idiotic to rise up
against the emperor. He did not, however, get a good response,
perhaps because he was too honest to ask for something from
which he could personally benefit. Neither did it make any difference
when he was backed up by a certain Antiochus, 'a Syrian who had
lived in Naples for a long time, making his living from sea trade, and
who was known in the town for being wise and honest'. Procopius
does not say whether Antiochus was part of the delegation or simply
one of the citizens who had gathered to listen to Stephen's speech, as
seems to be the case with others who are mentioned later. If Antiochus was one of the *optimates* sent to Belisarius, this would be an
important sign of his integration into Neapolitan 'high society'; but
even if he was not, the fact that he was treated as an authoritative
citizen of Naples can be seen as a perfect application of the *ius soli*,
which shows the Naples of the time to be an inclusive society,
relatively free from ethnic hierarchies. All the same, despite Antiochus' good reputation, he too failed to achieve the desired results, and
the assembly decided to go in a different direction.

This shift was achieved thanks to the skill of 'two lawyers named
Pastore and Asclepiodotus, who were distinguished among the Neapolitans, devoted to the Goths, and adverse to any change in the *status
quo*'.[15] They felt—as perhaps did the majority of the Neapolitans—that
the current situation was not such a bad one. The Goths were few in
number and did not create too much discomfort; they ensured a certain
amount of security, and life was relatively peaceful given the coexistence of different cultures and customs. This peaceful coexistence may

---

[15] For the reconstruction of the skilful 'parliamentary strategy' of Pastore and
Asclepiodotus see Procopius' account, *Gothic War* 1.9 ff.

indeed have been typical of all maritime port cities, but in this case was even more deep-rooted in the tradition of the city of Naples, where Greeks, Romans, and Italic peoples mixed happily with Jews, Goths, Syrians, Huns, and other people from all regions of Europe, Asia, and Africa. Why, then, did they have to risk changes and innovations when it was clear that the representatives of Byzantium were even more irritating and arrogant than the Uliari had proved themselves to be over the last forty years?

By describing the period immediately before the conquest of Naples, and reporting the latest negotiations between the opposing parties, Procopius both respected the classical historiographical law of the *verum* ('to respect and to account only the truth') and enriched the figure of Belisarius, excusing and absolving him from his ignoble actions during the siege and conquest of the city.[16] In this respect, the element that most concerns us—insofar as it relates to broader issues of reception and cultural memory—is the famous episode of the entry into the city via the city water supply, a stratagem devised by Belisarius (or rather by one of his Isauric soldiers), which ultimately led to the conquest of Naples. It is worth noting that some centuries later both Belisarius and Procopius were used as 'models' when King Alfonso of Aragon also used the aqueduct to enter and conquer Naples. At that time, the humanist Leonardo Bruni (1370–1444) congratulated Alfonso for this achievement, sending the king an excerpt of 'his' *De bello Italico adversus Gothos gesto* (1470), which spoke of Belisarius' entry into Naples almost a millennium earlier.[17] Meanwhile, Giovanni Gioviano Pontano (1429–1503) used Procopius' account of the war operations in Neapolitan territory as his main source for the archaeological-antiquarian appendix at the end of his *De bello Neapolitano*.[18] These two uses of the aqueduct thus give further evidence of the importance of the Neapolitan subsoil and its 'memories' in the long and multifaceted history of the city.[19]

But let us return to Procopius' story. After he had entered the city, and after a day of massacres, Belisarius recalled his troops and attempted to save whatever he could. He released the women and

[16] See Procopius, *Gothic War* 1.9–16.

[17] See Bentley (1987), 55. This work is both a translation and an abstract of Procopius' *De bello Gothico*; Bruni did not, however, declare his original source, thus meriting accusations of plagiarism from his contemporaries.

[18] See Iacono (2009).

[19] See also de Divitiis, Chapter 10 in this volume.

children who had been taken prisoner, and allowed the survivors to return to their homes. Things went well for the Goths (those who had survived the battle, which was the overwhelming majority, as there had been an immediate escape of the entire garrison apart from the soldiers located on the north side), because Belisarius saved at least 800 of them, and treated them in the same manner he treated his own soldiers. Nothing is said about the Jews, but the reasons for their persistence in fighting cause us to infer that hardly any would have managed to make it out alive. Procopius, instead, focuses with seeming enjoyment on the fate of Pastore and Asclepiodotus: the former died of a timely stroke, but the Neapolitans refused to believe he was dead (a situation with echoes in the later plays and films of Eduardo De Filippo and Totò), so they fetched his body from his house and hanged him in Palaepolis; meanwhile, the latter tried to save himself by going over to Belisarius, but Stephen identified him to the people and Belisarius handed him over to them, after which he was killed and torn to shreds.

The conclusion of Procopius' account of the taking of Naples recalls the peace that reigns in Warsaw: 'And so the Neapolitans were liberated' after no more than twenty days of siege; but despite Procopius' attempts to emphasize the generosity of Belisarius and minimize the massacres and damage, the consequences of the city's capture were serious. The 'Western' sources restore balance to the situation, for although they are likely to be biased in the other direction, they probably give a more accurate picture of the extent of the massacre.[20] In any case, Naples eventually returned into imperial hands when the last king, Theia, was defeated and killed at the Battle of Vesuvius in 553, and the last of the Goths in central and southern Italy (whose number has been estimated at close to 7,000) were closed in at Conza on the Ofanto, at the borders between Campania and Basilicata, where they surrendered to Narsetes in 555.[21] Although there was no further damage, everything that

---

[20] These sources include Jordanes, *The High Point of Time, or the Origin and Deeds of the Roman People* (*Romana*) 370 and *Getica* 311; the life of Pope Silverius in the *Liber Pontificalis* 1.290; Paul the Deacon, *Roman History* 16.16; Landolphus Sagax, *Historia Miscella* 18.15; *Monumenta Germaniae Historica* 2.273–4.

[21] Agathias 2.13.1; this number is usually considered to be too high, as is often the case with Agathias. Edward Gibbon had a terrible opinion of this author, and even Cameron (who tried to partially rehabilitate him) has her just criticisms about the information Agathias gives us: see Cameron (1970). On this occasion, it is quite

the city had suffered in the years between 536 and 553 left its mark. In Rome and Milan things had not gone much better, and these cities would also need a great deal of time to invent new roles for themselves. In Naples there was still a port, which—together with the safe conditions of sailing in the Mediterranean—guaranteed commercial opportunities for the city; there was also a Byzantine commander, who was able to maintain effective relationships with Constantinople and the other imperial settlements in Italy. After this it would be the strong Duchy of Benevento which would take possession of most of the hinterland and make an enclave that was not Lombard, but still very different from everything that surrounded it.

Naples, a city ravaged by disastrous events such as these, maintained her dedication to her classical heritage. For example, she held 'her' Virgil close, creating around him the extraordinary corpus of popular and literary legends that constitutes one of the marvels of Neapolitan cultural history. These legends attribute to Virgil the creation of a set of miraculous objects that was supposed to protect the city—but which, for one reason or another, did not succeed in defending it from the devastations described in this chapter. Naples then moved on, at her leisure, to create a new *populus* which included the Aligerni and Theodrics (who are recorded in Neapolitan documents up until at least the year 1000, and who imitated the older Gothic tradition as enthusiastically as they did the Byzantine Greek one), as well as the (Italian) Romans, the Jews, the Saracens, the Arabs, and then the Normans, the Swabians, the French, the Spanish, the Austrians, and all the very many others who, for the most varied reasons, have found themselves here in the city. These are the people who built the present—the different successive presents—on the walls of the past, destroying the past in order to preserve it, and preserving it in order to live and alter it. Similar processes have, of course, taken place in other Italian cities, but in Naples we find a multiplicity of connected or superimposed levels of history—as well as a multiplicity of sources that vary in their accuracy, but which have become 'true' because they have been *believed*. Ultimately, these sources have enabled the transmission to the Enlightenment and beyond of an

certain that the number was not only overestimated, but also included those who survived the Battle of the Volturnus and the events of the previous war, together with the Franks and the Alamans of Butilin.

attitude to history that is creative and respectful in equal measure—
the kind of attitude which allowed a refined artist like the Maestro
Roberto De Simone to write about Virgil with the same passion that
he brought to his work on sixteenth- and seventeenth-century music
and the tradition of *canzone napoletana*.[22]

---

[22] De Simone (1982).

Part II

Classical Naples After Antiquity

7

Marmora Romana in Medieval Naples

Architectural Spolia from the Fourth to the Fifteenth Centuries AD

Angela Palmentieri

The disappearance of most of Naples' classical monuments can be explained with reference to the transformations that took place in the urban landscape between late antiquity and the early modern period.[1] For instance, besides the damage caused by a long series of earthquakes and wars (including the Gothic War whose events have been recounted in Chapter 6 of this volume), the year 1566 saw the issuing of a royal prohibition against the construction of new buildings outside the city walls, which led to them being erected on top of the ancient monuments in the city centre.[2] Despite these losses, however, the ancient city has left a lasting impression on the modern *forma urbis*.[3] The Graeco-Roman layout, with its long and narrow roads, was reused in the medieval city; the three *plateiae* that run from east to west (Via Anticaglia, Via Tribunali, Via S. Biagio dei Librai) and the *stenopoi* that run from north to south correspond exactly with the roads that criss-cross Naples today (Fig. 7.1). The material culture of classical Neapolis has also survived through the reuse of fragments of

---

For Stefania Adamo Muscettola, *in memoriam*.

[1] On the history and topography of medieval Naples, see Capasso (1895); *Napoli antica* (1985); Skinner (1994), 279–99; Arthur (2002); Giampaola (2004).

[2] Pane (1949); Alisio (1980).

[3] On the topography of ancient Naples, see Beloch (1989 [1890]); De Caro and Giampaola (2008), 107–24.

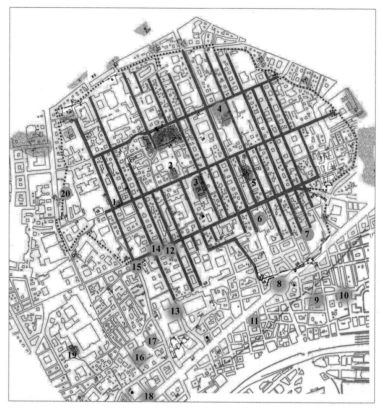

Fig. 7.1. Plan of Naples marked with locations of reused material. 1: Pietrasanta complex; 2: S. Paolo Maggiore—temple of the Dioscuri; 3: S. Lorenzo Maggiore; 4: S. Restituta, Duomo, and Stefania; 5: Carminello ai Mannesi; 6: S. Giorgio Maggiore; 7: S. Agostino alla Zecca; 8: Piazza Nicola Amore (temple of imperial cult; agonistic inscriptions; gymnasium); 9: S. Giovanni a Mare (the 'Capa di Napoli'); 10: S. Eligio Maggiore; 11: S. Agata degli Orefici; 12: Palazzo of Diomede Carafa; 13: Palazzo of Carlo Carafa; 14: Piazzetta Nilo (the 'Corpo di Napoli'); 15: S. Maria della Rotonda; 16: Pappacoda chapel; 17: S. Giovanni Maggiore; 18: Piazza Giovanni Bovio (marble arch); 19: S. Chiara; 20: S. Antoniello a Port'Alba.

Source: After F. Zevi (ed.), *Neapolis* (Naples, 1994).

ancient architecture and sculpture in later buildings: it is this phenomenon of Neapolitan *spolia*—and particularly the changing uses and meanings of classical fragments throughout the long period between the fourth and the fifteenth centuries—that will be the focus of the present chapter.

THE REUSE OF *SPOLIA* IN NEAPOLITAN ARCHITECTURE BETWEEN THE FOURTH AND TENTH CENTURIES

The history of reuse in Naples begins with Constantine and the bishops, who were the first to take charge of managing the architectural patrimony of the city.[4] In Naples, as elsewhere, the reuse of ancient marbles in the early Christian basilicas was essentially a dual process of conservation and renovation.[5] Following a tradition started in Rome, the white and polychrome marbles of pagan temples were used by the local church to preserve and pass on cultural memory.[6] This process is clearly visible in the basilicas that were built between the fourth and sixth centuries outside the central forum area, which continued to be the site of vibrant commercial activity.[7] Contrary to the assumptions of seventeenth- and eighteenth-century scholars, the churches of S. Restituta, the so-called Stefania basilica, S. Maria della Rotonda, S. Giorgio, S. Giovanni Maggiore, and the Pietrasanta basilica were not all built on the sites of pagan temples, despite their obvious reuse of Roman building materials.[8] Evidence discovered in excavations of the nineteenth and twentieth centuries can be set alongside the analysis of reused material from different monumental contexts, in order to find out more about the provenances of the *spolia* and the changing significance of these acts of reception.[9]

The fourth-century basilica of S. Restituta was—just like the first cathedral in Rome—built in honour of the Saviour. It stood in an area which in antiquity had been the site of a residential area near to a late imperial necropolis.[10] According to certain learned sources, the

---

[4] On reuse in Rome, see Liverani (2006), 235–44; Liverani (2011), 529–40.

[5] On the legislation and phenomenon of late antique reuse, see Anguissola (2004), 13–29; de Lachenal (1995); Kinney (1995), 53–67; (1997), 117–48; Brilliant and Kinney (2012).

[6] Arthur (2002); Amodio (2005); Savino (2006–7), 65–84. On *spolia* in Rome, see Wegner (1958); Esch (1969); Deichmann (1975); Alchermes (1994); De Blaauw (2001), 52–61; Barresi and Pensabene (2002), 799–842; Hansen (2003); Brandenburg (2004).

[7] Arthur (2002).

[8] D'Engenio (1623); Mormile (1670); Ceva Grimaldi (1857), 49; Venditti (1973), 177–88.

[9] A systematic study of Neapolitan *spolia* can be found in Palmentieri (2010a). For preliminary studies, see Pensabene (1990); Pensabene (1998); Pensabene (2005).

[10] Capasso (1892), 454–84; Di Stefano and Strazzullo (1972); Cesarini (2008).

ancient marbles that were incorporated into this building's fabric may have come from the ruins of a nearby temple of Apollo and Neptune; in their new context, these marbles became a sign of the 'rebirth' of Naples as a Christian city.[11] Fourteen columns from different imperial sites were arranged along the five aisles of the basilica and the baptistery of S. Giovanni in Fonte, in a manner consistent with the classical architectural tradition (Fig. 7.2).[12] A pair of fluted columns made from Phrygian marble were placed at either side of the absidal arch, while shafts made from *africano* marble, eastern granite, and cipollino were arranged symmetrically in the naves.

The same basic desire for uniformity seems to have governed the choice of the Corinthian columns and capitals in the so-called Stefania basilica, which was built next to the cathedral in the sixth century and named after its founder, bishop Stephen.[13] The highlight of this church's interior was a rich *ciborium* (container) with four porphyry

Fig. 7.2. The church of S. Restituta in Naples, detail of interior.
Source: Photograph: Angela Palmentieri.

[11] Celano (1692), 78.   [12] Pensabene (1998), 181–231.
[13] Lucherini (2005), 2–31; Ebanista (2009), 307–75.

shafts, and a basin made from the same material, which was (like similar examples at Rome) reused as a container for holy water.[14] The rectangular atrium is still visible today; the arches of its portico are supported by eleven columns in granite and white marble, with Attic bases and Corinthian capitals of the Western and Asiatic types that were characteristic in the northern part of the *insula episcopalis* around the second half of the fifth century (Fig. 7.3).[15]

Fig. 7.3. Portico of the Stefania basilica, Naples.

Source: Photograph: Angela Palmentieri.

[14] Adamo Muscettola (1996), n. 4. In the manuscript of Antonio Afeltro, *De nobilitate Neapolitana Compendiolum* (Biblioteca Nazionale di Napoli, segnatura IX, E, 13 nel tomo VIII al fo. 86) the font is said to be on the ground in the atrium, in front of the *porta maggiore* of the archbishop of Naples. See also Capasso (1892), 460 n. 1.

[15] Ebanista (2011), 383–418.

At this time, classical material culture was also being reused in other parts of the city, at varying distances from the area of the ancient forum. The church of S. Maria della Rotonda is one of six buildings traditionally attributed to Constantine.[16] This building was constructed on a Roman site known as the *Regio Nilensis*—the hilly area near Via Mezzocannone, where tufa blocks from the ancient fortifications and traces of a street axis were found at the end of the eighteenth century (Fig. 7.4).[17] The original octagonal plan of this church's interior incorporated eight column shafts of porphyry and granite, while at the entrance there stood a pair of white marble columns with reused inscribed bases: these inscriptions celebrated the restoration works carried out by a fifth-century AD consul, Postumius Lampadius.[18] Another example of *spolia* from this church is the cippus of the freedman Marcus Cocceius, which had been used in antiquity as the support for a monumental cup but then reused in S. Maria at some point during the fourth century as the base of a baptismal font.[19] This piece was unfortunately lost at the end of the nineteenth century, but we can see it at the bottom of the duke of Noja's 1775 map of Naples, where it appears alongside an image of ancient ruins.[20]

The study of *spolia* in Constantinian buildings can help us to clarify various aspects of the street plan of late antique Neapolis, as well as giving us some useful insights into the architecture of the early imperial period. Some of the reused marbles, like the column capitals of S. Restituta, can be dated to the Augustan and Julio-Claudian eras on the basis of comparisons with material from sites like the Forum of Augustus and the Basilica Aemilia in Rome.[21] Other capitals from the same complex are similar to examples from Pozzuoli, Nola, and Capua, indicating that they may have been executed by the same skilled workers.[22] A further series of capitals from S. Restituta is related to Roman models dating to the Flavian and Trajanic eras,

---

[16] D'Engenio (1623), 260; Capasso (1892), 480 s.; Altamura (1974), 96 ff.; Venditti (1967), 511.

[17] Carletti (1776), 24; *Napoli antica* (1985), 474, n. 66 pl. VI.

[18] Celano (1692), 115; Giannone (1823), 394; Camodeca (2010), 283 ff.

[19] *Napoli antica* (1985), 394, n. 117.2.

[20] Blessich (1896), 75–6; Alisio (1969), 223–6. For the loss of the piece, see Capasso (1892), 481.

[21] Leon (1971); Zanker (1988); Lipps (2011); Pensabene (2007).

[22] Heinrich (2002), 70, nos. K38 and K59.

Fig. 7.4. Excavations at S. Maria della Rotonda, Naples.

Source: Image used courtesy of the Ministero per i Beni e le Attività Culturali–Soprintendenza Speciale per i Beni Archeologici di Napoli e Pompei.

while other types dating to the Antonine period recall models in the theatre of Sessa Aurunca.[23] At both S. Restituta and the Stefania basilica we find capitals dating to the Augustan age which are similar to other Neapolitan and Campanian examples, while another locally made group (based on models made in Asia Minor) are of a type more normally found reused in the porticos of suburban villas. The majority of the reused columns have smooth shafts and are made of white marble, *bardiglio*, *africano*, and eastern granite, while a small

[23] Cascella (2009).

minority have fluted columns of white or coloured marbles. In
S. Maria and the Stefania basilica, the use of columns in porphyry
(a material strongly connected to the imperial ideology) is suggestive
of an elite clientele who were able to afford the costs of transportation
from Rome.[24] Meanwhile, the numerous columns in Assuan pink
granite used in the naves of S. Restituta are to be linked to a local,
Flavian tradition.

The churches of S. Giorgio and S. Giovanni Maggiore were built
between the end of the fourth and beginning of the fifth centuries in
two opposite parts of the city, at the edge of the eastern slope near the
ancient walls, and on the hilly promontory between Monterone and
the *canalone* of Via Mezzocannone. At each of these sites, the architecture was inspired by an eastern Greek aesthetic.[25] According to a
sixteenth-century text by Annibale De Capua, S. Giorgio was divided
into three naves by twenty marble columns, which were topped by
capitals dating from the imperial period.[26] In the cross vault there
were twelve column shafts made from alabaster and *africano* marble,
six of which divided the apse and the nave from the presbytery. After
the restoration of 1640, some columns were taken and reused in the
church of S. Maria delle Anime del Purgatorio ad Arco. A single pair
of columns in Egyptian granite remained in place at S. Giorgio; these
had bases of composite type and Corinthian capitals, and had originally adorned a building which dated to the second half of the first
century AD (Fig. 7.5). Other columns in this church are made from
coloured marble, and these may have come from a monumental
building of the early imperial period. In fact, shafts made in *africano*
marble—which was one of the first materials introduced to Rome in
the late Republican period—are often found in the theatres of ancient
Campania, such as the one in Capua (which was modelled on the
theatre of Marcellus at Rome) and the one in Nuceria, which is also
the provenance of the alabaster columns reused in the Byzantine
basilica of S. Maria Maggiore.[27]

[24] De Blaauw (1991); Ensoli and La Rocca (2000).
[25] For Byzantine architecture, cf. Johnson, Ousterhout, and Papalexandrou (2012).
[26] On Capua, see Capasso (1892), 18–21; Colonna (1892), 365–8.
[27] Pensabene (2005). On the links between the Capua theatre and the theatre of
Marcellus, see Bianchi (2010), 285–321. On the seventeenth-century reuse of shafts
from the Capua theatre in the church of Gesù Nuovo in Naples, cf. Palmentieri
(2010b), 61 n. 11.

Fig. 7.5. Detail of *spolia* in the church of S. Giorgio Maggiore, Naples.
Source: Photograph: Angela Palmentieri.

Where did the columns of S. Giorgio come from? Much of the archaeological material in the city dates to the time of the Flavian dynasty, when restoration work was carried out in the wake of damage suffered by buildings in the natural catastrophes of the second half of the first century AD.[28] Amongst the buildings of this period was the Roman theatre in the upper *plateia*, the ruins of which were known in the sixteenth century.[29] The theatre was in use until the mid-fourth century, when parts of its fabric may have been reused in Christian building projects like the church of S. Giorgio.

The paucity of ancient remains in the forum area can be linked to the traumatic events suffered by the city's Augustan monuments. However, one temple dating from the early imperial period has recently been discovered in the coastal area near to Piazza Nicola Amore, just a short distance from the church of S. Giorgio.[30] This

[28] The inscription *CIL* 10.1481 testifies to the intervention of imperial functionaries sent to Campania to assess the damages suffered by the monuments.
[29] Cf. Fabio Giordano's *Descriptio Campaniae Veterumque monumentorum et locorum in ea existentium, conservata* (MS Biblioteca Nazionale di Napoli, segnatura XIII, B 26), discussed in Fusco (1841), 9–20 and Rea (2013). On the theatre see Johannowsky (1985), 209–12 who puts forward the hypothesis of a first Augustan phase; see Longobardo and Zeli (2010) for the recent excavations.
[30] Bragantini (2010), 607–21.

temple has been connected to the Isolympic games that were instituted in honour of Augustus in AD 2, on account of the discovery at
the site of an inscribed list of winners of the *Italika Rhomaia Sebasta
Isolympia*.[31] Some monumental remains have also been excavated
from the site—namely three Corinthian capitals, a few fluted columns
in Luna marble, and fragments of marble cornices dating to the early
imperial age. These pieces evidently survived the raids that took place
from the mid-fourth century until the final destruction of the complex in the Gothic War (on which see Giovanni Polara, Chapter 6 of
this volume). Sculptures similar to those from the isolympic temple
are found reused in the porticos of the Stefania basilica and along the
naves of S. Restituta, suggesting that this site may have been used as a
source of building material. However, the types of architecture used
in S. Giorgio are absent from the isolympic temple, and instead may
have come from other neighbouring buildings such as the gymnasium, the stadium, and the hippodrome—which epigraphic sources
and sculptural finds connect to the area in front of the temple.[32]

The church of S. Giovanni Maggiore was built by Bishop Vincenzo
on the remains of a temple of Hercules and Antinous, as we know
from an inscription reused in the church.[33] The reused materials were
subsequently scattered in the restoration works of the sixteenth
century, but their extreme elegance is suggested by the term *praeful-
gida* ('resplendent') used to describe them by John the Deacon in his
Chronicles, as well as a set of drawings by Francesco di Giorgio.[34] The
seven sketches in the Uffizi represent fragments of the trabeation and
a *transenna* with a dolphin, both decorated with motifs of the mid-
imperial era similar to those found in certain other buildings in the
Phlegraean area.[35] Despite an evident desire for uniformity, these
spolia come from a range of different contexts. The pair of capitals
on the triumphal arch—reused here on tall shafts of *caristio* marble—
originally belonged to the canonical type of Corinthian column made
by Roman craftsmen working in Naples at the beginning of the

---

[31] Miranda (1990), 75–114; Di Nanni (2007–8); Miranda (2007).

[32] Lasena (1688); Miranda (1985b), 390–2.

[33] Capasso (1892), 473; Gagliardi (1888), 42; Borrelli (1967), 11–17; Miranda
(1990), 19–20, n. 5.

[34] Pane (1975), 24 ff.; Vasori (1981); Burns (1993), 366 ff.; Picone (2008), 50, fig. 19.

[35] *Transenne* with marine motifs are known, for example, in the *macellum* of
Pozzuoli, cf. Demma (2007), 331 n. 424.

second century.[36] A fragmentary capital made of Pentelic marble must have come instead from a building of the Augustan era, comparable with other Neapolitan and Phlegraean buildings.[37] Another composite capital finds no parallels amongst surviving Campanian examples and cannot easily be placed in the context of local traditions of the age of Caracalla; it should therefore be attributed to travelling craftsmen working in the traditions of Asia Minor.[38] Other reused sculptures include the pair of marble pilasters in the apse (Fig. 7.6), decorated with spirals of acanthus and animated by figures.[39] In addition to traditional subjects like birds, serpents, cupids, and animal protomes, we also find 'local' motifs such as the Siren, which could easily be absorbed into an ideological reinterpretation (Fig. 7.7).[40]

The conservatism of Roman architectural styles makes the identification of these sculptures' provenance difficult to ascertain. The rigid style of the decorative elements suggests local work of the first decades of the second century AD, but—despite the excellent state of preservation and the fact that the capitals and bases originally belonged together—there is no hard evidence that they were taken from the area underneath the church, even though the excavations have uncovered structures of ancient walls and mosaic pavements in this area.[41] The two pilaster capitals find parallels in an example that comes from the theatre; another Attic base of Julio-Claudian date attached to an adjacent column also appears to come from the same workshop. Stylistically, this base matches examples now held in the stores of the Naples Archaeological Museum, which themselves echo models from the theatre of Cherchel.[42] These pieces help to corroborate the hypothesis that there were links between the Augustan workshops operating in Rome, Ostia, and the cities of Mauritania, all of which belonged to a wider circle of production that also included centres of the Phlegraean Fields and southern Lazio, as well as the Parthenopean capital.[43] Ultimately, despite the elegance

---

[36] Pensabene (1998).   [37] Pensabene (1998); Heinrich (2002).

[38] On the restoration of a coastal road in AD 202 near the area under examination here, cf. Giampaola (2010), 20, fig. 2.

[39] *Napoli antica* (1985), 484, n. 153 with pl. 2; Mathea-Förtsch (1999), 129, n. 81 with pl. 44, 1–5.

[40] Ensoli and La Rocca (2000).   [41] Carletti (1776), 120.

[42] Schreiter (1995), 210, nos. 77 a–b, with figs. 92–3. For the example from the theatre, see Longobardo and Zeli (2010), 43, fig. 20.

[43] Pensabene (1982), 116–69.

Fig. 7.6. Pilaster decorated with vegetal and animal motifs, from the church of S. Giovanni Maggiore, Naples.

Source: Photograph: Angela Palmentieri.

of S. Giovanni's *disiecta membra*, the stylistic variety of the material suggests a progressive reduction in ancient elements that were available for reuse.

The marbles from the church of S. Maria Maggiore della Pietrasanta probably come from the forum area or from the remains of an earlier temple of Diana on the site. This church was built in 533 by bishop Pomponio.[44] Fabio Giordano records that it was situated on

---

[44] Schipa (1892), 25; Beneduce (1931), 11 ff.; Alisio (1964), 226–36; Guida (1969), 128.

Fig. 7.7. Detail of Fig 7.6.
Source: Photograph: Angela Palmentieri.

the *media plateia* in the *Regio Marmorata*, where remains of a late antique *domus* have been found, along with other monumental remains from the early imperial era.[45] The current church was modernized by Fanzago in the middle of the seventeenth century; it substituted the ancient basilica, which had been divided into three naves by eighteen spoliated columns.[46] Only a single Corinthian capital in the Flavian tradition and an Attic base remain, both of which are now used as elements of the modern baptismal font.[47] The excavations have intimated the existence of an atrium on the Via dei

[45] *Napoli antica* (1985), 417; Arthur (2002), 65.
[46] Alisio (1964), 228 ff.   [47] Guida (1969), 128, fig. 16.

Fig. 7.8. The Pietrasanta bell tower, Naples.
Source: Photograph: Angela Palmentieri.

Tribunali, on top of which the famous bell tower was built in *opus lateracium*, using many spoliated marbles (Fig. 7.8). Cippi, statue bases, and column shafts in Phrygian marble were used to define the corners of the tower's base and the first-level stringcourse. A pair of trabeations in Luna marble belong to the architectural tradition of the first and third centuries, and bear particular similarities with elements on the cornice of the isolympic temple, which is itself modelled on the Forum of Augustus in Rome.[48] Other *spolia* from

---

[48] Bragantini (2010), 611, fig. 5.

different contexts were used for decorative purposes in the upper levels of the tower: these include a fragment of a *trapezophoros* (table leg) with the protome of a griffin, a capital from a pilaster of the mid-imperial era (similar to other Neapolitan and Pompeian examples), and a pair of columns made from *tenario cipollino* and Proconnesian marble.[49] These *spolia* indicate that material was being taken from the surroundings area as well as from outside the city, in particular the necropoleis, which is where the inscriptions walled into the attic of the bell tower came from.[50]

The church of the Saviour (Chiesa del Salvatore) was built on the remains of an extra-urban villa in the *insula maris*—the island of Megaride, where according to tradition the tomb of the Siren was located.[51] This area had been connected to the mainland since the late Republican period by means of a network of steps and terraces belonging to the villa (*castrum*) of Lucullus.[52] Celano describes the Byzantine church as having three naves, which were divided by four granite columns of similar dimensions topped with Corinthian capitals of late imperial production.[53] Fragments of fluted columns in white marble divided the so-called Room of the Columns into three sections. The *spolia* came not only from the residential complex beneath the church, but also from public contexts—this is suggested by the fragment of cornice decorated with meanders which is reused as a shelf, since similar motifs are found in the first-century AD public monuments of Nola and Cuma.[54]

As far as late antique building practices are concerned, it is unclear whether the Neapolitan buildings were systematically plundered, with *spolia* being collected and kept in temporary storehouses, or whether quarries were set up to supply new construction works.[55] It seems reasonable to suppose that in these early centuries material was taken from nearby buildings, with additional material sometimes being

---

[49]   The pair of capitals with cornucopiae and theatrical masks were reworked in the medieval period. On the cornucopiae type, cf. Heinrich (2002), 80, no. S23. For the cipollino columns see Lazzarini (2006), 111, fig. 4.

[50]   CIL 10.3007: *D(is) M(anibus)/Threpto/Propinqui l(iberto) b(ono)/hic situs est/ sibi et suis*; of Phlegraean origin.

[51]   The sources for the cult of Parthenope are collected in Büchner, Morelli, and Nenci (1952), 406.

[52]   Mormile (1670), 49; D'Arms (2003).

[53]   Celano (1692), 65; Venditti (1967), 514.

[54]   Pensabene (2003), 104, fig. 45; Nuzzo (2010), 339.

[55]   On the figure of the late antique architect, see Venditti (1966), 86–9.

brought in from elsewhere for certain prestigious works—such as the church of S. Gennaro extra Moenia.[56] This church was built in the fifth century in an area previously occupied by necropoleis and residential villas; it is unlikely that this location would have yielded monumental material of the sort found in the church, like the pair of fluted columns in white marble and the capitals reused in the absidal arch, which were originally executed for a public building of the Augustan period.[57] These sculptures can be compared with the material from S. Restituta and the temple of Augustan Fortune in Pompeii, which were made in the same workshops by Roman sculptors operating in Naples, Pompeii, and other Campanian centres.[58]

Different types of reuse are attested in Byzantine civil architecture. Recent excavations in Piazza Giovanni Bovio have brought to light fragments of decoration in relief, as well as cornices and Corinthian and Ionic capitals, all of which were reused in the Byzantine fortifications.[59] These marbles were taken from a monumental arch that may have stood on the Via Litoranea, which was reorganized under the emperors Septimius Severus and Caracalla.[60] The reuse of marbles as simple building materials suggests a certain lack of interest on the part of the local ruling class; alternatively, it may be that the urgent need to build fortifications in late antiquity meant that marbles that *were* perceived as valuable nevertheless had to be used in this way.[61]

The construction in the early ninth century of the medieval church of S. Paolo Maggiore on the ancient temple of the Dioscuri signals a turning point in how the city's classical heritage was used to construct political and social prestige.[62] In contrast to the late antique practice of reusing pagan monuments as 'quarries' of fragmentary building materials, the building of S. Paolo involved the wholesale recuperation of a Roman temple—a project that was in line with broader

---

[56] Amodio (2005); Savino (2005).
[57] Chierici (1934), 203–16; Ebanista (2010), 127–74, fig. 15.
[58] Heinrich (2002), 64, no. K7; Palmentieri (2013).
[59] Giampaola (2010). The city walls were restored under Valentinian III (425–50), *CIL* 10.1485. In 536 there was an intervention by Justinian, who reinforced the perimeter with seven towers; destroyed by the Goths in 543, these were restored a decade later under Narsetes, cf. Venditti (1967), 471.
[60] Giampaola (2010).   [61] Kinney (1995); Kinney (1997).
[62] The Church in Naples may have suffered some crisis between the seventh and eighth centuries, since there are no attestations of new ecclesiastical foundations at this time. Arthur (2002), 60, fig. 4.1.

Carolingian engagements with the classical tradition.[63] While the conversion of pagan buildings into Christian churches had begun in the wider Campanian region in the fifth–sixth centuries (as we can see from the case of the temple of Augustus at Pozzuoli, which was reused between the end of the fifth century and the early medieval era, as well as from the Doric temples of Paestum), such practices seem to begin later in Naples, perhaps on account of the fact that the bishops of Rome forbade the reuse of pagan temples.[64] At S. Paolo, although the floor plan signalled a return to early Christian models (it was divided into three naves by eighteen columns of oriental granite topped by capitals that had been taken from the ruins of the temple and surrounding buildings), the reuse of the antique assumed a new ideological valence, which was especially evident in the pediment with its mythical subjects.[65] The importance here of S. Paolo (which Celano dubs as 'la più bella e antica macchina' in Naples) lies not only in its reuse of architectural *spolia*, but also in the restoration of the ancient ruins and their incorporation into the new Christian image of Naples.[66] The early medieval 'return to the antique' involved the renovation of an area that in antiquity was strongly characterized by its public functions. The Tiberian temple of the Dioscuri on the *plateia mediana* was situated in the ancient forum, onto which faced other civic and religious buildings. As part of a programme initiated at the beginning of the sixth century (when Bishop Giovanni II commissioned a basilica on the ruins of the Roman market), the area of the forum was progressively converted into a site of memory of the city's pagan past, which was nevertheless now seen through the lens of the new Christian tradition.[67]

---

[63] Pensabene (2003), 166–95; Liverani (2004), 383–433; Guidobaldi and Pensabene (2005–6).

[64] On other Campanian examples of reuse, see Maiuri (1951); Settis (1977).

[65] Adamo Muscettola (1985), 196–208.

[66] Celano (1692), 151. On Naples' new image, see D'Engenio (1623), 84. A description of the facade with its six columns can be found in Mormile (1670), 10–12, where he identifies amongst the sculptures a naked Apollo leaning on a tripod, and personifications of Earth and the Sebeto River, near Jupiter and Mercury (but cf. the different reading of Rabun Taylor in Chapter 3 of this volume). In Chapter 12 of this volume Fulvio Lenzo provides a full discussion of this church's history and its evolving relationship to antiquity.

[67] The temple's elegant pair of Pentelic marble columns with their ornate capitals and Attic bases suggest a close link between this Neapolitan monument and certain Augustan buildings of Rione Terra, Pozzuoli, and the forum at Cuma. See Zevi and Cavalieri Manasse (2005), 269–94; Valeri (2005); Nuzzo (2010), 388, figs. 15–16. The

THE RECOVERY OF ANTIQUITY BETWEEN THE
MEDIEVAL PERIOD AND THE RENAISSANCE

So far this chapter has suggested that, while the *spolia* reused in the churches in Naples between the fourth and tenth centuries can rarely be traced back to specific architectural contexts, they still constitute a rich body of evidence which can help to shed light on the form of the ancient city, as well as on the processes of urban adaptation that took place in Naples in this period.[68] The process of transforming the city and its ancient material culture continued well into the early modern period, and examining buildings built in post-medieval times can give further insights into the phenomenon of reuse. Because of the continuous occupation of Naples, medieval sites tended to be built on earlier palaeo-Christian churches; they often incorporated architectural material from the earlier buildings, while in some cases *spolia* were taken from other Campanian contexts. In many cases, antiquity was used to create and reinforce the social status of the new ruling classes.[69]

One excellent example of the Norman attitude to antiquity is the Jerusalemite church of S. Giovanni a Mare, which was built during the reign of William II of Sicily (1166–89).[70] Here, antiquity is referenced through the use of the early Christian floor plan, which was divided by six column shafts (in cipollino, grey marble, and Proconnesian marble) topped with capitals from different traditions, which in some cases were reworked to give the impression of greater uniformity (Fig. 7.9). Certain pieces were used for functions very different from those they held originally, like the fragment of a large spiral-form column reused as the base for another column, an inscription of imperial age recut as the abacus of a column capital, and a pair of marble cornices from the Augustan period used in the piers of the triumphal arch. Although some of the material from

four column bases of the facade are of similar dimensions but are made from different materials (Luna and Pentelic marble), a common feature of Campanian architecture of the Augustan era. On the Cumaean material see Nuzzo (2010).

[68] For similar processes in other Campanian centres, see Palmentieri (2010a).

[69] On the medieval ideology of reuse, see Settis (1986); Pensabene (1990); de Lachenal (1995) and (1999); Esch (1998); Ideologie e pratiche del reimpiego (1999); Bernard, Bernardi, and Esposito (2008); Greenhalgh (2008); Brilliant and Kinney (2012).

[70] Radogna (1873); Pensabene (2005).

Fig. 7.9. Detail of the interior of the church of S. Giovanni a Mare, Naples.
Source: Photograph: Angela Palmentieri.

S. Giovanni must have come from the surrounding ruins, we also find in this building the first examples of *spolia* from the Campanian countryside being used in urban monuments.

The wider Phlegraean area offered many marble resources, thanks to the widespread abandonment of monuments that had been damaged by Bradyseism and the various raids of late antiquity. The early medieval age saw the creation of groups of *marmorarii* (marble workers) who specialized in the demolition of ruins, and who targeted Pozzuoli and Baia in particular.[71] Following the example of Abbot Desiderio, who had built the monastery at Montecassino with marbles from Rome and the ruins of Minturno, reuse of Phlegraean *spolia* extended to the two great coastal centres of medieval Campania— Naples and Salerno.[72] The variety of the *spolia* used in S. Giovanni a Mare shows that the building's patrons had the financial means to transport precious marbles by sea. The symmetrical arrangement of different types of capital (predominantly Corinthian and composite)

[71] Palmentieri (2005); Pensabene (2005).
[72] On Montecassino, see Pensabene (1990); Esch (1998); Romano and Enckell (2007); Mesolella (2012). On the Phlegraean provenance of material now in Amalfi and Salerno, cf. Esch (1998); Palmentieri (2005); Palmentieri (2010a).

along this church's naves recalls the early Christian aesthetic of the Constantinian basilicas, while we also find Ionic architecture being used in the naves for the first time. One elegant capital with a *hypotrachelion* decorated with a palmette *antemion* was reminiscent of Greek prototypes from the Heraion of Samos and the eastern portico of the Athenian Erechtheion. Similar prototypes had also been used in Julio-Claudian monuments like the Athenian temple of Augustus and other buildings of Rome, including S. Maria in Trastevere, the Lateran, and Palazzo Venezia.[73] There are also close formal analogies between this Neapolitan capital and a Hadrianic example from the baths at Baia, from which site the Neapolitan capital may itself have been taken at some point during the medieval period. Another capital in S. Giovanni, made from Pentelic marble, comes from a Phlegraean or Sorrentine context; this takes up a Greek decorative tradition, which is also attested in architecture of the first and second centuries in Miseno, Sorrento, and Sessa Aurunca.[74] The decorative syntax of this Neapolitan example was in fact taken as a model by the Swabian and Angevin craftsmen at the site of S. Lorenzo Maggiore. At the same time, however, when compared with the city's Norman architecture, the building programme promoted by the Angevin dynasty between the second half of the thirteenth century and the first decades of the fourteenth century points to the gradual abandonment of the classical tradition, and the development of an autonomous architectural language that was not rooted in antiquity.[75]

The church and convent of S. Lorenzo Maggiore presents a compelling case study because of its clear archaeological stratification.[76] The area that was conventionally known as the *regio fori* or *augustalis* was, according to Fabio Giordano, occupied by a series of monuments from the *forum rerum venalium*.[77] The public nature of this area in antiquity seems to be confirmed by the antiquities used in the Angevin works.[78] Only twelve of the sixteen marble capitals that divided the sixth-century church into three sections remain; these are

---

[73] Barberini (2008), 145, no. 15. On the parallels with the Greek monuments, see Pensabene (2005), 133, no. 4d; Gruben (2006), 7–16.
[74] Lljenstolpe (1997–8), 117; Pensabene (2005), 131, no. 1d; Palmentieri (2010a).
[75] De Castris (1986); Gardner (1989); Bruzelius (2005a); Vitolo (2008).
[76] *Napoli antica* (1985), 185–95.   [77] Greco (1985b).
[78] Roncella (1996), 111 ff.; Bruzelius (2005a), 1–16; Bruzelius (2005b).

reused in the Gothic pilasters in the great hall of the basilica and in other spaces, where they seem to take the form of erudite citations. In this church we also find columns of varying diameters topped with a variety of different capital types, including examples from the Antonine and late imperial periods, and composite types from the Julio-Claudian period similar to those used in S. Restituta (Fig. 7.10). Other pieces have parallels at Campanian sites, such as the three capitals *a calice* which were made in the first century, and which are similar to spoliated marbles used in S. Matteo at Salerno and SS. Crocifisso in Amalfi, which come from the ruins of Paestum.[79] The capitals from all three sites may have been products of the same workshops, which were operating from the middle of the first century along the Campanian coast. Another two capitals from S. Lorenzo also suggest this: one of these, which is now held in the museum of Opera, was produced by a workshop active at the start of the second century and which specialized in the re-elaboration of the Attic models that were used

Fig. 7.10. Detail of the interior of the church of S. Lorenzo Maggiore, Naples.
Source: Photograph: Angela Palmentieri.

[79] On S. Matteo, see Heinrich (2002), no. S25a; on SS. Crocifisso, see Palmentieri (2010a).

in the Augustan theatres of Herculaneum and Nuceria.[80] In this case, similar subjects can be found in the medieval churches of S. Benedetto in Salerno and in S. Pietro alli Marmi in Eboli.[81] The second capital, which is reused in the Charterhouse of S. Lorenzo, recalls a series from Salerno: four examples from this series are now in the cathedral of S. Matteo, six are in the church of S. Massimo, and a final pair are in the complex of S. Sofia in Benevento.[82] An unpublished drawing by the French architect François Debret records the nineteenth-century discovery in Paestum of another fragment identical to the Salernitan ones.[83] These fourteen Proconnesian marble capitals were made by the same local craftsmen of the Antonine period, who specialized in the simplification of the composite type. The fact that a high percentage of capitals from S. Lorenzo conforms stylistically to the marbles reused in other Campanian sites helps to corroborate the hypothesis that there was a local antiquities market which may have been instituted in the early medieval period to supply certain sites which were not urbanized in antiquity and which were thus lacking in sculptural materials.[84] It is also worth mentioning that, in addition to the reuse of Classical and early Christian monuments, the importance of past models for Angevin architects is also demonstrated by the reworking or creation of new objects based on the classical forms of the Neapolitan *spolia*.[85]

The Franciscan complex seems almost to have used residual materials from the early Christian basilica as an indicator of the changing occupation of the site; the new Angevin cathedral, too, incorporated marbles from earlier buildings from the Stefania complex, including approximately forty-six columns of granite that were used to divide the naves and two columns of porphyry on the facade.[86] Similar architectural formulae were used in the construction of the new complexes of S. Agostino alla Zecca, S. Chiara, and the Incoronata. Two mid-imperial capitals decorated with eagles reworked into the

---

[80] Johannowsky (2000), 17–32.   [81] Palmentieri (2010a).

[82] Palmentieri (2010a).

[83] A sketch of the capital can be seen in the notebook *Le Voyage en Italie de François Debret* (1777–1850), preserved in the Bibliothèque de l'École Nationale Supérieure des Beaux-Arts, NUM PC 77832 (07), fo. 222.

[84] Manacorda (1979); Palmentieri (2013).

[85] On medieval reworkings, see D'Onofrio (2003); Bona Castellotti and Giuliano (2008).

[86] Bruzelius (1999), 187–95; Romano and Bock (2005); Vassallo Zirpoli (2008).

emblem of the Angevin house were reused in the Charterhouse of S. Agostino, on top of a pair of spoliated columns.[87] A third capital appears in the portico of the Stefania basilica as part of the thirteenth-century restoration works, which saw the division of the atrium into two *aulas* by a line of columns. Columns and capitals were reused in their classical function in the monastic complex of S. Chiara, in which precious materials were exhibited almost as a symbol of the survival of the imperial past.[88] Other reused marbles at S. Chiara come from Phlegraean provenances, like the inscription of the goddess Faustina reused as a door jamb.[89] Meanwhile, the blocks of limestone used in the basement of the bell tower come from a Capuan building (perhaps the amphitheatre), and thus echo similar examples of reuse in the bell towers of Salerno, Capua, Amalfi, and Nola.[90] Instead, the church of the Incoronata near the Roman port area alternated some rather modest ancient marbles with new ones, exemplifying the Angevin tendency to merge elements of local ancient culture with new traditions (Fig. 7.11).[91] One can discern in the words of Petrarch tones of disapproval in the face of such utilitarian reuse of antiquity, which he thought degraded monuments and indicated the poverty of local historical memory.[92]

The first decades of the fifteenth century saw the dawn of a new interest in the material traces of antiquity in Naples, thanks in part to the literary rediscoveries of the humanistic age.[93] The interest in Roman architectural remains blossomed in this climate, and the local ruins began to be interpreted as signs of a lost magnificence.

---

[87] For the capitals with eagles, see von Mercklin (1962), 221–9 nn. 543–58. On the church, see Venditti (1973), 724; Russo (2002), 35; Bruzelius (2005a), nos. 42 and 63 with fig. 25.

[88] Bruzelius (1995), 69–100; Bruzelius (2005b). On the columns, see Maresca (1888), 115. On the reception of antiquity in the Swabian and Angevin periods, see Bona Castellotti and Giuliano (2008).

[89] de Franciscis (1954), 277–83; *Napoli antica* (1985), 225–7.

[90] Palmentieri (2010a). On the theatre provenance see Palmentieri (2010b).

[91] On the recent finds from the port of Neapolis in the area of Piazza Municipio, see Giampaola (2004), 39–50.

[92] Cf. the *Hortatoria a Cola di Rienzo e al popolo romano* of 1347, reproduced in Dotti (1978), 892–919: *Itaque nunc heu dolor! Heu scelus indignum! De vestris marmoreis columnis, de liminibus templorum, (ad quae nuper ex toto orbe concursus devotissimus fiebat) de imaginibus sepulcrorum, sub quibus patrum vestrorum venerabilis cinis erat, ut reliquas sileam, desidiosa Neapolis adornatur.* Cf. Adamo Muscettola (1996), 580 and n. 52; Catudella (2006); Picone (2008).

[93] Mustilli (1952), 431 ff.; Pane (2008).

Fig. 7.11. Portico of the church of the Incoronata, Naples.
Source: Photograph: Angela Palmentieri.

All'antica monuments were now made using spoliated materials, which suggested for their observers the idea of the restoration of the ancient past.[94] One striking example is the bell tower built in 1415 by the eminent personality Artusio Pappacoda, adviser to King Ladislao (Fig. 7.12).[95] This edifice was constructed on the model of a Roman building, using Roman *spolia*; its design mirrored many aspects of the nearby complex of S. Giovanni Maggiore, creating an aesthetic and conceptual link between the two sites. The walls were built from blocks of tufa in the Roman *opus reticulatum* style, while the facades

---

[94] See the various chapters in Warr and Elliott (2010).
[95] Adamo Muscettola (1994), 101. For a study of the elite of this period, see Vitale (2003).

Fig. 7.12. The Pappacoda chapel, Naples.
Source: Photograph: Angela Palmentieri.

incorporated a selection of marble objects that came from different Campanian sites. These included a marble mask of Dionysian type, the front panel of a sarcophagus representing the scene of the rape of Proserpina and part of an acrolithic statue of Athena.[96] Both the architectural style and the type of material reused echo the famous *Porta* of Federico II in Capua, on the attic of which were

---

[96] For a study of acroliths, see Ghisellini (2004). This author is currently working on a publication of the *spolia* from the Pappacoda chapel.

Fig. 7.13. Detail of the Pappacoda chapel, Naples.
Source: Photograph: Angela Palmentieri.

displayed ancient sculptures including a reworked ancient acrolith—the so-called *Capua fidelis*.[97] On another facade of the Pappacoda bell tower were displayed the head of a female divinity and a pair of marble funerary stelae (Fig. 7.13). The reuse of stelae in particular evoked the earlier bell tower of the Benevento cathedral, where the images of the dead served as a form of 'genealogical memory', legitimizing the social status of the local elite.[98]

An even more radical example of reuse is found in the arch of the clock tower belonging to the church of S. Eligio Maggiore, which was modelled on the arch of Augustus at Rimini.[99] Built in the second half of the fifteenth century, this structure embodied the classicizing impulse of the Aragonese court.[100] It also marked the start of a new 'proto-Renaissance' style, which involved the reproduction of ancient architectural models, and which often took on the role of celebrating

---

[97] Willemsen (1953); Bologna (1989); on the *spolia*, cf. Bona Castellotti and Giuliano (2008).

[98] Settis (2008).   [99] De Maria (1988); Palmentieri (2010a).

[100] Bruschi (2008).

ancient history.[101] Like the Augustan model, which incorporated four *clipei* portraits of divinities (Jupiter, Apollo, Neptune, and Roma), the Neapolitan arch included four ancient marble portraits in the guise of *imagines clipeatae*. The emperor Antoninus Pius and a poet appeared on one side of the arch, while the images on the other side represented the deified Plautilla and a philosopher (Fig. 7.14). The imperial portraits were based on ancient sculptures, while the other two portraits—which are carved from a finer quality of marble—may have come from herms of the Hadrianic age.[102] Further Hadrianic herms of Hercules and Homer on the pilaster may have come from the surrounding area.[103] Images of this kind were often used to decorate stadia and gymnasia in the imperial period.[104] It is very probable that the marbles from S. Eligio came from the ruins of an agonistic building of the second half of the second century, even if no evidence for their provenance has yet been found.[105]

Another intriguing reception of antiquity is found in the palazzo of Diomede Carafa, which was built on the *plateia inferiore*.[106] In line with the political, cultural, and ideological programme at the court of the time, the facade of this house incorporated certain iconic sculptures, including an imperial portrait of Vespasian wearing the civic crown (Fig. 7.15) and one of Matidia the Elder.[107] These two portrait images—which were probably intended as allegorical representations of the owners of the house—were paired with images of the hero Diomedes and the city's founding figure Parthenope, in line with a new interpretative paradigm which drew on the past for the purposes of self-fashioning.[108] Similar dynamics can be perceived in the construction of the palazzo of Carlo Carafa in the *sedile di Nilo*, which

---

[101] Summonte (1640); Croce (1892b).

[102] These unpublished imperial sculptures date from the second half of the second century, cf. Fittschen (1999). On the typology of herms, see Palma (1998); Piekarski (2004).

[103] Capasso (1905), 264; *Napoli antica* (1985), 414, n. 119.2.

[104] On the Athens stadium, cf. Gasparri (1973).

[105] Johannowsky (1960); *Napoli antica* (1985), 484, pl. IX (an archaeological plan of the finds from this area); Bragantini (2010).

[106] On Carafa see Ceci (1893), 149–52; de Divitiis (2007) and Chapter 10 of this volume; Dodero (2007).

[107] An analogous portrait of Vespasian from Minturno is in the Museo Nazionale Romano. Cf. Wegner (1966), 79; for a portrait of Matidia now in the Palazzo dei Conservatori in Rome, see Wegner (1956).

[108] On the beginnings of the first collections of antiquities, cf. Iasiello (2003); de Divitiis (2007).

Fig. 7.14. View of the clock tower of the church of S. Eligio Maggiore, Naples.
Source: Photograph: Angela Palmentieri.

incorporated the remains of a building from Nola, demonstrating a wider fashion for the reuse of antiquities amongst the Campanian nobility.[109] Crucially, in this period we see a reduction in the spoliation of Roman buildings for a collective, public use, and a corresponding increase in the use of antiquities in private palazzi, where figurative

---

[109] On the use of ancient materials in Capuan and Nolan palazzi, see Palmentieri (2010a). On the Palazzo of Carlo Carafa, see Leone (1514).

Fig. 7.15. Portrait of Vespasian, reused in the palazzo of Diomede Carafa, Naples.
Source: Photograph: Angela Palmentieri.

sculptures such as stelae, portraits, and inscriptions were used to support the construction of new social identities.

   In conclusion, this chapter has traced the reuse of antiquity in Naples from the late antiquity until the Renaissance, bringing to light some previously unpublished or unknown examples, and suggesting some of the symbolic and ideological meanings of these various acts of reuse. In the medieval and early modern periods, the material culture of classical antiquity seems to have been used to construct the identity of the city and its ruling class. Interestingly, while texts like the fourteenth-century *Cronaca di Partenope* and the fifteenth-century *Historia Neapolitana* of Fabio Giordano testify to a contemporary consciousness of the past, they do not mention the reuse of ancient sculptures, despite the fact that many examples could have been seen in the city.[110] In the sphere of art and architecture, however, the material memory of ancient Neapolis was admired and drawn on by many, with the *spolia* being taken as models in many different circumstances.[111] Meanwhile, the seventeenth century witnessed a growing interest in Parthenopean culture as a whole, which (in the words of Giuseppe Mormile) was 'wonderful for the ancient ruins, the sculptures, columns and epigraphs that were reused in the palazzi of the nobles and scattered in the streets of the town' ('meravigliosa si rende anco per le gran vestigie d'antiche fabbriche, delle tante statue, colonne, & epitaffi,

Fig. 7.16. The 'Capa di Napoli' ('head of Naples').
Source: Photograph: Angela Palmentieri.

[110] Unlike Ambrogio Leone, who speaks about the Roman antiquities used in the bell tower of Nola cathedral (1514). On reuse at Nola, see Palmentieri (2010a).

[111] The dedicatory inscription from the temple of the Dioscuri was copied for the Malatesta temple of Rimini, cf. Adamo Muscettola (1984). Lecora (1999/2000) presents a study of drawings of Neapolitan *spolia*.

che si veggono tanto nei palagi de' Signori, quanto sparsi per la Città').[112]
The antiquities that emerged from the subsoil in this period, like the
'Corpo di Napoli' and the 'Capa di Napoli' (a sculpture that has been
connected to the cult of the Siren Parthenope), became protagonists
of erudite fantasy and popular imagination, serving as examples of
cultural continuity of the most remote origins (Fig. 7.16).[113]

---

[112] Mormile (1670), 10.

[113] On the 'Capa di Napoli', see de la Ville sur-Yllon (1894); Adamo Muscettola
(1984), 2–10. On the 'Corpo di Napoli', see De Caro and Spinosa (2003).

8

Virgiliana Neapolis Urbs

Receptions of Classical Naples in the Swabian and Early Angevin Ages

Fulvio Delle Donne

There are many different reasons why a city might become a capital. It could be that its geographical location makes it particularly well suited to that role, or it might gradually acquire a position of economic, and therefore political, pre-eminence. Alternatively, a city's ascent to capital might owe something to the strength of its ancient cultural traditions—whether these happen to be real or invented. It was probably a combination of these reasons that led to Naples becoming the capital of the Kingdom of Southern Italy during the Swabian and early Angevin periods (that is, between the middle decades of the thirteenth century and the beginning of the fourteenth century).

Certainly, when Frederick II of Swabia made his entry into the Kingdom after the imperial coronation in 1220, Naples was simply one city among many, and was perhaps even less important and influential than other cities like Palermo (the old capital city of the Norman Kingdom), or Foggia (perhaps the city most beloved by the Swabian emperor), or Capua, which was dubbed *caput Apulie* ('the capital city of southern Italy') by the chronicler Andreas Ungarus.[1] Eighty years earlier, in 1139, Frederick's maternal grandfather, the Norman king Roger II of Altavilla, had subdued the Duchy of Naples.

---

[1] Cuozzo and Martin (1995). For Capua, see Delle Donne (2014), p. 40, ch. XLII.1.

That event had not only been a prologue to the ensuing unification of southern Italy, but it had also put on display the social, religious, and linguistic differences of what was an incredibly heterogeneous territory. These were differences that could not easily be smoothed over by prescriptive solutions imposed from above; and so at the moment when the Italian Mezzogiorno was first united under the Norman monarchy, the area lacked a strong cultural tradition that might be drawn on in order to unite different populations. Armies may conquer people, but it is only when arms are laid down that populations and territories can be organized and given unity and a recognizable identity.

This chapter will look at how leaders and writers operating during the reigns of Frederick II of Swabia (1194–1250), Charles I of Anjou (1226–85), and Charles II of Anjou (1254–1309) helped to reinforce the role of Naples as the capital of the Kingdom, through researching, strengthening, or even inventing the city's ancient cultural traditions. It will focus primarily on the importance of classical antiquity to one key figure of the period: Manfred of Swabia (1232–66), the illegitimate son of Frederick II, who reorganized the university that his father had founded in the city in 1224, and who supported the translation and the transmission of many ancient texts. At the same time, it will also highlight some distinctive aspects of classical reception in this period, focusing on the 'non-literary' or 'symbolic' reception of authors in contemporary texts, which provide a broader context for the contemporary development of the myth of the writer-magician Virgil—one of the most distinctive and enduring aspects of Naples' classical heritage.

NAPLES AND THE FIRST STATE UNIVERSITY

After Manfred of Swabia was crowned king of Sicily on 11 August 1258, he took it upon himself to reorganize the Kingdom of Naples with great energy and authority.[2] One of his most pressing tasks was the reopening of the *studium*—that is, the institution that we now

---

[2] Not all sources agree on the date of Manfred's coronation. Nicolas of Iamsilla (1726), 583 has the date as 11 August, which was a Sunday. The *Annales Cavenses* (Delle Donne (2011b), 59) say instead that the coronation took place on the feast day

know as the University of Naples. In a letter that can probably be
dated to the spring of 1259, Manfred invited students to come to that
institution, noting that the brilliance of *philosophia*—that 'venerable
mother and teacher of virtues' (*reverenda genetrix et magistra
virtutum*)—had been tarnished by the war that had set the Kingdom
ablaze after the death of his father Frederick II.[3] And he expanded on
his decision in the following way:

> Therefore, we who ardently desire to raise again to her earlier state that
> venerable mother [i.e. philosophy], who rules kings with cautious
> prudence and sustains the dominions with perpetual strength [...]
> have agreed to embellish, with the reopening of the university, the
> Virgilian city of Naples, which was of old a deep well of science and
> an ocean of poetic ingenuity.[4]

This description of the city of Naples is extremely suggestive, but its
seductive phrases need some contextualization—starting with the
references to philosophy and the state of abandon in which that
discipline had been left. The University of Naples was the most
important urban institution of the period, and the first state university (previous higher learning institutions having been under ecclesiastical influence).[5] It had been founded by Frederick II in 1224, but
since then it had suffered various hardships: it had been closed on
several occasions, and in 1252 had even been transferred to Salerno
by Manfred's brother Conrad.[6] The Neapolitan institution may have
remained closed from that point, and its reopening after seven years
would therefore have been an extremely important occasion—one
that would have brought esteem to the city as well as bestowing

---

of S. Lorenzo, which falls on 10 August. On this issue, see Böhmer, Ficker, and
Winkelmann (1881–1901), no. 4670, and Delle Donne (2010b), 513–15.

[3] This document is published in Delle Donne (2010a), 127–9, doc. 19, where it is
also contextualized and dated.

[4] *Nos igitur venerandam matrem ipsam, que sue cautele prudentia regit reges et
fulcit perpetuo robore principatus, ardentes in statum pristinum suscitare [...],
Virgilianam Neapolim urbem, ubi fuit antiquitus scientiarum abissus et pelagus poetice
facultatis, restauratione studii providimus decorandam.* Delle Donne (2010a), 128,
doc. 19.

[5] For the University of Naples as the first state university in history, see
Winkelmann (1880), 12; Hampe (1923), 3 n. 1; Delle Donne (2010a), 9–10.

[6] On events pertaining to the history of the *studium* in the Swabian era, see Arnaldi
(1982); Arnaldi (2005); Violante (2002); Delle Donne (2010a).

prestige on the Kingdom and its sovereign, who was presented as someone who Philosophy herself 'calls and invokes' (*clamat et invocat*) for help in returning from her long and silent exile.[7]

We will return to discuss Manfred's specific invocation of Virgil at the end of this chapter, but the rest of his letter underlines in more than one respect the contemporary importance of classical philosophy and knowledge, which were not only seen as illuminating the mind and soul, but were also perceived as routes to dignity, honour, and riches.[8] When Frederick II had founded the *studium* in 1224, he had hinted at the convenience of the location for scholars of the Kingdom, who were now able to study in a place near to their homes; he had also suggested that these scholars might be favoured by hope and expect 'multiple gifts' (*bona plurima*).[9] In Manfred's text, the motivations for study are made more concrete and precise: we learn that the study of philosophy might lead not only to riches, but also to nobility—a 'nobility of soul' (*nobilitas animi*) comparable to the 'nobility of blood' (*nobilitas sanguinis*) of the princes.[10] To reach such heights, however, this intellectual diligence had to be channelled into the government of the realm.[11]

THE RETURN OF ARISTOTLE

The importance of classical philosophy to Manfred is also attested by a letter that was sent to the teachers at the Paris *studium* (the most

[7] Delle Donne (2010a), 128, doc. 19.

[8] Delle Donne (2010a), 128, doc. 19: *hec est autem illa scientia, que diligentibus eam thesauros aperit et ad divitias pontem facit*; 'this, however, is the science that will yield treasures for those who love it, and build bridges towards riches'. This entire phrase is reused on different occasions, for instance by Peter of Prezza, an imperial notary who will feature later on in this chapter: cf. Müller (1913), 133 and 135, docs. 13 and 15. For numerous examples of the reuse of texts of this type in the environment of the European royal chanceries, see the extensive treatment of Grévin (2008).

[9] Delle Donne (2010a), 86–7, doc. 1.

[10] Similar ideas are expressed in relation to the *studium* in other documents of Conrad IV (son of Frederick II and half-brother of Manfred). Cf. Delle Donne (2010a), 112 and 115, docs. 13 and 14.

[11] On the concept of nobility at the court of Frederick, see Delle Donne (1999). It may have been the new opportunities offered by the politics of Frederick II that led to the reinvigoration of debates about how to define nobility, which was seen as determined by individual virtue, not by birth.

acclaimed centre for the study of philosophy at this time) along with some logical and mathematical treatises of Aristotle and other authors translated from Greek and Arabic into Latin. This letter, which has sometimes been attributed to Frederick II, was in fact certainly written on behalf of Manfred around 1263, and it records a lasting passion for study and knowledge that seems to have been nourished from childhood.[12]

> We do not allow the little time we are able to snatch from family chores to pass in idleness; instead, we dedicate it willingly to the pleasures of reading.[13]

The translated texts that were sent along with the letter give some insight into the type of literature that Manfred himself enjoyed. The characterization of Manfred as philosopher is particularly important when we consider the contrasting emphasis that his father Frederick placed on ancient legal texts, which he regarded as more appropriate and useful topics of study.[14] While Frederick found in law the means for his subjects to serve God and please the sovereign (who was understood to have been chosen by divine will to guide the kingdom and its subjects), for Manfred such functions were reserved for the wisdom (*sapientia*) gained from the study of philosophy (*philosophia*).[15] And he made specific reference to the study of philosophy in the letter sent to the Parisian teachers, in which he noted that his own library also contained texts of Aristotle and other authors writing in Arabic and Greek. The letter states that the translation of these texts into Latin was still 'work in progress', although the careful work of the

---

[12] Cf. Böhmer, Ficker, and Winkelmann (1881–1901), no. 4750; Zinsmaier (1983), no. 4750. The letter may have been drafted for Frederick II first, before being reworked by his son Manfred: note, though, that this hypothesis has been rejected by H. M. Schaller (1986), 103–4. For a thorough treatment of this issue, see Schaller (1956).

[13] *Quidquid tamen temporis de rerum familiarium occupatione decerpimus, transire non patimur otiosum, sed totum in lectionis exercitatione gratuita libenter expendimus.* Delle Donne (2010a), 132, doc. 21.

[14] Delle Donne (2010a), 87–8, doc. 1.

[15] The expression *lex animata in terris* ('living law on earth') was used by Frederick in April 1237: Böhmer (1870), 264, doc. 299. Furthermore, the phrase *iurisprudentia est divinarum atque humanarum rerum notitia*, appears in the Code of Justinian, in *Digestum*, 1.1.10.2 and in *Institutiones*, 1.1.1. On Frederick II's conception of justice, and the connected sacred representation of power, see De Stefano (1952); Kantorowicz (1957), 97–107; Schaller (1974); as well as Delle Donne (2005), 81–3.

translators had permitted the completion of some books, which the sovereign had decided to send to the teachers in Paris.[16] Unfortunately, there is no way of knowing for certain which translations Manfred sent to Paris, but his words suggest that the organization of an active centre of translation from Greek and Arabic at the University of Naples facilitated a new circulation of works of Aristotle—one that was destined to revolutionize the history of Western thought.[17]

POETICA FACULTAS, CLASSICAL RHETORIC, AND THE ARS DICTAMINIS

The discussion of this chapter so far has focused on the value of classical philosophy to Manfred, drawing attention to his role in transmitting some ancient texts connected with that theme. In a sense, these texts reconnected Naples (and her university, where their translations were prepared) to classical antiquity; however, this was not the only reason for Manfred's reference to antiquity in his invitation letter of 1259. There, he referred to Naples *antiquitus* as 'a deep well of science and an ocean of poetic ingenuity'. As we have seen, these *scientiae* may well be identified with classical philosophy, which was relaunched through the translation and circulation of ancient texts. The mention of 'poetic ingenuity', though, points towards another distinctive facet of classical reception in Angevin and Swabian Naples.

Interestingly enough, it does not seem that classical poetry was particularly popular in the thirteenth century, either in the Kingdom of Sicily in general or in the city of Naples in particular. In the historiographical tradition, Frederick II of Swabia has always enjoyed great fame as a man attracted by culture and the *scientiae* but (as

---

[16] Gauthier (1982) provides a thorough study of this issue, and advances the hypothesis that the translations sent by Manfred were not those of Averroes but were perhaps made by other translators who worked at his court, for instance Bartholomew of Messina, or, even more probably, Steven of Messina or John of Dumpno, which were specifically astronomical in focus. For an alternative hypothesis, see Delle Donne (2007b).

[17] On the importance of the discovery of Aristotle and the Thomistic philosophy, see the classic study of Gilson (1965), with further bibliography.

I have argued elsewhere) this is for the most part a mythicization.[18] Certainly, the Swabian Kingdom inherited the emphatic linguistic pluralism of earlier eras, in which Latin and the Vulgate were used in everyday parlance together with Arabic, Greek, Hebrew, German, and Gallo-Roman idioms. However, this did not lead to a literary movement with strong classical characteristics. The work of the so-called Sicilian School of poetry (the 'scuola poetica siciliana') to which the foundation of Italian literature is attributed bears no significant traces of ancient authors, and neither does the work of Latin chroniclers like Richard of San Germano or Nicolas of Iamsilla.[19] It is true that among the historians of the preceding generation there had been Geoffrey Malaterra (end of the eleventh century) and the so-called 'Falcandus' (mid-twelfth century), whose works reveal a fairly recognizable use of Sallust's *Bellum Catilinae* and *Bellum Iugurthinum*.[20] It is also true that in the only surviving codex of the *Liber ad honorem Augusti* by Peter of Eboli (end of the twelfth century) we find visual representations of Virgil, Lucan, and Ovid, who are shown unrolling their works to allow glimpses of the first verses of the *Aeneid*, the *Civil War*, and the *Ars Amatoria* respectively.[21] However, while these illuminations aim to graphically evoke the ancient sources used by the author of the codex, a close reading of the works suggests that this reuse is more 'ideal' than 'real', since the written text itself contains no traces of such classical works.[22] We might also consider the *Historia Destructionis Troiae* by Guido de Columnis, which judging from its Latin title alone would seem to have more direct links with antiquity. In reality, this text is a translation of the *Romance of Troy* (*Roman de Troie*), a French Vulgate version of the fall of Troy by Benoît de

---

[18] See Delle Donne (2012). For a comprehensive treatment of culture at the time of Frederick, see Niese (1912) and De Stefano (1950).

[19] See Garufi (1937–8); Nicolas of Iamsilla (1726). On this last work, which probably dates to the beginning of the fourteenth century, but which was compiled from earlier works, see Delle Donne (2011a).

[20] See Cantarella (1993), 832; D'Angelo (2003), 134–42.

[21] Cf. Kölzer, Stahli, and Becht-Jördens (1994), 35, where c. 95r of codex 120 from the Bern Burgerbibliothek is reproduced. At a later time, another hand added three more verses: under line 1.1 of the *Aeneid* he put l.2.490 of the *Georgics*; under line 1.1 of Ovid's *Ars Amatoria* he put line 3.653 of the same work; under that of Lucan the verse 'Lucanum queras, qui Martis proelia dicet' ('ask Lucan, who will sing of the battles of Mars'), and an extract from the *Disticha Catonis* ii, Prol. 5.

[22] On this text's use of the Old Testament Book of Isaiah and the Sibylline Books rather than the fourth *Eclogue* of Virgil in the representation of the divine birth, see Delle Donne (2005), 37–40.

Sainte-Maure, which mediated between Guido de Columnis and the ancient Greek and Latin sources.[23] In a similar way, Richard of Venosa's elegiac comedy *De Paulino et Polla*, written around 1232, may enter into a genre of texts which return to Plautus and Ovid, but it does not reveal any real or concrete links with those two ancient authors. In this case, the direct models are the Pseudo-Plautine *Querolus* and the elegiac comedies that were produced in west-central France in the twelfth century.[24]

Similar observations can be made of two other distinctive literary genres produced by intellectuals in the area of southern Italy in the thirteenth century: epistolography (the art or practice of writing letters) and the *ars dictaminis* (the art of prose composition), which in that period had become almost exclusively rhetorical in nature.[25] In the case of these texts, which were probably produced in the environment of the Neapolitan University, even ancient authors working in the same genre were not always considered to be essential or unmalleable source material. Although Cicero's works (including the *Rhetorica ad Herennium*, which was attributed to him) were studied in Italy in this period, their author is generally treated as a shadowy tutelary deity, who is cited by name, but whose work itself fails to leave obvious traces on the receiving texts. It also seems that students were more frequently exposed to recent treatises of *ars dictaminis*, which appeared much more relevant to the students' practical goals, insofar as they included examples that functioned as models to imitate and follow.[26]

These treatises were undoubtedly studied alongside collections of letters by the most famous *dictatores* of the period.[27] In this way, the teachers of *dictamen* like Thomas of Capua or Peter de Vinea (an imperial notary who taught at the *studium*) became the main reference points for their contemporaries, often taking the place of Cicero

---

[23] The only edition of the Latin text is that of Griffin (1936). However, there are numerous Vulgate versions including, for instance, the Italian version edited by de Blasi (1986).

[24] Cf. Pittaluga (1986).

[25] On the *ars dictaminis*, see Murphy (1974), 194–268; Camargo (1991). See also Schaller (1980). For the bibliography on this topic, see Murphy (1971); Worstbrock (1989). For a review of studies, see Sivo (1989). A catalogue of texts can be found in Worstbrock, Klaes, and Lutten (1992); a catalogue of manuscripts is in Polak (1993).

[26] On this style of teaching, see Delle Donne (2007c). On the influence of Ciceronian rhetoric in this period, see Ward (1978); Alessio (1979); Reeve (1991).

[27] See e.g. Schaller (1956), 235 ff., where he describes some manuscripts of the letter collection of Peter de Vinea.

and Quintilian: their refined, luxuriant, expressive, and often obscure styles became the models from which it was impossible to depart. Furthermore, it soon becomes clear from reading the letter collections of these *dictatores* that the principal reference texts used by their authors were not classical but rather liturgical. Other works that were drawn on included the Bible, the *Corpus iuris*, Christian texts of a theological nature, and comments on sacred scripture—all of which sit alongside scant traces of classical authors. To understand the situation better, we might turn to a particularly representative letter written by Nicholas of Rocca the Younger. Nicholas was a cleric active in the papal circles, who may have studied the art of rhetoric in Naples and thus received the same teachings as the other *dictatores*.[28] In this letter, Nicholas invites into 'the steadfastness of the faith' the young monarch John of Castrocielo, who was already destined to take up an important position within the ecclesiastic hierarchy.[29] His invitation takes the form of a long theological digression, supported by (often unacknowledged) citations. Some of these citations come from books of the Bible—primarily those that were well known from the Sunday and festive liturgies—as well as other Christian works including those of Prudentius and Bernardus Silvestris. Others come from the work of classical authors, such as Juvenal, Seneca, and above all Ovid. When we look closely at the classical citations, we see the complete decontextualization of the passages used, as well as their frequent 'misinterpretation', in the sense that they are adapted for a meaning that contrasts with the original one. While some phrases of Juvenal and Seneca are quite congruous with the sense of Nicholas's letter, the same cannot be said of the citations of Ovid.[30] For instance, we find the following two couplets cited after the words *iuxta Nasonis quoque sententiam* ('also in the opinion of Ovid'): *est Deus in nobis et sunt commercia celi: | sedibus ethereis spiritus ille venit*, and *est Deus in nobis, agitante calescimus illo, | impetus hic sacre semina mentis habet*.[31] The close juxtaposition of these reused verses raises

---

[28] Delle Donne (2003), 141–4, doc. 120.

[29] On this figure, see Mercantini (2000).

[30] In the first instance, examples can be found in the citations of Juvenal's Satire 15.146 (*sensum a celesti demissum traximus arce*—'we took from the heights of heaven this sensibility'), and Seneca's *Epistle* 4.31.11 (the so-called *tuba moralis*), about a god hosted in a human body (*deum in humano corpore hospitantem*).

[31] Respectively from *Ars amatoria* 3.549–50 ('There is a god in us, and our dealings are with the heavens: | this inspiration comes from ethereal heights') and *Fasti*, 6.5–6

the possibility that Nicholas (perhaps led astray by the similar beginnings of the hexameters) believed that they belonged to the same work. At any rate, one begins to doubt that the verses were read directly from the work of Ovid, and this suspicion may find some support in the fact that they get interpreted by Nicholas as descriptions of a Christian divine power. In fact, in the original text both couplets are used by Ovid to describe the inspiration which guides the process of poetic composition: the first couplet, for the most part, refers to the 'profane' love of women, which in Nicholas's letter becomes confused with the 'sacred' love for God, which the author is attempting to render more solid in the soul of his correspondent.

FLORILEGIA AND THE RECEPTION
OF CLASSICAL TEXTS

This example of Nicholas of Rocca's letter helps us to understand something of the general cultural background of Neapolitan intellectuals in the era and environment under discussion in this chapter.[32] In particular, it shows that these intellectuals often had a classical background, but also indicates the possible use of a *florilegium*—that is, a compilation of excerpts from the works of ancient authors. *Florilegia* were produced and copied in the period that has been defined as the *aetas Ovidiana*; they collected, in more or less alphabetical order, citations that may also have been used in sermons.[33] The use of *florilegia* was common and widely diffused, and they constituted instruments of work that were both accessible and manageable. The *florilegium* functioned as a useful surrogate for the complete work of the *auctores*, which was often not easily available

---

('There is a god in us: when he stirs we kindle, | That impulse sows the seeds of inspiration').

[32] Another comparable example is a love letter attributed to Peter de Vinea, in which every phrase seems to end with a verse taken from the works of Ovid and the elegiac comedy *Pamphilus*: Huillard-Bréholles (1865), 417–21, doc. 104. This letter is contained in only one of the four versions of the collection *Larger in Six Books*.

[33] The use of *florilegia* or perhaps school textbooks is suggested in part by the recurrent citation of certain sententious verses, like the 413 of Horace's *Ars poetica*. On the use of Ovid in the twelfth and thirteenth centuries, see Battaglia (1960). On schoolbooks and medieval teaching cf. Black (2001).

to consult.[34] The classical citations contained within the *florilegia* were often used to embellish a text that strived for elegance, rather like cameos.

Although it is important to draw attention to the existence and use of *florilegia* or schoolbooks at this time, it is certainly not my intention to argue here that the Classics were never read in Naples in this period, or that manuscripts of ancient authors did not exist at the court of the Swabian sovereigns.[35] On the contrary, the chronicler Rolandinus of Padua recounts that Peter de Vinea took inspiration for one of his public orations from a precise and contextualized passage of Ovid.[36] Meanwhile, we also find imperial documents that contain accurate citations from classical authors such as Horace and Juvenal.[37] Two letters by Peter of Prezza, an imperial notary who probably studied in Naples before being exiled to Saxony after the defeats of Manfred and Conradin (in 1266 and 1268 respectively), seem to attest to the fact that some classical texts were sought after and admired in this period. In the first letter, which probably dates to 1248, he addresses an unknown interlocutor in the following way:

> I ask at your discretion, with all the deference I can, that you lend me willingly for some days the book of Titus Livius, if you have it, or other histories of the Romans, which I know for certain that you possess, because, if this thing is possible, I will become even more indebted to you than I already am, and even more devoted, while, thereby, I collect the little flowers of pleasure and obtain some useful fruit of knowledge.[38]

---

[34] Delle Donne (2003), 8 and 62, docs. 2 and 40; Delle Donne (2007a), 154, doc. 144.

[35] See Villa (1997), 333–4, who makes reference to some codices which may have been copied in that environment. However, it is worth bearing in mind that conclusions based exclusively on codicological or art historical analyses are always uncertain.

[36] Fiorese (2004), 198, 4.10. This is the most recent edition of the *Cronica*, with an Italian translation. The lines cited are from Ovid, *Heroides*, 5.7–8. See also Artifoni (1995), 179–80.

[37] Cf. Weiland (1893), 361, doc. 262, on which see Böhmer, Ficker, and Winkelmann (1881–1901) no. 3495, where ll. 180–1 of Horace's *Ars poetica* (*Epistles* 2.3) are cited; as well as Epistle 5.2 of Peter de Vinea, on which see Böhmer, Ficker, and Winkelmann (1881–1901), no. 3768, which ends with a citation from Juvenal 13.208–10.

[38] *Vestram discrecionem . . . rogo propensius, quoad possum, quod librum Titi Livii, si forsan habetis eum vel alias historias Romanorum, quas pro certo comperi vos habere, mihi per dies aliquot hilariter commodetis, quod, si posset esse, propterea*

In the second letter, which probably dates to the same period and which is perhaps addressed to the same interlocutor, we find the following passage:

> I ask for your paternity, with the cordiality that I can, or rather with more cordiality than I can, that you deign to lend me the work of Isidorus on synonyms and etymology, Tullius, Seneca, which I know for sure are found in your monastery, and also other books, above all those authors who with their treatises move freely in the pleasant fields and the flowery meadows of pleasing rhetoric, knowing for sure that they will be sage, as if they were gold or of inestimable value, for your consent.[39]

It is impossible to say for sure to whom these letters were addressed, although the monastery to which Peter refers cannot be far from Parma, where he may at that time have been a prisoner.[40] In any case, a preference is declared for the history of rhetoric, and above all for pleasant stylistic models, from which Peter might perhaps have hoped to take inspiration (and here we should note the pairing in the first letter of *delectatio* and *utilitas*, in which a Horatian influence might be detected).[41] A similar interest also seems to be attested in an exchange of letters that took place in 1281 and 1282 between John of Castrocielo, archbishop of Beneventum, and Steven of S. Giorgio, who would eventually become an influential adviser to the kings of Naples and England, as well as to the pope.[42] These letters regard a manuscript of the letters of Cyprian, which John had brought with him 'from the deepest regions of Emilia' (*de ultimis Emilie partibus*). This work—which was 'magnificent in its gracious eloquence, distinguished for its elegant phrases' (*eloquentia gratiosa magnificum,*

---

fiam de vestro vestrior et devocior de devoto, dum ex hoc et delectacionis flosculos colligam et utilitatis aliquos in scienciam fructus sumam. Müller (1913), 134, doc. 13.

[39] *paternitatem vestram rogo precordialiter, quoad possum, immo precordialius plus quam possim, quatenus Isidorum de synonimis et ethymologiis, Tullium, Senecam, quos in vestro monasterio pro certo comperi reperiri vel aliquos eciam libros alios ex illis precipue, qui suis tractatibus per agros amenos et prata florencia delectantis rhetorice spaciantur, mihi dignemini commodare pro certo scituri, si essent aurei vel inestimabiliter preciosi iuxta vestrum beneplacitum, salvi fient.* Müller (1913), 135, doc. 14.

[40] In Alessio and Villa (1990), 501–2, and Villa (1997), 334–6, it is suggested that the monastery was in Verona. It needs to be underlined that the dating and context of the letters are only hypothetical.

[41] Alessio and Villa (1990), 503–4, put forward the hypothesis that citations from the preamble to the first book of Livy appear in Schminckius (1745), 4–5 para. 7.

[42] Cf. Delle Donne (2004).

elegantia sententiarum illustre)—was apparently so interesting and important that John had wanted to acquire it and take it with him. However, since the codex was written in an ancient script that was difficult to decipher, he asked Steven to recopy it. We do not know if Steven complied with this request, and it is not possible to track down surviving copies of any such manuscript. All the same, these letters clearly show that scholars of the period still gravitated towards rhetorical texts, while John's judgement of Cyprian's prose helps us to understand that his aim in reading Cyprian was ultimately to find inspiration and stylistic examples which he could integrate into one of the many collections of *dictamina* (models of rhetorical epistles), ready to be decontextualized and reused at every available opportunity.

THE TWO FACES OF VIRGIL

This discussion of the various types of engagement with classical literature in the Angevin and Swabian periods suggests that it is not possible to talk of a wholesale 'recovery' of literary memory by Neapolitan intellectuals at this time, or even a simple renewal of these texts' intense appeal for contemporary audiences.[43] Instead, we find the texts of the ancient *auctores* being copied, cut, and reduced to *florilegia*, a treatment that enabled their reuse as peculiar and decontextualized citations, formulae, or rhetorical models. This suggests a literary parallel to the contemporary reuse of ancient columns and other marble *spolia* discussed by Angela Palmentieri in Chapter 7 of this volume, which served to embellish more recent architectural constructions while conferring on them the noble allure and alterity of antiquity. A similar function was served in literary texts by the 'exemplary' mention of an ancient *auctor*. Amongst the authors most frequently mentioned is Cicero, who is often cited by name alone as an example of an insuperable mastery of language and rhetoric, as in the eulogy (*praeconium*) of Nicholas of Rocca the Elder, or that of Peter de Vinea.[44] Cicero's citing by name alone may be due to the fact that

---

[43] This is the hypothesis proposed in Alessio and Villa (1990), 496–506; Villa (1997); Villa (1999); and Villa (2001).

[44] Delle Donne (2003), 6 and 34, docs. 1 and 15.

his works were not read directly, but were rather mediated through other, later texts.[45] But perhaps the best example is Virgil, whose work certainly was read, albeit in a way that produced erroneous, symbolic, and esoteric meanings.[46]

It was undoubtedly well known in this period that Virgil had enjoyed a long stay in Naples and that his tomb was located in the city. Other chapters in this volume mention the corpus of legendary stories that constructed the poet as a tutelary deity—a beneficent magician who was able to protect the population through his powers (cf. in particular Chapter 11 by Harald Hendrix).[47] The first attestation of this fantastic transformation dates from the early Swabian era, when Conrad of Querfurt (chancellor of the emperor Henry VI, father of Frederick II) wrote a letter from Sicily to the prior of the convent of Hildesheim.[48] In this letter of 1194, Conrad stated that Virgil himself had founded Naples and erected the city walls, adding that he had given the Neapolitans a phial containing a *simulacrum* (image) of their city, which would not suffer any damage while the *simulacrum* remained whole. Other miraculous works of Virgil mentioned in Conrad's letter included a bronze horse which stopped the city's real horses from getting worn out, a bronze fly which kept real flies away, an abbatoir in which meat stayed fresh for long periods, an iron gate behind which Virgil had closed all the snakes, the statue of an archer that prevented Vesuvius from erupting, and the baths of Baia and Pozzuoli, whose waters had the power to cure all illnesses.

These stories enjoyed a wide diffusion, as is attested by Gervase of Tilbury's *Otia imperialia*, which was written around 1210 for the emperor Otto IV, and which contained versions of many of the

---

[45] One example may be found in a text written by the imperial notary Henry of Isernia, who had a similiar fate as Peter of Prezza, and who was forced to go into exile in Bohemia, where he was responsible for the diffusion of Swabian *dictamina* and rhetorical teachings coming from Italy. In one of his letters, he cites the book *De bono oratore*, a reference that he may have found in the *Planctus Naturae* of Alain of Lille. Hampe (1910), 70, doc. 1.

[46] It is tempting to draw parallels here with the enigmatic Castel del Monte near Andria in Apulia—the octagonal castle built by Frederick II, in which certain scholars are always inclined to find esoteric and fundamentally erroneous meanings. See Villa (1997), 336–8.

[47] On this issue, see the still-unrivalled study by Comparetti (1941), particularly the second volume, but also Ziolkowski and Putnam (2008).

[48] The letter is transmitted by Arnoldus Lubecensis, see Lappenberg (1869), 193–6.

same stories.[49] However, it is in the fourteenth century that we find the most comprehensive versions of the Virgilian legends, including the problematic *Cronaca di Partenope*.[50] This work, which stands at an important crossroads in the medieval diffusion of that tradition, explains that the Castel dell'Ovo on the island of Megaride owes its name to a magical egg made by Virgil and hidden in its foundations, which would protect the castle from destruction; it records, too, that the aqueducts, fountains, wells, and drains of the city had been made by Virgil; that Virgil had been the one to institute the 'gioco della Carbonara' (a type of warlike game); and that it was again Virgil who had fabricated a copper cicada that squashed all the real cicadas of Naples, as well as other powerful talismans capable of protecting the city. Such legends had an incredibly wide diffusion, and made the historical figure of the poet practically indistinct from the fantastical figure of the magician (famously, when Petrarch was asked by King Robert of Anjou whether he thought that Virgil had made the grotto of Pozzuoli, Petrarch replied sardonically that he had not known that Virgil was a 'stone-breaker').[51]

THE BIRTH OF A (CLASSICAL) CAPITAL

These stories about Virgil had already been formed in the twelfth century, if not earlier: they attest to the existence of a rich folkloric patrimony, and must have helped to fabricate a strong sense of urban identity rooted in the classical past—an identity that was cemented by the foundation of the *studium* and its various reopenings.[52] These stories also take us back full-circle to Manfred's letter of 1259, helping us to understand why the name of the ancient poet was invoked at the moment in which Manfred decided to reopen the *studium* in Naples. Just as Frederick II had used references to the Roman Empire and its culture to justify and legitimate his great power, so Manfred used Naples' classical heritage (and particularly his celebration of the city as Virgilian) to lend support to decisions that had in reality been motivated by a combination of political and economic factors.

---

[49] Binns and Banks (2002), 576–86.
[50] Altamura (1974), 71–83; Kelly (2011), 184–200.
[51] Lo Monaco (1990), 58.   [52] Cf. Vitolo (2006), 36–7.

In fact, the initial choice of Naples as home of the university—the first in history to be founded by a sovereign—is not as obvious and predictable as one might imagine. Certainly, by the Swabian age Naples already had a long pedagogic tradition, having been the home of various academic institutions throughout the medieval period.[53] But at the same time, it was not yet politically and economically important enough to become the capital of the Kingdom, as would happen in the Angevin era. Manfred's father Frederick had justified his choice by referring to the amenity of the site, along with the salubrity of the air, the abundance of 'everything that a student could need', and the affable customs of its inhabitants.[54] These motivations are, however, rather vague, and furthermore draw on standard topoi which can be found in many descriptions of other late-medieval cities. Interestingly, the very same characteristics were attributed to Salerno when the *studium* was transferred there for a brief period in 1252. For instance, letters written by Conrad of Swabia at this time dub Salerno the 'home of studies' (*domus studii*) and 'ancient mother' (*antiqua mater*), using a Virgilian tone that may have been deliberately provocative, given the fact that Naples had rebelled against Conrad.[55]

We might suspect, therefore, that motives other than those admitted by Frederick influenced his choice of location for the university. If Frederick wanted his new *studium* to attract students from all over the Kingdom and Empire (as we know was the case), it had to be located in a central region that was easily accessible. Campania—whose territory, we should remember, did not map onto that of the modern region, but in fact included the southern part of modern Lazio too—was evidently deemed to be suitable in this respect, since it occupied a position on the northern borders of the Kingdom, and also enjoyed a central location on existing trade routes as well as a famously favourable climate. In addition to these geographical and economical reasons, a significant number of functionaries of the imperial chancellery who would later study law at the university

---

[53] For the high medieval period, see Salvioli (1898), 114; De Stefano (1950), 284 n. 7; Riché (1966); Riché (1979), 154–7, 174–9; Riché (1989). See also Alessio (1992). There does not seem to be any evidence for schools in Naples after AD 1000, although they must have existed.

[54] Delle Donne (2010a), 86 and 96, docs. 1 and 4.

[55] Virgil *Aeneid* 3.96: *antiquam exquirite matrem* ('Follow the ancient mother'); Delle Donne (2010a), 113, 115, and 119, docs. 13, 14, and 15.

came from the region of Campania. While before 1212 the notaries of the Swabian chancellery tended to come from Sicily and Puglia, the number of Campanian functionaries increased in the years immediately after this date, and this tendency was only reinforced in later years.[56]

Campania, then, was arguably the most obvious choice of region for the location of the university. But within Campania there were different cities that could contend with Naples for the privilege of becoming the cultural centre of the Kingdom. Among these was Salerno, the home of the ancient and prestigious medical school, as well as Capua, which had produced numerous orators and literary figures—including Peter de Vinea, whose work has already been discussed here. Frederick's ultimate choice of Naples may well be explained with reference to his desire for peace. Naples had been the last city to concede defeat to Roger II (in 1139); since then, it had resisted for three years against the siege of Henry VI, before rebelling against Frederick's move to the party of Otto IV in 1211.[57] It was probably his awareness of Naples' strength and tenacity that motivated Frederick's original choice of Naples instead of Salerno, a city that, in other ways, was perceived to share many of the same characteristics.

At the same time, when Naples rebelled against Conrad in 1252, it was Salerno that was chosen as the temporary seat of the university. And it may have been the competition of Salerno that pushed Manfred, some years later, to celebrate the memory of the Parthenopean city in such a way as to oppose the *Virgiliana urbs* to the *antiqua mater*—that is, by appealing to Naples' classical tradition as a means to justify its renewed political importance. In any case, the decision to reopen the *studium* in Naples was a very fruitful one, both in economic terms (insofar as the growing presence of teachers and scholars attracted commerce and wealth to the city), and from the point of view of cultural development. Certainly, the presence of the university in Naples made the city into one of the most important centres of humanism, thereby enabling the expansion of scholarship from a relatively narrow focus on judicial texts into the areas of the liberal arts, philosophy, and classical texts.[58] At the same time, however, as

---

[56] Schaller (1957), 210, 229, 238, and *passim*.   [57] Cilento (1980), 313.

[58] As attested in the texts of *dictatores* such as Henry of Isernia. On this figure, already mentioned, see H. M. Schaller (1993). For an examination of classical citations

this chapter has shown, the survival of the classical texts in this period seems to have been facilitated, not only by their in-depth study at the university, but also by what we might call their 'non-literary' or even 'symbolic' reception in the form of legends, exemplary mentions, and decontextualized uses to embellish later texts. Such symbolic forms of classical reception nevertheless served to cement and corroborate Neapolitan pride in an identity firmly rooted in classical antiquity, and the construction of lasting cultural memories—possibly fantastic, but certainly ancient.

in his works, see Šváb (1978), 45–50. For a comprehensive overview of Neapolitan culture in the Angevin era, see Sabatini (1975).

9

Naples—A Poets' City

Attitudes towards Statius and Virgil in the Fifteenth Century

Giancarlo Abbamonte

Even today Naples has preserved its fame as a 'City of the Arts' by continuing to inspire poets and musicians. Although from the eighteenth century onwards it was music on which the city's artistic reputation rested, in earlier centuries Naples had been famous for its poetry.[1] Certainly, Naples' early fame as a city of poets has gained much from the fact that the Roman poet Virgil lived and was buried there. As Domenico Comparetti's wonderful volume *Virgilio nel Medioevo* as well as many other scholarly works published over the last century have shown, the poet from Mantua was well known not only in Neapolitan intellectual circles, but also among working-class people, due to the aura of magic which had come to envelop the Roman poet and which rendered his tomb a sacred place.[2] A medieval tradition based on an erroneous interpretation of a passage in Pliny the Elder even claimed that the city of Naples had been handed

[1] I wish to thank Lucia Gualdo Rosa, with whom I discussed the present work. On the tradition of Neapolitan music, see the chapter entitled 'Musikkultur und –Industrie', in Pisani and Siebenmorgen (2009), 371–411.
    [2] See the second volume of Comparetti (1941), entitled *Virgilio nella leggenda popolare*, and Ziolkowski and Putnam (2008), 829–60. For references on Virgil and Naples, see Stok (1993), esp. 231 with n. 1.

over to Virgil by Augustus himself, making him master (*dominus*) of the town.[3]

However, we should not forget that ancient Naples produced another famous Latin poet too—Publius Papinius Statius. Of course, Statius' fame as a Neapolitan citizen cannot be compared to Virgil's, since it neither started as early nor did it reach beyond the circles of the well-educated.[4] Nevertheless, during the 1470s a number of intellectuals who were connected to the so-called Accademia Pontaniana and who were close to the Aragonese court made an attempt to alter the urban poetic canon by putting Statius on a par with, or even above, Virgil. This chapter will discuss several documents that may shed light on this phenomenon, its protagonists and causes.

Over the course of the fifteenth century and the first decades of the sixteenth century, Naples had become home to a thriving humanistic production in Latin. The Aragonese kings at Naples, first and foremost Alfonso the Magnanimous (1443–58), contributed decisively to this recovery of the *studia humanitatis* and encouraged numerous humanists from all over Italy to settle at the court of Naples. These humanists included the Sicilian Antonio Beccadelli, known as 'il Panormita', the Roman Lorenzo Valla, the Ligurians Giacomo Curlo and Bartolomeo Facio, and later the Umbrian Giovanni Gioviano Pontano.[5] Neapolitan humanism was therefore characterized and shaped from the start by such great poets as Panormita, Pontano, Michael Marullus, Sannazaro, and others who sojourned at the Aragonese court.[6] It was these humanists and poets who laid the foundation of Naples as a 'City of Poetry'.

---

[3] See the Preface of the so-called *De rebus Rogerii Siciliae Regis libri IV*, written by Alexander of Telese (died before 1143), now published in Ziolkowski and Putnam (2008), 922–3.

[4] One of the reasons for this delay is certainly the confused and confusing medieval biographical tradition about Statius, which suggested that Toulouse was his home town (on which see further below). A late example of Statius' appreciation in Naples is discussed in Abbamondi (1906). He does not, however, analyse its origins.

[5] See Garin (1966), 161–6, who maintains that Alfonso the Magnanimous, on his arrival in Naples, was struck by Italian humanist culture and thus continued to patronize it. See Cappelli (2007), 278–9 for a collection of more cautious opinions on Alfonso's relationship with humanism.

[6] To appreciate the role that Neapolitan Latin poetry from the Aragonese period played in the 'bigger picture' of Italian Latin poetry of the time, one only needs to consult the long sections on 'Neapolitan' poets in the 1,200 pages of the anthology edited by Arnaldi, Gualdo Rosa, and Monti Sabia (1964), where the poems of

During the reign of Alfonso the Magnanimous (the first Aragonese king to govern Naples) the most illustrious poet at the Naples
court was doubtlessly Panormita (1394–1471).[7] During the long
reign of Ferrante (1458–94) and then under the last Aragonese
kings (1495–1503), humanistic Latin poetry flourished under the
guidance of Ferrante's secretary Giovanni Gioviano Pontano
(1429–1503), who had developed the so-called Accademia Pontaniana (also called the 'Porticus Antoniana' in honour of its founder,
Panormita), a place where humanists gathered to read and study
Latin works. Pontano was followed by Jacopo Sannazaro (1455/
6–1530), whose poetic works in both Latin and Italian were taken
as a model by humanists all over Europe.

The fame of the Latin poets from the Aragonese period was by no
means only local, but spread rapidly throughout the peninsula and,
from here, throughout the rest of Europe, where their poetry was
influential at least until the eighteenth century. Their success is
evident in Lilio Gregorio Giraldi's (1479–1552) *Dialogi de poetis
nostrorum temporum*, which was written in Rome between 1514
and 1515, and which contains one of the first histories of neo-Latin
poetry. In the first of those 'dialogues' Giraldi explicitly points out
that the new Latin poetry has its origin in the works of Giovanni
Pontano and the members of his academy, and he compares the
brilliant poets emerging from this academy with the warriors coming
out of the Trojan horse:

> Pontano produced some famous poets and orators, and this is why
> Pontano's Academy is now commonly called 'a Trojan Horse'. In the
> Academy Sannazaro is now approaching old age – though it may be
> better to say that he is now flourishing! I have read wonderful poems
> that are testimony to his genius [...]. From this same academy of
> Pontano came Michael Marullus and Manilius Rhallus. Both of these
> were born of Greek parents, but were brought up in Italy. They
> were friends and both were more steeped in Latin literature than in
> Greek [...]. Gabriele Altilio came from the same Academy. Although
> I have read little of his work, he nevertheless displays marvelous and

Panormita occupy 28 pages, Pontano's poems 476 pages (307–783), Giovanni
Antonio Campano's works 60 pages, and Sannazaro's works 105 pages (1102–1207).

[7] For background information on Panormita, see Cappelli (2007), 300–4.

outstanding erudition as well as eloquence in the wedding poem that he wrote for Isabella of Aragon, the king's daughter.[8]

During the first decades of the sixteenth century, Sannazaro and many other writers nostalgically celebrated the rebirth of Latin poetry under the Aragonese kings as a golden age of the city of Naples. This poetic sentiment was strongly linked to an evaluation of the new political situation, since the fall of the Aragonese dynasty had led to the city's integration into the Spanish imperial system and the loss of its central role both politically and culturally. As the court of Naples lost its independence, many intellectuals left Naples, thereby casting the city's cultural life into a profound crisis.[9]

Although Pontano, Sannazaro, and the other members of the Accademia Pontaniana were certainly conscious of their own poetry's value, they frequently underlined the connections which linked their works to the two great Latin authors from ancient times, who had, in turn, linked their own names to the city of Naples: Virgil and Statius.[10] Of course, Virgil was not actually Neapolitan by birth, but had been born in the area around Mantua. The reason why he adopted Naples as his 'city of choice' may have been connected to the fact that the area between Herculaneum and Naples boasted the two main schools of his beloved Epicurean philosophy. And it was in Naples that he chose to be buried. Statius, in contrast, had been born in Naples, where he was educated by his father, a well-known master

---

[8] *A Pontano non nulli profluxere tum in poetica, tum in arte dicendi celebres, unde et Pontani Academia nunc vulgo ut Troianus equus dicitur, in qua nunc senescit, ni potius floret Actius Syncerus Sanazarius, cuius ingenii exquisita quaedam monumenta legi [. . .]. Ex eadem Pontani Academia fluxere M. Marullus et Manilius Rhallus ambo parentibus Graecis nati, in Italia enutriti, Latinis tamen literis magis imbuti, atque invicem amici, uterque epigrammatum poeta [. . .]. Ex eadem Academia fuit Gabriel Altilius, cuius licet pauca legerim, in nuptiali tamen carmine in Isabellam Aragoniam regis filiam miram habet et singularem cum eruditionem tum facundiam. Dialogi de poetis nostrorum temporum 1.37–51.* Eng. trans. by Grant (2011), 37–41.

[9] Galasso (1994) and (1995) emphasized the role of Naples in what he termed the 'Spanish imperial system'. However, his conclusions have been partly reconsidered by Musi (1994).

[10] See the last lines of Pontanus' *Actius* in Previtera (1943), 238–9, while Vecce (1998), 71–7 and van Dam (2010), 939, have shed light on Sannazaro's attitude towards Statius' works. For the parallels that Sannazaro draws between his own poetry and that of Virgil, see *Elegia* 9.17–20, while his epigram 1.2 (*Ad villam Mergillinam*) makes use of a type of poetry we are familiar with from Statius' *Silvae* 1.3 and 2.2, which describes and praises the private villas of personal friends.

of rhetoric. Later on he and his father moved to Rome, where Statius achieved his fame as a writer.[11] Nevertheless, Statius never lost touch with his home town, and his bonds with Naples were certainly fostered by some of his patrons, who were aristocratic Neapolitans living in Rome or on the bays of Naples and Pozzuoli. Furthermore, Statius himself frequently points out the links between his own poetry and that of Virgil. Of course, the parallels he draws never amount to any kind of emulation; instead, he contents himself with references to a 'shared Neapolitan experience'.[12] Statius also mentions Naples and its surroundings in a number of those *Silvae* dedicated to his Neapolitan patrons and relatives. At times these references take the form of allusions to geographical places, while at other times he mentions some of the countless myths surrounding this area of the region of Campania which the Romans loved so much.[13]

In short, the biographies of the two poets seem to mirror each other in reverse: Virgil was not born in Naples but chose to live there because the city offered him a peaceful and secluded life (*otium*) and gave him the opportunity to practise Epicurean philosophy and to compose poems. Statius instead was born in Naples, but left the city as a young man and never returned other than for brief visits to his local patrons.[14] His city was Rome, a capital as elegant and exciting as a writer hungry for success could wish for. Only at the end of his life, and perhaps due to his humbling defeat at the Capitoline games (AD 90 or 94), did Statius consider retiring to Naples, as he himself tells us in *Silvae* 3.5, a poem addressed to his wife in which he tries (unsuccessfully, it seems) to persuade her to leave Rome.[15]

The very different imprints that these two poets have left in the Neapolitan cultural memory or *Kulturgeschichte* have undoubtedly

---

[11] See Statius, *Silvae* 5.3, a poem written in memory of his dead father, where Statius mentions the role of the father in his education.

[12] See Nauta (2008), 156.

[13] See Statius, *Silvae* 1.2 (*Epithalamion in Stellam et Violentillam*), and in particular ll. 260–5 on Violentilla and her birthplace, Naples. Cf. the two poems devoted to Pollius Felix, namely *Silvae* 2.2 (*Villa Surrentina Pollii Felicis*), and *Silvae* 3.1 (*Hercules Surrentinus Pollii Felicis*), as well as *Silvae* 3 *Praef.*, where Statius focuses on his patron's *villa Surrentina*, but also mentions Pollius' Neapolitan villa at Posillipo (see e.g. *Silvae* 2.2, ll. 79–82).

[14] See e.g. *Silvae* 2.2, ll. 6–12 about Statius' visit to Pollio at Sorrento.

[15] The date of the quadrennial games, where Statius was defeated, is disputed: see Kytzler (1960), 350.

been influenced by the very different natures of their relationships with Naples, as well as by the diverging paths of transmission that their works took over subsequent centuries. Although Virgil only dedicated a few lines to the city, Naples upheld his memory for centuries.[16] This was a memory that went far beyond his fame as a poet, a memory of almost mystical or magical qualities, which continues to live on in the city's collective consciousness.[17] Statius, instead, takes a very different place in Naples' cultural memory. His fame and his connection with the city never penetrated Neapolitan popular culture, and even his place in the 'ideal gallery of Neapolitan poets' was far from secure until the second half of the fifteenth century. Interestingly, this 'misfortune *in patria*' does not correspond to a widespread cancellation of Statius' memory during the Middle Ages. We must not forget that his *Thebaid* was one of the most well-known and well-read texts throughout the medieval period and that Statius himself was considered an *auctor* of almost equal importance as Virgil.[18]

The air of oblivion which surrounded Statius during the Middle Ages in his own home town was, then, by no means caused by a general decline of his reputation or a lack of appreciation for works like the *Thebaid*.[19] Instead, one of the most important reasons for the city's long and seemingly unmotivated ungratefulness to its gifted son can be found in the medieval tradition of Statius biographies, which confused Statius the poet with Lucius Statius Ursulus, a Gallic rhetorician from the Claudian era who had been born in Toulouse.[20] Naples' interest in Statius was rekindled when his *Silvae*—a collection of verses containing numerous references to Naples as the author's city of origin—were rediscovered in Italy in the second half of the

---

[16] Virgil only mentions Naples (*Parthenope*) in the last lines of the *Georgics* (4.563–6), on which see further below.

[17] Numerous testimonies of this phenomenon have been analysed in Comparetti (1941).

[18] This can be seen in Dante's *Commedia* where Virgil, being a pagan, is forced to leave the traveller at the summit of Purgatory, but entrusts him to the poet Statius who—so one medieval legend has it—converted to Christianity at the hour of his death.

[19] Recently Alfano (2011) has found traces of Statius' *Thebaid* in Boccaccio's Neapolitan works, in particular in the *Teseida*. This is one of the rare testimonies of Statius' continued (if obscure) local presence during the Angevin period. It does not warrant any awareness of his Neapolitan origins.

[20] See e.g. Dante, *Purgatorio* 20.88–90, and a list of passages in Abbamondi (1906), 32–4; Anderson (2009); and Pade (2014). Statius' Neapolitan origins were noted in some MSS of the *Silvae*: see Reeve (1977), 225 with n. 101.

fifteenth century.[21] We might refer here to one of Panormita's epi-
grams presumably written for a statue of Statius which was said to
have been erected in Naples during the Aragonese period as a
reminder of Statius' Neapolitan origins. In this epigram, Panormita
not only rejects Statius' link to Toulouse, but also engages in a
controversial debate with the French, who in Aragonese Naples,
were identified with the loathed Angevin dynasty:

> With this statue is honoured Statius who sang of Thebes and died
> shortly after he had started to sing of Achilles. Naples gave birth to
> him and rejoiced in such a son, although Toulouse may tell the tale that
> he is hers. If vainglorious Gaul should claim that Statius is her poet, go,
> honest reader, and read once more the *Silvae*. Naples itself, fertile
> mother, has brought forth the poet Stella too, so that she may not
> shine through this poet alone.[22]

After Statius' death in *c.* AD 96, the five books of the *Silvae* had
continued to be circulated and read until late antiquity, and had
been taken as a model by poets such as Ausonius, Claudianus,
Paulinus of Nola, and Sidonius Apollinaris. However, after the fall
of the Roman Empire it seems that the *Silvae* gradually disappeared
from the scene. Evidence of their circulation is rare and uncertain
throughout the High Middle Ages; there are some echoes of the work
at Charlemagne's court, while Statius seems to have been forgotten
entirely between the tenth and fourteenth centuries (with the exception of a single document dating from the tenth century).[23]

---

[21] On the description of Naples in Statius' *Silvae*, see Szelest (1972).

[22]
> *Qui cecinit primo Thebas, mox orsus Achillem*
> *occidit, hac colitur Statius in statua.*
> *Hunc genuit tali gavisa Neapolis ortu,*
> *ipsa Tolosa licet blacteret esse suum.*
> *Quod si vana suum contendat Gallia vatem*
> *Silvarum relegas, candide lector, opus.*
> *Hanc eadem peperit Stellam fecunda poetam,*
> *ne sit in hoc uno splendida Parthenope.*

Panormita, *Carm.* 7, in Arnaldi, Rosa, and Sabia (1964), 24. In his study of Statius'
Vitae, Anderson (2009) does not mention Panormita's epigram about the statue of
Statius; the statue is, however, mentioned in van Dam (2010), 937.

[23] For the transmission of the *Silvae* between the second and fourteenth centuries
AD, see Reeve (1977); Courtney (1990), pp. v–ix; Anderson (2009), 65–121; and van
Dam (2010), 933–5. The tenth-century document containing a paraphrase of *Silvae*
2.7 is the MS Florence BML 29.32: see van Dam (2010), 936.

It was Poggio Bracciolini who rediscovered a manuscript containing the *Silvae* during the last years of the Council of Constance (1414–18). It is likely that he came across the manuscript in the area of Lake Constance, although the concrete circumstances of its rediscovery are still unknown.[24] Poggio had the medieval manuscript copied, and this copy has come down to us as MS *Matritensis* 3678, preserved today in the Biblioteca Nacional de España in Madrid. Our knowledge of the *Silvae* depends entirely on this first copy. From Constance, Poggio sent the newly made copy to Italy, where further copies began to circulate only after a couple of decades.[25] These new copies were created by Italian humanists who included their own emendations in an attempt to reconstruct corrupt passages of the text. This was the beginning of a long tradition of *Silvae* exegesis, which naturally took place in Naples, newly rediscovered as Statius' home town.[26]

Thus, while Virgil's memory remained vivid in the area of Naples throughout the Middle Ages, Statius had to wait until the second half of the fifteenth century for his rehabilitation as a Neapolitan poet, when a new era of *Silvae* research was finally launched as a result of Poggio's rediscovery. It is after this rediscovery that we witness in the

---

[24] On Poggio Bracciolini's mysterious discovery of the *Silvae*, see his letter to Francesco Barbaro (November 1417), edited by Clark (1899). Different hypotheses about the date and place of the discovery can be found at Sabbadini (1914), 76–82 (who could not draw any certain conclusion); Reeve (1977), 202 (Switzerland 1417); Reeve (1983), 397–9 (before 6 July 1417, when he announced the discovery of Silius Italicus' *Punica*); van Dam (1984), 10 (St Gall or Reichenau, 1417); Courtney (1990), pp. viii–xi (who does not draw any certain conclusion); van Dam (2010), 939 (who does not draw any certain conclusion).

[25] Niccolò Niccoli kept Poggio's manuscript until 1430, when he returned it to Poggio, who did not part with it again until a later date—either 1453, the year he moved from Rome to Florence, or 1459, the year he died. The first MS of the *Silvae* copied after the *Matritensis* is dated 1463 (Rome). See van Dam (2010), 937.

[26] See Reeve (1977). In the preface to the first printed commentary on the *Silvae*, published in Rome by A. Pannartz (13 August 1475, ISTC 00697000), the humanist Domizio Calderini explicitly underlines the fact that his was the first printed commentary: *Tum incidi in quinque libros sylvarum Statii Papinii, opus granditate heroica sublime, argumento varium, doctrina remotissimum, quod nemo ante aut ausus est aut potuit attingere* ('Then I came across the five books of Statius' *Silvae*, a work of literature elevated in heroic grandeur, the variety of its arguments, and its refined erudition, which none previously had the courage or was able to touch'). In fact, his enemy, the humanist Perotti, had already written a commentary on the *Silvae* around 1472, which is partially preserved in MS Vat. Lat. 6835; see Mercati (1925), 74–84, 156–8, and Abbamonte (1997). On the tradition of the fifteenth-century commentaries on the *Silvae* see Abbamonte (2013), and Coppini (2013).

1470s an attempt by the intellectuals of the Aragonese court to place Virgil and Statius side by side—and even in some ways to substitute Virgil with Statius as the representative of Neapolitan poetry. Such a rehabilitation, which can be traced in works by writers connected with the Aragonese court, fits perfectly within the broader cultural and political programme of the time. Many scholarly works have shown that the Aragonese monarchs chose to surround themselves with Italian humanists and strove to create libraries based on Greek and Latin classics, in order to foster their power both within and beyond Naples. It seems that their aim in doing so was to prove themselves to be culturally equal to other Italian rulers and, at the same time, to distance themselves through the use of the classical heritage from the Gothic-scholastic tradition of the preceding Angevin monarchy.[27]

As far as Naples' cultural memory is concerned, the recovery of intellectual figures from the city's Graeco-Roman past who were some-how connected to local cultural traditions was vital for the creation and fostering of a new cultural identity based on antiquity rather than the Middle Ages. Of course, Statius lent himself perfectly to this purpose, since his Neapolitan origins had remained obscure during the Middle Ages and his *Silvae* had survived 'uncompromised' by the Angevins.

The development of a new poetic production in Latin which took place at the Aragonese court of the time also provoked a new debate about poetry and its genres. Neapolitan humanists began once again to use certain traditional forms such as epic and didactic poetry, as well as the epigram, satire, and Virgilian pastoral poetry, which was also recast in the new form of the *ecloga piscatoria* ('eclogue of fisher-men') inaugurated by Sannazaro.[28] In addition, Giovanni Pontano and the other members of his academy injected new life into the form of Statius' *Silvae* itself—a genre characterized by its eulogistic nature, its quick and casual mode of creation and the poignancy of its form and content. Another reason why the genre of the *silvae* presented a suitable model for the courtly environment and its tastes and demands was the fact that Statius had written the *Silvae* in order to

---

[27] For the literature see Cappelli (2007), 277–304. The bibliography on Aragonese classicism in architecture, sculpture, and manuscript manufacture and illumination is endless.

[28] On Bartolomeo Facio's historical work dedicated to Alfonso and its classical models see Abbamonte (2011).

praise aristocratic patrons. In Neapolitan humanism, certain humanists linked to the Accademia Pontaniana studied Statius' *Silvae* with the intention of adapting some aspects of this ancient work to the context of the modern court. That was one of the reasons, and not the least important, why Statius was regarded as somehow preferable to Virgil.[29]

Unsurprisingly, among the arguments used to promote such a 'substitution' we find appeals to Statius' role as Naples' very own son, which the *Silvae*'s rediscovery had authorized. Apart from the aforementioned epigram by Panormita about Statius' statue, the earliest evidence of this can be found in a letter at the end of a text entitled *De priscorum proprietate verborum*, a lexicographical work in Latin written by the Neapolitan humanist Giuniano Maio (*c*.1430–93) and published in 1475 in Naples in a printed book edited by the author himself.[30] Maio taught at Naples University and was also active as a private educator for a number of aristocratic Neapolitan families, including the royal one.[31] His Latin lexicon enjoyed a certain success, as can be judged from five subsequent reprints outside Naples.[32] In the letter at the end of *De priscorum proprietate verborum*, Maio first sings the praises of the Aragonese dynasty which, according to him, could rightly claim to have brought culture to Naples. He then continues to trace Naples' grand poetic tradition, which reaches all the way back to antiquity:

> We shall not mention all the others, but will pride ourselves only with the help of those who called Naples a learned city. But most of all

---

[29] On the poetry of the *Silvae*, see Nauta (2002), 249–56; on their influence on modern poetry, see van Dam (2010); and, for Spanish culture in particular, Kallendorf and Kallendorf (2000). Naturally, Pontano was indebted to Virgilian poetry for styles and genres, as evident in the *Actius* (a treatise on literary theory). Neither did Pontano undervalue Virgil in his lectures, as Iacono (2005), 31–9, has shown.

[30] Napoli, Mathias Moravus, 1475, H* 10539 IGI 6036 ISTC im00095000. On this incunable, see Fava and Bresciano (1911–12), ii. 92–4, no. 108.

[31] On Giuniano Maio, see Caracciolo Aricò (2006) and Palumbo (2012), 27–31. Documents relating to his life and works were published by Percopo (1894), 111–27, and studied by de Frede (1960), 46–57, and Ricciardi (1968).

[32] Further editions of Maio's work are the following: Treviso, Bernardus de Colonia, 1477, H* 10540 IGI 6037 ISTC im00096000; Treviso, Bartholomaeus Confalonerius, 31.III.1480, HC* 10541 IGI 6038 ISTC im00097000; Venice, Octavianus Scotus, 03.VI.1482, HC 10542 IGI 6039 ISTC im00098000; Venice, Peregrinus de Pasqualibus et Dionysius Bertochus, 8.X.1485, HC* 10543 IGI 6040 ISTC im00099000; Venice, Johannes Rubeus Vercellensis (Giovanni Rosso), 23.II.1490, HC* 10545 IGI 6041 ISTC im00100000.

I believe that we should be proud of this most erudite poet, our compatriot Papinius Statius. He imitated Virgil so well that he was able to fully absorb and reproduce his poetry. What should I tell you of Virgil, this extraordinary pupil of our town and Naples' tenant? Here he spent almost his whole life and wrote the greater part of his most famous works. Thanks to his blessed and almost divine inspiration he surpassed all other poets who ever existed and ever will. Nevertheless he was able to achieve all this due to our city's gentle climate.[33]

The location of this passage in the text—that is, the fact that it was part of a paratextual section that the author could have circulated independently of the *De priscorum proprietate verborum*—gives Maio's words an almost programmatic meaning and force. By inserting the letter at the end of his book, Maio was pointing towards his work's place at the end of a long line of humanistic studies that had been based in Naples ever since antiquity.[34] During his reconstruction of the city's cultural tradition, the author makes a number of loaded choices and provides pieces of information that cannot be considered 'neutral', although from a present-day viewpoint not all of them are immediately perspicuous. For instance, his use of the noun 'Neapolis' and the related adjective 'Neapolitanus' contrasts with the classical poetic tradition, in which the city is usually called 'Parthenope', and in which 'Neapolis' and its related forms are very hard to find.[35] Virgil refers to the city by name only once, in the famous

---

[33] *Nam ut caeteros taceam, gloriabimur plurimorum testimonio qui doctam Neapolim appellarunt, sed magis gloriandum puto ob doctissimum uatem ciuem nostrum Statium Papinium, qui Virgilium ita potuit imitari ut eum totum exhauserit atque effinxerit. Quid de magno nostrae ciuitatis alumno Virgilio, inquilino Neapolitano, dicam, qui hic omne fere euum* [sic] *pleraque clarissima suorum operum lumina scripserit? Qui, quamuis foelici atque diuino prope ingenio omnibus qui fuerunt quique futuri erant praestiterit, multum tamen nostrae Neapolis clementia coeli addere potuit?* (Maio, *De prisc. propr. uerb.*, f. 367v).' Maio's text is quoted according to Ricciardi (1968), 304, who revised the text printed in 1475.

[34] In the previous lines Maio says: *quae quidem gloria propter litterarum studia atque praeclara ingenia quasi hereditaria huic civitati iam pridem parta* ('the glory which the city created for herself many years ago, both for her literary studies and her famous and inspired poets can be called almost innate to her').

[35] *Neapolis* occurs only eleven times in ancient Latin poetry up to late antiquity, while we count forty-four instances of *Parthenope* and its related forms. We might note that Panormita used both *Neapolis* and *Parthenope* in his epigram (see above), whilst Pontano entitled his collection of elegies *Parthenopeus*: see Iacono (1999).

closing lines of his *Georgics*, and here he uses the word *Parthenope*.[36] Statius in his *Silvae* follows this model in nine instances.[37] Nevertheless he does use the name *Neapolis* once, when he says *Nec solum festas secreta Neapolis aras | ambiat* ('And let not Naples only in isolation surround the festal altars').[38]

Unfortunately, we do not have sufficient evidence to know whether Maio's linguistic choice here was a conscious one, or whether he was simply following the custom of the time. But more understandable and certainly deliberate was Maio's choice to begin his discussion of Neapolitan poets with Papinius Statius, whose birth in Naples he is proud to point out. What is more, he praises Statius by saying that his poetry would have been a match for Virgil's—an allusion to the last lines of his *Thebaid*, where Statius himself had already established a relationship between his epic poem and Virgil's *Aeneid*, albeit one that emphasized his inferiority to Virgil.[39] In his brief eulogy, Maio insists on two concepts, that of *gloria* and that of a city which was *docta* and a poet who was *doctus*. These terms are also part of Statius' vocabulary in his *Silvae* and are essential elements of that poetic genre, which was designed to celebrate the (commissioning) patron in the most refined way possible.[40] Maio does mention Virgil immediately after Statius, and calls him 'the pride of Naples': nevertheless, his praise is somewhat lessened by the fact that Virgil appears second—an effect that is

---

[36] *Georgics* 4.563–4: *Illo Vergilium me tempore dulcis alebat | Parthenope studiis florentem ignobilis oti* ('In those days I, Virgil, was nursed by sweet Parthenope, and rejoiced in the arts of inglorious ease'; trans. Fairclough and Goold (1999) 259). The form *Neapolis* can be found in the Ps.-Virgilian *Aetna* 430.

[37] See the occurrences of *Parthenope* in Statius' *Silvae*: 1.2.261, 2.2.84, 2.6.43, 3.1.93 and 152, 3.5.79, 4.4.53, 4.8.3, 5.3.105.

[38] *Nec solum festas secreta Neapolis aras | ambiat. Silvae* 4.8.6–7; Eng. trans. Shackleton Bailey (2003), 295.

[39] See Statius, *Thebaid* 12.810–19.

[40] The attribute *doctus* occurs twenty-four times in the *Silvae*. See e.g. the attribute *docta* when he speaks about the *carmina* of his addressees Stella (*Silvae* 1.2.171–2 and 259), Rutilius Gallicus (1.4.23), Pollius Felix (2.2.97), or those of Lucretius (2.7.76 and 119) and, obviously, of his father Statius the Elder (5.3.156). *Docta* are the Epicurean *otia* of Marcellus (1.3.108), and artists like Myron are *docti* (4.6.25 and 44). Naples is called *docta* in Colum. 10.134 and Mart. 5.78.14. See also Rostagni (1952), 355, who connects the attribute *doctus* to the long-standing tradition of literary games held in Naples since the Augustan age. *Gloria* instead occurs twelve times in various contexts in the *Silvae*.

underlined by Maio's description of Virgil as *inquilinus Neapolita-nus* ('tenant of Naples').[41]

Moreover, Maio also attributes part of Virgil's success to Naples, by insisting that the poet was influenced and inspired by the city's mild climate (*clementia caeli*). This mention of Naples' favourable meteorological conditions was itself part of a tradition going back all the way to antiquity when the area of Campania was particularly loved by Romans for its mild climate.[42] This image may have been suggested to Maio by sources such as Strabo (see Lorenzo Miletti, Chapter 2 of this volume), as well as by Virgil's *Georgics* themselves, where the author speaks about *dulcis Parthenope*.[43] Nevertheless, Maio's use of the noun *clementia* to refer to natural and atmospheric phenomena does not occur in Virgil, nor does it appear in any other writer before Lucan, who was the first to use the expression *clementia caeli* in this way in poetry, albeit in reference to the Far East rather than to Campania. Interestingly, it is Statius who makes constant use of the noun (and its related forms) when talking about a mild climate. In the poem dedicated to Pollius Felix' villa at Sorrento, Statius even uses the adverb *clementius* to refer to the winds of the Bay of Naples:[44]

> Wonderful is the calm of the sea; here the weary waters lay their rage aside and the wild south winds breathe more gently [*clementius*]. Here the headlong tempest bates its daring; the pool lies modest and untroubled, imitating its master's manners.[45]

---

[41] Maio's peculiar definition of Virgil as *inquilinus Neapolitanus* was probably influenced by the malicious expression *inquilinus civis urbis Romae* which occurred as a negative reference to Cicero in Catiline's speech at the Senate house reported by Sallust (see *Cat.* 31.7). The word *inquilinus* was transliterated into Greek by Appian in a passage about Catiline and Cicero (see *Civ.* 2. 2. 5).

[42] On the topos of Campania's weather in the ancient sources, see especially Stärk (1995), but also Rostagni (1952), 346, and Borca (2003), 144.

[43] Erren interprets *dulcis* as a reference to the Siren Parthenope's song, as well as to the pleasantness of his visit: Erren (2003), 1002. There is no hint of this reading in Servius' comment *ad locum*.

[44] The expression occurs only once in Lucan: *emollit gentes clementia caeli* (8.366), while for Statius see *Thebaid* 3.527 (*clementia Nili*), 5.468 (*clementior Auster*), 7.80 (*aestivi clementior aura Lycaei*).

[45]

> *Mira quies pelagi: ponunt hic lassa furorem*
> *aequora, et insani spirant clementius austri;*
> *hic praeceps minus audet hiems, nulloque tumultu*
> *stagna modesta iacent dominique imitantia mores.*

Silvae 2.2.26–9; Eng. trans. Shackleton Bailey (2003), 125. On literary models for these lines, see Szelest (1972).

The poem continues by pointing out that Pollius' villa had favourable effects on its owner's poetic inspiration, thanks to its numerous amenities—including the climate (of course the connection between *ingenium* and a favourable natural environment occurs so frequently in classical literature that it can be considered a topos). And in Statius' famous poem addressed to his wife Claudia, in which the author tries to convince her to move back to Naples, the favourable climate is again one of the arguments used to justify the move. Although the term *clementia* does not itself occur in the lines dedicated to the question of climate, Statius seems to paraphrase it by pointing towards the absence of both excessive heat or cold during the summer and winter months:

> This is the dwelling place (for I was not born in barbarous Thrace or Libya) to which I am trying to bring you, tempered by mild winter and cool summer, washed by the lazy waves of an unwarlike sea. Peace secure is there, the leisure of a quiet life, tranquility undisturbed, sleep that runs its course.[46]

In this way, Maio's words allude to a topos that would certainly have been well known to intellectuals and poets in Naples at the end of the fifteenth century, given that the habit of praising the city's climate was part of a long-standing ancient literary tradition. During the Middle Ages, this tradition had been revived by a legend disseminated through texts such as Peter of Eboli's *De balneis Puteolanis*, which was written at the beginning of the thirteenth century.[47]

One last piece of evidence for Naples' new interest in Statius comes from beyond the kingdom, and shows how widespread this tradition was even in circles quite remote from Naples and the Aragonese court. The humanist Domizio Calderini (1446–78) was the author

---

46

> *Has ego te sedes (nam nec mihi barbara Thrace*
> *nec Libye natale solum) transferre laboro,*
> *quas et mollis hiems et frigida temperat aestas,*
> *quas imbelle fretum torpentibus alluit undis.*
> *Pax secura locis et desidis otia vitae*
> *et numquam turbata quies somnique peracti.*

Silvae 3.5.81–6; Eng. trans. Shackleton Bailey (2003), 231.

[47] According to this legend it was the poet Virgil himself who had founded the famed thermal baths at Baia-Pozzuoli. See Vitolo (2006).

of the first continuous commentary on Statius' *Silvae*, a work printed in Rome in 1475.[48] At the end of the commentary's preface we read a short composition in hendecasyllables dedicated to Francesco d'Aragona (1461–86), son of Ferrante, king of Naples, in which the humanist exhorts Statius to return to his home town:

> Domizio invites Papinius Statius to return to his home town Naples, where he will be welcomed by Francesco d'Aragona, son of King Ferrante.
>
> Until only a little while ago you were unknown in this city: neglected, ragged, and with disorderly hair. Now, groomed once more, you have been restored to your previous looks: brilliant, intact, elegant, clean. What infinite number of kisses will you receive with happy gaze? The nine sisters wish to sit down in your fair woods; here, even Apollo would like to sing with you, Papinius, his Castalian canto. Go quickly now, towards the Euboean Penates where the singing virgin [the Siren Parthenope] rising from her tomb will make known to all the noble name and that of its descendants. There, everybody will welcome you and the earth will strive to make the people's applause resound. Youth will offer you those beverages which it drinks after it has dug them up with its nails and the royal lineage will favour you [. . .]. Once you have become familiar with the costumes, the nature, the grace, and the beauty of the royal family, you will be happy to have been dead for some time, so you could be reborn at this moment.'[49]

---

[48] On Calderini, see Nordera Lunelli and Dunston (1984), and Campanelli (2001). On Calderini's commentary on the *Silvae*, see n. 26 above.

[49] *Domitius hortatur Statium Papinium, ut redeat Neapolim in patriam, ubi ei blandietur Franciscus Aragonius Regis Ferdinandi filii:*

> *Nuper non fueras in urbe notus*
> *incultus, lacer, horridus, retonsus,*
> *nunc vultus reparatus in priores*
> *splendens, integer, elegans, politus.*
> *O quot millia fronte basiorum*
> *gaudenti excipies? Novem sorores*
> *tam laetis cupiant sedere sylvis.*
> *Hic tecum pariter velit, Papini,*
> *Phoebus Castalium novare carmen.*
> *I nunc Euboicos celer penates,*
> *qua surgens tumulo canora virgo*
> *nomen nobile pandit et nepotes.*
> *Illic nam tibi cuncta blandietur*
> *et tellus popularibus sonabit*
> *certans plausibus. Hos dabit iuventus*
> *fossos quae bibit ungula liquores,*

That the poem refers to the *Silvae* is evident from the first lines, in which Calderini alludes to the work's vanishing for centuries and its recent reappearance under mysterious circumstances. With ill-concealed pride Calderini intimates that it was he himself who rendered the text presentable. In the central part of the poem he imagines the poet's triumphant return to his home town, represented by the ancestral gods (*penates*), and his festive reception by the citizens of Naples, including the royal family, while in the poem's final part Calderini underlines Francesco's personal interest in the *Silvae*. The whole composition reveals that even outside the kingdom of Naples—in Roman circles, for instance—other humanists were aware of the strong interest that Neapolitan intellectuals took in Statius and the *Silvae*, as well as the fact that the poet's increased appreciation was seen as connected to the Aragonese dynasty. At the same time, we must note that, apart from the dedicatory poem to Francesco d'Aragona with its clear intention of celebrating his qualities as a ruler, Calderini's commentary pays little attention to Neapolitan elements, or even to those elements related to the general geography of Campania.

From the testimonies of Maio and Calderini, then, it seems clear that the 1470s witnessed a growing interest in Statius amongst Neapolitan intellectuals. The main focus of this interest seems to have been the *Silvae*, which had aroused curiosity not only because of their interesting form as occasional and eulogistic poetry, but also on account of their history of transmission, which had required humanistic emendations. In Maio's writings we also note a reversal of fortunes of Naples' two ancient poets: Statius, who had been hardly visible in Angevin Naples (and then only thanks to his *Thebaid* and *Achilleid*), rises to the top while Virgil, whose memory had remained alive both in popular circles and among intellectuals, starts to lose importance.

These documents also allow us to correct an opinion shared by many modern scholars—that is, that it was Politian (or, more generally, the Florentine humanist circles around Lorenzo de' Medici) who

> *proles regia, te fovebit illa [. . .].*
> *Huius quom bene noveris, Papini,*
> *mores, ingenium, decusque, formae,*
> *tum gratum fuerit perisse quondam.*
> *Huic nunc ut liceat tibi renasci.*

was responsible for the renewal of interest in Statius' *Silvae*. According to this opinion, the revived interest in Statius only reached Naples in the 1480s, when Francesco Pucci, one of Politian's students, started to teach there (1483), with Maio, Sannazaro, and Parrhasius being in his 'audience'.[50]

Even leaving aside the role played by Roman humanists like Pomponius Laetus, Niccolò Perotti, and Calderini who, at the end of the 1460s, had already started to work on the *Silvae*, the writings of Maio and Calderini presented here have demonstrated that Neapolitan humanists connected to the Aragonese court had rediscovered Statius and his *Silvae* well before Pucci's arrival.[51] The context outlined here seems to suggest that Statius' rehabilitation in Naples had already started with Panormita and that it had formed part of Pontano's cultural and political stratagems for depicting the Aragonese court as an important centre of humanist research on a level with other such centres. Unfortunately, no documents (related to Pontano or otherwise) have survived to lend further support to this hypothesis.

The work of the humanist Aulus Ianus Parrhasius (1470–1521) allows us yet another glimpse of the *Silvae*'s changing fortunes under the Aragonese dynasty. The case is particularly significant, because one of the protagonists is Pontano, who was assumed to have played a leading role in Statius' relaunch. Parrhasius, who stayed in Naples between 1491 and 1497, was little more than 20 years old and had just arrived in the city when Pontano invited him to deliver a lecture on the *Silvae* at one of the gatherings at the academy (*c.*1492). A trace of this lecture remains in Parrhasius' *Oratio ad patricios Neapolitanos*, which was probably delivered in front of the academy's members:

---

[50] Politian's role in the *Silvae*'s fortune during the humanistic period is stressed by De Robertis (1988), 519–29, and van Dam (2010), 932–3. On Pucci, see Fera (1995), 452–66. On his influence on Neapolitan humanists, see van Dam (2010), 937. Tuscan influence can be felt instead in another city of the Aragonese kingdom, Cosenza, where a humanist from the Marche, Tideus Acciarini, taught (Parrhasius was one of his students). It is possible that he himself acquainted his students with the *Silvae*, which he could have learned of from his correspondence with Politian. On Tideus Acciarini, see Lo Parco (1916), Praga (1960), and D'Episcopo (1985).

[51] Around 1469–70, Pomponius Laetus wrote an unpublished commentary on the *Silvae*, preserved in MS Vatican Lat. 3875. He also possibly wrote the earlier commentary preserved in MS Rome Vallicelliana C. 95: see Fera (2002), 74, and Accame (2008), 95–6. Politian's commentary on Statius' *Silvae*, ed. Cesarini Martinelli (1978), heavily depends on Calderini's commentary: see Fera (2002), 72–3, and Abbamonte (2003), 146–53.

Now, my noble lords, while I have been everywhere in your wonderful state as part of my duty to visit friends, I was completely unable to take my leave from them after a couple of days, for they claimed to enjoy my company too much. Thereafter they never ceased to tempt me until I, overcome by their ardent requests, promised that I would analyse for them Statius' *Silvae*—not completely but single passages, since he is doubtlessly the most learned of all poets of whom this thriving city may pride itself in front of the whole world, to wherever the fame of the Latin language extends.[52]

In defining Statius as the most *doctus* of ancient poets, Parrhasius makes use of Statius' own vocabulary as well as highlighting once again an image already used by Maio. Both Parrhasius and Maio underline Statius' bond with Naples. Nevertheless, while Maio still mentions Virgil, Parrhasius—perhaps because of his lecture's focus on the *Silvae*—simply crowns Statius the best ancient poet without referring to Virgil at all. Parrhasius' statement also confirms that his audience at the Accademia Pontaniana was more interested in Statius' *Silvae* than in his epic works, a phenomenon to which the attitudes of Maio and (according to Calderini) Francesco d'Aragona testify as well.

In the decades to come Parrhasius did not return to Naples, unless it was for brief visits. Instead, he seems to have drifted between various humanistic centres in northern Italy (Milan, Vicenza, Padua, Venice, and, in the end, Rome) in the hope of finding somewhere to settle down. Nevertheless, he did not relinquish his interest in the *Silvae*, which remained at the heart of his teachings in both Milan and Rome. The most conspicuous evidence for Parrhasius' prolonged interest in the *Silvae* is MS Napoli, BNN, V.D.14, a continuous commentary that was never published, in which Parrhasius' various reflections and musings on the *Silvae* have been brought

---

[52] *At in praesentiarum, viri patritii, cum offitii causa, ut amicos inviseremus, ad vestram rempublicam ornatissimam undique versum me contulissem, ab eisdem post aliquot dies missionem impetrare haudquaquam potui, quod dicerent nostrae consuetudinis iucunditate teneri, nec unquam a me contendere desierunt quousque, assiduis eorum vocibus expugnatus, P. Papini Stati, poetarum oppido quam doctissimi, quem urbs haec florentissima universo terrarum orbi, quocumque Latini nominis fama percrebuit, non iniura queat imputare, Silvarum opus haud omnibus obvium, singulis lectionibus, enodaturum promiserim.* (MS Bibl. Naz. Napoli V.D.15 fos. 27r–28v.) Parrhasius' *Oratio ad Patritios Neapolitanos* is edited by Lo Parco (1899), 119–23, who gave this title to the oration which is untitled in the MS.

together.[53] However, this commentary cannot concern us in the present context. Of course, it constitutes an important testimony of Parrhasius' ongoing interest in Statius, and we cannot deny that he owed much to the Neapolitan humanistic school. However, the manuscript was put together during periods of Parrhasius' life that were spent far from Naples. At most, then, it can testify to the profound cultural crisis suffered by Naples at the beginning of the sixteenth century, when the fall of the Aragonese dynasty and the end of its court caused many of the city's humanists to search for refuge in other Italian regions, where some of them continued to study and comment on the *Silvae* of Statius and, in this way, kept alive the memory of Statius' Neapolitan origins.

---

[53] A list of Parrhasius' documents which refer to Statius' *Silvae* can be found in Abbamonte (2003), 136–46. MS Napoli, BNN, V.D.14 consists of 384 large pages (213 × 315 mm) as well as numerous smaller ones which the author added in various different time periods. On this commentary of Parrhasius, see the dated and unsatisfactory work of Abbamondi (1906). In Abbamonte (2003) I examined the sources of Parrhasius' commentary.

10

Memories from the Subsoil

Discovering Antiquities in Fifteenth-Century Naples and Campania

Bianca de Divitiis

From its foundation in the fifth century BC until the present, the ancient centre of Naples has never been abandoned and the city has continued to build on itself without interruption. In the fifteenth century, the ground underneath Naples already concealed twenty centuries of history and its layers were part of the daily life of its inhabitants. This chapter will focus on how this uninterrupted continuity with the ancient past was drawn on in the second half of the fifteenth century, at a time when the territory of Naples—both its soil and subsoil—was becoming an important source for collections of ancient sculptures, for antiquarian studies, and for the production of works of art and architecture executed in a new *all'antica* style.

The constant interaction between the city's ground and underground levels in this period is already evident from the steady flow of antiquities that surfaced as soon as any excavations began. As is already known for Rome, in Naples too ancient statues and epigraphs emerged from the subsoil during work on building sites or after earthquakes, attracting the attention of noble patrons who subsequently put them on display in their new *all'antica* palaces.

The research leading to these results has received funding from the European Research Council under the European Community's Seventh Framework Programme (FP7/2007–13)/ERC Grant agreement n° 263549; ERC-HistAntArtSI project, Università degli Studi di Napoli Federico II, Principal Investigator Bianca de Divitiis.

On 10 October 1467 an ancient marble milestone inscribed with a dedication in honour of the emperor Trajan was discovered in the ditches along a road from Pozzuoli to Naples. News of this discovery was reported by two direct witnesses of the event, the Florentine merchant Angelo Manetti (who was in Naples at the time), and the humanist Giovanni Pontano, who has appeared in other chapters of this volume.[1] The 'beautiful marble column [...] with two bases' described in Manetti's codex soon entered the collections of the count of Maddaloni, Diomede Carafa (*c.*1406–87), who used it at the entrance of his property near Porta Reale, near the modern Piazza del Gesù.[2]

Diomede Carafa also used ancient finds to adorn his magnificent *all'antica* palace on the *plateia Nidi* (modern Via S. Biagio dei Librai). For example, he obtained an ancient head of Antinous that had appeared amongst the ruins of the Basilica of S. Giovanni Maggiore after the 1456 earthquake.[3] Meanwhile, during building works on the foundations of his own palace, Diomede found an inscription dating to the Roman imperial period that recorded the ancient name of the quarter in which he lived, which he then arranged amongst the other antiquities in his collection (Fig. 10.1).[4]

In those same years Suardino de' Suardi displayed on the facade of his palace the 'larger than life' marble images of the emperors Vespasian and Titus that had been excavated from under his property, which was built on the site of the two ancient theatres of Naples.[5]

---

[1] *CIL* 10.6928. See Codex Magliabechiano 25.62, fo. 141: *Praeclarum divi Traiani monumentum in via quadam Neap. A fossoribus compertum a. 1467 die 10 Oct. atque his litteris in marmorea pulchraque columna conscriptum. Columna vero est altitudinis IIII cum duabus basibus.* Manetti's codex draws on Pontano's now-lost epigraphic sylloge. Pontano himself records the inscription in his treatise on aspiration, without noting the provenance. Pontano, *De aspiratione* (1538), 2.70. On the *De aspiratione* and its relation to Manetti's codex, see Germano (2005), 222–3.

[2] See *CIL* 10.6928. The location of the milestone at the entrance of Diomede Carafa's property is recorded in Giovanni Giocondo's sylloge: *Neapoli in quadam columna extra portam Regalem in porta cuiusdam horti comitis Matalonae.* Fra Giocondo da Verona was in Naples from July 1488 to 1494. Ciapponi (1961), 143–6; Pagliara (2001), 326–38; de Divitiis (forthcoming, a). Diomede Carafa's property near Porta Reale is mentioned in his will: *Item in quodam jardeno cum nonnullis domibus sito et posito extra et prope Neapolim, ubi dicitur ad Porta Reale, iuxta bona Monasterii Sancte Clare de Neapoli, iuxta [...] viam publicam et alios confines.* See Persico (1899), 321.

[3] De Divitiis (2007), 108–9.

[4] *CIL* 10.2609. On the inscription, see Tutini (1644), 28; Romanelli (1815–19), 60; de Divitiis (2007), 101.

[5] The information is recorded in a letter sent from Pietro Summonte to Marc'Antonio Michiel in 1524: 'In le case del signor Annibale di Capua, in le case di messer Soardino de' Suardi si discernono doi teatri, dove sono ancora altri vestigi d'immensa

Fig. 10.1. Inscription from the foundations of the palazzo of Diomede Carafa in Naples.

Source: Museo Nazionale di Napoli (inv. 3214).

Furthermore, the ancient statue representing the river Nile, which is still one of the most important symbols of the city, was unearthed at

fabrica. Qua è stata defossa la imagine marmorea di Vespasiano e di Tito, maior del naturale; e, quantunque qua ci sia adnexa e supraddita molta fabrica moderna, pur, quando sete dentro vi accorgete della verità e di quelli membri antiqui di quelli fornici grandi.' Nicolini (1925), 173–4; Iasiello (2003), 143–4.

the beginning of the sixteenth century in the area of the Seggio of Nido, one of the five meeting places of the Neapolitan nobles at this time, located on the *plateia Nidi* (now S. Biagio dei Librai; for the statue see Fig. 1.1).[6]

Another important record of the great number of antiquities that came to light during building works in this period is the collection of transcriptions of epigraphs compiled by the architect and antiquarian Fra Giocondo da Verona (1433–1515). Of the forty inscriptions recorded during his sojourn in Naples between 1488 and 1494, at least eight are described as being on marble slabs or lead *fistulae* that he had inspected *ex fundamentis*—that is, in the foundations of Neapolitan palaces (to which he may have been called to give his opinion on the finds).[7] Similarly, in 1488, the Florentine architect Giuliano da Sangallo (1443–1516) was called to inspect the torso of an ancient statue which had come to light during works on the palace belonging to the count of Venafro, Scipione Pandone, and to consider its appropriateness as a gift for Lorenzo de' Medici.[8]

Besides such chance discoveries, the contemporary awareness of the ancient treasures concealed in the subsoil (treasures that could be used for purposes of both domestic decoration and humanistic research into the city's past) is demonstrated by the new excavations that were commissioned in the fifteenth century by the elite, in the territory surrounding Naples, and beyond, in the more remote regions of the Kingdom. Again, Diomede Carafa acquired a property in Pozzuoli which yielded antiquities that he could then display in his palace in Naples, and he was also renowned for ordering excavations in other parts of the Kingdom, as demonstrated by the statue of Scipio Africanus from Linternum (modern Lago Patria) and the statue of the

---

[6] The discovery of this statue has been dated to between 1476 and 1507, when the new home of the Seggio of Nido was being built. However, Benedetto di Falco's description of Naples suggests instead that the statue was found in the Seggio when the street was being repaired in 1534: 'Una statua di marmo con una imagine d'una gran donna con molte poppe che lattava molti fantolini novamente ritrovata nel seggio cavandosi la terra per amattonar la strada' (Di Falco (1548), fo. Fv). See de la Ville sur-Yllon (1894); Capasso (1905), 159–61 n. 22; Middione (1993), 23–7. On the building of the Seggio of Nido, see Di Stefano and Santoro (1961–2), 187–92; Di Stefano (1964–5), 12, 16–17.

[7] *CIL* 10.1757, 1764, 2880, 1496, 1947, 3115, 1700, 1900.

[8] Fusco and Corti (2006), 304–5, docs. 93 and 96. De Divitiis (forthcoming, b).

Fig. 10.2. Relief of Mithras killing the bull from the Crypta Neapolitana.
Source: Museo Nazionale di Napoli (inv.6764).

ancient poet Torpilio from the town of Sessa Aurunca.[9] Duke Alfonso of Calabria collected in Castel Capuano some impressive ancient pieces excavated from across the Kingdom, probably with the help of the knowledgeable antiquarian Fra Giocondo. In addition to a relief depicting Mithras killing the bull that had been found in the Crypta Neapolitana in Naples (Fig. 10.2), his princely residence was adorned with several inscriptions that had been found in Pozzuoli, as well as an ancient statue of a nude satyr that had come to light during the works on the castle in Gaeta and a marble calendar excavated in Venosa.[10]

[9] On Diomede's property in Pozzuoli and the statue of Scipio, see de Divitiis (2007), 101. For the statue of Torpilio from Sessa, see Sacco (1640), 89: 'Torpilio Poeta comico, quale havendo consumato il lume di questa presente vita a Sinuessa, gli fu eretta da Sessai suoi compratioti una statua di marmo, con l'epitaffio di sotto, acciò delle sue illustri virtù non andasse in oblio l'onorata memoria. La statua è in Napoli nel palagio del Duca di Maddaloni e dell'epitaffio resta sin'ora un fragmento nella città, fabricato presso il muro dell'antico tempio di S. Silvestro (già profanato) in questa somigliante guida.'

[10] De Divitiis (2013). The relief is now in the National Archaeological Museum in Naples (inv. 6764). Fra Giocondo recorded the inscription on the upper and lower cornices of the relief and reported that it was in *Neapoli apud illustrissimum ducem*

Fig. 10.3. View of the palazzo of Carlo Carafa in Naples.
Source: Photo: Fulvio Lenzo.

And at the end of the fifteenth century, Carlo Carafa built his palace in Naples using the ancient blocks excavated from the so-called temple of Mercury in Nola, which are still visible today in the base that runs along Via Paladino (Fig. 10.3).[11]

As these examples show, the subsoil of Naples and the rest of the *Ager Campanus* teemed with ancient objects as well as entire monuments which, as the Nolan humanist Ambrogio Leone recounts, could even be felt under the feet or detected through the 'swellings' of the soil.[12] But while the excavation of classical antiquities

Calabriae advectum ex Pausillipo. Antonio Augustín reported that the inscription was *in lapide invento in monte Pausilypo, per quem est illa crypta Neapolitana.* See *CIL* 10.1479. Vecce (1998), 59; de Divitiis (2013). On the relief, see Vollkommer (1992), 599, no. 131. For the findings in Gaeta and Venosa see de Divitiis (2013).

[11] A contemporary account of the discovery of the ancient marbles and their transfer to Naples for the construction of the palace is given by Ambrogio Leone and Pietro Summonte. Leone (1514), bk. 1, ch. 8, fo. xiii; cf. Ruggiero (1997), 178–9; Nicolini (1925), 174. On the *De Nola*, see de Divitiis (forthcoming, c).

[12] Throughout his *De Nola* Ambrogio Leone often refers to the *solus extumescens*, that is, the swelling of the soil which concealed antiquities. See e.g. Leone (1514), bk. 1, ch. 8, fo. xii; bk. 2, ch. 14, fo. xxxvi. See Ruggiero (1997), 167 and 178.

contributed to the new physical appearance of the fifteenth-century palaces, another contemporary engagement with the Neapolitan subsoil set up a permanent contact between below and above, between the ancient past and the present. Since antiquity, the subsoil of Naples had been characterized by a dense network of underground paths and spaces, which had been executed at different times and with different aims. Galleries, crypts, aqueducts, cisterns, tombs, and catacombs—whose construction had been enabled by the natural characteristics of a soil composed of yellow tufa and volcanic stones—made the subsoil accessible in many different ways and created a parallel subterranean life in continuous contact with the ground level above.

During the fifteenth century the Neapolitan subsoil was still accessible through the two ancient aqueducts: the Bolla, which collected the springs of Monte Somma and the waters of the river Sebeto and which served the historical centre of Naples, and the Serino, once thought to be the aqueduct of the emperor Claudius, which started from the springs on the plateau in Irpinia before passing through Nola, Acerra, and the northern part of Naples and finally terminating in the monumental *Piscina Mirabilis* in Miseno.[13] Nearly 2 metres high and about 1 metre wide, the tunnels of the aqueducts meandered underneath the whole city, linking large cisterns for the collection of water and creating a subterranean urban network at approximately 14 metres below sea level that was used for centuries (Fig. 10.4).[14] It was thanks to the Bolla aqueduct that Alfonso of Aragon succeeded in conquering Naples after eight years of war against the Angevins in 1442: on the night of 1 June a group of 200 soldiers loyal to the Aragonese party had penetrated the city, which was under siege from the French troops, via the tunnels of the aqueduct, emerging from a well in the courtyard of a house near Porta S. Sofia.[15] The troop was guided by the young Diomede Carafa, who during the operation

[13] On the subsoil of Naples, see Melisurgo (1889); De Stefano (1961). On the two aqueducts, see Elia (1938); Potenza (1996); Montuono (2008); Riccio (2002); De Rosa (2008). This aqueduct was named after the emperor Claudius up until the seventeenth century, although it has now been ascertained that it was built under the emperor Augustus.

[14] Melisurgo (1889); De Stefano (1961), 106.

[15] The event is recounted by Bartolomeus Facius, *De rebus gestis ab Alphonso primo* (1562), bk. 7, 176–80. Belisarius also conquered the city by entering through the aqueduct in 537 (see Giovanni Polara, Chapter 6 in this volume).

Fig. 10.4. Channels of the aqueduct in Naples.
Source: Photo courtesy of *Napoli sotterranea*.

acquired a severe injury that affected his leg permanently.[16] This exceptional episode, which led to the Aragonese conquest of Naples, provides us with evidence that the ancient aqueduct was still in use in the fifteenth century, and demonstrates the importance of the structure for the city—not only for the water supply, but also as a means to access and control urban space.

Both aqueducts had functioned without interruption throughout the centuries, although tumultuous political events and frequent wars had necessitated several restoration works during the medieval period. This was also the case in the fifteenth century. We know from Panormita's work that once Alfonso I had re-established the peace in 1442, he carried out consistent restoration of the subterranean aqueducts, cleaning and rebuilding channels and drains, as

---

[16] Archivio di Stato di Modena, Estero. Carteggio di Principi e Signorie. Napoli e Sicili. Letter of 4 April 1477. See Moores (1971), 3: 'So' stato più de uno mese non ò possuto esir da una camara, con poca freve, ma ebe primo dolore de stena, poi calò a la gamba dove ebbe la ferita quando trasivemo in Napoli; et utanto ad dicta ferita como per tucto g eave curso omore e doglya.'

well as restoring the existing fountains and building new ones.[17] Fifty years later, his nephew Alfonso II had envisaged extending the aqueduct in order to transport water to individual houses, public fountains, and troughs, with the aim of making Naples the cleanest and most splendid city in Europe. As the humanist Pietro Summonte recalls in a 1524 letter to his Venetian friend Marcantonio Michiel, Charles VIII's 'barbarian invasion' of Naples in 1494 prevented Alfonso from accomplishing his plans.[18] Alfonso II's programme of urban improvement as recounted by Summonte reflects the broader urban politics of the Aragonese court, where the maintenance and improvement of the aqueducts had been a matter of central import- ance. During the years of Aragonese rule the aqueducts had become the object of study and research connected to the improvement of the supply of water, as well as to the new antiquarian and humanistic interests. It is not by chance that our most detailed images of the two ancient aqueducts in the fifteenth century come from the work of two humanists. In the sixth book of his *De bello Neapolitano*, Giovanni Pontano offers a very interesting and detailed description of the Bolla aqueduct, which he considers, together with the city walls, to be an 'extraordinary document of a certain ancient magnificence'.[19] Pontano not only mentions that the aqueduct served public wells, fountains, and the palaces of the Neapolitan nobles, but he also explains how the water, flowing 'like a gravelly river through the very wide and not at all rectilinear channels', actually cleaned itself—a process that en- sured Naples received only the purest water.[20] Pontano must have witnessed this process with his own eyes: we know from the later

---

[17] Panormita, *De dictis et factis* (1589): *aquaeductus subterraneos expurgavit ac refecit, veteres fonts instauravit, novos nonnullos extruxit, aquas publicas diu jam magna ex parte dispersas in quae ductus alveum reduxit.* See Vitale (2005).

[18] Nicolini (1925), 171–2.

[19] Pontano, *De bello Neapolitano* (1509), bk. 6, A/3v–A/4r: *Priscae quoque urbis magnificentiae propter ipsa moenia maximo est indicio fluvius intra urbem inductus excavato saxo, in quo vetus urbs tota inerat fundata, eaque cuniculatio atque effossae specus deductae subter maxime celebres urbis vias atque ad singula quadrivia, in quae urbs quondam omnis distribuita erat, excisi putei e quibus vicinia hauriat. Ab hac autem ipsa cuniculatione deducuntur ad alia urbis loca aedesque nobilium aquae tum ad puteorum usum tum etiam fontium in urbis iis partibus quae vergunt ad mare. Ipsa vero cuniculata effossio ductilesque aquarum cavae et latae sunt admodum et decursu minime recto quo dum ad angulos saepius aqua refringitur, reddant salubrior, quo circa et decurrit et strepit sonorum in saxosi modum fluminis antiquum sane opus ac priscae cuiusdam magnificentiae praeclarum testimonium.* See Iacono (2009), 571–2.

[20] Pontano (1509), bk. 6, A/3v–A/4r.

accounts of Giovanni Antonio Summonte that the aqueduct was easily accessible, and included small balconies which allowed viewers to look down onto the flowing water without getting wet.[21] In the treatise *De magnificentia*, Pontano gives a description of the Serino aqueduct, reporting that he had inspected 'the lead pipes of incredible width bearing the name of the emperor Claudius' found between Baia and Pozzuoli. The humanist also describes the spectacular continuous path of the aqueduct, which stretched for 40 miles through a terrain that alternated between ground-level brick structures and underground caves.[22]

Pontano's accounts find echoes in the descriptions given by his friend Ambrogio Leone, another humanist from Nola. In the dialogue *De nobilitate* (1525), Leone gives a brief but detailed description of the Serino aqueduct which, following Pontano, he considers to be a work of the emperor Claudius.[23] Using the aqueduct as an example of the superiority of architecture over the sister arts, the Nolan humanist describes its exceptional extension made of 'uninterrupted brick work and innumerable arches' which, so it seemed from the parts that were still visible, 'never lost their regularity despite the steep and rough

[21] Summonte (1640), 281–2; Hersey (1969), 96.

[22] Pontano, *De magnificentia* (1498), bk. 11: *Memoria mea multis in locis inter Baianas atque Puteolanas reuinas fistulae plumbae mirae crassitudinis inventae sunt, in quibus Claudii Augusti nomen scriptum erat. Vestigia enim ipsa lateritiae substructionis in Sarnensibus, Nolanis atque Acerranis finibus, ac tum subterranei specus, tum montes pluribus locis perforati ostendunt a quadraginta millibus passuum continuatum et quidem amplissimum aquarum ductum, qui Neapolim primo, deinde Puteolos, Baias, Cumas et sparsa per litus aedificia derivatus est.* See Tateo (1999), 186–7.

[23] Leone (1525), ch. 42: *Et in aquae ductibus mirandum quoque huius artis ingenium, praesertim in eo quem Campania ad divum Claudiuum* [sic] *referunt; is enim a Montorio oppido sex millia passuum a Sarno versus Salernum distante fabricatus est; transiens inter Nolam ac radices Vesuvii montis et inter Acerras Neapolimque usque ad Puteolos contendit. Longitudo est circiter triginta millia passuum opere perpetuo et lateritio, cuius canalis supra arcus innumeros tanta iustitia et tenore substructus est, quemadmodum in partibus eius ostenditur, ut nullo in loco eum vel tantulam depressionem eminentiamve contorquere umquam invenietis, quamvis natura loci fere tota inepta et procliviosa sit, quae intra montem aliquando est. Quid non admiremini eos aquaeductus, qui Neapoli adhuc videntur? Nam fere per maximam partem urbis subducuntur, interea per viginti pedes depressi, ubi tam placide quieteque suffluunt aquae, ut per aequatum iustumque alveum se labi arguant. Quod opus miram habet difficultatem atque rationem, neque plures referre opus est, nam plures haberem Romae dicendos, singularem illum veterinum* [sic pro veternum?] *prope Salernum, ubi stupescunt adventantes.*

nature of the site and the presence of mountains'.[24] Leone also describes those parts of the aqueducts that ran underground in Naples, possibly referring to both the tunnels of the Serino aqueduct that crossed the northern part of the ancient centre and those of the Bolla aqueduct, noting, as Pontano had done, the flow of the water. In his final eulogy of the design of the ancient aqueducts, besides mentioning the numerous examples in Rome, he makes an exceptional reference (unique in surviving sources) to the 'notable and ancient' aqueduct in Salerno, which had been built in the tenth century by the Lombard prince Arechi, and which—according to Leone—amazed all those who saw it.

Even if Pontano and Leone had, over time, acquired a profound technical knowledge which enabled them to understand the most complicated aspects of ancient infrastructures, it is possible that their descriptions of the Serino and Bolla aqueducts were the result of inspections made in the company of the architects who were in the city at the time and with whom they were in contact, such as Francesco di Giorgio and Fra Giocondo da Verona.[25] These two architects would have been very interested in the aqueducts, both from an antiquarian point of view and a technical one. The aqueducts presented a rare, unmissable opportunity to see an ancient infrastructure still in use—exceptional ancient source material that could be compared with the ancient text of Vitruvius (on which both Fra Giocondo and Francesco di Giorgio were working during their stay in Naples). In particular, the structure and functioning of the aqueducts would have offered Fra Giocondo the chance to collect structural and visual evidence for his later editions of Vitruvius' *De architectura* (1511) and Frontinus' *De aquaeductibus* (1513).[26]

Apart from admiring the barrel-vaulted channels carved into the tufa banks, the walls in *opus reticulatum*, and the facing in *cocciopesto*, Fra Giocondo and Francesco di Giorgio would almost certainly have

---

[24] See n. 23, above.

[25] For Fra Giocondo da Verona, see n. 3 above. Francesco di Giorgio was in Naples intermittently between 1491 and 1495 to work on the defensive system of the Kingdom of Naples. See Percopo (1997 [1893–5]), 298–304; Hersey (1969), 73–4; Adams (1993), 126–62.

[26] *M. Vitruvius per Iocundum solito castigator factus cum figuris et tabula ut iam legi et intelligi possit* (Venice: Ioannis de Tridino alias Tacuino, 1511). *Vitruvius Iterum (de Architectura) et Frontinus (de Aquaeductibus urbis Romæ) a Iocundo revisi repurgatique quantum ex collatione licuit* (Florence: Philippus de Giunta, 1513).

noticed the redeployment in the aqueducts' channels of ancient sculptural pieces. In his updated edition of Carlo Celano's description of Naples, Giovan Battista Chiarini recounts that the channel of the aqueduct under the *plateia mediana* (the modern Via dei Tribunali) was partly made from marble blocks, amongst which he noted 'a statue of white marble lying prone, of which one could observe an uncovered knee and a pleated dress from the chest to the knees', a Corinthian cornice, the remains of a column, as well as other pieces of which he could only see the unworked rear face.[27] The aqueducts clearly excited Fra Giocondo's antiquarian interests—like Pontano, he inspected the inscriptions carved on the lead *fistulae* in Naples and surrounding areas, transcribing them in his sylloge.[28] When Francesco di Giorgio arrived in Naples he already had plenty of experience of working underground: he had been involved since at least 1469 in the construction of the system of water supply for the city of Siena, where he had developed a way of cleaning the channels and extending the aqueduct by 25 kilometres.[29] The system of self-cleaning water described by Pontano would therefore have provided an interesting ancient precedent for Francesco di Giorgio to study, which would have informed his continued work in Siena (where he kept his title of 'Camerlingo delle acque' even during his stay in the Kingdom of Naples), as well as his work for the Aragonese royals.[30]

Even if we do not have any evidence that directly connects Fra Giocondo and Francesco di Giorgio to work on the Neapolitan aqueducts, it is highly probable that they were involved in the restoration works carried out during the second half of the fifteenth century. We know that the Bolla aqueduct and its secondary branches were lengthened in order to bring water to public fountains, as well as to the many public and private baths in function at the time and to the palaces where water was needed for both domestic use and water games. The capillary water supply in the ancient centre enabled

---

[27] Celano (1692 [1856–60]), 409–14; De Stefano (1961), 106.

[28] *CIL* 10.1496: *Neapoli in domibus D. Fernandi Ianuarii iuxta castrum Capuanum reperti sunt acquaeductus plumbei in ruinis aedificiorum quorundam in quibus scriptum est. CIL* 10.1900: *Neapoli in aquaeductum plumbeo: in quodam vico Puteolano repertum a fossoribus.*

[29] Adams (1993), 126–7.

[30] Francesco di Giorgio's ongoing role as 'Camerlingo delle acque' in Siena emerges from the letters of Alfonso, duke of Calabria to the Balia of Siena sent from Naples in 1492. Gaye (1839–40), i. 317–20.

Diomede Carafa to create in his *all'antica* palace a garden dedicated to the nymphs, where he installed what seems to have been the first recreation of an ancient nympheum in the city.[31] In 1479 a new branch of the aqueduct was designed, which began from the palace of the royal secretary Antonello Petrucci.[32] Between 1487 and 1488, the duke of Calabria (the future Alfonso II) intervened on the Bolla aqueduct so that the two branches into which it divided before reaching Naples would serve his three residences. One branch entered the city and ran underneath the new Porta Capuana: this supplied water to both Castel Capuano (where Alfonso had created a bath and large fountains) and the splendid dwelling of the Duchesca, built in the gardens of the castle, where he created a nympheum with a fountain representing the Siren Parthenope sprinkling water from her breasts, and where the guests were entertained during banquets by sudden floods in the central courtyard.[33] The other branch of the Bolla aqueduct serviced the newly built villa of Poggioreale outside the city walls.[34] As Pietro Summonte pointed out in the letter to Marcantonio Michiel, Fra Giocondo and Francesco di Giorgio were both involved in the building of Poggioreale.[35] In particular, it seems that Fra Giocondo was responsible for the sophisticated hydraulic system, which consisted of small hidden channels that enabled the instant flooding of the courtyard and also of the open columnar *all'antica* space in the garden (later called 'La Venetia') where the duke entertained his guests.[36]

Apart from Poggioreale, both Francesco di Giorgio and Fra Giocondo were involved in the main building and military projects of Ferrante and Alfonso—projects that made a knowledge of the aqueducts indispensable for the development and the security of the city. Alfonso's conquest of Naples in 1442 had demonstrated that the knowledge of the aqueducts and the network of paths was an

---

[31] De Divitiis (2007), 86–90.

[32] In a notary act dated 12 November 1478 the Lombard builder Morilino promised that he would construct an acqueduct between the puteals in the house of Antonello Petrucci and the house of a 'messer Salvatore', which pass through the puteals of several other Neapolitan noble families. Filangieri ((1883–91), vi. 197); Rotolo (2003), 22; de Divitiis (2012), 99–122.

[33] On the Duchesca, see Colombo (1884), 563–4.

[34] De Divitiis (forthcoming, b).

[35] Nicolini (1925), 171–2. See also Fontana (1988), 21–3; Pagliara (2001), 329–30. For an updated bibliography on Poggioreale, see Lenzo (2006a), 271.

[36] Fontana (1988), 35–6; Pagliara (2001), 326–38.

important military secret; therefore, it is highly probable that the supervision and improvement of the aqueducts were duties in which Fra Giocondo and Francesco di Giorgio were involved, and it is possible that they also had a role in Alfonso's project of extending the aqueduct. Furthermore, while exploration of the subsoil channels was essential for an architect who wanted to come into close contact with traditional construction history and local materials such as tufa, lapilli, and pozzolana, it may have also offered them the chance to develop military operations, like the underground mine that Francesco di Giorgio exploded under Castel Nuovo in 1495, when he was trying to stop Charles VIII's invasion.

The interest in the aqueducts and the Neapolitan subsoil in general is also reflected in the humanists' literary work. Pontano's technical description of the Bolla aqueduct was transfigured in the fourth *Pompa* of his first *Eclogue*, where he describes the nymph Labulla and her daughter Formello, an evident reference to the 'Formale reale'—the name used for the section of the aqueduct that went from Poggioreale to Naples.[37] The subterranean journey that Sannazaro describes in his *Arcadia* does not only contain echoes of classical sources, such as Virgil's description of Aristaeus' underworld journey in the fourth book of the *Georgics*, but also traces of years of surveys and study of the Campanian aqueducts as well as wider historiographical problems concerning the subsoil of Naples and of the surrounding territory, such as the position of Pompeii and the path of the ancient river Sebeto.[38] The journey of Sannazaro's alter ego Sincero in the company of the nymph along 'secret ways' (*occolte vie*) and through valleys and mountains seems like a literary transfiguration of a walk in the company of his fellow humanists and architects across the subterranean channels of the aqueduct of the Bolla and along the overground and underground paths of the Serino aqueduct (Fig. 10.5).[39] It is surely not a coincidence that the subterranean journey is part of prose 12, which was added to the initial manuscript of the *Arcadia* in 1492—that is, in the very years in which Fra Giocondo and Francesco di Giorgio were in Naples and in which

---

[37] On Pontano's *Eclogue* and in particular on the *Lepidina*, see Monti Sabia (1973).

[38] Sannazaro, *Prose* 12; Vecce (2013), 289–306. For Aristaeus' underground journey, see Vecce (2013), 9–40.

[39] Sannazaro, *Prose* 12; Vecce (2013), 300–2.

Fig. 10.5. Sincero meets the nymph of the stream who leads him underground back to Naples. Engraving from Francesco Sansovino's edition of *Arcadia* (Venice, 1578).

Sannazaro was in close contact with Pontano.[40] In one passage, Sincero finds himself surrounded by water; he passes from one grotto issuing water to another whose arches were all made of rough pumice stones, with crystal stalactites above and earth floors covered with a fine and thick green; this description reflects the appearance of the real aqueduct as it may still be seen today when walking though 'Napoli sotterranea'.[41] In the literary text, the alternation of narrow tunnels and wide spaces reflects the passages from the channels to the

---

[40] On the dating of *Prose* 12, see Vecce (2013), 33–4.
[41] Sannazaro, *Prose* 12.15–24; see Vecce (2013), 294–6.

cisterns that characterize the Bolla aqueduct below the ancient centre of Naples.

If Sannazaro had walked through the underground of Naples just like Pontano had done, according to the later testimony of Pietro Antonio Lettieri (1560), he also had a direct experience of the Serino aqueduct, fragments of which he had inspected near Palma Campania.[42] The part of Sincero's journey that led from Arcadia (located in the Peloponnese) to Naples via the underground ruins of Pompeii reflects the exceptional length of the Serino aqueduct, which served multiple cities and reached ancient Naples with one of its branches before getting buried underground.[43] By depicting the ancient and mythical river Sebeto as a fluvial god lying in a cave together with two nymphs, Sannazaro offers a poetic transfiguration of a historiographical problem relating to the sources and the original path of the Sebeto, Sincero's 'Neapolitan Tiber'.[44] This river's path had been described by Virgil, Statius, and Columella, but its route was already partially lost in the fourteenth century when Boccaccio and Petrarch had tried to retrace it.[45] The two nymphs of the Sebeto who bring Sincero/Sannazaro out of the cave represent the two branches into which the river divided itself, one leading towards the country and the other leading through a 'secret way for the commodity and ornament of the city'. Here, Sannazaro is evidently demonstrating his knowledge of how the water of the river still flowed outside the eastern walls of Naples in the open air, as well as nourishing the subterranean channels of the Bolla aqueduct.[46] It is not by chance that, after having saluted the nymph representing the Bolla, Sincero ends his

---

[42] Lettieri (1803), 399: *Et me ricordo che me disse più volte il quondam ep. Messer Ciccio de Loffrido che ad tempo che vivea lo Sanazaro il quale fo in Nola per causa dela peste che era in Nap[oli], et quando vedde certi formali che sono nel piano di Palma [Campania]le disse per quelli lo Sebetho flueva in Napoli. Et lo semele me han detto havernolo audito da bocca del pred[etto] Sannazaro, lo venerabile Don Constantio Sebastiano monacho de monte oliveto, che al presente vive; et lo magnifico signor Mario Galeotha.* See Lenzo (forthcoming). For the part of the Roman aqueduct near Palma Campania, see Cosimi (2008).

[43] Sannazaro, *Prose* 12.32; Vecce (2013), 298–9. On the aqueduct in Pompeii, see Ohlig (2001).

[44] Sannazaro, *Prose* 12.37–42; Vecce (2013), 299–300.

[45] Monticello (1830).

[46] Sannazaro, *Prose* 12.46; Vecce (2013), 301. The two branches of the aqueduct were already personified in Pontano's *Lepidina*. See Vecce (2013), 299–300.

subterranean journey across the 'secret ways' by emerging from a fountain where the water 'boiled'.[47]

Apart from the aqueduct, the underground topography with nymphs and divinities described in the journey from Arcadia to Naples also recalls the naturally porous subsoil of Naples and the Phlegraean Fields. Sannazaro's knowledge of the Phlegraean Fields was profound, and he often guided the important guests of the Aragonese court around the area. It is already well known that the humanist went on antiquarian tours in Pozzuoli with Fra Giocondo, and it may also be possible that Sannazaro assisted the other architects who stayed in Naples in their attempts to associate real sites to those mentioned in classical texts. This activity is attested, for example, by the classical and mythological references added by the Tuscan architects Giuliano da Sangallo and Francesco di Giorgio to their surveys of the area.[48]

Full of underground tunnels cut into the soft and compact tufa stone, as well as lakes, mountains of sulphur, and grottoes pouring water—just like the one where Sincero met the personification (or the god) of the Sebeto—the Phlegraean Fields brought together the mythological allure of ancient cults of nymphs and divinities with the therapeutic effects of the ancient thermal baths.[49] Celebrated in the poetical and literary works of Pontano and Sannazaro, the baths between Pozzuoli, Baia, and Miseno were intensely frequented in the fifteenth century by the Neapolitan elite and royals, who were able to enjoy there an authentic experience of *all'antica* bathing.[50] The illuminations of Peter of Eboli's *De balneis Puteolanis* and other works on the baths produced between the medieval period and the end of the fifteenth century show how most baths in the Phlegraean Fields

---

[47] Sannazaro, *Prose* 12; Vecce (2013), 301. According to Carlo Vecce, the fountain where Sannazaro emerged in Naples can be identified with the Fountain of the Sellaria, located near the house of the poet. Vecce (2013), 37.

[48] On Jacopo Sannazaro as guide in the Phlegraean Fields, see Vecce (1998), 60; de Divitiis (forthcoming, a). For Sannazaro's antiquarian surveys in the Phlegraean Fields, see Percopo (1997 [1893–5]), 49; Fontana (1989), 111–12. For Francesco di Giorgio in the Phlegraean Fields, see n. 25, above. For Giuliano da Sangallo, see de Divitiis (forthcoming, b).

[49] Kaufmann (1959); Petrucci (1979).

[50] See Rodney (2006); Putnam (2009). For the use of the baths by the Aragonese royals, see Keller (1973). On Diomede Carafa and the baths of Pozzuoli, see de Divitiis (2010).

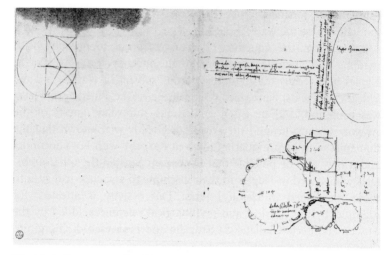

Fig. 10.6. Francesco di Giorgio, Topographical sketch of the 'Lago Chumano'.

Source: Florence, Gabinetto Disegni e Stampe degli Uffizi, U329.

still preserved their original ancient structure within a cave, as well as their original decoration.[51]

A wider interest in the underground structures and in the porosity of the soil of the Phlegraean Fields is testified by the architectural and topographical sketches of Francesco di Giorgio who, apart from drawing a thermal bath under the mountain adjoining Lake Avernus, also surveyed the cistern below Cape Misenum and the so-called Crypt of Cocceius, which connected Lake Avernus with the ancient city of Cuma (Fig. 10.6).[52] Renowned since the time of Strabo, the Crypt of Cocceius was part of a network of ancient tunnels which were still in use and at least partly accessible at the end of the fifteenth century: these included the so-called 'Crypt of the Sybil' that connected Lake Avernus and the *Portus Iulius* on the sea, as well as the

---

[51] Kaufmann (1959).

[52] The relevant drawings are the Uffizi, Gabinetto di Stampe e Disegni, U329 Av; U331 Ar. See Burns (1993), 342–3, 346. On the U329 Av Francesco di Giorgio describes what seems to be the Crypt of Cocceius as a 'cave, that is a street below the Mount Avernus that passes from one side to the other above the lake; approximately a mile and a half long, 14 feet wide and 20 feet high' ('chava hovero strada soto mo(n)te Avernus / pasa da luna banda alaltra sopra a lago / longa cjrca a un mezo mjgljo larga p(piedi) 14 / alita p(iedi) 20').

so-called Roman crypt between the acropolis and the port of Cuma.[53] A similar system of underground paths physically connected the Phlegraean Fields with Naples. In his *De magnificentia*, after having described the 'two famous caves on the Lake Avernus', Pontano himself draws a parallel between the crypts in the Phlegraean Fields and the two ancient tunnels existing in Naples, the so-called Crypta Neapolitana and the Crypt of Sejanus, comparing them on the grounds of their similar nature and their belonging to the same underground network.[54]

The reference to the Neapolitan crypts made in *De magnificentia* finds a parallel in the *De bello Neapolitano*, where Pontano celebrates the 'twin crypts that pierce the mount of Posillipo'.[55] The tunnel of Sejanus had been created to connect the villa of Augustus in Posillipo with Pozzuoli. After describing the tunnel as being 'on the protruding part of the mountain facing the sea', Pontano recounts how at the end of the fifteenth century the crypt was 'for the most part fallen due to its antiquity'.[56] The Crypta Neapolitana was instead 'located along the *via Puteolana* and almost at the beginning of the promontory', and offered an alternative connection between the western side of Naples and Pozzuoli to the longer road that went through the hills (Fig. 10.7). Recalled by ancient authors such as Strabo and Seneca, the crypt had been used throughout the medieval period; according to Pontano, at the end of the fifteenth century it was still an 'admirable structure and convenient for those who travel'.[57] A vivid example of the continuing

---

[53] On the Crypt of Cocceius, see Maiuri (1959); Caputo (2004); Basso (1997).

[54] Pontano (1498), bk. 11: *In agro Cumano et secundum Avernum lacum simili opere duobus in locis nobilissimae extant cryptae, quas vetustas magna ex parte confecit. Quae quidem mirum artificium, ingentes sumptus, magnum publici boni studium prae se ferunt.* Cf. Tateo (1999), 188–9.

[55] Pontano (1509), bk. 6: *Sunt geminae etiam cryptae perforato monte Pausilypo, altera ad viam Puteolanam in ipsoque fere promontorii principio, quae ab Alfonso rege fuit non modice amplificata, altera ad montis in mare prominentiam atque ad ipsius exitum eaque maxima parte ab vetustate labefacta.* See Iacono (2009), 571–2.

[56] Pontano (1498), bk. 11: *Refertur ad Marcum Cocceium (nesciam an is fuerit Marcus Cocceius Nervae Augusti avus, qui Romae aquarum curam habuit, tulitque maximam architecturae laudem), refertur, inquam, ad hunc sive ad alium Cocceium crypta Neapolitana (sic enim ad accolis vocatur), mirum quidem opus et iter facientibus commodum. Extat altera etiam crypta, quae Seiani dicitur, qua parte Pausilypus mons in mare protenditur, cuius transitus ob ruinas impeditus est.* See Tateo (1999), 188–9.

[57] Pontano (1498), bk. 11. See Tateo (1999), 188–9. On Strabo's account of the crypts in Naples and in the Phlegraean Fields, see Lorenzo Miletti, Chapter 2 in this volume.

Fig. 10.7. View of the entrance of the Crypta Neapolitana.
Source: Photo: Bianca de Divitiis.

use of the crypt is offered by a contemporary of Pontano, the Venetian historian Marin Sanudo, who defined it as being 'large enough to allow the passage of four horses in pairs', describing how one needed to 'cross it with lit torches and a real light as there was much obscurity and much dust'.[58]

The first pictorial representation of the crypt appears as one of a small handful of Neapolitan sites on an engraved map of Nolan territory published in 1514 in Ambrogio Leone's *De Nola*, which was produced within the humanistic milieu to which Pontano belonged (Fig. 10.8).[59]

---

[58] Sanudo (1873), 246–1: 'Et mia do lontano de qui è una montagna concavata, longa mezo mio, et larga vi pol andar 4 cavalli a paro, alta meza lanza, et in alcuni luogi una lanza e meza, è di sorte di sasso di tuffo, si va con torza accese e vero lume per essere obscurità et assà polvere: la qual concavità fo fatta, come si dice per Lucullo romano.' See de Divitiis (2011).
[59] Leone (1514). See Lenzo (forthcoming). On the *De Nola*, see de Divitiis (forthcoming, c).

Fig. 10.8. Girolamo Mocetto and Ambrogio Leone, *Detail representing Naples with the Crypta Neapolitana (bottom) from the map of the* Ager Nolanus *in Leone,* De Nola (1514), engraving.
Source: ERC/HistAntArtSI project.

Pontano attributes the execution of the Crypta Neapolitana to an architect called Cocceius, without specifying his first name.[60] This attribution was probably based on Strabo's *Geography* (5.4.5), where the ancient author recalls that Lucius Cocceius Auctus was responsible for creating the crypt on Lake Avernus and the crypt that connected Naples to Pozzuoli. Already in 1484 the Florentine

---

[60] Pontano (1498), bk. 11. See Tateo (1999), 188–9. On the identity of Lucius Cocceius Auctus, see Valeri (2005), 40–1.

humanist Francesco Pucci, chief librarian of the Aragonese royal library, had relied on the *Geography* to prove that the Crypt of Sejanus and the Crypta Neapolitana were works of a Lucius Cocceius Auctus.[61] The architect was already renowned among the humanists as being the creator of the temple of Augustus at Pozzuoli, and it is no coincidence that the humanist Agustinus Tyfernus included the Crypta Neapolitana among the seven wonders of the world after transcribing Lucius Cocceius Auctus' signature on the temple in Pozzuoli.[62]

As Pontano recalled, Alfonso I had notably improved the crypt by 'widening a considerable part'.[63] Commemorated by a marble inscription dating to 1455, the works on the ancient gallery consisted in the widening of the entrance, the lowering of the ground level by approximately 11 metres, and the opening of new shafts for light.[64] We do not know if on this occasion the part of the Serino aqueduct that crossed the hill in a channel parallel to the crypt was also restored. It was possibly during further works on the crypt, or else perhaps during a simple inspection carried out at the end of the century, that Fra Giocondo found the large marble relief of Mithras that was taken away and put on display in the residence of Duke Alfonso of Calabria in Castel Capuano (Fig. 10.2). The discovery of this relief suggested the existence of an ancient Mithraeum in the Crypta Neapolitana, which provided a further example of how the underground cavities of the city may have hosted ancient cults, just like those of the Phlegraean Fields. This is also the case with the so-called caves of Platamone located near the sea, which Sannazaro identifies in his fifth *Piscatory Eclogue* as the *antrum*

---

[61] Francesco Pucci's letter is published by De Marinis (1947–52), ii. 254–5.

[62] Vienna, Österreichische Nationalbibliothek, cod. 3528, fo. 29. *Longitudo crypte Luculliane sub villa Virgili Maro / nis poete, excavata per montem ex solido lapide apud / Neapolim Puteolos versus, sunt passus MC / LX, qui faciunt stadia IX passus XXXV, opus inter / septem mirabilia mundi numerandum.*

[63] Pontano (1498), bk. 11. See Tateo (1999), 188–9.

[64] The inscription was on the right-hand wall of the entrance to the gallery; it bears the royal arms and the name Bruno Risparella (probably the person in charge of the restoration): 'OPVS DOMINI PRVNO RESPARELLE D NAPOLI / SUB ANNO DNO MCCCCLV / SUB REG IHE / NE DNI NRI DNI ALFONSI REGIS VTRIVSQ. SICILIE 2°C.' Another ruined and irregular inscription in front of the tomb of Virgil dated to 1455 apparently recalled an ancient inscription carved after Virgil's death. See Trapp (1984); D'Ovidio (2006), 57–60; D'Ovidio (2012), 329.

sacred to Serapis, and which Pontano also describes as a site of ancient banquets.[65]

Compared to other caves in the area, the Crypta Neapolitana represented an exceptional case of continuous and stratified use from antiquity to the fifteenth century. Between the twelfth and fourteenth centuries, the crypt was connected to the myth and cult of the ancient poet Virgil, whose tomb had been identified in a nearby columbarium.[66] Envisaged at the time as a magician well disposed towards the city, Virgil was recorded in the *Cronaca di Partenope* as being responsible for a series of incredible enterprises, including the perforation of the Posillipo hill with the magnificent tunnel. A trace of the connection between the cult of Virgil and the crypt can be found in a fifteenth-century fresco located in an aedicule at the entrance of the tunnel: this portrays a man with a long white beard, holding the bowl used typically by painters but also by chemists to mix their powders, who can be identified with the ancient poet in the guise of a magician.[67] Even if the legend of Virgil as a magician had faded since Petrarch's visit to the crypt in 1341, the portrait of the poet at the entrance would still have reminded fifteenth-century travellers that the tunnel had once been thought of as the work of Virgil himself.[68] For at least part of the thirteenth century, the 'pagan' cult of Virgil had coexisted in the crypt with the Christian cult of S. Maria dell'Itra, to whom a rock chapel was devoted at the entrance of the tunnel. Elements of this chapel are still recognizable today, including traces of the frescoes and a tufa block (which was probably used as an altar) located next to the portrait of Virgil. Further evidence comes from a votive aedicule cut in the tufa walls on the opposite wall, decorated with painted images of the Virgin and Child, St John the Baptist, and another saint (probably Luke).[69] The rock chapel attracted a notable

---

[65] Sannazaro, *Fifth Piscatory Eclogue* (5.5). See Putnam (2009), 134. Pontano (1509), bk. 6: *Secundum maritimam vero oram quaedam etiamnum visuntur monumenta Luculli piscinarum, qui locus Lucullianus hodie quoque dicitur. Post quem sunt et Platamoniae excavatae ad litus ac manu hominum factae specus, quas vetustas ipsa salsaque maris aspergo magna e parte consumpsit temporum ipsorum iniquitas, loca nimirum ad voluptatem aestivasque deambulationes atque convivia excogitata.* See Iacono (2009), 571–2.

[66] Trapp (1984); D'Ovidio (2012), 338–41.

[67] D'Ovidio (2006), 72–3.

[68] Petrarch, *Itinerarium ad sepulcrum Domini nostri Iesu Cristi ad Iohannem de Mandello*, 37. See D'Ovidio (2012), 336.

[69] D'Ovidio (2006), 65–74.

devotion, and seems to have fallen into disuse only after the restoration works carried out by Alfonso, which lowered the original level of the ground, thereby isolating the chapel under the vaults of the ancient tunnel.[70]

Further underground locations connected to sacred cults of saints could be found in the Neapolitan catacombs, where the later cultural use was associated with the original funerary function. The use of artificial cavities cut into the tufa banks for burial had been a widespread phenomenon between late antiquity and the Middle Ages, when the creation of Christian cemeteries next to the burials of saints led to a further series of underground monuments, whose branches spread throughout the north-western subsoil of Naples.[71] An idea of contemporary perceptions of the catacombs at the end of the fifteenth century comes from a hitherto unnoted account given by the Nolan humanist Ambrogio Leone. While discussing the burial practices of his city of origin, Ambrogio recalls how in Naples, as in Syracuse, 'in the bowels of the mountain and of the earth there was a city of the dead [...] where one goes through tunnels [...] made during the age after the ancient one, although neither in our time nor in the past have people been buried in them'.[72]

At the end of the fifteenth century, then, the Neapolitan catacombs were recognized as one-time cemeteries, no longer used for burial. Leone probably had in mind the catacombs of S. Gaudioso and S. Severo, but he would not have missed the monumental catacombs of S. Gennaro extra Moenia, a vast subsoil complex on two levels used as both a place of worship and as a cemetery (Fig. 10.9).[73] The most venerated of the relics preserved at the site were the bones of S. Gennaro. It was on account of the presence of these bones that bishops and church dignitaries were buried in a *confessio* built above

---

[70] D'Ovidio (2006), 68.   [71] Sanchez (1833).

[72] Leone (1514), bk. 3, ch. 2, fo. xxxxii: *Neque in excavatis in monte verrucave aliqua magnis concameratisque cuniculis quae aliquanto tractu semota sint ab urbe, incavantur sepulcra singulis defunctis, quae sicuti casae longa serie ac sibi haerented ordinatae, tum in dextro tum in laevo cuniculi latere soloque calle, qui in medio est cuniculo relictus, discriminante structa spectantur. Quam orbem in visceribus montis terraeve facta esset veluti civitas defunctorum atque tanquam per vicinias, ita per cuniculos tumulatorum iretur. Quemadmodum aetas quae secuta est illam priscam, fecisse comperta est, utque Neapoli atque Syracusis eiusmodi mortuorum civitates excavatas etiam nunc est cernere, quamquam neque tempestate hac neque longis anteactis temporibus quisque in eis conditus sit.* Cf. Ruggiero (1997), 407–8.

[73] Fasola (1975); Ebanista (2012); Ebanista and Amodio (2008), 118–32.

Fig. 10.9. View of the catacombs of S. Gennaro extra Moenia.
Source: Archivio dell'arte/Luciano Pedicini.

the tomb of the saint, known as the 'Cripta dei Vescovi' after the *clipei* portraits of the first fourteen bishops of Naples that were once painted in the vault.[74] The relics of S. Gennaro were stolen from the catacombs in the ninth century by Sico, the Lombard prince of Benevento; it was not until the year 1497, six centuries later, that the Neapolitan cardinal Oliviero Carafa managed to bring them back to Naples from the monastery of Montevergine near Avellino.[75] In order to provide a permanent resting place for the recovered bones, Olivero commissioned the Succorpo, a magnificent new underground chapel made almost entirely from marble, which was created by excavating 3 metres below the thirteenth-century apse of the cathedral of Naples (Fig. 10.10).[76] The Succorpo was conceived as a *confessio* made in the new *all'antica* style and directly inspired by

[74] Fasola (1975); D'Ovidio (forthcoming a).
[75] Vitale (1989); Norman (1986), 331–7.
[76] Norman (1986), 331–7; Del Pesco (2001); Dreszen (2004); de Divitiis (2007), 170–81.

Fig. 10.10. View of the chapel of the Succorpo in the Cathedral of Naples.
Source: Photo courtesy of Mimmo Iodice.

the catacombs of S. Gennaro extra Moenia. The niches with altars on the side walls of the chapel recall the familiar structure of the *arcosolii* in the tunnels of the catacombs; meanwhile, a specific reference to the figural catalogue of the 'Cripta dei Vescovi' can be found in the half-bust *clipei* portraits of the seven bishops and patron saint of Naples that were sculpted in the marble ceiling of the chapel.[77] Furthermore, Oliviero's ambitious liturgical project of reuniting the relics of the main martyrs of Naples in the lateral altars of the chapel was probably intended to recall the concentration of venerated remains of the underground cemetery.[78]

Twenty years after Oliviero's commission, the porosity of the Neapolitan subsoil, with its caves inhabited by stratified cults, inspired the creation of another new underground structure—the church of S. Maria del Parto that was commissioned by Jacopo

---

[77] Norman (1986), 343.
[78] Norman (1986), 342; de Divitiis (2007), 172.

Fig. 10.11. Giovanni da Nola, *Presepe*, church of S. Maria del Parto in Naples.
Source: Photo: Bianca de Divitiis.

Sannazaro in 1520.[79] Unusually, this church was conceived of as two superimposed cult buildings with distinct dedications and functions. The upper part, which was built against the cliffs of Mergellina and hosted Sannazaro's funerary monument, was dedicated to S. Nazario; meanwhile, the lower part, which was created by excavating an artificial cave in the tufa banks, was dedicated to the Nativity (Fig. 10.11).[80] The lower church seems to have been the fulfilment of a promise to the Virgin to raise an 'altar in the solid rock', made by Sannazaro in a manuscript copy of his *De partu Virginis*. In fulfilment of this vow, a wooden crib was carved by the sculptor Giovanni da Nola in 1524, and placed behind the lower church's main altar.[81] In erecting his burial place in proximity to a grotto, Sannazaro may have wanted to imitate the location of Virgil's tomb near the Crypta Neapolitana; at the same time, the creation of a lower church that was expressly meant for the use of fishermen and that attracted the devotion of pregnant women may reflect the further intention of

---

[79] Croce (1892a); Laschke and Deramaix (1992).
[80] Laschke and Deramaix (1992), 29–31.
[81] Laschke and Deramaix (1992), 29–31.

creating a new underground cult similar to that of Virgil in the Crypta Neapolitana and that of Serapis in the caves of the Platamone, which had just been rediscovered within the Neapolitan humanistic ambience.

The chapel of the Succorpo and the lower church of S. Maria del Parto were thus conceived as magnificent modern 'caves' for the performance of contemporary cults—the revived cult of S. Gennaro and the Nativity. The presence in Naples of old and new underground sites of veneration can thus be set alongside the uninterrupted use of the ancient aqueduct and tunnels, as well as the discovery of ancient sculptures and epigraphs, all of which testify to different fifteenth-century interactions with the Neapolitan underground. Each of the examples discussed in this chapter indicates that the identity of the city in this period was built on a vital and reciprocal relationship between below and above, between past and present. Memories of classical antiquity unearthed from the city's subsoil nourished the humanistic debate in Naples and the antiquarian culture of patrons and architects, and contributed to making the city one of the most active cultural centres in fifteenth-century Europe.

11

City Branding and the Antique

Naples in Early Modern City Guides

Harald Hendrix

This chapter explores the descriptions of Naples and its immediate surroundings that were produced from the early sixteenth century onwards, focusing on how the city's classical heritage was incorporated into a wider process of identity construction. Thanks to these antique resonances, Naples could feature prominently amongst the main attractions in the new phenomenon of the educational tour of Italy as it was propagated from the 1570s onwards by northern humanists like Stephanus Pighius, who in his *Hercules Prodicius*— based on a trip to Italy in 1573–5—praised and promoted Naples as the *Paradisus Italiae*.[1] Visits to Naples and its district even came to typify the exemplary educational trip in one of the first and most influential treatises on early modern travel, Hieronymus Turler's *De peregrinatione et agro Neapolitano libri duo*, published in 1574 and immediately translated into English as *The Traveiler*.[2] Naples also figured prominently in what was to become the foundational text in the rapidly expanding Grand Tour publishing industry, Franciscus Schott's guide to Italy issued for the Holy Year 1600, *Itinerarii Italiae*

---

[1] Pighius (1587), 454. The *Hercules Prodicius* offers a detailed account of the Italian tour undertaken between 1573 and 1575 by the young German prince Charles Frederic of Cleve and his tutor, the Dutch humanist Stephanus Pighius (1520–1604). For Naples and its district, see Pighius (1587), 452–518. On this trip, see Laureys (2000).

[2] Turler (1574); Turler (1575).

rerumq. Romanarum libri tres, which echoes the earlier text by Pighius.[3]

The classical heritage highlighted in the early modern descriptions of Naples, however, was not altogether stable, nor was it undisputed. Although it is beyond doubt that the antique roots of Neapolitan culture dominated and even motivated the numerous city eulogies, descriptions, and guides that were produced from the 1530s onwards (first by Neapolitans themselves, but soon after this by other Italians and even foreigners), it is also clear that attitudes towards this heritage evolved over the years. These shifts occurred partly as the result of the intrinsic dynamism of a recently established genre, where new texts both continued and countered the ones that had preceded them. But they were also motivated by external considerations linked to the political and ideological undertones of the genre of city descriptions and its effect of identity branding, as well as to changing cultural attitudes towards issues such as the significance and interpretation of urban heritage.

This chapter aims to reconstruct and contextualize these shifts in attitudes to the ancient past of the city.[4] A central concern of this analysis is the assessment of the changing balance between an orientation on classical heritage grounded in literary memories on the one hand and archaeological exploration on the other, especially insofar as this corresponds to ambitions to connect the legacy of antiquity with elements in contemporary culture and society. Such a theme arises from one of the first and best-known instances of renewed interest in Naples' classical heritage, Petrarch's visits to the locations associated with Virgil, since these prefigure later practices that would inform the writing of city praises, guides, and descriptions. Petrarch was driven by his admiration for the Latin poet, whom he tried to imitate in forging a literary and intellectual profile of his own in view of his 1341 coronation as poet laureate by King Robert of Anjou. During his two

---

[3] Schott (1600); the *Iter Neapolim versus* is on pp. 340–420. The guide was reprinted twenty-five times before the end of the seventeenth century, with slightly varying titles in various languages and mostly in updated versions. On this commercial success, and the book's indebtedness to Pighius (1587), see De Beer (1942).

[4] This essay details and elaborates on some of the notions presented earlier in Hendrix (2013). While recent scholarship has produced critical editions of some of the texts here discussed, more comprehensive studies are lacking. A general outline of early modern Neapolitan city guides was first presented in a 1992 exhibition at the Neapolitan Palazzo Serra di Cassano; cf. Amirante (1995).

trips to Naples, the poet had visited various locations distinguished by their connections to Virgil or his works: the tunnel at Posillipo, allegedly created by the poet's legendary magical powers (spring 1341), and various places near Baia that he knew from the descriptions given in *Aeneid*, book 6 (autumn 1343).[5] Petrarch's attitude towards the antique resonances of these Neapolitan locations combined sheer admiration based on the authority of classical texts with a more critical stance linked to personal, 'on the spot' observations. He could hardly suppress his emotions while viewing the sites celebrated by his classical forebear (*vidi loca a Virgilio descripta*[6]), but he was not without scepticism and even sarcasm with regard to the alleged magical powers of the poet. Not only was Petrarch unaware of any textual evidence for Virgil's powers as a sorcerer, he was even able to discern traces of edged tools in the tunnel's sides—proof that it had been fabricated by hard work rather than by magic.

When it came to identifying the Latin poet's grave, however, Petrarch's eagerness to forge a personal connection with his admired predecessor seemed to overcome his probing disposition.[7] His reservations about the rather unprecise reports about this site, preserved in earlier texts whose documentary accuracy he considered questionable, were balanced by his own explorations during the 1343 trip and supplemented by the testimonies of some locals he consulted. This enabled him to identify a Roman columbarium near the Piedigrotta entrance to the Posillipo tunnel as being the tomb of his great predecessor, an identification that has maintained authority ever since, despite the fact that its legendary status has long been demonstrated (Fig. 11.1). As of the early sixteenth century, in fact, this identification would become central to the project of Neapolitan identity formation as reflected in the incipient production of city descriptions. It is, however, nothing but a projection of literary memories and associations, which were inscribed into some physical remains of antiquity that were otherwise difficult to document, and which therefore had little independent meaning.

---

[5] Petrarch reports his first visit to Naples much later, when he includes memories of that trip in his *Itinerarium Syriacum* of 1358; cf. Cachey (2002), 27, 49 n. 110, fo. 10r.col.1. Details of his second trip are reported in his *Familiares* 5.4, addressed to Giovanni Colonna; see also *Metricae* 11.7 to Barbato da Sulmona, and *Metricae* 11.15 to Rinaldo da Villafranca.

[6] *Familiares* 5.4.5.

[7] Trapp (1984), 7–10.

Fig. 11.1. Virgil's grave at the Piedigrotta entrance of the Posillipo tunnel. Anonymous engraving, from Scipione Mazzella, *Sito ed antichità della città di Pozzuolo e del suo amenissimo distretto* (1591; Naples, 1606), 199.

This example of Virgil's tomb not only signals the dominance of a literary perspective in the revival of Naples' antique heritage, but also indicates a desire to connect this heritage to contemporary needs and ambitions. Petrarch considered Virgil his alter ego, and wanted to feel close to him in a material as well as a literary sense: this involved visiting the locations where Virgil's presence was most intensely felt, whether this meant his body (as with the legendary tomb) or the places mentioned in his literary works (as with the Baia locations described in the *Aeneid*). Such material closeness to an ancient model had more than a memorial function: it also served to provide new inspiration, urging the 'receiving' poet to compete with this model and surpass it.

A similar kind of Janus-faced view, looking to the past as well as to the present and the future, characterized the growing interest in antiquity at the court of Robert of Anjou, which itself provided the broader context for Petrarch's stay in Naples and his explorations into the city's ancient heritage. On his trips to Virgilian locations, Petrarch was accompanied by King Robert himself (in 1341), as well as by some of his more knowledgeable courtiers, notably Giovanni Barrili (in 1341 and 1343) and Barbato da Sulmona (in 1343), who from that time forth were counted amongst Petrarch's closest friends.[8] It was Barrili in particular who, besides actively promoting the modern re-enactment of the ancient poet laureate ceremony, acted as a well-informed guide to the Virgilian locations, thus demonstrating the Angevin court's ambition to establish a relationship with the city's antique heritage through its interest in Virgil and the sites associated with that poet. This same ambition informed the *Cronaca di Partenope*, which was compiled around 1350 in circles close to the Angevin court. The *Cronaca* was clearly motivated by a new curiosity for the city's antique history, and particularly for the mediating function of a figure like Virgil who—although still primarily interpreted in a legendary key—in this chronicle was firmly established as an emblematic presence capable of connecting past and present.[9]

---

[8] For Barrili and Barbato, see Walter (1964); Campana (1964).

[9] On the *Cronaca di Partenope*, see Kelly (2011). The figure of Virgil dominates chs. 16–32 (Kelly (2011), 182–200); on his grave and the Posillipo tunnel, see Kelly (2011), 192, 195–7. On the rise of an interest in the city's antique heritage at the Angevin court in relation to Petrarch's visits, see Kelly (2011), 52.

It was only a century or so later that this interest in the city's antique heritage was transformed into a fairly systematic project of identity construction. This first occurred in some of the distinguishing habits of self-fashioning developed by the group of late fifteenth- and early sixteenth-century humanists traditionally known as the Accademia Pontaniana. Their example was decisive in inspiring the appearance, from the 1530s onwards, of more or less comprehensive city descriptions and guides, in which what had started as a personal or at most collective project of humanist self-fashioning was turned into a more elaborate scheme of city branding.

Here, as in the case of Petrarch, literary associations were once more essential in fostering a new perspective on Naples' classical heritage. But in their cultivation of such memories, the humanists active at the Aragonese court were keen to exploit the potential of these associations for public as well as private agendas. Characteristic in this regard is the Neapolitan trajectory of an alleged relic of Livy's arm, which was found or produced in the Latin author's native Padua. This relic was brought back to Naples in 1452 by the king's confidant Antonio Beccadelli ('il Panormita') as a diplomatic gift from one of his missions; it then moved from the royal collection to the private estate of Giovanni Pontano (Panormita's friend and his successor as moderator of the learned conversations at court) who interred it in the altar of the private chapel he built in 1490 to commemorate himself and his family.[10]

Pontano's private building projects indeed denote an outspoken ambition to establish an intellectual and personal connection to antique heritage, and to mould his public persona on templates full of classical associations. The architecture of the Cappella Pontano strictly follows Vitruvian principles and is richly adorned with elaborate epigraphical material, alternating antique *spolia* with modern imitations. But in his less monumental and commemorative projects too, Pontano accentuated his interest in classical culture in a manner that may be considered programmatic. In the 1470s he turned a delapidated Roman tower on the Via Nilo—a gift from his patron King Ferrante—into a private dwelling known as the Palazzo dell'-Arco, where he hosted the erudite conversations of his circle of humanist friends, the Accademia Pontaniana. In these same years

---

[10] On this episode see Bentley (1987), 131; Filangieri di Candida (1926).

he acquired a garden on the Vomero hill, along the ancient road that connected the city to Pozzuoli (the Roman *Via Puteolanis per colles*), which he turned into his Villa Antiniana, thereby associating it with the mythical nymph Antiniana.[11]

While Pontano's uses of the classical past—which included evocations of Vitruvian principles, antique itineraries, and classical mythology—remained rather generic, in the later case of Iacopo Sannazaro (Pontano's friend and successor in the Academy) these references gained a more specifically local character. When in 1499 his generous patron King Federico offered him the means to build a villa, Sannazaro selected a location on the seashore near Posillipo that not only commanded associations with mythological nymphs—in this case Mergellina, another nymph who was well known locally— but also evoked a direct and very material connection to the prestigious Virgilian heritage materialized in the nearby tomb at the entrance to the Piedigrotta tunnel.[12] Sannazaro did not hide his desire to mould his own poetic persona on that of his venerated forebear, erecting his own sepulchral monument in a chapel on this estate in the immediate vicinity of Virgil's legendary grave.[13] This merging of the identities of the modern and the classical poet was later eloquently epitomized in the epitaph dictated by Pietro Bembo after the poet's death in 1530: *Da sacro cineris flores: hic ille Maroni Sincerus Musa proximus ut tumulo* ('Bring flowers to the holy ashes: here lies Sincerus [Sannazaro], close to Maro [Virgil] in his grave as in his art') (Fig. 11.2).

The steadily increasing engagement with Naples' classical heritage that we observe in the circles of the local Accademia Pontaniana from its earliest beginnings at the time of Panormita to its later phase under Sannazaro can be seen as dominated and driven by a project of contemporary identity construction.[14] In this period, engagements with the material heritage of the city were motivated by indications given in literary texts, rather than by antiquarian or archaeological approaches. Cultural memories based on the contents of classical texts (both fictional and non-fictional) were projected onto the

---

[11] On Pontano's villa see Percopo (1921); Kidwell (1991), 104–7, 130–1, 215–17.

[12] The building history of Sannazaro's villa is documented in Percopo (1931), 132–7, 194–5. See also Divenuto (2009).

[13] On this chapel, see Carrella (2000), as well as Deramaix and Laschke (1992) and Addesso (2005).

[14] On the Accademia Pontaniana and its locations, cf. Furstenberg-Levi (2006).

Fig. 11.2. Sannazaro's grave and sepulchral monument, S. Maria del Parto, in Pompeo Sarnelli's *Guida de' forestieri curiosi di vedere e d'intendere le cose più notabili della Regal Città di Napoli e del suo amenissimo distretto* (Naples, 1685), *ante 334.*

material remains of antiquity. This led to techniques of labelling and appropriation that were intrinsically symbolic, and which aimed to give lustre to contemporary realities—whether individual identities (as in the cases of Pontano and Sannazaro) or the urban identity of the city of Naples itself.

Such a symbolic reading of the city and its surroundings is indeed paramount in what may be considered its first modern chorographical description, Ioan Berardino Fuscano's *Le stanze del Fuscano sovra la bellezza di Napoli*, published in 1531. This poetic text explicitly aimed at praising the city through a description of what it called 'l'amenissimo sito napoletano', echoing a well-coined phrase from Sannazaro's recent *Arcadia*.[15] In his two books of stanzas, Fuscano offered a highly literary view of Naples, which was closely related to and indeed grounded in the ideas elaborated by Sannazaro and his circle.[16] The text describes a one-day itinerary of two friends, Philologo and Alpitio, whose names denote the allegorical nature of their enterprise from its very start. They cross the city from east to west (without, however, giving any details on the specific locations visited), heading for what turns out to be the ultimate goal of their journey— the Posillipo hill, which as a result of Sannazaro's endeavours is considered 'the temple of the sacred Mergellina'.[17] In book 2, the friends participate in a festive ritual on this hill, which is promoted by a group of nymphs and attended by a large number of contemporary Neapolitan poets, all of whom were close to the Accademia Pontaniana. This solemn feast intends to celebrate poetry in a location that epitomizes artistic creation: Virgil's grave close to the Piedigrotta tunnel, the only spot that the poem describes with a certain amount of precision, albeit still in a highly allegorical vocabulary appropriate for evoking the metaphysical processes of inspiration and creation that happened there.[18]

---

[15] *Arcadia* 11.2: 'Udendo ragionare de l'amenissimo sito del mio paese'.

[16] Fuscano (1531), now also available in the critical edition by C. A. Addesso (2007).

[17] Addesso (2007), 44–5 (book 1, 100–1): 'ti astringo a venir meco a quell'aprica | piaggia vicin, che Pausilippo è detta, | sol per diporto de le ninfe eletta. || Iv'è quella minuta et ricc'arena | ch'in vago giro il mar Tireno lava, | ivi sovente s'ode la sirena| in qualche scoglio, o in qualche grotta cava, | ivi sta mia foresta tutta piena| d'arbor, ch'Apollo et Citerea ne ornava| il tempio de la sacra Mergellina, | ch'or gode al tremolar de la marina.'

[18] Addesso (2007), 72 (book 2, 76–7): 'Eran le ninfe giunte a un picciol piano,| ch'a due a due venian con lenti passi, |dov'era un spatio, più ch'uom trae con mano, | d'una valletta fra duo poggi bassi. | Ivi un vestigio, come d'alcun fano| che mostr'antiquità,

In identifying what distinguished Naples as a city, Fuscano focused on its great men of letters, following both a widespread convention of *uomini illustri* historiography and Pontano's and Sannazaro's lessons in connecting modern poets to their antique models. Hence the rare concrete ingredients present in Fuscano's praise of the city relate to the only place where this carefully constructed connection between classical and modern culture materializes: the 'new Parnassus' of the Posillipo hill. While designating this specific location as an iconic place of Neapolitan urban identity, Fuscano was clearly voicing a sentiment that was shared more widely by his near-contemporaries. Such a sentiment is testified, for instance, in the oldest known carto-graphic representation of Naples, which gives a factual rather than a symbolic survey of the geographical situation: an image of the erup-tion of Monte Nuovo engraved shortly after this dramatic event in September 1538. The remarkable *Vero disegnio in sul propio luogho ritratto del infelice paese di Posuolo* shows a panoramic map of the Gulf of Naples, naturally focused on the Pozzuoli section where an explosion created this new mountain while destroying the small village of Tripergola (Fig. 11.3).[19] But alongside the obvious geo-graphical indications (Baia, Solfatara, Bagni, Lake Agnano), it also shows the iconic places that the men of letters in and around the Accademia Pontaniana had successfully constructed as *lieux de mém-oire* of Neapolitan urban identity: Virgil's grave, the Piedigrotta tunnel ('La Grotta'), and Sannazaro's villa at the Mergellina seaside.[20]

This labelling of Posillipo and by extension Naples as a place where antique and modern cultures met and mingled would indeed prove a lasting success, well beyond the circles of the Accademia Pontaniana where it had originated. It can be found in virtually all city descrip-tions of Naples up until the end of the seventeenth century, where it

solingo stassi, | d'arbori cinto et sempre esposto al sole, | pien tutto di ligustri et di vïole. || In mezzo v'era un'alta pino annosa, | la qual sorgea per dentr'un sasso rotto, | entrar là dentro alcun già mai non osa, | si non è spirto assai ben colto et dotto.'

[19] For this map by an artist known only by his monogrammatic name G.A., see Pane and Valerio (1987), 34–6. Contemporary reports on the eruption of the Monte Nuovo are in Falconi (1539) and Toledo (1539). The report by Pietro Giacomo da Toledo contains a graphic representation of the event (*c.* [8]) that is clearly more schematic than documentary.

[20] The correlation between this map and Fuscano's *Stanze* is additionally under-lined by the fact that the map highlights the royal villa at Poggioreale, the only modern location to be recorded specifically by Fuscano, apart from Sannazaro's villa; see Addesso (2007), 25 (book 1, 27).

Fig. 11.3. G.A., *Il vero disegnio in sul propio luogho ritratto del infelice paese di Posuolo* (Naples, 1540).

Source: Bibliothèque nationale de France.

often served as an introduction to a virtual tour of the city itself.[21] It also figures prominently in the visual representations accompanying such texts, such as Joris Hoefnagel's attractive and much-copied image of his entry into the city of Naples, together with his friend and employer, the cartographer Abraham Ortelius, for whose 1578 version of the *Theatrum Orbis Terrarum* this engraving was produced (Fig. 11.4).[22] On their two-year journey around Italy, the two Antwerp friends began their visit of Naples at the western entrance of the Posillipo tunnel—as their compatriot Stephanus Pighius (and doubtless most other contemporary tourists) had done just a few years earlier

[21] References to the connected Virgil–Sannazaro memorials in Mergellina-Posillipo are in Di Falco (1548); Alberti (1550); De Stefano (1560); Schott (1600); Capaccio (1607); Mormile (1670); Capaccio (1634); Sarnelli (1685); Celano (1692). On this success, see Trapp (1984), but also Capasso (1895) and Fino (2008), 201–21.

[22] Cf. Pane and Valerio (1987), 62–3, 69–70. Based on his 1578 trip with Ortelius to Naples, Hoefnagel produced five images, all focused on the city's district. Reductions of all these in a more simple engraving technique were used to illustrate the guide by Schott as of its 1601 edition, together with a map of Italy: see De Beer (1942), 65.

Fig. 11.4. Joris Hoefnagel, 'Neapolis et Vesuvii montis prospectus', in Georg Braun and Franz Hogenberg, *Theatrum orbis terrarum* (Cologne, 1578).
Source: Bibliothèque nationale de France.

in 1574—going straight on from there to the alleged grave of Virgil on the other side of the tunnel, and then on to the Sannazaro villa and chapel, as the 1600 guide by Frans Schott would recommend.[23]

While this framing of Naples and its surrounding district in a discourse centred on the meeting and mingling of antique and modern local cultures would have lasting success, the literary associations at the heart of this erudite invention would however gradually fade and give way to different interpretations of Naples' antique legacy. In a somewhat minor praise of the city like the one offered in the mid-1540s by the Sorrento-based Bernardo Tasso to one of his Neapolitan correspondents, we still find an emphasis on Neapolitan literary prestige—mainly ancient but with some digressions into contemporary culture—that is clearly responsive to the lessons of

[23] Pighius (1587), 455; Schott (1600), 359.

the Pontano–Sannazaro circles.[24] But in these same years other much more elaborate and systematic city descriptions were being conceived, in which the emphatic focus on Naples' antique heritage was now balanced by a conventional literary perspective that paid more detailed attention to the material remains of the city's classical legacy, and which conveyed rather different ideological interpretations and appropriations of this heritage.

Indeed, a considerably more comprehensive interest informs the ambitious *Descrittione dei luoghi antiqui di Napoli* published in 1548 by Benedetto di Falco (Fig. 11.5). This work, which was reprinted many times until well into the seventeenth century, had a major impact on early modern perceptions of Naples and its surrounding district.[25] In introducing the city, Di Falco still adheres to the conventions of erudite literary branding, starting his itinerary from Posillipo and Mergellina while elaborately recording these locations' literary associations and linking them almost automatically to the accomplishments of contemporary Neapolitan poets. Pre-eminent here is the figure of Sannazaro, whose project to memorialize his image by connecting it to Virgil's reputation and alleged sepulchral presence is celebrated at length, since—as Di Falco complacently notes—'places are usually recorded because of the graves of excellent and extraordinary men'.[26]

However, Di Falco then goes on to describe in some detail not just the city's antique history, but also its original urbanistic layout along the three main *decumani*. He contrasts this with later developments that could be observed in the contemporary city, highlighting the situations where this had produced a hybrid mix of antique and modern, as, for instance, the antique theatre still visible in the house of the duke of Termoli:

[24] Tasso's city praise is contained in a letter to Giovambattista Peres, published in Nicolini (1904); it can be dated to 1543 or 1545.

[25] Di Falco (1548); for a modern edition of Di Falco see Grippo, Toscano, and Toscano (1992). Quotations here are taken from the edition Di Falco (1589). On the dating of the work, see Masi (1996), 305 n. 16. On Di Falco, cf. Formichetti (1991); Toscano (1991).

[26] Di Falco (1589), 25–6: 'Fe ancora l'otiosa e dotta Napoli, Poeta nobile e chiaro Giovanni Pontano, il Sannazaro, il Gravina, Statio che è nel numero de gli antichi, & altri. Sogliono i luoghi nominarsi per li sepolcri d'huomini eccellenti e rari, come Hierusalem per il santo sepolcro di Cristo, e 'l monte Cascio nella Soria per il tumulo di Pompeo, Sigeo per la tomba d'Achille, e la nostra gloriosa Napoli per la sepoltura di Virgilio.'

Fig. 11.5. Benedetto di Falco, *Descrittione dei luoghi antichi di Napoli* (Naples, 1598 edn.), title page.

In the mountain area was the theatre where the learned men living in Naples in those times long gone used to recite Greek and Latin poems. Its ancient remains and high walls nowadays can be seen in the palace of the duke of Termoli. In this theatre Emperor Nero sang when he returned from Greece, as Suetonius writes in his biography. Nor did he reject the office of giving recitals, when the Neapolitans offered it to him, since Nero held the liberal arts flourishing at that time in Naples in great esteem.[27]

---

[27] Di Falco (1589), 75: 'Nel seggio della Montagna era il teatro dove si recitavano tutti componimenti greci e latini delli studiosi ingegni che in quella etade fiorivano in Napoli, le cui vestigie antiche e l'alte mura del che paiono hoggidì nel palazzo del Duca

While exploring this fusion of antique and modern elements in the urban fabric, Di Falco shows a particular interest in the documentation of epigraphic material, both ancient and modern. He puts considerable energy into providing Italian translations for the Latin and sometimes Greek texts, even when this is not an easy task, as is the case with the obscure epitaphs he finds on Pontano's former house, the Palazzo dell'Arco.[28] His book is therefore clearly positioned not towards an erudite readership of humanists like his colleagues in the (by now waning) Accademia Pontaniana but towards a general audience that was not particularly knowledgeable about the significance of such antique traces.

This orientation helps us to better grasp the ambitions underlying Di Falco's project, as do some of the sections of this still rather incoherent city description. Di Falco alternates chapters on the classical roots of Naples and Pozzuoli with lengthy paragraphs on the city's modern churches and its district's celebrated thermal infrastructure; he also inserts digressions on the etymology of city names, on the lining of streets with trees and plants, as well as on contemporary and antique aristocratic conventions in table setting. His final chapter, though, which is devoted to the praising of Naples, not only states that the work is dedicated to Charles V (and here he invites the emperor and king to personally visit his capital), but also explains that it serves to contradict the allegations against Neapolitans being disloyal subjects which had been voiced by Pandolfo Collenuccio in his recently published *Compendio de le istorie del Regno di Napoli*.[29] In coming to the defence of his countrymen's civic and political reputation, Di Falco elaborates a strategy he is familiar with: stressing the city's connection to a prestigious antique heritage still to be seen in its urban fabric, a legacy that had materialized most significantly in the contemporary city's intellectual accomplishments. Not forgetting the suggestions offered by his forerunners in the Pontano and Sannazaro circles, Di Falco unsurprisingly closes his

di Termole. In questo theatro Nerone imperatore ritornando da Grecia musicalmente cantò come scrive Suetonio nella sua vita, né disprezzò l'ufficio del recitare offertogli dai napoletani, considerando esso Nerone l'eccellenza degli honorati studi che fiorivano in Napoli di tutte l'arti liberali.'

[28] Di Falco (1589), 76–7.

[29] On Di Falco's position towards Collenuccio, see Masi (1996). Collenuccio's text dates to *c*.1498. It was first published in 1539 (Venice, Michele Tramezzino), but was previously well known thanks to a wide manuscript circulation.

Descrittione with a paragraph on the city's modern academies and on the by-now topical monuments that testify to their glory: the graves of Virgil, Sannazaro and his friend Parrasio, and the chapel and house of Pontano.[30]

Di Falco's endeavour was not to remain without consequence, although the reactions to his book took a turn that was perhaps not what he had expected or hoped for. It was not his polemical stance on Neapolitans being loyal citizens that caused consternation, but rather his emphatic stress on the city's antique heritage as its priviliged and almost exclusive pathway to glory. Some ten years later, other Neapolitan intellectuals took upon themselves the task of writing city descriptions that clearly aimed to supplement and problematize Di Falco's erudite template, by offering more contemporary perspectives on the city. Such antagonistic motivations are all but manifest in the 1560 text by Pietro De Stefano that even echoes Di Falco's title: *Descrittione dei luoghi sacri di Napoli*.[31] In claiming that Neapolitan urban identity was grounded as much in the city's modern religious architecture as in its antique heritage, De Stefano intended to correct and supplement but not negate his predecessor's perspective. In order to do this, he offered an elaborate and detailed inventory of the epigraphical material that he had been able to record during his systematic exploration of the city's religious buildings, which had been driven by the urge to save this material from elimination by its exposure to the elements.[32] This project had produced an impressive collection of inscriptions present in the urban landscape, which was clearly meant to be comprehensive and hence to include even materials without religious connotations or, in some instances, material that dated from classical antiquity.[33] As in Di Falco's model, De

---

[30] Di Falco (1589), 132–4.

[31] De Stefano (1560), critical edition in D'Ovidio and Rullo (2007).

[32] On this motivation, see D'Ovidio and Rullo (2007), 244: 'Acciò dunque, che il tempo, solo consumator del tutto, col suo continuo rivolgimento consumando le lettere scolpite in questi sassi, come in alcune ha già cominciato, non le defraudi del suo nome, m'ha parso (come ho detto) brevemente annotarle a tal che da questa ingiuria siano al tutte libere, et io quanto posso non me dimostri ingrato et ala patria mia et all'industria deli antiqui, ch'in ogni modo si sono forzati nobilitarla come l'han fatto.' De Stefano includes very recent data, such as the epitaph to Portia Capece, who died in 1559, in the Rota chapel in S. Domenico: see the edition by D'Ovidio and Rullo (2007), 144–5.

[33] De Stefano even feels obliged to apologize for his ambition to be exhaustive: 'Ho seguito la natia favella per non mostrarmi affettato e per farmi intender da tutti, e se

Stefano gives Italian translations of all these inscriptions, and thus addresses a similarly general audience. However, since his information is systematically organized according to the building types of urban religious architecture, he does not offer any itineraries; his text thus lacks the qualities of a city guide that were instrumental in De Falco's project of urban identity branding.

In De Stefano's 1560 representation of Naples, associations with the city's antique heritage are still present, but they are not as prominent as they had been in the work of authors belonging to the earlier humanist circles around the Accademia Pontaniana. References to iconic places like Virgil's grave and Sannazaro's villa and chapel are relegated to more moderate positions, as mere elements of what aims to be a comprehensive systematic exploration of the contemporary urban landscape.[34] This shift in Neapolitans' perceptions of their urban identity must have been widely shared, since it reappears only a few years later, and in an even more blatant manner, in Giovanni Tarcagnota's 1566 praise of the most recent urban innovations, entitled *Del sito et lodi della città di Napoli*.[35] Although this dialogue is primarily concerned with presenting a lengthy and rather conventional narrative of the city's history from ancient times to the end of the fifteenth century—most of which is based on earlier chronicles like the controversial one by Collenuccio—it is remarkable for its opening paragraphs: these present an itinerary of the modern city centre which highlights the ambitious urbanistic projects that had only very recently been executed by viceroy Pedro da Toledo.

In this celebration of Naples as a state-of-the-art modern capital, conventional elements like praise of the city's antique heritage are not lacking, but they are relegated to a clearly secondary position. Interestingly, this causes a fundamental inversion in the conventional association of Sannazaro and Virgil, since now it is no longer the

forse alcuni più delicati harrebono voluto più sceltura neli epitaphii, io ho voluto obedire al apostolo Paulo, il quale ne dice che non ad alcuni soli, ma a tutti siamo tenuti a compiacere. Dirrò ben questo perché, se alcuno epitaphio vi è quale al gusto comune non piaccia, non è posto per l'elegantia, ma o perché ne manifesta qualche persona illustre, overo ne scopre qualche sententia notando e christiana.' See the edition by D'Ovidio and Rullo (2007), 251–2.

[34] The descriptions of Virgil's grave and Sannazaro's villa and chapel are in the edition by D'Ovidio and Rullo (2007), 109–10 and 213–15.

[35] Tarcagnota (1566), with anastatical reproduction in the edition by Strazullo (1988). On Tarcagnota, and specifically on his activities as editor of chorographical texts, see Tallini (2012).

classical but the modern poet who receives most credit.[36] As a consequence of this status reversal, Tarcagnota's interest in these poets' memorials is predominantly focused on Sannazaro's tomb in S. Maria del Parto (Fig. 11.2), which by its own merit and no longer by its association with Virgil's grave becomes emblematic of the glory of modern Naples.

> Going eastwards on the other side, there is the delightful Mergellina, particularly praised by Sannazaro, who, as we mentioned before, has been buried on this spot in the church he erected to honour the Holy Virgin of the Nativity. If Naples ever had anything that added to its lustre, then it was in our days this divine spirit who with his learned writings made it so famous that other cities might feel envious, like Mantua and Smyrna, even if they pride themselves on having given birth to the first geniuses of poetry.[37]

One of the best illustrations of this development of an interest in the contemporary city can be found in the magnificent map produced in these very years by Étienne Du Pérac, which is the first to detail the city's intricate urban layout and to highlight those urbanistic projects eulogized by Tarcagnota: the Via Toledo and the *quartieri*, as well as the imposing new defensive structures and the many monumental city gates (Fig. 11.6).[38] At the same time, this very accurate map also

---

[36] 'Et Virgilio anchor che Lombardo fosse, non visse egli qui un buon tempo, come in luogo, nel quale sentia maraviglioso contento? Onde benche poi altrove morisse, volle esservi nondimeno sepolto. Ioviano Pontano cosi celebre oratore & poeta, anzi in ogni faculta dottissimo, & per cio à gli Re di Aragona in questo regno carissimo, se bene egli non vi nacque, non ne visse ancho egli in Napoli quasi tutto il tempo della sua vita? Anzi fattone cittadino vi lasciò con la sua ornata cappella honorata memoria. Archia Poeta, & maestro di Cicerone non fu ancho egli fatto con suo molto contento di animo cittadino Napolitano? Questo istesso si potrebbe dire di molti altri eccellenti letterati. Ma tutti sono stati di gran lunga avanzati dal signor Giacomo Sanazaro nostro cittadino, che tanto nella poesia si avanzò, che co' migliori antichi gareggia di maggioranza.' Strazullo (1988), fos. 33v–34r.

[37] Strazullo (1988), fo. 31r: 'Dall'altra parte verso Oriente è la dilettevole Mergellina celebrata tanto dal Sanazaro, che in questo luogo, come poco avanti dicevamo, nella chiesa da lui sotto nome di Santa Maria del Parto edificata giace sepolto. Onde se hebbe mai Napoli cosa, che la illustrasse, la ha questo divino ingegno nella età nostra co' suoi dotti scritti fatta così celebre, che gliene possono havere invidia et Mantova, & Smirna, anchor che de' primi ingegni della poesia si vantino.'

[38] Strazullo (1988), fos. 10r–14r. On this map, see Pane and Valerio (1987), 37–45. The map was engraved by Du Pérac and printed, certainly before 1572 but perhaps already in 1566, by the Rome-based typographer Antoine Lafréry. As Giulio Pane argues (Pane and Valerio (1987), 42), the map may be a direct result of the surveys and measurements undertaken as part of the viceroy's urbanistic building policies.

Fig. 11.6. Antoine Lafréry and Étienne du Pérac, *Quale e di quanta importanza e bellezza sia la nobile Cita di Napole* (Rome, 1566).
Source: Bibliothèque nationale de France.

signals the rise of an interest in Naples coming from outside the city, based in erudite circles that shared a passion not only for detailed topographical knowledge, but also for outspoken antiquarian interests. The map was printed at the Roman press of Antoine Lafréry, who in these very years and often in collaboration with the engraver Étienne Du Pérac specialized in the production of lavish representations of Rome's antique heritage, which from the early 1570s on were collected in series, from the *Speculum Romanae Magnificentiae* to *I vestigi dell'antichità di Roma*.[39] The international audience addressed by such costly commercial enterprises focused on Roman antiquities was clearly thought to be interested in Naples as well, and this must have motivated the printer to include the monumental Neapolitan map in his available stock.

In doing so, the cartographic entrepreneur in Lafréry could rely on the rapidly growing inclination of wealthy foreigners to include a visit to Naples and its district in their educational tour of Italy, a practice

---

[39] For these projects see <http://speculum.lib.uchicago.edu>, as well as Besse (2009).

only very recently established and propagated by northern humanists like Turler and Pighius, as we saw at the beginning of this chapter. But in their explorations of this area, these new visitors (who often came from far away) were not guided by the recently forged Neapolitan self-image that was focused on the city's modern identity as a capital full of imposing new buildings and state-of-the-art public infrastructures. Instead, these visitors showed an unmistakable enthusiasm for the region's antique heritage, which recalled the earlier perspectives of local humanists such as Pontano and Sannazaro. However, in contrast to the predominantly symbolic interpretation of their home town's antique heritage proposed by these earlier generations, these visitors from beyond Naples showed a more inquisitive disposition, motivated by a clear-cut passion for antiquarian exploration. And whereas the intellectuals of the Accademia Pontaniana had been interested in using the prestigious connotations of their city's antique heritage in order to forge a new identity of their own, the travellers from out of town felt less bound by such constraints and were thus able to develop more disinterested and neutral attitudes towards the antique remains they encountered.

This type of antiquarian curiosity informed most of the chorographical texts that were produced from the 1570s onwards in response to the new travelling habits that would develop into the Grand Tour. It was, though, already evident in one of the foundational texts of this genre, Leandro Alberti's *Descrittione di tutta Italia*, and even so with particular insistence in the pages devoted to Naples and its district.[40] Published in 1550 after a long process of elaboration, the book reflects the author's personal travel experiences gathered in the decade between 1525 and 1535. Alberti offers a profile of Naples that is partly based on a compilation of information taken from earlier texts, including again Collenuccio's chronicle as well as Flavio Biondo's *Italia illustrata* of the previous century.[41] This information is then supplemented and tested by data collected personally on location, not just from reading local publications perhaps less known elsewhere, but primarily through conversations with knowledgeable local

---

[40] Alberti (1550). The reprint of the 1568 edition in Prosperi (2003) includes a range of case studies dedicated to specific aspects of the text; the description of Naples and its district is at fos. 180v–188v. On Alberti, see also the essays in Donattini (2007).

[41] On Alberti's sources and working methods, see Petrella (2004).

experts as well as site visits (sometimes made in the company of these same erudite men).[42]

As Alberti's treatment of the Piedigrotta tunnel and the Virgil–Sannazaro *lieux de mémoire* on the Posillipo hill characteristically demonstrates, such a composite basis then produces a hybrid text which is clearly indebted to the suggestions of the members of the Accademia Pontaniana circle that Alberti doubtlessly met when in Naples (where he stayed between 1525 and 1528), but which is then counterbalanced by his personal investigations grounded in a down-to-earth empiricism. Alberti presents all the topical elements, and follows the conventional itineraries, from Pozzuoli and the villas of Cicero and Lucullus to the Piedigrotta tunnel and from there to the grave of Virgil and the Sannazaro villa. But he reports and weighs up the various opinions on the historicity of some of these elements, and does not hesitate to perform investigations of his own, for example by measuring the exact dimensions of the Piedigrotta tunnel, which had not yet been recorded by the authorities consulted on this matter:

> Then there is the entrance to the said Grotto, which has been skilfully pierced in the mountain, conducting the road through the inside of the mountain I mentioned before, right up to the other side. On this Strabo says: 'Between Pozzuoli and Naples there is a cave that has been dug in the mountain, much like the other one that leads to Cuma, many *stadi* long, and so wide as to allow two chariots to pass through easily together.' Because of my curious disposition, I wanted to see this cave, and then took measurements, noticing it to be more than 12 feet wide, and equally high. And measuring it from its entrance to its exit, it turned out to be 2,000 feet long, followed by another 500 feet of roofless mountain passage, in the direction of Naples. Which means that the total equals a modern mile, or 1,000 steps, all pierced and cut in the mountain's rock.[43]

---

[42] In his description of the eruption of the Monte Nuovo, for instance, Alberti uses information gathered from the contemporary reports by Falconi (1539) and Toledo (1539). He is also familiar with Leone's recent book on Nola, Leone (1514); cf. Prosperi (2003), fo. 190r.

[43] Prosperi (2003), fos. 181v–182r: 'Vedesi poi l'entrata dell'antidetta Grotta, la quale è tutta cavata artificiosamente nel sasso, che continua la via per le viscere del prefato monte infino all'altra parte. Di cui dice così Strabone: "Ritrovasi fra le Dicearchia & Napoli una spelunca nel monte cavata, fatta à simiglianza di quell'altra per la quale si passa da Cuma, molti stadij lunga, & tanto larga, che insieme vi possono agevolmente passar due carra". La qual'io curiosamente volendo vedere, la misurai, & la ritrovai esser larga oltre di 12 piedi, & altrettano alta, & lunga, cominciando dalla

Of course, this combination of antiquarianism and scepticism recalls the attitude adopted by Petrarch on his visit to the Virgilian locations two centuries earlier: this parallel was probably recognized by Alberti, although he does not include the poet's report in his list of the many authorities used while preparing his own visit and text. But whereas Petrarch's engagement with Naples' antique heritage was not disinterested, in Alberti it is hard to see any particular urge towards self-fashioning. The antique remains that he meticulously investigates challenge him to compare his personal observations with his existing notions of the classics. This was a curiosity-driven activity in which scholarship and exploration met: for such erudite enquiries, the city of Naples and its surrounding district offered an ideal playground.

Although Alberti did not conceive of his book as a travel guide, it quickly came to be perceived as such.[44] After its reprinting in a quarto format (from 1551) and subsequent translation into Latin (1566), it soon became a national and international success, not only in a commercial sense, but also through its use as a reference text by both real and 'armchair' travellers. The book found its way into most major private and public libraries of the period all over Europe, and the information it contained was pillaged undeferentially.[45] Hence it became a gold mine for the new commercial enterprises which, from the 1570s onwards, started to develop products specifically aimed at the educational travellers who were touring Italy in ever-increasing numbers. Indeed, we find clear traces of the Neapolitan section of the book in early Italian commercial chorographies like Francesco Sansovino's succinct *Ritratto delle più nobili e famose città d'Italia* of 1575, but also in such monumental products as the famed *Theatrum Orbis Terrarum* atlas, which was assembled and organized by Abraham Ortelius in the 1570s.[46] As mentioned earlier in this chapter, Ortelius visited Naples and its district together with his friend the engraver Joris Hoefnagel in 1578, but even before that explorative trip, the first edition of his atlas in 1570 included an introduction to the region that was virtually a paraphrase of Alberti.[47]

---

foce per la quale s'entra alla foce per la quale si esce al scoperto, 2000 piedi, et da detti foci caminando al scoperto, ma però nel sasso tagliata verso Napoli 500 che risulterebbano in tutto alla misura d'un perfetto miglio de' nostri tempi, tutto quello cavato & tagliato nel sasso, ò di mille passa.'

[44] On the book's printing history, see Prosperi (2003), 27–44.
[45] On the international reception of Alberti's text, see Gaiga (2014).
[46] Sansovino (1575), fos. 78v–83r.   [47] Gaiga (2014).

It comes as no surprise that the northern humanist authors like Turler and Pighius who advocated this educational tour of Italy included Alberti's text amongst the many authorities used in constructing their descriptions of Naples and its antiquities.[48] But what is quite remarkable is the fact that this 'outsider' view of Naples also appealed to local intellectuals interested in representing their home city, to the extent that it came to overshadow the techniques of urban self-fashioning developed just a few decades earlier—both the older literary view of Neapolitan identity and its modern urbanistic counterpart proposed more recently by Tarcagnota. The local city guides published after Tarcagnota's 1566 *Del sito et lodi della città di Napoli* do not, in fact, mirror his model, but on the contrary find inspiration in that elaborated by Alberti, which they adopt as their default template while supplementing it with elements taken from various other sources, including the complementary city descriptions by Di Falco and De Stefano.

This process is apparent in the ambitious project by the Neapolitan historian Scipione Mazzella, who between 1586 and 1591 produced a two-volume description of the Kingdom of Naples so heavily dependent on Alberti that it provoked serious allegations of plagiarism that would end in court.[49] Elaborated in the early 1580s, Mazzella's description reworks and assembles a wide range of source materials into a systematic exploration of the whole kingdom, with particular reference to the city and its district. Whereas the first book presents itself as an encyclopedic work on southern Italy and its constituent cities, supplementing and detailing the model offered by Alberti, the second book (*Sito, ed antichità della città di Pozzuolo e del suo amenissimo distretto*) is clearly intended as a traveller's guide to the antiquities in the Pozzuoli district, even including a series—the first of its kind—of fifteen illustrations. It is this last detail in particular that exemplifies the strong commercial aspirations underlying this

---

[48] Turler (1574); Pighius (1587).

[49] Mazzella (1586) gives a systematic description of the whole kingdom, including the city of Naples, while Mazzella (1591) concentrates on Pozzuoli and its district. Mazzella (1601) gives an expanded version of the volume on the kingdom, whereas Mazzella (1606) complements the visual illustrations of the original edition with a separate map of the whole Pozzuoli region. The first volume on the kingdom was published in English in Mazzella (1652). Costo (1595) substantiates his accusations of plagiarism voiced over the preceding years, thereby provoking a legal case for slander. On Mazzella, Costo, and their polemics, see Ventura (2008); Lettere (1984); Hendrix (2014).

project, which were determined by the incipient Grand Tour interest
in the region. Such a market-oriented nature would indeed distinguish all subsequent guides to Naples, from Giulio Cesare Capaccio's
well-known *Il Forastiero* (1634) and the highly successful *Guida de'
forestieri curiosi di vedere e d'intendere le cose più notabili della Regal
Città di Napoli e del suo amenissimo distretto* by Pompeo Sarnelli
(1685) through to the celebrated 1692 *Delle notizie del bello, dell'antico e del curioso della città di Napoli per gli signori forastieri* by Carlo
Celano.[50]

Mazzella's books, however, do not only show how local entrepre-
neurial men of letters quickly responded to the opportunities created
by the recent growth of travellers visiting their region. They also
suggest how far this situation challenged them to adopt attitudes
towards their own city's antique heritage that were close to those
cherished by the educational travellers from outside, for whom they
now primarily conceived their city guides. While still eager to collect
antique epigraphical materials, a passion shared by Neapolitans and
visitors alike, Mazzella does not bother to make these more accessible
by giving translations, as his local predecessors Di Falco and De
Stefano had done; instead, he follows the proto-archaeological habits
of humanist authors like Stephanus Pighius and Laurentius Schrader
to meticulously document all such evidence.[51] Unlike his Neapolitan
predecessors, Mazzella clearly felt no urgency to create links between
the city's antique heritage and its modern identity. In his discussion of
what his predecessors had constructed as the topical *lieux de mémoire*
of local identity, the combined Virgil–Sannazaro memorial on Posillipo hill, any reference to Sannazaro or modernity is missing.[52]

---

[50] Capaccio (1634); Sarnelli (1685); Celano (1692).

[51] Pighius (1587), *passim*; Schrader (1592). Most of the inscriptions collected by
Pighius remained unpublished, but are in the Codex Pighianus (Staatsbibliothek
Berlin, MS Lat. fol. 61a).

[52] Mazzella (1606), 206–7: 'Ma è cosa degna da non tacersi d'un albero grosso di
laoro che nella sommità della cupula di detta capella è naturalmente nato, percioche le
sue radici si veggono che stanno attaccate alle fissure del muro onde pare che la madre
natura l'habbia fatto nascer detto lauro come per segno che ivi giace la cenere di quel
gran poeta stupore del mondo, & oltre di questo la detta capella si vede coperta e di
mortelle e di hedre che fanno una bellissima vista, il che rende maraviglia ad ogn'uno
che considera il luogo, & a ma pare che simili cose l'havesse ivi la natura prodotte, sì
per ornar' il luogo à un tanto grande huomo, come anco per mostrare la grandezza
sua, poiche vedendo essere stato il tumulo di esso poeta spogliato de gli belli e ricchi
marmi, ha voluto che non li mancasse honore, e che ogn'uno respettasse il detto luogo.
Essendo sei anni sono andato à diporto in questi luoghi, in compagnia del signor

Fig. 11.7. Commemorative plaque (dated 1544) near the alleged grave of Virgil, Naples, with graffiti by Stanislaus Cencovius (1589) and other visitors.
Source: Photograph: Harald Hendrix.

Instead, the cult of Virgil's grave is enacted in a manner that interprets fashionable modalities introduced by the international audience of 'investigatori dell'antichità' that the site now attracted in great numbers: that is, by admiring the picturesque laurel tree springing from the tomb's roof (Fig. 11.1), reciting verses and even creating poetry of one's own—to celebrate not Virgil, but the laurel on his tomb—or leaving graffiti, as a foreign traveller like the Polish nobleman Stanislaus Cencovius would do in 1589 (Fig. 11.7).[53]

Geronima Colonna & del Dottore Fabio di Giordano, e di Paolo Portarello persone tutte di molto sapere e di gran dottrina ornati & investigatori dell'antichità, così il signor Colonna volle che ciascuno di noi di là non partissero che prima non havessimo fatto in lode del detto lauro alcuni versi. E perche io di tutti quanti era il più giovane me disse che per regola legale a me conveniva dire prima. E così fra poco spatio di tempo vi feci questi versi.'

[53] Cencovius left his signature in a marble plaque that a few decades earlier, in 1554, had been installed near the alleged grave of Virgil by the owners of the land, the Lateran canons of S. Maria di Piedigrotta, in order to give the tomb an appropriate epitaph. See Trapp (1984), 12.

12

Ex dirutis marmoribus

The Theatines and the Columns of the Temple of the Dioscuri in Naples

Fulvio Lenzo

S. Paolo Maggiore is one of the largest churches in Naples, and it contains many important works of art dating from the seventeenth and eighteenth centuries (see Fig. 3.1). The church also preserves traces of a much older, classical past, for it was constructed by Theatine priests on the remains of the ancient temple of Castor and Pollux.[1] In 1538, the Theatine Order settled in the medieval church that had been built in the ninth century behind the remains of the temple; fifty years later they began the rebuilding of that church, which was carried out in three main phases. The transept and the apse were built in 1583–4, inspired by the city's Angevin churches; the nave and the facade were built between 1589 and 1591 after a new design by the architect Giovan Battista Cavagna, and finally the aisles were erected from 1623 to 1639 under the architect Giovan Giacomo Conforto. The temple's marble pronaos remained standing until it was destroyed in an earthquake in 1688, with its six columns on the facade, and two other columns on either side supporting the temple

The research leading to these results has received funding from the European Research Council under the European Community's Seventh Framework Programme (FP7/2007–13)/ERC Grant agreement n° 263549; ERC-HistAntArtSI project Università degli Studi di Napoli Federico II.

[1] See Lenzo (2011) for a more detailed chronology.

pediment. The pediment itself preserved almost all of its original sculptures, apart from a central void (the reconstruction of which is discussed by Rabun Taylor in Chapter 3 in this volume), and a Greek inscription on the entablature, which commemorated the building's original dedication by Tiberius Julius Tarsos to the Dioscuri.[2] At the time of the church's construction, then, the ancient pronaos was still almost whole, and—as this chapter will show—its presence, the allure of its antiquity, and its symbolic meaning guided the Theatines' choice of this site for their new church.

The discussion here will focus on two central episodes in the history of the church of S. Paolo, both of which have the potential to give us insights into the evolving relationship between the Theatines and classical antiquity. The first is the initial choice in 1538 of the temple as the site of the Theatines' home in Naples, when the antiquity and fame of the temple were used to give prestige to the new church. At this time, the ancient building was seen as providing incontrovertible evidence of the glorious classical past of the city, whose historical roots—both ancient and early Christian—were shown to be even deeper than those of the city of Rome. The second episode dates to a few decades later, in the year 1576, when a new staircase was built to replace the ancient marble steps at the front of the building. Here, the evidence suggests that, while the legacy of the classical past was not entirely rejected, it now posed certain problems for contemporary audiences, and needed to be 'Christianized' before it could be incorporated into Church history. For above the doorway through which visitors gained access to the staircase a new inscription was placed, which affirmed that the Theatines had built the new steps out of the ruined marbles that had once been dedicated to the false pagan idols Castor and Pollux, and which had now been rededicated to the Christian saints Peter and Paul. As we shall see, these two distinct moments in the history of this important Neapolitan church not only give insight into how Naples' ancient past was used to create a new religious identity for the city but, taken together, they also echo a broader shift in sixteenth-century attitudes to classical antiquity and its material culture.

---

[2] See pp. 39–40 of this volume for the text and translation of this inscription.

THE CHOICE OF S. PAOLO AS THE THEATINE
CHURCH IN NAPLES (1538)

The Order of the Theatines was founded in Rome in 1524 by Gaetano
Thiene, a priest from Vicenza, and the Neapolitan Gian Pietro Carafa,
then bishop of Chieti.[3] After the sack of Rome in 1527 the Theatines
sheltered in Venice, before Thiene and some other brethren moved to
Naples in 1533. Here, they first settled in the church of S. Maria della
Misericordia, just outside Porta S. Gennaro.[4] This church, however,
failed to fulfil the needs of the Theatines, and before long they began
to search for more suitable accommodation. Gian Pietro Carafa
belonged to a well-connected Neapolitan noble family and so was
able to help in this matter, although he himself remained in Venice as
the leader of that city's Theatine convent. In 1534, he wrote a letter to
Gaetano Thiene in which he raised the possibility of obtaining the
medieval church of S. Paolo. Carafa explained that this church could
be a good choice for the Theatines, on account of its 'respect for the
Apostles' (*apostolica reverentia*), its 'venerable antiquity' (*veneranda
vetustate*), and its location in a prominent part of the city (*celeberrimo
urbis loco*).[5]

The Theatines had to work hard to gain possession of the medieval
church of S. Paolo, but four years later they succeeeded, thanks in part
to the direct intervention of the viceroy Pedro de Toledo (after they
had threatened to leave Naples for good). Their persistence reflects
Carafa's strong desire to obtain this particular church, which was
small and poor, but which had been built inside the ancient temple. It
is important to note here that Carafa's response to classical antiquity
was more complex than one of simple adulation, and must be considered within the wider context of the sixteenth-century debates
about the (often uneasy) relationship between classical antiquity
and Christianity. On the one hand, while the medieval tradition had
celebrated the destruction of the pagan idols by Pope Gregory the
Great in the sixth century as the triumph of Christianity over paganism, from the time of Petrarch onwards the end of Roman civilization
began to be regarded of the beginning of a 'dark age' in human

---

[3] Carafa was to become cardinal in 1536, and Pope Paul IV in 1555. See Paschini
(1926); Monti (1923).
[4] Paschini (1926).   [5] Paschini (1926), 187–94.

history.[6] The lamentation over the lost artistic heritage of classical antiquity became a common topos of humanistic culture: the words of Petrarch were later echoed by Fra Giocondo and Raphael, and by the beginning of the sixteenth century similar ideas were being expressed by cardinals and popes. On the other hand, this was also the period in which Martin Luther condemned Rome as a new Babylon, and its great buildings, both ancient and modern, as the visible expression of such moral decay (he wrote, for instance, that the Pantheon could not have been built without the help of the Devil).[7] These Protestant attacks aroused a new feeling of uneasiness amongst Catholics, to such an extent that, in his *Enarrationes* of 1552, the Dominican priest Ambrosio Catarino Politi imagined a Devil who was pleased by collections of pagan statues.[8] Meanwhile, the Spanish bishop of Alife, Antonio Agustín—himself an antiquarian and collector of ancient inscriptions—acknowledged in 1566 that the many statues of Venus and other 'lustful' antiquities displayed in the garden of Pope Julius III shocked pilgrims from the north of Europe on their visits to Rome.[9]

In 1536 Pope Paul III promoted Gian Pietro Carafa to the office of cardinal, and in 1542 appointed him head of the Tribunal of the Inquisition—that is, the most severe and conservative institution that emerged from the Catholic Counter-Reformation. This choice was not accidental, because Carafa had made himself known as a fierce supporter of the 'hard line' in what he defined the 'spiritual fight' against the heretics: his main concern was to eradicate the 'plague of heresy', and to restore the papal authority—which, in his own words, should be 'able to shake the highest mountains into the abyss'.[10] In his role as Grand Inquisitor he persecuted some famously learned cardinals, such as Reginald Pole and Giovanni Morone, and later, once he had become pope (in 1555), he damaged European culture once again by issuing the first *Index of Prohibited Books*, which condemned not only books written by Protestant authors, but also all the Italian translations of the Bible, as well as the entire literary production of Erasmus.

That such a man chose the site of the pagan temple of the Dioscuri for the church of the religious order he had founded might seem

---

[6] Buddensieg (1965); Weiss (1969).
[7] Battisti (1963).   [8] Scavizzi (1981), 286.
[9] Agustín (1765–74), viii. 248. For Agustín as antiquarian, see Crawford (1993).
[10] 'Atta a far tremare li gran monti infino a l'abisso.' See Prosperi (1969), 264.

curious, to say the least. But despite his strict religious policies, Carafa was no enemy of classical culture. His grandfather Diomede was renowned for having assembled one of the first antiquarian collections in the Italian peninsula.[11] Meanwhile, his uncle, Cardinal Oliviero Carafa, had been an enlightened patron of art and architecture, both in Rome, where he commissioned the wooden ceiling of S. Lorenzo Fuori le Mura and the new cloister of S. Maria della Pace that was built by Bramante, and in Naples, where he restored the ancient church of S. Gennaro extra Moenia and built a new chapel under the apse of the cathedral. This crypt, known as the Succorpo of S. Gennaro, is one of the most striking examples of *all'antica* architecture in the city.[12] Oliviero Carafa also took charge of the education of his nephew Gian Pietro, whose knowledge of the Classics and fluency in Latin and Greek is said to have astonished even Erasmus.[13] According to his earliest biographers, Gian Pietro Carafa commissioned Pirro Ligorio to make a bronze tabernacle for the papal chapel, and suggested that they use for this purpose a collection of ancient coins that he kept in a basket in his chamber (an offer refused by Ligorio). This episode, perhaps more than any other, sheds light on the ambiguous relationship between Carafa and pagan antiquity. For although Carafa was apparently willing to destroy the valuable ancient coins, the fact remains that he possessed such a collection in the first place, and that he kept it in his private chamber as a personal treasure. Another sign of Carafa's affinity with antiquity is his (failed) plan to enlarge the cloister of S. Silvestro al Quirinale in Rome, by enclosing several ancient Roman remains within the new building.[14] Furthermore, Gian Pietro Carafa was a Neapolitan, and therefore likely to have been well aware of the profound symbolic meaning that the ancient temple of the Dioscuri and the adjoining church had in his city.

In this regard, we have a great deal of evidence that attests to the importance of the temple and its reception since Angevin times, when Niccolò Deoprepio of Reggio—who was active as physician and translator at the court of King Robert of Anjou—translated the Greek inscription into Latin. Around 1323 his translation was inserted into the first part of the *Cronaca di Partenope*, the late

---

[11] de Divitiis (2007); de Divitiis (2010); Dodero (2007).
[12] Norman (1986); de Divitiis (2007), 171–81.
[13] Paschini (1926), 31.
[14] Caracciolo (1612), 138–9; Castaldo (1615), 153.

medieval chronicle in which many older legends were collected.[15] This is the first known translation from classical Greek into Latin in early modern Western Europe, and it provides evidence of the Angevin interest in monumental inscriptions and their ancient use as a means of commemorating the founders of buildings.[16] Some years later, King Robert and his wife Sancia of Mallorca followed this example by inlaying a long marble inscription at the top of the basement of the bell tower of S. Chiara, which celebrated the church's foundation.[17] From the fifteenth century onwards, the Greek inscription of the temple of the Dioscuri was copied by many Neapolitan and foreign antiquarians. Nicolò Signorili inserted it into his 1409 manuscript collection of ancient epigraphic texts, although he had probably never seen the temple itself.[18] Cyriac of Ancona, instead, could copy the inscription directly from the monument during his stay in Naples in 1432.[19] The Greek text also attracted the interest of Lorenzo Valla, who between 1420 and 1428 amended the translation of the *Cronaca di Partenope*, and of Fra Giocondo, who arrived in Naples in 1489.[20] The earliest known reproductions of the architecture of the ancient temple also date from the fifteenth century, when the building appears in the background of a relief representing the triumph of King Alfonso of Aragon over the inner door of the Sala dei Baroni in Castelnuovo (Fig. 12.1), and in an illuminated manuscript of the *De dictis et factis Alphonsi Regis Aragonum* dating to *c.*1460.[21] In the last years of the fifteenth century, the Florentine architect Giuliano da Sangallo accurately measured and drew the details of the bases of the columns.[22] In 1506–7, the temple was drawn by Agustinus Prygl

---

[15] Lo Parco (1910); Altamura (1974); Kelly (2011).

[16] Weiss (1950); Weiss (1969).   [17] Gaglione (1998); Bruzelius (2004).

[18] Campana (1973–4), 87.

[19] *Kyriaci anconitani itinerarium* (1742), 23–4; Campana (1973–4); Mitchell and Bodnar (1996); Lenzo (2006b).

[20] Ziebarth (1905), 232; Koortbojian (1993). On Valla's amendment, see Campana (1973–4); Valla (1984), 241–3 n. 19.

[21] BAV, *Vat. Lat.* 1565, fo. 123v. See Helas (2009), 163–84, 203. The text was composed in 1455 by Antonio Beccadelli ('il Panormita'). The relief dates to 1452–7. See Kruft (1972), 20–1 n. 42; Kruft and Malmanger (1975), 213–305; Caglioti (2008), 97–8 n. 30; Helas (2009), 150–8, 197.

[22] BAV, *Barb. Lat.* 4424, fo. 67v: 'Questa base è a San Pagholo di Napoli tempio anticho e ogni parte è meno 4/5 chel proprio, misurato apunto'. See Hülsen (1984 [1910], fo. 67v). The drawing only occupies one corner of the sheet, and it is possible that the architect intended to draw the plan or the elevation of the temple in the central space.

Fig. 12.1. Domenico Gagini, *The Triumph of King Alfonso*, formerly in the Sala dei Baroni of Castelnuovo, Naples. The temple of the Dioscuri and the Roman theatre are depicted in the background.

Source: From Burger (1907).

Fig. 12.2. Agustinus Prygl Tyfernus, facade of S. Paolo Maggiore in Naples.
Source: Vienna, Österreichische Nationalbibliothek, codex 1528, fo. 57r.

Tyfernus (Fig. 12.2), and in 1526 it appeared in a prominent position in the city view of Naples, which was used as the frontispiece of the second printed edition of the *Cronaca di Partenope* (Fig. 12.4)[23].

Once the Theatines had settled in the church of S. Paolo in the middle of the sixteenth century, drawings of the temple and copies of its inscription soon began to increase in number. The Neapolitan humanist Pietro Summonte gave only the briefest of descriptions of the temple to his Venetian colleague Marco Antonio Michiel, refraining from transcribing the inscription because he assumed that

---

[23] *Chroniche de la inclyta cità de Napole*, 1526.

Michiel already knew it from his earlier trip to Naples.[24] The temple
was well known in Venice, where Carafa was living, as well as in
Rome. Baldassare Peruzzi (1481–1536), who certainly visited Naples,
included it at the end of a list of the most important ancient buildings
still surviving in his lifetime.[25] In 1540, the temple and its inscription
were drawn by the Portuguese artist Francisco d'Ollanda (see
Fig. 3.2).[26] Manuscripts by the epigrapher Jean Matal dating from
around 1547 record that the Greek inscription had previously been
copied by the Spaniard Jean Hermengol, and then by many French
and Flemish scholars associated with the Accademia Vitruviana of
Rome, such as Louis Budé, Abel Portius, Antoine Morillon, Simon de
Vallambert, and Guillaume Philandrier.[27] Stephanus Winandus Pighi-
ius from Kempen was also a member of the circle of the Accademia
Vitruviana of Rome; he saw the temple of Castor and Pollux for the
first time during his journey to Italy in 1548, and again in 1574 when
he travelled to Naples in the company of the young prince of Cleves.
After the death of the prince, he published a diary of their travels,
mentioning the temple of the Dioscuri amongst the many ancient and
modern monuments they had seen.[28] In 1550 the inscription was
copied by the English humanist Thomas Hoby (the first translator of
the *Cortegiano* of Baldassare Castiglione) on his travels through Italy
in company of his friends Peter Whitehorne, Henry Parker, and
William Barker.[29] Some years before this, the Neapolitan painter,
architect, and antiquarian Pirro Ligorio had transcribed the Greek
text and drawn a restoration of the ancient temple.[30] Between 1545
and 1547 Andrea Palladio used Ligorio's sketches as the starting point

---

[24] Pietro Summonte, letter to Marco Antonio Michiel (Naples, 20 March 1524):
'Nel mezzo di questa città, quasi in *umbilico urbis*, dove oggi è l'ecclesia di San Paulo, è
tutto intiero ancora lo pronao e frontispicio dell'antiquo templo di Castore e Polluce,
di certe colonne grandi e ben striate, con quel bello fastigio e con la greca inscriptione,
quale non vi mando, perché penso la abbiate lecta'. See Nicolini (1925), 173.

[25] Uffizi A 489r: 'Templu[m] castor epollucjs nea/polj.' See Wurm (1984), 337.

[26] Madrid, El Escorial, cod. 28-I-20, fo. 45v. See Correra (1905); Tormo (1940);
Schreurs (2000); Schreurs (2006); and Rabun Taylor, Chapter 3 in this volume.

[27] BAV, *Vat. Lat.* 6039, fos. 129(=355)v, 211(=443)v. See Lenzo (2011), 40–4, pls.
35–6.

[28] Pighius (1587), 456.

[29] Powell (1902). The inscription does not appear in the published fragment of his
diary. For the manuscript, see Bartlett (1991); Bartlett (1993); Bartlett (2006).

[30] Turin, Archivio di Stato, MS a.III.14 (vol. 12), fos. 23v, 169r. See Mercando
(1996); Schreurs (2000), 70–1, 461; Schreurs (2006); Lenzo (2011), 44–50; Lenzo
(2012).

for his reconstruction of the temple facade and of the architectural details, which was later published in his *Quattro Libri dell'architettura* (1570).[31] This book ensured that the Neapolitan temple gained great renown throughout Europe, and in 1614 the building attracted the interest of Inigo Jones, who wrote his notes directly on his copy of Palladio's book (he was deeply impressed by the temple, and wrote that it was '[one] of the best things I have seen').[32]

Even this brief survey should be enough to show what Carafa meant when he wrote that the site chosen by him for the Theatines was 'celeberrimo'. All the same, the interest that the Neapolitan temple held for foreign travellers and architects was principally an antiquarian one. For Neapolitans—including Carafa—the ancient building embodied a far more complex and multifaceted set of meanings. The building was, for instance, the topic of numerous medieval stories and legends, which survived into early modern times thanks to their inclusion in the *Cronaca di Partenope*. While the inscription's reference to the *polis* may originally have meant that the temple was dedicated to Castor, Pollux, and the *polis* (embodied in the form of its tutelary deity, the Siren Parthenope), in the *Cronaca di Partenope* the word was understood to mean that the patrons of the temple (Tiberius Julius Tarsos and Pelagon) were, at the same time, the founders of the new town of Neapolis.[33] Another story suggested that the absence of sculptures in the middle of the pediment was due to the miraculous intervention of St Peter, who stopped in Naples on his way to Rome, and made the images of the pagan gods to whom the temple was dedicated fall to the ground—an act that was considered to have been St Peter's first step in converting the city to Christianity (Fig. 12.3).[34] Even Pope Clement VII knew this particular story, and alluded to it in a letter to the Theatines in 1533 in which he urged them to found a new house of the Order in Naples, as demanded by

---

[31] Palladio (1570), lib. iv, 95–7. See Lenzo (2011), 50–6; Lenzo (2012).

[32] Oxford, Worcester College, B. 3:13, p. 96. See Jones (1970), ii. 61. On Jones's stay in Naples, see Newmann (1980); Chaney (1998), 168–202. Over the next few decades many other foreign travellers drew or described the temple, including Richard Symonds in 1651 (Oxford, Bodleian Library, Rawlinson D. 121, fo. 23r; drawing reproduced in Lenzo (2011), fig. 39), and Ferdinand Delamonce, who saw it in 1719; see Vallet Mascoli (1984).

[33] Kelly (2011), 171–2, 288–9. For the dedication to the *polis*, see Taylor, Chapter 3 in this volume.

[34] Summonte (1601), i. 301; Capaccio (1634), 80; Scherillo (1859).

Fig. 12.3. Massimo Stanzione, *St Peter Makes the Pagan Statues of Castor and Pollux Fall*, fresco (1642), formerly on the ceiling of S. Paolo Maggiore (destroyed 1943).

Source: Foto Alinari, from the archive of the Soprintendenza per i Beni Ambientali e Architettonici di Napoli e Provincia.

the city's deputies.[35] Meanwhile, older chronicles held that the church behind the ancient temple had been constructed during the time of

[35] The pope wrote that Naples was 'a very faithful city, which accepted the Catholic faith from St Peter, the prince of Apostoles, as there it is believed, and ever preserved it in the more loyal way' (*fidelissima civitatis, quae fidem catholicam, ab ipso beatissimo Petro apostolorum principe, ut pie ibi creditor acceptam, semper*

Duke Antimo (801–17) as a vow of thanks to St Paul, who had helped the Neapolitans to defeat the Saracen invaders.[36]

In this way, the temple of Castor and Pollux materialized some important links between the city's classical past and its early Christian history. The pronaos was one of the few ancient monuments in Naples that had been preserved almost in its entirety, and the huge quantity of marble that was still visible evoked the richness and splendour of the ancient city of Neapolis. In many ways, the fabric of the building embodied the whole of the city's long history: its inscription was written in Greek and named a Roman emperor, while the absence of sculptures in the middle of the pediment was considered as material evidence for St Peter's visit to Naples, and the little medieval church built behind it reminded viewers of the later victories of the Neapolitans against the Saracens. The importance of the temple for the Neapolitans is evident in the etching reproduced at Fig. 12.4, which was issued in 1526, just a few years before the Theatines' arrival in the city. Here, the temple is represented at a disproportionately large scale, emerging from among the much smaller buildings of the city, which is itself shown enclosed inside the walls that had been built by the Aragonese kings. On the temple frieze we see some nonsensical signs that can nevertheless be understood to allude to the Greek inscription: meanwhile, two figures are represented within the pediment (whose complex scene is thus condensed), while the gap in the middle of the pediment is also represented clearly and schematically. The temple is thus presented as a kind of metaphor for the whole city of Naples, which is able to summarize its entire history from the Greek foundation until modern times. Only by considering all these different layers of history and meaning can we begin to understand why Carafa wanted the church of S. Paolo for the Theatines, and what he meant when he wrote that he would have to fight to obtain the church (*ecclesiam ab harpys auferre*), because of the *apostolica reverentia*, the *veneranda vetustate*, and its location in a *celeberrimo urbis loco*.

A similar interest in antiquity seems to have governed Carafa's choice of a third, Roman site of the Theatine Order. After he became pope, Carafa granted to his brethren the church of S. Silvestro al

---

constantissime, fidelissimeque servavit). See Caracciolo (1612), 216–19; Lenzo (2011), doc. I.2, 175–6.

[36] Capasso (1881–92), i. 205, 347–8; Altamura (1974), 112; Kelly (2011), 238–9, 311.

Fig. 12.4. Frontispiece from the *Chroniche de la inclyta cità de Napole emendatissime. Con li bagni de Puzolo et Ischia. Novamente ristampate, stampate in la inclita cità de Neapole, per m. Evangelista di Presenzani de Pavia*, adi xxvii de Aprile 1526.

Source: From Lenzo (2011).

Quirinale in Rome, which was not far from his family villa.[37] This church had been built in an area crowded with ancient remains, including the temple of Serapis (also known as the tower of Maecenas), the baths of Constantine, and the two marble statues of Castor and Pollux, which at the time were believed to be works of the Greek artists Phidias and Praxiteles. In 1558 Carafa commissioned

[37] For the church of San Silvestro, see Negro (1985); Torresi (1989); Torresi (1994). For the Villa Carafa, see Coffin (1982); Parlato (1990).

Michelangelo to restore the ancient stairway of the Serapis temple that ascended to the top of the hill, which passed between Carafa's villa and the Theatines' church.[38] This ambitious plan remained unrealized, but it nevertheless provides us with some further evidence of Carafa's interest in classical antiquity. Furthermore, it is interesting to note that in Rome, as in Naples, the Order of the Theatines was connected to the figures of Castor and Pollux: this repeated classical link may well have been intended to recall the Order's distinctive feature of having two founders, rather than a single one.

Returning to Naples, in 1538 the church of S. Paolo and the temple of Castor and Pollux were two distinctive buildings that were separated by a garden, whose contours are easily visible in the drawing by Tyfernus (Fig. 12.2). Still, in the eyes of the Theatines, the church of S. Paolo clearly gained prestige from its juxtaposition with the ancient marble columns of the temple, which were viewed not only as remains of classical antiquity, but also as key monuments of both Christian memory and Neapolitan civic identity.

REBUILDING THE ANCIENT STEPS (1576)

The church that the Theatines obtained in 1538 was a medieval building.[39] Documents and written descriptions of the time inform us that it had three aisles separated by arches resting on eighteen marble columns, and that four other columns—two of marble and two of granite—supported the 'arch of the choir'.[40] This probably means that the church had an ambulatory behind the altar, as was the case in other early medieval Neapolitan churches, such as S. Giovanni Maggiore and S. Giorgio Maggiore. At the time of the Theatines' arrival, the church was in very poor condition; contemporary guides

[38] Del Tufo (1609), 52–3; Castaldo (1615), 147–8; Ancel (1908), 70; Ackerman (1988 [1961]), 327–8; De Maio (1965), 110; De Maio (1981), 372–3; Argan and Contardi (2007 [1990]), 350.

[39] In the ninth-century *Sanctae Neapolitanae Ecclesiae* we read that the first church had been built during the government of Duke Antimo (801–17); from other documents we know that in 991 it was one of the six main parish churches of Naples and that in 997 it was served by a congregation of priests. See Capasso (1895), 109–10.

[40] ASNa, *Mon. Sopp.*, 1135/a, fo. 11r–v; ASNa, *Mon. Sopp.*, 1071, p. 7. See Lenzo (2011), 24–5, 145.

of Naples describe it as 'abandoned as a cave'.[41] After undertaking some initial repairs, the Theatines modified the inner space in order to make it fit their liturgical needs. They built a longitudinal wooden paling to separate the congregation into men and women; closed the choir with a curtain behind the main altar, and moved all tombs to the exterior of the church. Then, the garden between the ancient columns and the church was transformed into a graveyard.[42] The Theatines avoided any secular interference in their affairs, even if this choice meant that they would forgo the income gained from conceding chapels to private families. The early years of the Order's residence in Naples are characterized by a strong pauperism, although this was to change over the next decades. Since the time of the Order's foundation, the Theatines had been obliged to respect chastity, obedience, and above all poverty; the older manuscript and printed chronicles of the Neapolitan community often emphasized the poverty of the fathers, who lived in very small rooms made of wooden boards.[43] After the promotion of Carafa to pope, the politics of the Theatines became increasingly ambitious, and in 1555 the community of S. Paolo started to build a cloister to enlarge the convent. Only when the cloisters were finished in 1576 did they plan the refashioning of the main entrance of the church. Here, the Theatines faced a problem, since the open ancient marble steps ascending from the street to the level of the columns were often used as a meeting point by the 'idlers' of the town, who spent time there gambling, fooling around, and blaspheming.[44] Their solution to this problem was to

---

[41] Di Falco (1548), folios not numbered: 'Nella più bella parte della città fu dagli antichi edificato il tempio di Castore e Polluce, come in Roma, il quale li christiani consecraro a San Paulo. Questo tempio gran tempo è stato abbandonato a modo di spelunca, poi, per la bontà de' Napoletani, li quali sempre hanno a riverenza i luoghi sacri, vi hanno collocati li venerabili et onestissimi preti teatini.' De Stefano (1560), 26: 'Mi pareva detta chiesa essere abandonata (et non sò per che essendo in si alto, e bello luogo) à modo di spelunca; poi per bontà & pietà de Napolitani, i quali sempre hanno à reverenza i luoghi sacri, vi hanno collocati i religiosi et honestissimi Preti Teatini.'

[42] Llombart (1962); Lenzo (2011), 76–92.

[43] Paschini (1926); Andreu (1945). For a detailed analysis of pauperism in the Counter-Reformation period, see Schofield (2002).

[44] Valerio Pagano, *Breve relatione del principio e progressi de la religione de chierici regolari e delle attioni d'alcuni di essi padri notate da don Valerio Pagano dell'istessa religione*, manuscript dated 1616, Naples, Biblioteca Nazionale 'Vittorio Emanuele III', manuscript *San Martino* 564, fo. 113r: 'La porta magiore de la chiesa di San Paolo di Napoli si teneva dalli padri sempre serrata, perché le scale di essa che erano trenta sei stavano patente, et aperte al pubblico, e tanto scomodo, che non si ci saliva da

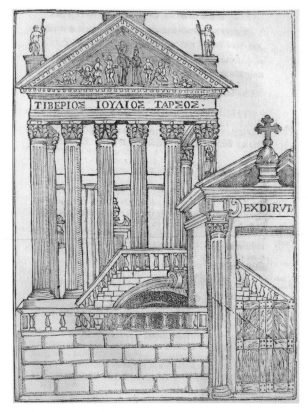

Fig. 12.5. The pronaos of the temple of the Dioscuri converted into the porch of S. Paolo Maggiore and the new staircase built by the Theatines.

Source: From Summonte (1601) (the figure is taken from the later 1675 edn.).

build a new staircase, which would be separated from the street by a wall (Fig. 12.5).

This area of the city was, however, under the control of the Eletti. These were deputies who were elected every year by the six Seggi of Naples (the Seggi were the councils where the members of the families of the local elite gathered to take decisions regarding the

niuno fuorché da gente bassa solo li vennerdì di marzo, et in quelle scale ci dimoravano continuamente persone otiose, e dissolute li quali ci giocavano, e ci facevano altre actioni sconvenienti da un si fatto luogo, in modo che publicamente era solito a dire per la città li marioli de le scale di San Paolo.'

government of the town). In Naples there were five Seggi of Noble-men (Capuana, Nido, Montagna, Portanuova, and Porto) and one of Commoners—each of which appointed one or two Eletti.[45] The Theatines needed the Eletti's approval before beginning work, so from 17 July until 3 August 1576 they went around the different Seggi presenting a three-dimensional cardboard model of the new staircase, while issuing assurances that the work would be paid for by the Theatines—even though the new staircase would be an ornament for the whole city.[46] Each of the Seggi approved the project, and thereby allowed the Theatines to reuse the ancient marble steps. The Seggio of Capuana, however, specifically forbade the sale of any ancient marbles, while the Seggio of the Commoners added that no alterations could be made to the columns of the pronaos.[47] We might argue, then, that although the Seggi allowed the Theatines to change the staircase, they did not abdicate their control over one of the main antiquities of the town (in Naples, as in the other cities of the Kingdom such as Capua, Sessa, Sorrento, and Barletta, the Eletti of the Seggi had a special power over antiquities, especially when the ancient monuments were considered of particular importance for civic memory).[48]

[45] On the Seggi of Naples, see Tutini (1644); Schipa (1908); Galasso (1998), 61–110; Visceglia (1999); Vitale (2003); Vitale (2010); Santangelo (2013); Lenzo (2014).

[46] The model was presented to the Seggio of Capuana on 27 July, to the Seggio of Nido on 28 July, to the Seggio of Montagna 29 July, to the Seggio of Porto and to that of Portanuova on 31 July, and finally to that of the Commoners on 3 August. See Lenzo (2011), doc. II.1–6, 180–1.

[47] ASNa, *Mon. Sopp.*, vol. 1135, fo. 201: 'purché nel fare detta nova gradiata se habiano da servire dell'istessi marmi ch'al presente vi sono [. . .] et con espressa conditione che l'arco et colonne di dett'ecclesia non se debiano ne possano toccare o mutare in modo alcuno dall'essere in che al presente se ritrovano'. See Lenzo (2011), doc. II.6, 180–1. For the legislation against marble reuse, see ASNa, *Mon. Sopp.*, vol. 1135, fo. 197: 'ne si alienerà alcuno di marmi antiqui anzi vi si aggiongeranno de gl'altri'. See Lenzo (2011), doc. II.1, 180–1.

[48] In the buildings hosting the Seggi of Naples there were small public collections of antiquities: in the Seggio of Nido there was the ancient statue of the river Nile (see Fig. 1.1), in that of Capuana there was a female statue thought to be a portrait of Parthenope, while in that of Montagna an ancient Roman inscription naming the emperor Constantine the Great and his mother Helena was preserved. It should be noted that collections of antiquities are documented in the Seggi of many other towns of Southern Italy, such as Sessa, Nola, Capua, Sorrento, and Barletta. See Lenzo (2014).

It was during the excavations undertaken for this work that two Roman male torsos were found in the area underneath the old staircase (cf. Fig. 3.7). The decrees of the Eletti stipulated that these stones had to be preserved rather than sold, but rather than simply hand them over to the Eletti, the Theatines decided to display the fragmentary statues at the entrance of the church, under the ancient columns. The torsos were soon identified as the *simulacra* of Castor and Pollux, which—according to the medieval legend—St Peter had caused to fall from the top of the temple. For that reason they were proudly displayed by the Theatines, in a way that was similar to how ancient Romans used to display trophies won in battle. This 'triumphalist' interpretation is given support by the new inscription that was carved on the gate that gave access to the staircase from the street, the text of which explicitly opposed St Peter and St Paul, the two princes of the Apostles, to the pagan twins Castor and Pollux:

EX DIRUTIS MARMORIBUS CASTORI ET POLLUCI FALSIS DIIS DICATIS NUNC PETRO ET PAULO VERI DIVIS AD FACILIOREM ASCENSUM OPUS FACIENDUM CURARUNT CLERICI REGULARES. MDLXXVIII.

By using the ruined marbles formerly dedicated to the false gods Castor and Pollux, now consecrated to the true saints Peter and Paul, the Theatines made [this stairway] for an easier ascent. 1578.

This new inscription, which recalled the Greek one carved in the pediment of the temple, gave a new Christian meaning to the whole building complex without physically altering the ancient remains. The ruined marbles, the columns of the temple, the sculpted pediment, and the inscription—all of which were once dedicated to the pagan idols—were now *re*dedicated to the *veri divis*, St Peter and St Paul. In this way, they ceased to be simple proof of the ancient magnificence of the town, and became a *signum* of the triumph of the Christian Church over the pagan religion.

The operation undertaken in Naples by the Theatines reflects a broader shift in the relationship between antiquity and Christianity, and it was to be followed a few years later in Rome by Pope Sixtus V (1585–90). The total condemnation of pagan antiquity at the time of Sixtus' predecessor Pope Gregory XIII is encapsulated in the fresco painted on the ceiling of the Sala di Costantino in the Vatican Palace, which represents a broken statue of Mercury lying on the soil in front of a golden cross.[49] Sixtus V, instead, understood that it was impossible to purge Rome of its past, and introduced a new way of negotiating the relationship between antiquity and Christianity, by regarding the preserved remains of classical antiquity as the material expression of the Christian Church's triumph over the pagan religion. He commissioned his architect Domenico Fontana to place statues of St Peter and St Paul at the top of the spiral columns of Trajan and Antoninus Pius (the latter of which would later be reidentified as the column of Marcus Aurelius), and he also reinstated many fallen Egyptian obelisks, topping them with crosses.[50] In Rome, as in Naples, such operations meant that antiquities could be Christianized and treated as trophies of a victory over paganism. Furthermore, this victory could be also read as an allusion to the new challenges that the Catholic Church of Rome was facing in the conflict with the Reformed Churches of northern Europe.

The new entrance to the church of S. Paolo was completed in 1591, and at this time the nave was also rebuilt and extended up to the ancient pronaos. The burial area that had until then separated the church from the ancient columns was transferred under the porch, where a crypt (*succorpo*, or *confessione*) was then excavated.[51] On the same occasion, the gap at the centre of the ancient pediment was sealed with a new wall, on whose surface a fresco depicting the figures of Castor and Pollux armed with shields and spears was painted.[52] By converting the marble pronaos into the porch of the church, the ancient columns became a part of the new building, and history was incorporated into the present.

The creation of a crypt that could be accessed from the street was an adaptation of the early Christian model of Roman *confessiones*, a model that was at that time being renewed by Cardinal Cesario Baronio in the restoration of the churches of SS. Nereus and Achilleus and S. Cesareo de Appia in Rome.[53] Baronio was a historian who had spent many years researching the early history of the Church, and who eventually published the monumental *Annales Ecclesiastici* in twelve volumes from 1588 to 1607.[54] His work sparked a new interest

---

[49] Chastel (1989); Buddensieg (1965).
[50] Mercati (1589); Fontana (1590); Madonna (1992); Curcio, Navone, and Villari (2011).
[51] Lenzo (2011), 141–4.   [52] Summonte (1601), i. 92.
[53] Herz (1988).   [54] De Maio, Giulia, and Mazzacane (1982).

in early Christianity, and the crypt of S. Paolo Maggiore can be interpreted as an example of this. The connection with Baronio is more than simple coincidence: the Roman cardinal had lived for a time in the convent of S. Paolo Maggiore during his stay in Naples in 1582, and during this time he had become a friend of the Neapolitan Theatine priest Marco Palescandolo, who was responsible for many architectural works undertaken by his Order in Naples as well as in other cities.[55] Palescandolo promoted a new trend in the architecture of the Order, which is well evident in the design of the second cloister of the convent of S. Paolo Maggiore, which was built in 1608.[56] This cloister reflected early Christian models insofar as it incorporated arches resting on ancient marble columns—an association that had been condemned as incorrect since the time of Leon Battista Alberti's *De Re Aedificatoria*, but one that could now find a prestigious model in the *quadriportici* of the first Roman Christian churches.[57] Furthermore, the marble columns of the cloister were those that had been removed by the Theatines from the medieval church of S. Paolo when they started building the new church between 1583 and 1591.[58] It must have been clear even in 1608 that the columns, before being incorporated into the medieval church, had been used in the interior of the temple of the Dioscuri. During the rebuilding of the staircase, the sentence written over the doorway had been enough to communicate the new ideological meaning; in this last phase, the architectural choices also communicate a revival of early Christian models.

EPILOGUE: THE COLLAPSE OF THE PRONAOS (1688) AND THE AFTERLIFE OF THE COLUMNS

In 1671 Gaetano Thiene was proclaimed saint, and the Theatines of S. Paolo Maggiore decided to celebrate the event by building a new facade, which they commissioned from the architect Dionisio Lazzari.

---

[55] For the stay in Naples, see Del Tufo (1616), 49; Engenio Caracciolo (1624), 87; Osbat (1982).

[56] Del Tufo (1609), 127–9, 131, 197–209; Del Tufo (1616), 50, 84–7; Silos (1650–66), i. 528, 590, 648. On Palescandolo and architecture, see Borrelli (1967), 33–9; Savarese (1986), 29–48; Piazza (2003); Lenzo (2011), 108–10, 129–30.

[57] Lenzo (2011), 144–6.

[58] ASNa, *Mon. Sopp.*, 1135/a, fo. 11r–v; ASN, *Mon. Sopp.*, 1071, 7.

The small private buildings that leaned against the sides of the pronaos were bought and pulled down, and a new barrel vault was built between the ancient columns and the church facade. Statues of St Paul and St Peter by the sculptor Andrea Falcone were placed inside niches in the aisles of the facade, and the two busts of Castor and Pollux were encased into the wall under their feet (Fig. 12.7).[59] Once again, as in the earlier construction of the staircase, the motivations for this arrangement were explained in accompanying inscriptions.[60] Under the statue of St Peter, the inscription read:

AUDIT VEL SURDUS POLLUX / CUM CASTORE PETRUM; / NEC MORA: PRAECIPITI MARMORE / UTERQUE RUIT

Let's hear, indeed, dumb Castor and Pollux: not wrongly did Peter make your marble statues fall down.

Meanwhile, the following inscription appeared under the statue of St Paul:

TYNDARIDAS VOX MISSA FERIT / PALMA INTEGRA PETRI EST / DIVIDIT AT TECUM PAULE / TROPHEAE LIBENS.

O Paul, the voice emitted wounds the Tyndarides [i.e. Dioscuri], the glad palm of Peter's victory is fully shared with you.[61]

Unfortunately, however, the ancient structure of the pronaos was not able to support the new barrel vault that had been built by Lazzari and, after having been damaged by the earthquake of 1687, it collapsed almost entirely in the earthquake of 5 June 1688 (Fig. 12.6).[62] Previous works undertaken in 1635 and completed in 1639 had slightly damaged the corner of the temple, meaning that part of the inscribed entablature had to be replaced, but the damage of 1688 was so great that this kind of restoration was unthinkable.[63] Only four columns remained standing, while the other marbles (the columns,

---

[59] The two ancient torsos were only removed from this position in 1972, when work undertaken in the crypt of S. Gaetano led to the discovery of a marble leg belonging to one of the statues. They are now on display in the Museo Archeologico Nazionale. See Adamo Muscettola (1985).

[60] Rizzo (1984b), docs. 4, 6, 35; Savarese (1986), 65–6. On the statues of St Peter and St Paul by Andrea Falcone, see Rizzo (1984a), 373, doc. 5.

[61] Castor and Pollux were also called 'Tyndarides', from Tyndarus, king of Sparta and husband of their mother Leda. See Harris (1903); Harris (1906).

[62] Celano (1692), ii. 158–9; Chiarini (1856–60), iii. 214–15.

[63] Spinazzola (1901); Lenzo (2011), 21, 151.

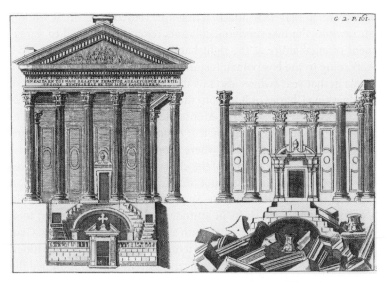

Fig. 12.6. Engraving after a drawing of Arcangelo Guglielmelli, S. Paolo Maggiore before and after the earthquake of 1688.
Source: From Celano (1692).

entablature, and pediment) fell down: these remained on the ground in front of the church for several years, until 1712, when Andrea Avellino, another member of the Theatine convent of S. Paolo, was proclaimed saint.[64] On this occasion the Theatines decided to refurbish the church, and commissioned the painter Francesco Solimena and the architect Domenico Antonio Vaccaro to do so. They rebuilt the entrance step (which had been damaged by the collapse of the columns), constructed the new chapel of the Frasconi family, and added a marble revetment to the pilasters of the nave and the *hypogeum* sepulchral chapel of S. Gaetano.[65] Significantly, all of this work was completed using the ancient marbles that had fallen down in the earthquake, along with two of the four columns that had remained standing. Records of payments made to the workers inform us that even the reliefs of the pediment were cut up so that the background

[64] *Diario della casa di San Paolo Maggiore*, BNN, *San Martino*, MS 682, folios not numbered under the date 25 April 1687 and 5 June 1688. See Lenzo (2011), doc. I.2, 210–11.
[65] Lenzo (2005); (2011), 165–71, 212–13.

slab to which they were attached might be reused for the new work.[66] Meanwhile, the two surviving columns remained attached to a fragment of entablature at the right-hand side of the facade until 1734. According to the Neapolitan historiographer Bernardo De Dominici, it was in that year (which also saw the triumphal entry into Naples of the new king Charles of Bourbon) that Ferdinando Sanfelice, architect and member of the Seggio of Montagna, convinced the Theatines to preserve the memory of the ancient temple by arranging the columns at both sides of the doorway, where they still stand today.[67]

In conclusion, the history of the church of S. Paolo Maggiore gives us some valuable insights, not only into the strong connection between the Theatines and the ancient temple of the Dioscuri, but also into the broader shifts in attitudes to pagan antiquity that took place over the course of the sixteenth and seventeenth centuries. Gian Pietro Carafa's decision to use the temple as the site of the Theatines' church in Naples was highly significant, since it both conditioned the subsequent building history of the new church, and helped to shape the identity of the Theatine Order itself. Carafa has always been regarded as a hero of the Catholic Counter-Reformation, but this little-known episode of his life sheds new light on his antiquarian interests. At the same time, while in 1538 the ancient temple was able to give prestige to the new church without requiring any justification, after the conclusion of the Council of Trent in 1573 the use of these evidently pagan remains was felt to be much more problematic. It is for this reason that the Theatines looked back to the first centuries of Christianity for a solution, to the time when many pagan temples had been transformed into Christian churches. Anticipating a more

[66] Archivio Storico del Banco di Napoli, *Banco della Pietà, Giornale copiapolizze n. 1300*, under the entry for 24 December 1712: 'A Francesco Capece Minutolo ducati 19.13 e per lui a Domenico Antonio Vaccaro sono cioè ducati 15.13 per il marmo bardiglio posto in opera nel marmi seu pilastri di base posti sopra nella chiesa di San Paolo Maggiore dei padri teatini e ducati 4 per la secatura della statua antica e con detto pagamento resta soddisfatto.' See Rizzo (2001), 236, doc. 230.

[67] De Dominici (1742–5), iii. 653: 'li padri teatini di S. Paolo volevano levar via le due colonne, che stavano per cascare, che erano rimaste dell'antico tempio di Castore, e Polluce, ma ad istanza di esso Sanfelice amante dell'antichità colla direzione del medesimo l'han situate una per parte nel prospetto della loro chiesa avendo esso don Ferdinando non solo fatto contribuire qualche cosa dalla città, ma anche posto il complimento di suo proprio danaro per mantenere a' posteri tal memoria'. See Ward (1988), 199.

Fig. 12.7. S. Paolo Maggiore, Naples. Columns of the temple of the Dioscuri and statue of St Paul. Until 1972, one of the two ancient marble torsos of the Dioscuri was encased in the niche under the statue.

Source: Photograph: Fulvio Lenzo.

general trend that would start in Rome some years later, these ancient statues and architectural remains of the pagan temple of the Dioscuri in Naples were presented by the Theatines as a trophy—in other words, as material evidence of Christianity's victory against paganism.

13

Reshaping the Past, Shaping the Present

Andrea de Jorio and Naples' Classical Heritage

Annalisa Marzano

> Beyond this, the questions that foreigners are always asking we
> Neapolitans about the meaning of one behavior or another . . .
> have increased our determination . . . to illustrate, as far as we
> can, even the apparently disreputable aspects of the very inter-
> esting customs of our country that are, in reality, full of phil-
> osophy, and could be said to be *Roman, Greek, Natural.*[1]

With these words Andrea de Jorio, canon of the cathedral of Naples,
archaeologist, and curator of the Gallery of Etruscan Vases at the Real
Museo Borbonico in Naples, explained one of the motivations behind
his 1832 treatise on ancient and Neapolitan gesture, *La mimica degli
antichi investigata nel gestire napoletano.*[2] De Jorio's book was the

---

[1] 'A tutto ciò, per dare il colmo alla nostra determinazione, si aggiungeva così il
sentire le continue domande, che gli esteri fanno ai nostri, sul significato di tale, o tal
altro atteggiamento . . . ci invitava ad illustrare, per quanto era in nostro potere, anche
questa apparentemente disprezzabile parte degl'interessantissimi usi del nostro paese,
che sono in realtà pieni di filosofia, che potrebbe dirsi *Romana, Greca, Naturale*.' De
Jorio (1832), p. vii; all English translations of de Jorio's text present in this chapter are
by A. Kendon, quoted from De Jorio (2000). The original 1832 book can be consulted
from the Internet Archive (<http://archive.org/details/lamimicadeglian03jorigoog>,
last accessed July 2013).

[2] The Real Museo Borbonico was the precursor of the current Museo Archeologico
Nazionale. It was created in 1777 when the Museo Ercolanese at the Royal Palace of
Portici and the Museo Farnesiano at the Royal Palace of Capodimonte were merged

first (and for decades to come remained the only) study of Neapolitan gesture; it took an ethnographic approach to the subject,[3] discussing gesture as a 'culturally established communicative code analogous to language'.[4] *La mimica* is still one of the most complex treatises ever written on the topic of gesture, and it remains of great interest to modern scholars of language and semiotics.[5] In part, this is because de Jorio explores the broader nature of the relationship between the physical form of a gesture and its meaning, and tackles the question of how to describe something that is both a physical action and a significant act.[6] This is not the only work by de Jorio; he was a prolific writer and published several books on topics such as the antiquities of Cumae (*Gli scheletri cumani*, 1810), the collections of the Real Museo (the *Galleria de' vasi del real museo Borbonico*, 1825 and the *Guide pour la galerie de peintures anciennes*, 1830), the site of Puteoli (*Guida di Pozzuoli e contorno*, published in 1817 and in a second enlarged edition in 1822), and, of course, Pompeii (*Plan de Pompéi, et remarques sur ces édifices*, 1828, later published in Italian with the addition

and moved into the monumental building the museum still occupies. After the unification of Italy in 1861, the name was changed to 'Museo Nazionale'. The 'Etruscan' vases in de Jorio's care were, in fact, Greek vases, which had been made either in mainland Greece or in the Greek colonies of southern Italy. This kind of vase had been first discovered in Etruscan tombs in Tuscany and was thus thought to be of Etruscan manufacture. In the late eighteenth century it was understood that they were in fact Greek vases, but the label 'Etruscan' continued to be used: Momigliano (1950).

[3] As noted by Carabelli (1996), 101, several Neapolitan intellectuals of the late eighteenth/early nineteenth century combined antiquarian interest with interest in the people and customs of their own region. Connections between traditions and practices of antiquity and the present were, for instance, made in works such as Nicola Valletta's *Cicalata sul fascino volgarmente detto jettatura* (1787), which marked the start of several studies on the ancient cult of Priapus and modern folklore published in Naples; see Carabelli (1996), 95–6. Michele Arditi (who was in the early 1800s director of the Real Museo Borbonico and 'Sopraintendente degli scavi di antichità del Regno') also wrote a work on ancient gesture (*Simile sul pantomino degli antichi*), which, however, remained unpublished: de Rosa (1841), 25.

[4] Kendon in de Jorio (2000), pp. xx, xxii; Kendon (2004), 45–50. The book was used as a reference work by various academic writers of the nineteenth century, including Garrick Mallery, author of *Sign Language among North American Indians compared with that of Other Peoples and Deaf-mutes* (1880) and Wilhelm Wundt, author of *Völkerpsychologie* (1900). On more recent, popular appreciations of *La mimica* see Ceserani (2012), 149.

[5] Magli (1986).

[6] Kendon in de Jorio (2000), pp. xx, lxxii–lxxiii: Kendon notes that de Jorio's view that gestures have a 'double aspect' (i.e. they are both physical and meaningful acts) is reminiscent of Saussure's description of the linguistic sign 'in which the sound pattern or the *significant* is inseparable from what it signifies, the *signifié*' (p. lxxiii).

of plans of several buildings that had been discovered in the inter-
vening period). His writings followed a well-established Neapolitan
tradition of writing guidebooks which incorporated recent scholarly
advances.[7]

The aim of *La mimica*, as de Jorio declares in the introduction to
the volume, was to provide scholars of Graeco-Roman antiquity with
a tool that would help them to understand the gestures and poses
depicted in ancient figurative media and described in Greek and Latin
literary texts.[8] His methodology was underpinned by a conviction
that the ordinary people of the Naples of his time had preserved in
their culture—and in their gestures—the traditions of the earlier
Greek and Roman inhabitants of the region. De Jorio had developed
the idea for his treatise while he was curator of the Real Museo
Borbonico. He wrote of this time:

> We found ourselves in charge of giving verbal explanations to those
> who came to admire the numerous Greek painted vases collected in the
> Real Museo Borbonico. As a result, we had many opportunities to
> observe ancient gestures in these vases, and to note that they were in
> every way similar to our own.[9]

The gestures of the 'common folk' of early nineteenth-century Naples
were thus presented as an interpretative tool that might help viewers
to reach a deeper understanding of the figurative art of classical
antiquity—the vases, frescoes, mosaics, and sculptures that had
'revealed' classical antiquity to the world, particularly after the discoveries at Pompeii and Herculaneum of the preceding century. In de
Jorio's mind, the everyday habits of the city's living population
opened a window onto the populations of the past: as has been

---

[7] Ceserani (2012), 147. On de Jorio and the cultural context of his time see also:
Carabelli (1996), 102–6; Schnapp (2000), 164–6; Ceserani (2012), 147–53.

[8] As Kendon reports (de Jorio (2000), p. xxxi), according to his biographer, de
Jorio was sought out by cultivated people of every class, and as soon as foreigners
arrived in Naples they would seek an appointment with him. On artistic literature of
the sixteenth–eighteenth centuries focusing on 'how to read' works of art see Haskell
(1993), 131–58; 155–8 for a discussion of de Jorio's work. At p. 145 Haskell notes that
treatises on expression and gesture (e.g. J. Bulwer, *Chirologia or the natural language
of the hand* (London 1644)) were popular in the mid-seventeenth century in connection with the interest in oratory and theatre.

[9] 'Ritrovandoci nell'incarico di dare qualche verbale spiegazione a coloro, che
venivano ad ammirare la numerosa raccolta de' vasi Greci dipinti nel R.M.B. non
mancavamo nelle opportunità di far essi osservare alcuni antichi gesti, dell'intutto
[*sic*] simili ai nostri.' De Jorio (1832), p. v.

noted above, his attempts to link archaeology and ethnography constitute another highly original aspect of *La mimica*. It is true that during the eighteenth century several studies (most of which were written in French) had noted similarities between the customs of the American Indians and those of ancient Greeks and Egyptians, and that in this period there had been a broader growth in interest in the customs of the 'common folk' of Europe.[10] However, de Jorio was more systematic in his attempts to link ethnography with archaeology in order to create a new method of enquiry. As noted by Schnapp, while de Jorio was influenced by, amongst others, the baron d'Hancarville, his approach to everyday life in Naples differed from that of French and English scholars and was 'from the inside rather than with condescending detachment'.[11] De Jorio's experience of explaining to illustrious foreign visitors the meaning of the gestures they saw in the ancient works of art collected by the Bourbon kings on the basis of parallels drawn from the typical—indeed even nowadays stereotypical—characteristic of the Neapolitans to express themselves colourfully in speech and gesture, is encapsulated in one passage from the writings of Winckelmann, quoted by de Jorio himself.[12] Winckelmann, in a letter on the discoveries of Pompeii and Herculaneum, turned his attention to a small statuette from Herculaneum depicting Priapus. He noted that

Priapus appears to make a kind of gesture very common among the Italians but entirely unknown to the Germans: consequently I will have difficulty in making understood the description I will give of it.[13]

---

[10] Kendon in de Jorio (2000), pp. xxi, lxviii; see also Cocchiara (1954); Pucci (1993).

[11] Schnapp (2000), 164; on d'Hancarville and Hamilton see most recently Heringman (2013), 125–54; also 165–75 for some discussion of de Jorio's work.

[12] De Jorio (1832), 176–7. On Neapolitan gestures, see e.g. the following comment by Goethe: 'To return to the lower populace of Naples . . . Their language is said to be figurative, their wit very shrewd and cutting. The ancient Atella lay in the neighbourhood of Naples, and seeing their favourite Punchinello still continues those celebrated diversions'. Goethe (1885), 337. Kendon (de Jorio (2000), p. xxii) notes that Neapolitans were known for the complexity of their use of gesture (e.g. J. J. Blunt *Vestiges of Ancient Manners and Customs Discoverable in Modern Italy* (1823)—a work that was probably unknown to de Jorio, since he does not mention it), but that it was de Jorio's book which drew attention to this aspect of Neapolitan life.

[13] De Jorio quotes from J. J. Winckelmann, *Recueil de lettres sur les découvertes faites à Herculanum, à Pompeii, à Stabia, à Caserte & à Rome, avec des notes critiques: Traduit de l'Allemand* (1784). The passage he quotes in French reads: 'Ce Priape paroît faire une espèce de gestes fort ordinaire aux Italiens, mais entièrement inconnu

The ancient gestures that are discussed in *La mimica* come not only from figurative arts, but also from literary texts. In discussing the five distinct signs used to ask for something (whether material or mental objects), de Jorio refers to lines from the comedies of Terence and to the miniatures of the Vatican Terence (the *Codex Vaticanus Latinus* 3868).[14] The passage is worth citing, for it shows how he describes the gestures and how he validates the antiquity of a very common gesture that was used in his time (and that is, in fact, still used today):

> 3. *The fingers extended and joined in a point, turned upwards* (see Plate XX, no. 6). The hand held thus is raised a little towards one's own face, and one moves it several times directly from this position towards the person with whom one is speaking. Perhaps the meaning of this gesture arises from the fact that it is often used when questions are asked of persons who speak much, without making themselves understood or who, in their presentation do not explain well what they are talking about... In this case, by uniting the tips of the fingers together into a single point, one is understood to be saying: 'bring your ideas together, collect all your words together in one, or in brief, in one point, and tell me, what is that you wish to say?' In short: 'What are you talking about?'
>
> 4. *Thumb and index finger joined at their tips, the other fingers indifferently open.* Lifting the hand up, arranged in this manner and moving it back and forth, means the same as the preceding gesture, being only the diminutive of it.
>
> There are many examples in antiquity both of this sign and the preceding one. This in the often cited passage from Terence, *Eunuchus* Act IV, sc. V, Pythias, saying *an abiit iam a milite?* (Has she left the Captain's yet?) makes the present gesture. Again, in *Heauton* ('The Self-Tormentor'), Act III. Sc. III, Chremes does the same as he asks *Quid istuc quaeso?* ('Pray, what is the meaning of this?'). Gesture n. 3 is also frequently found in this scene. Likewise, in *Andria* ('the girl from Andros'), Act I, Sc. 1, Sosia says to Simo: *quid est, quod tibi mea ars efficere hoc posit amplius?* ('What more can a cook's art do for you, sir?') and makes this gesture as he does so.)[15]

aux Allemans: conséquemment j'aurai peine a leur faire entendre la description que j'en vais faire.'

[14] Kendon in de Jorio (2000), 130–3: he probably had seen the miniatures in one of the three editions of Terence available at this time, which also reproduced the miniatures of the Vatican Terence.

[15] '3. *Dita allungate e riunite in punta, rivolte in su (v. tav. 20. n. 5)* [*NB. This is a mistake on De Jorio's part, the gesture he refers to is number 6 of plate XX*]. La mano così disposta si alza un poco verso il proprio volto, e si agita più volte direttamente da

De Jorio evidently believed that the illustrations provided in the manuscript derived from very ancient archetypes and offered examples of the gestures that would have been performed by the actors when performing the plays (thus functioning in the manuscript as a sort of 'stage direction'). While his view is not completely correct, he was right to believe that these gestures had been in use for many centuries. Modern scholars agree that the illustrations in the manuscript (and hence the gestures depicted) have an origin in classical antiquity, although there is no agreement on a specific date.[16]

In addition to the novelty of its topic and methodology, De Jorio's monograph was important for another reason. By establishing a direct link with the gestures of the much-admired classical antiquity, he gave dignity to ordinary Neapolitan people, transforming their gestures into a topic worthy of scholarly study, as well as rehabilitating the customs of a population that was often portrayed as dirty, poor, and idle in the writings of Europeans on the Grand Tour. Sometimes, these negative comments referred to Italy as a whole, as in the following passage from a 1743 text:

questo alla persona con la quale si parla. Forse il significato di questo atteggiamento nasce da che spesso tali domande si fanno a persone, le quali sogliono parlare molto, senza farsi comprendere, o vi si presentano non ispiegandosi bene . . . su quello che chiedono. In questo caso con riunire in un punto tutte le dita della mano s'intende dir loro = *riunite le vostre idee: raccogliete le tante parole in una, e in breve, in un punto, e ditemi cosa volete?* In somma, *di che si tratta?* 4. *Pollice ed indice riuniti ne' loro estremi, le altre dita indifferentemente aperte.* Portando in su ed agitando nel descritto modo la mano cosi atteggiata, dinoterà anche lo stesso che l'antecedente, non essendo il presente gesto che un diminutivo di quello. Sono molti gli esempi dell'antichità di questo segno, come del precedente nello spesso citato Terenzio, *Eun.* Att. IV. Sc. V. *Pythias,* dicendo, *an abiit jam a milite* fa il presente gesto, e nell'Heaut. Att. III. Sc. III Cremete domandando, *Quid istuc quaeso?* Fa lo stesso: il gesto n. 3 è anche frequente nelle dette scene, come nell'*And.* Att. I. Sc. I Sosia dice a Simone. *Quid est, quod tibi mea ars efficere hoc possit amplius?*' De Jorio (1832), 86.

[16] Kendon in de Jorio (2000), 130–3, with relevant bibliography. The Vatican manuscript dates to around the early ninth century AD; it was produced at the Abbey of Corbie in Picardy by the copyist Hrogdarius and the miniaturist Adelricus. Its texts and illustrations are a copy of an earlier work, probably dated to the fifth century AD, which is itself believed to have been a copy of an earlier manuscript. Because of the stylistic connections between these miniatures and ancient paintings and mosaics of theatrical subjects known from Herculaneum, and the affinity with gestures described in the first-century AD work on oratory by Quintilian, some date the miniatures' archetypes to the first century AD. Others think a fourth-century AD date is more likely.

> The Italians are so intirely [*sic*] taken up with what the People and
> Country were seventeen hundred years ago that they neglect the present
> Condition of both. Their cities are now thin of Inhabitants, their soil
> barren and uncultivated, and themselves a pusillanimous, enervate, lazy
> people.[17]

By the mid-eighteenth century, it had indeed become commonplace
amongst northern Europeans to denigrate contemporary Italy and
Italians; comparisons were frequently drawn with the country's glorious past—both the remote past of classical antiquity and the more
recent splendour of the Renaissance. These negative comments
belonged to a broader cultural discourse that divided Europe into
North and South and made these geographical points of reference
into 'charged moral categories'.[18] De Jorio cuts into the midst of this
discourse, which had begun some eighty years before the publication
of his work and which continued for the best part of the nineteenth
century. In the works of historians, philosophers, poets, and other
writers, northern countries and their populations were represented as
industrious, civilized, and orderly. Southern countries, on the contrary, were seen as chaotic and rather uncivilized—their people were
depicted as lazy and as given over completely to the enjoyment of
material pleasures such as eating and drinking. The climate and
environment were thought to be the determining factors that shaped
these differences between countries and people. Of course, such ideas
had already been explored in classical Greek texts, and they had also
been at the core of later works such as Montesquieu's 1748 *De l'esprit
des lois*.[19] In book 17, Montesquieu had presented climate as the
principal factor underlying the strength of Europe and the corresponding weakness of Asia. Interestingly, Italy occupied an ambiguous
place in this work: it was part of Europe, but had affinities with Asia.[20]
Following on from Montesquieu's influential work, the notion that
climate was a determining factor in shaping nations—together with

[17] Mead (1914), 270: the reference he gives is simply *Travels* 11.4, with no author name.
[18] Moe (2006), 13.
[19] Moe (2006), 23–7. Herodotus' *Histories* often explains the different characters of populations in terms of the climate of the region where they live; see Pinna (1988) for an overview of the evolution of the 'climate explanation'.
[20] The ambiguity was reinforced by the example of the despotic rule of Ottoman Turkey, which Montesquieu used to illustrate the shortcomings of the Italian repub-lics (in book 11).

the related notion of a North–South divide—occurred frequently in the writings of European intellectuals. Goethe, who spent time in Naples in 1787, reacted to accusations of idleness by pointing out that common people in Naples did in fact work, but that they did so with a very different predisposition, because of the blissful climate and the natural fertility of their environment:

> The inhabitants of the North are compelled by nature to forethought, to making provisions for the future . . . Unquestionably, the influences of rigorous nature operating for thousands of years have gone to the formation of the character of the northern nations so worthy of honour in many respects. On the other hand, from our point of view, we are apt to judge the natives of the South, towards whom the skies have been so lenient and indulgent, by too strict a rule . . . it would then perhaps be remarked that the so-called *Lazzaroni* are not a hair less active than any of the other classes, that they all in their way do not work simply to live, but to enjoy, and that they are intent on enjoying themselves even while at work.[21]

In fact, at the end of the eighteenth century other positive views of Italy began to emerge, which nuanced the image of an idle and uncivilized South. The lack of 'orderly civilization' and the favourable Mediterranean climate were seen as signs of a more natural world which could regenerate its visitors: the search for and appreciation of the 'picturesque' had begun. In contrast with the depiction of Italy as a land hopelessly sunken in poverty and weakness, many eighteenth-century tourists were enthusiastic about the delights to be found there, dubbing Italy 'the garden of Europe'.[22] The recognition of the country's beautiful natural surroundings and excellent climate did not, however, change the prevailing negative view of its inhabitants. Anna Jameson expressed such ambiguous perspectives in her travel journal, published in 1826:

> Let the modern Italians be what they may . . . a dirty, demoralized, degraded, unprincipled race, centuries behind our trice-blessed, pros-perous, and comfort-loving nation in civilization and morals . . . I am

---

[21] Goethe (1885), 335–6. *Lazzaroni* in this period indicated the urban plebs and also street people who made their living with 'odd jobs'. In 1799 they were at the centre of a popular revolution against the king, who had provoked the war with the French and had then fled Naples, and the French invading army, heroically trying to defend the city. On the history of the *lazzaroni* see Basile and Morea (1996).

[22] Mead (1914), 271.

not come to spy on the nakedness of the land, but implore from her healing airs and lucid skies the health and peace I have lost.[23]

Later in the journal, she states that while civilization and comfort are excellent things, 'they are sworn enemies to the picturesque: they have banished it gradually from our towns . . . but in Italy the picturesque is everywhere, in every variety and form'.[24]

As far as Italian contributions to this discourse are concerned, late eighteenth-century Italian intellectuals reacted and responded to European ideas about Italy, reflecting on their place within Europe and, in some cases, recognizing the country's 'backwardness'.[25] On the contrary, during the Risorgimento, Italian thinking on Italy tended to claim some kind of primacy over the rest of Europe in one field or the other, as is the case in Gioberti's *Del primato morale e civile degli Italiani* (1843), which proclaimed the spiritual superiority of the country as the birthplace and home of Catholicism.[26] De Jorio was well connected in Italian and European intellectual circles, and would have been keenly aware of such ideas and debates.[27] He exchanged correspondence with members of the international community of archaeological scholars, as well as being a fellow of several learned academies in Naples, Rome, Sicily, England, Scotland, and France. He was also a founding member of the Istituto di Corrispondenza Archeologica created in 1829 and based in Rome, which regularly published a *Bulletin* and a *Journal*, in which considerable space was given to discussion of the archaeological developments occurring in Naples.[28] The Istituto was promoted by the Prussian diplomat Christian Bunsen and had received the support of the crown prince of Prussia, the future kaiser Frederick William IV; de Jorio acknowledges in another of his works the valuable conversations about ancient vases that he had enjoyed with the archaeologists Edward Gerhard and Theodor Panofka.[29] De Jorio had also lived

---

[23] *Diary of an Ennuyee*, passage quoted in Moe (2006), 18.
[24] Moe (2006), 19.   [25] Moe (2006), 21.
[26] Moe (2006), 22; Natali (1917). 'Risorgimento' denotes the social, political, military, and cultural events between the late eighteenth century and 1861 that led to the birth of one unified and independent Italian state.
[27] Ceserani (2012), 147–8. His family was also well connected and of some importance, comprising prominent men of law and clergymen: Kendon in de Jorio (2000), pp. xxv–xxvii.
[28] Kendon in de Jorio (2000), p. xxxvii.
[29] *Galleria de' Vasi* (1825), p. v: Kendon in de Jorio (2000), p. xxxvii. De Jorio was made Knight of the Red Eagle of Brandenburg by Frederick Wilhelm of Prussia; he

through several major cultural and political disturbances that affected his city: the rise of Neapolitan Jacobinism, the French invasion of Naples, the creation of the short-lived Neapolitan Republic in 1799 and its violent aftermath, the rule of Napoleonic kings, and the second Bourbon restoration.

This complex cultural and political background clearly shaped the writing of de Jorio's monograph on gesture and can help to shed light on the multiple aims of the text. De Jorio, with *La mimica*, subtly proclaimed Naples and its inhabitants as direct descendants of the classical civilizations that were most highly regarded and admired in the Europe of his time. In this process of legitimization, he ignored entirely the cultural contributions made over the centuries by more recent, foreign rulers of the city, representing Naples and contemporary Neapolitans as the sole Italian heirs of the (ancient Greek) civilization that had created democracy and given birth to the greatest philosophers in history. Interestingly, despite the fact that many of the ancient depictions he describes in *La mimica* relate to Roman objects discovered in Pompeii and Herculaneum, his text clearly places more emphasis on the city's *Greek* past.[30] For example, when discussing how the grammatical form of the superlative is rendered in spoken language and Neapolitan gesture, he refers to the mode that sees the change of the ending of a word to make it into a superlative as the 'Greek superlative'. The following explanation for the label is given:

> In distinguishing the process of forming the superlative by changing the ending of the positive, it is appropriate to call it Greek because of the nobility and antiquity of this princely Idiom, notwithstanding that such a use also has a place in other languages, such as Latin, Italian, etc.[31]

---

dedicated *La mimica degli antichi* to the kaiser. On the influence that de Jorio's work and Neapolitan antiquarianism had on Gerhard see Ceserani (2012), 150–3.

[30] In the book, the customs of de Jorio's time are explicitly connected to both Greeks and Romans (e.g. de Jorio (1832), 234: 'noi eredi de' Greci insieme e de' Romani'); however, in a number of places the understood superiority of Greek culture is implicit, thus making this the most important element inherited from the past. Ceserani (2012) investigates in detail the history of the idea of 'Greekness' in relation to southern Italy; pp. 152–3 on de Jorio's clear interest in the Greek element in his text *Metodo per rinvenire e frugare i sepolcri degli antichi* (1824).

[31] 'Nel denominare il superlativo che si forma col cambiamento della desinenza del positivo, è piaciuto chiamarlo *Greco* per la sola nobiltà, ed antichità, di questo Idioma principe, non già che un tal uso non avesse luogo anche negli altri Idiomi, come Latino, Italiano, ec.' De Jorio (1832), 308.

This idea, which underlies the text of *La mimica*, is explicitly stated in a letter written by the *regio revisore* (royal censor) Giuseppangelo Del Forno, in which he recommended the book's publication. Del Forno clearly based his description of the book's content on a careful reading of *La mimica*; his summary of De Jorio's work partially reveals the subtext of the book, as well as indicating how the work was perceived and had been received by the learned circles in Naples:

> Further, he has made every effort to demonstrate with very convincing reasoning, that the Gestural Expression used by them fully corresponds to the expressions of the Neapolitan people, once a Colony of glorious Athens, accompanying his happy attempts with tasteful erudition, delighting the reader with a sprinkling of Attic salt.[32]

The importance given by de Jorio to the Greek heritage of modern Naples needs to be seen in relation to the work of Johann Joachim Winckelmann, one of the founders of the discipline of Art History. Winckelmann is often said to have been the first scholar to make a clear distinction between Greek and Roman art and to forcefully argue for the purity and superiority of Greek art and architecture, which he saw as the cornerstone of the Western artistic tradition. His major work, *Geschichte der Kunst des Alterthum* (1764), presented a comprehensive, chronological account of all ancient art; it also introduced certain influential ideas that would shape subsequent developments in the discipline—such as the idea that art reflected the maturity or decline of the civilization that produced it, and the view of Roman art as a derivative body of imitations of Greek masterpieces.[33] The political, cultural, and social conditions that allowed the creation of great works of art in ancient Greece were stressed in Winckelmann's work, which thus implied the overall superiority of

---

[32] 'Si è sforzato inoltre con ragioni convincentissime dimostrare, che la Mimica da esso loro usata abbia tutto il rapporto, ed ogni convenienza con gli atteggiamenti del popolo Napoletano, Colonia un tempo della gloriosa Atene, accompagnando i suoi felici tentativi con dell'erudizioni di tutto gusto, ed asperse di sale Attico da recare sommo diletto ai leggitori.' De Jorio (1832): the letter, and the positive reply it received, were included in the published book after the indices (the end of the last index is on p. 380), but were not numbered according to the page number sequence of the book.

[33] See Bianchi Bandinelli (1976) for a synthetic overview of Winckelmann's role in the birth of Classical Archaeology; Potts (1994) has a biographical study of Winckelmann. Cf. Harloe (2013) on Winckelmann's work and the history of classical scholarship in eighteenth-century Germany.

this civilization compared to others. The German scholar had inter-mittently spent time in Naples between 1758 and 1767, and had been very critical of the methods used in the archaeological investigations at Herculaneum. De Jorio knew his work well, and he accepted Winckelmann's value-laden framework as the foundation of his work on gesture.[34] The preface to *La mimica* contains statements about de Jorio's city being 'full of philosophy' and about the common people possessing 'natural philosophy' which serve to emphasize the fact that the Greek cultural inheritance was alive and well in the customs of eighteenth-century Naples.[35] This remarkable use of the classical past engaged in direct dialogue with the intellectual discourse that had unfolded and was still unfolding in the cultured circles of Europe about the assimilation of the South with the Other, with the Uncivilized, with the Barbaric. I would also argue that it provided a way into rethinking Naples' role within peninsular Italy itself, in the crucial years of the Risorgimento.

Italy's classical past had been brought to light during the Renais-sance, both through the finding, reading, and publication of Greek texts that had been lost (in the West), and through the rediscovery of the physical vestiges of ancient architecture, sculpture, and painting. Renaissance architecture was greatly influenced by the extant monu-ments of ancient Rome and the theorization of architecture found in Vitruvius' *De Architectura*; meanwhile, the discovery in the late 1400s of the frescoes of the Domus Aurea (Nero's lavish palace erected in the middle of Rome) gave birth to a specific decorative style called *a grottesche*, which was employed in the decoration of upper-class palaces. Interest in ancient art and thought had flourished throughout the Renaissance, especially in Florence and Rome, where noble fam-ilies engaged in the active collecting of ancient works of art and acted as patrons of contemporary artists inspired by these same ancient works.[36] Although Renaissance Italy was politically more fragmented than the Italy of the eighteenth and early nineteenth centuries, the appreciation of Roman (and, in Tuscany, Etruscan) remains fostered

[34] Kendon in de Jorio (2000), pp. xxxv–xxxvi.
[35] De Jorio (1832), pp. vii, xiii. Ceserani (2012), 115–28 on the changing frame-works used to interpret the 'Italian pasts' (with particular relation to the South) in the period.
[36] For the influence of ancient thought, see the example of the Neoplatonist Ficino, who was active at the court of Lorenzo de' Medici, and who greatly influenced Poliziano's poetic production. See Martelli (1995).

the creation of an embryonic sense of belonging to the same glorious past: in this respect, the rediscovery of Rome's glory started to shape a sense of belonging in modern Italians.[37] However, the most notable discoveries of Roman antiquities did not take place in Rome, but in the Kingdom of the Two Sicilies, when the buried cities of Herculaneum and Pompeii were rediscovered in the eighteenth century.[38] These discoveries excited Europe, influencing architecture, figurative arts, furnishings, and even female fashion (see the 'empire style' in vogue in Napoleonic France).[39] As has already been mentioned, these same discoveries also attracted a large number of foreign visitors, who often ended their Grand Tour of Italy in Naples with trips to Vesuvius, Pompeii, and the collection of the Real Museo, which was housed at the Royal Palace of Portici before being transferred to Naples.[40] Despite such notoriety, allusions to Pompeii and Herculaneum and to other famous standing monuments of Roman Campania, such as the Arch of Trajan at Beneventum, are strangely absent from the Italian rhetoric of the Risorgimento.

The civilization of ancient Rome indeed became one of the key elements evoked in the shaping of Italian national identity during the Risorgimento. Political writers and nationalistic poets such as Pascoli,

---

[37] At least in central Italy—Venice in this period looked more to the Mediterranean East than to the Roman past, and to Byzantium and Greek works of art that arrived in the city from the Aegean.

[38] In 1738 some statues from the ancient theatre of Herculaneum were discovered when digging a tunnel; the engineer Alcubierre, who was in the service of the king of Naples, realized that something important was buried under the modern city, since farmers had also reported the frequent discovery of marble fragments and other ancient objects when digging for wells. Alcubierre managed to convince the king to start excavating in the area and Herculaneum was subsequently discovered. Meanwhile, excavations were also begun in Pompeii and Castellammare di Stabia. A synthetic overview of the discoveries is found in Rossano (2001). Detailed accounts can be found in Ruggiero (1885) and Ruggiero (1888).

[39] Haskell and Penny (1981); Irwin (1997); Thornton (2000). Cf. also the chapter on 'The Enlightenment and Neoclassical Theory' in Mallgrave (2005), 13–43.

[40] The Accademia Ercolanese, created for the purpose of studying the objects that were emerging from the excavations, undertook the publication of a large work entitled *Le antichità di Ercolano esposte* in an attempt to catalogue the discoveries. The first volume in the series, entitled *Le pitture antiche d'Ercolano e contorni incise con qualche spiegazione*, was published in 1757, and was instrumental in spreading news of the Roman frescoes around Europe. Soon, smaller and more economic editions appeared in various European countries, translated into different languages (English edn., 1773; German, 1778; French, 1780). The volumes of this work can be consulted in digitalized format from the library of the University of Heidelberg (<http://digi.ub.uni-heidelberg.de/diglit/ercolano1757ga>, last accessed July 2013).

Carducci, and D'Annunzio often referred to the past glory of Rome and to specific examples of Roman towns, and they foresaw an imminent second era of glory that would unite the Italian soil once again under one political leadership. They did not, however, allude to Pompeii or to Roman Campania. The reasons behind this exclusion were purely political. Pompeii and, by extension, the whole of Roman Campania, was a symbol of the Bourbon Kingdom of the Two Sicilies, not of a unified Italy under the leadership of Piedmont and the Sabaudian royal house. To quote Braccesi, 'La località di Pompei nel passato e presente ... è troppo intimamente connessa alla storia politica e culturale di Napoli' ('The site of Pompeii in both the past and present ... is too intimately connected to the political and cultural history of Naples').[41]

Therefore, while the discovery of a bronze statue of Victory from the Roman Capitolium at Brescia (Roman Brixia) in northern Italy in 1826 was welcomed with triumphal celebrations and immortalized in one of Carducci's odes, any reference to that same classical past in Naples and Campania was left out of the discourse of the Italian intellectuals who argued for national unity outside of the Kingdom of the Two Sicilies.[42] This omission also formed part of the Italian response to the European discourse on the moral qualities of northern and southern countries. In 1825, the Lombard Melchiorre Gioia, a leading Italian economist of the time (as well as a statistician, entrepreneur, and patriot), had published an article in the *Annali universali di statistica* in reply to Bonstetten's 1824 book *L'Homme du midi et l'homme du nord, ou l'influence du climat*.[43] Bonstetten's stress on the influence of climate on people's national character was inspired directly by the work of Montesquieu. Bonstetten took the Alps as the dividing element between North and South and presented the populations living on the opposite sides of the mountain chain, and the societies they had created, as embodying opposite characteristics. It is worth reproducing here the scheme by which Moe synthetically summarizes Bonstetten's sociocultural dichotomy:[44]

---

[41] Braccesi (2008), 72.
[42] Members of the local Ateneo di Scienze, Lettere e Arti, which had overseen the excavation, participated in the Risorgimento movement. Carducci's Ode is *Odi barbare* 5, entitled *Alla Vittoria, tra le rovine del tempio di Vespasiano in Brescia*. The same discovery prompted the rebuilding of the *cellae* of the Capitolium in order to house the Museo Patrio.
[43] Gioia (1825).   [44] Moe (2006), 28–9.

Man of the North	Man of the South
lives in monotonous environment	lives in varied and fecund environment
reason, reflection	imagination, feeling
industry	effortless subsistence off the earth
lives indoors	lives outdoors
fixed routines	no fixed routines
planning	no thought for the future
social opinion	egotism
can be educated/reformed	cannot be educated/reformed

Gioia reacted to this collection of commonplaces by generally defending the modernity of Italy as a whole, an argument that he presented from a number of different angles. At the same time, however, in a number of places Gioia adopted Bonstetten's North–South framework by proposing a more nuanced perspective. He stressed that Bonstetten's observations applied to only certain parts of the Italian peninsula. In particular, he responded to the comment that Italians did not plan for the future by moving the North–South demarcation further south. Gioia's words are explicit:

> In short, the author attributes *to all of Italy a custom which he observed in the noble houses of Rome and Naples.*[45]

It therefore seems likely that de Jorio, with his book, was not only responding to 'foreign' views of Naples and its customs, but also to northern Italian writers like Gioia who stressed that northern Italy belonged to Europe, while the South was closer to Africa or Asia in climate, as well as in the character of its people and the nature of their society.

The sociocultural dichotomy described here, which is ultimately rooted in the geographic-climatic theory, is still very much present in contemporary Italy. Political movements such as the Lega Nord, which argue for an independent North, are based on the idea that the hard-working and industrial northern Italy is more akin to other northern European countries than to the rest of Italy, particularly Rome and the South. The South is often represented (either in explicit derogatory terms or as a matter-of-fact statement) as part of North

---

[45] Gioia (1825), 10; English trans. by Moe (2006, 30); emphasis in the original article.

Africa, reflecting in part the large presence of illegal immigrants from Africa in cities such as Naples. At the same time, the direct association between Neapolitan traditions and the city's Greek past that de Jorio makes in his work can also still be found in contemporary thought about the place of Naples in modern Italy, with the classical past still being used to morally elevate the inhabitants of a wonderful city plagued by profound social and economic problems. Recent generations of southerners will remember the popular success enjoyed in the mid-1980s by the film adaptations of Luciano De Crescenzo's book *Così parlò Bellavista*.[46] A central message of these works was that Neapolitans were 'natural philosophers' and Epicureans, who were able to live more joyfully than the stoic, suffering, and self-sacrificing northern Italians. The opposition that De Crescenzo constructs between the 'Milanese' and the 'Neapolitan' characters therefore constitutes one recent example of how the ancient past continues to be pressed into the service of the long-lasting discourse about the North–South divide in Italy.[47]

CONCLUSIONS

De Jorio's text was clearly informed by his deep knowledge of the antiquities of Naples and surrounding territories, as well as his commitment to publishing guides and books that illustrated them to scholars and foreign visitors alike, his attentive analysis of details, and the clear love he had of his city, its people, and their distinctive customs. *La mimica* was an innovative work on multiple levels. The book marked the first time that ethnography was systematically used as a key to archaeological exegesis, and the first time that the

---

[46] The titles of the films are *Così parlò Bellavista* (1984) and *Il mistero di Bellavista* (1985).

[47] After all, Neapolis in the first century BC had been the location of the school of the Epicurean philosopher Siro, a friend of another famous Epicurean, Philodemus of Gadara, who also spent part of his life on the Bay of Naples. Philodemus was part of the retinues of L. Calpurnius Piso Caesoninus, Caesar's father-in-law, and spent time between Naples and Herculaneum. It is believed that the Villa of the Papyri in Herculaneum, in whose library several scrolls of works of Philodemus were discovered, was Piso's villa.

understanding of gesture as a culturally specific language was expounded along the lines of what we now call semiotics. The openly stated aim of the book was to offer an interpretative guide to ancient gestures for those scholars, philologists, or archaeologists who could not fully understand them because they did not have the benefit of the knowledge of modern Neapolitan gesture. However, this was only one of de Jorio's goals in compiling such a work. His assumption that contemporary Neapolitans preserved the culture and gestures of the earlier, classical inhabitants of the region (and especially the Greeks) led to a re-evaluation of Naples and Neapolitans in the eyes of cultured northern Europeans. Ancient Greek civilization was recognized in de Jorio's time to have reached the highest levels, both in the arts of the mind (such as philosophy and political thought) and in the figurative arts; so by claiming that Greek culture was very much 'alive' in the Naples of his time, de Jorio disassociated the city from the 'uncivilized South'—an image which had been predominant in the culturally determined discourse on the North–South divide. Furthermore, in the context of the political situation of his time, his book represented a southern, Bourbon reply to those in support of a unified Italy under the (northern) leadership of the royal house of Piedmont. If Naples had been a colony of democratic Athens, and if the Neapolitans had preserved the cultural inheritance of their Greek past, the next inference to make was that they were also culturally and politically superior to the northerners. To those who exalted the Roman past of the regions of northern and central Italy with the aim of cementing an Italian identity, while ignoring that same past in the Bourbon South, the learned de Jorio answered by stressing the Greekness of Naples and the unique interpretative tool Neapolitan customs offered to understand classical antiquity. Even the Neapolitan dialect was, in his opinion, a better tool than Italian to get closer to the spirit of certain ancient texts, such as Virgil's *Aeneid*.[48] In a topographical study in which he tried to identify the localities around Cumae described in *Aeneid* book 6, he often referred to Nicola

---

[48] This opinion may have rested on the fact that Virgil had spent time in Neapolis, where he had studied with the philosopher Siro. Philodemus was also a friend of Virgil and dedicated some of his works to him. See Fulvio Delle Donne, Giancarlo Abbamonte, and Harald Hendrix (Chapters 8, 9, and 11 in this volume) for the role of Virgil in Neapolitan visions of the past.

Stigliola's translation of the poem into Neapolitan.[49] The classical heritage and past of Naples was thus used by de Jorio—as by so many of the other people that we have already met in this volume—to reinterpret and reshape the present in a subtle and clever manner that still has resonances in the charged social and political climate of Italy today.

---

[49] De Jorio (1825), p. x: 'Lo spirito poi, non che il vero senso che tal volta è stato necessario con istento colpire, l'ho rinvenuto felicissimamente espresso nell'inimitabile traduzione che dell'Eneide abbiamo in lingua Napoletana.' The work to which he refers is the *Eneide di Virgilio Marone trasportata in ottava rima Napoletana da Giacomo Sitillo* (an alias for Nicola Stigliola).

14

'No Retreat, Even When Broken'

Classical Ruins in the Presepe Napoletano

Jessica Hughes

For anyone with an interest in the complex relationship between the classical and Christian pasts, the city of Naples offers no shortage of fascinating case studies. Numerous examples have been introduced in this volume already, from the use of Roman *spolia* in medieval churches (Angela Palmentieri, Chapter 7) to the juxtaposition of the thirteenth-century cult of the magician Virgil with that of S. Maria dell'Itra in the Crypta Neapolitana (Bianca de Divitiis, Chapter 10). This chapter will focus on another example from the religious material culture of more recent periods—the world-famous and highly theatrical representations of Christ's Nativity that are displayed in the city's homes and churches every Christmas, the components of which are sold throughout the year in the shops on Via S. Gregorio Armeno in the historic centre. These miniature tableaux, which are known as *presepi* (singular *presepe*), 'cribs', set the Nativity against an eclectic and bustling pageant of Neapolitan life across the ages, performed by a cast of characters drawn from history and contemporary popular culture. Every year, the Holy Family is joined by new local and global personalities, from musicians and actors to politicians and footballers. Perhaps unsurprisingly, it is the presence of these anachronistic and often humorous figurines that has dominated the attention of most observers; this chapter, however, shifts the focus onto the scenographic background of the *presepe*, and in particular the representations of classical ruins against which this definitively Neapolitan version of the Nativity is enacted.[1]

The chapter begins by laying out some brief historical background to ruins in the *presepe*, moving from the scattered and partial glimpses in texts of the seventeenth and eighteenth centuries to the much fuller material record of the nineteenth, twentieth, and twenty-first centuries. After introducing this evidence, it moves on to explore the following question: *why* did classical ruins become—and remain—such a central component of the *presepe napoletano*? The answer to this question is multi-layered for, as we shall see, ruins in this context have several possible functions and meanings. For instance, while the popularity of ruins in the eighteenth century can be seen to reflect a broader contemporary interest in classical culture, inspired by the rediscovery of sites such as Pompeii and Hercula-neum, these models also link the *presepe* to much older religious uses of ruins as symbols of Christian victory over paganism; meanwhile, within the unique context of the *presepe*, the classical ruins contribute to a more general sense of historical anachronism that many com-mentators have seen as the genre's most distinguishing feature. In recent times, the popularity of 'esoteric' approaches to the *presepe* has confirmed the ruins' role as a bearer of symbolic meaning, while—as the study of individual examples can show—the inherent ambiguity and polyvalency of the ruin have allowed it to be continuously adopted and adapted into new visual narratives about other sorts of contemporary decline *and* survival. In this way, the chapter brings our study of Neapolitan receptions of antiquity right up to the present day and into popular culture, showing how the classical past of Naples continues to be reshaped by the city's inhabitants and given powerful and provocative new meanings.

---

[1] A good starting point for study of the *presepe napoletano* in English is the collection of essays in Dickerson and de Cavi (2008). Mancini (1983) is an invaluable source of historical accounts of *presepi* from the eighteenth century to 1955. The historical and art-historical development of the *presepe* has been the central theme of most existing studies: see e.g. Borrelli (1970); Borrelli (1991); Borrelli (2001); Catello (1991); Griffo (1996); Grillo (1998); De Caro (2007). De Simone (1998); Forte (1999); Niola (2005); and Franchesi (2006) provide more theoretical and anthropological perspectives. Calaresu (2013) looks at *presepe* figurines in the context of a broader study of the representation of street life in eighteenth-century Naples.

A BRIEF HISTORY OF RUINS IN THE
PRESEPE NAPOLETANO

Most existing descriptions and historical studies of the *presepe* focus
not on scenographic elements like the ruins but on the figurines
(*pastori*), which are normally discussed and illustrated in isolation
from their 'backdrops'.[2] This dominant, decontextualized approach
to the figurines can be explained in part by the fact that *presepi* are
traditionally dismantled and remade on an annual basis, which of
course increases the chance that the figurines will become permanently separated from their original display contexts. In turn, the
backdrops themselves are often fabricated from relatively cheap,
ephemeral materials such as cork, wood, and papier mâché, so conservation is also an issue. In fact, only a handful of historic examples
of *presepe* scenographies survive—others have left traces in other
written or visual sources, most of which are collected in Gennaro
Borrelli's detailed 2001 study of the *Personaggi e scenografie del
presepe napoletano*. One of the earliest scenographies of which we
have record was erected in 1627 by the Padri Scolopi in their church
of the Nativity of Jesus; nothing survives of the backdrop itself, but an
account written in 1721 by the Jesuit priest Giuseppe Patrignani
mentions that it included a scene of the annunciation to the shepherds and 'una prospettiva in lontananza'.[3] Near-contemporary
descriptions of other *presepi* record representations of the *osteria*
(often transformed into a representation of one of the city's many
taverns) to which Mary and Joseph were refused access, and—most

---

[2] This is despite the fact that these backdrops—often elaborate, multi-part
constructions—have been of crucial importance in defining the genre, and in distinguishing the *presepe napoletano* from other crib traditions both around Italy and
internationally. On the relationship of the Neapolitan *presepe* to other European
Nativities see Dickerson and de Cavi (2008), 1–5; Fittipaldi (1979), 13. For an
introduction to the very different traditions of Nativity scenes from other parts of
Italy see Ruggiero (1988). Franchesi (2006) takes a case-study approach to *presepi* in
the province of Padua. For a comparative view of Nativity scenes from around the
world, see Govan (2007).

[3] Patrignani (1721), 34. See Borrelli (2001), 23 with the reconstruction drawing at
fig. 1. As Borrelli explains, this *presepe* inspired a series of similar cribs in Naples over
subsequent years, including the one set up by the Jesuits in 1630 in the church of Gesù
Nuovo, another assembled in 1633 by the notary Andrea Cassetta (one of the first
recorded 'domestic' *presepi*), and the *presepe* erected at Christmas 1661 in a hut in the
church of S. Paolo Maggiore.

importantly for us—of sparse, natural landscapes, dotted with the ruins of classical buildings.[4]

Some of the earliest examples of classical ruins in the *presepe* are found in a painting made in the last quarter of the seventeenth century, for display in the church of S. Giovanni a Carbonara.[5] Executed by an unknown artist, it formed a replacement background for a series of life-size wooden figures sculpted in the fifteenth century by the brothers Pietro and Giovanni Alemanno. These wooden figures are preserved today in the Museo S. Martino in Naples, and comprise one of the most precious documents in the history of the *presepe napoletano*. Unfortunately, the painted backdrop itself was destroyed in the Second World War, but reconstruction drawings made from pre-war photographs indicate that it included a bare landscape with a scattering of dead trees and a tower amongst a few rural farm buildings. In the background are hills and the remains of a Roman aqueduct. As Gennaro Borrelli points out in his discussion of this image, the scene draws on the seventeenth-century tradition of Neapolitan landscape painting, but is also reminiscent of 'real' local landscapes, such as the countryside visible beyond the Via Foria, which included the remains of the Roman aqueduct known today as the 'Ponti Rossi'.

While scattered references suggest that ruins did occasionally appear in early eighteenth-century *presepi*, we have much more evidence for the later part of that century.[6] For instance, we know that ruins appeared in what was perhaps the most famous domestic *presepe* from that period—that belonging to the Terres brothers, a family of booksellers and publishers with a workshop in Via S. Biagio dei Librai, opposite the church of SS. Filippo e Giacomo.[7] Designed in April 1785 by the architect and *presepista* Francesco Viva, it was subsequently viewed and described by several elite visitors to the city.[8]

---

[4] Borrelli (2001), 24. He notes that the earliest record of a tavern scene occurs in the context of a *presepe* that the Saavedra family exhibited from 1656 in their chapel in the church of St Peter of Murcia in Spain (where many Neapolitan *presepi* were sent).

[5] Borrelli (2001), 24 with fig. 2a.

[6] The first half of the eighteenth century yields few references to classical ruins, although Borrelli suggests that a drawing of a fantastical ruined building signed by the Neapolitan artist Luca Giordano may have been a preparatory design for a *presepe*— possibly that erected in the church of S. Brigida by Razionale Antonio Ciappa. Borrelli (2001), 25 with pl. 1.

[7] Borrelli (2001), 29–30; Niola (2005), 63–5.

[8] For Viva, see Fittipaldi (1979), 22.

Fig. 14.1. Dominique Vivant Denon, family group. The inscription reads 'Preso dal presepio de S.i Terres compost da Francesco Viva Napoli nel mese d'Aprile del anno 1785'.

Source: Naples, Museo Nazionale di San Martino. Reproduced courtesy of the Fototeca della Soprintendenza per il PSAE e per il Polo Museale della Città di Napoli.

An engraving by the French artist Dominique Vivant shows a detail taken from the Terres crib: it depicts a family resting next to a ruined classical column covered with lichen and plants; just visible in the background to the left is a circular temple vaguely reminiscent of the temple of Cybele in Rome (Fig. 14.1). A description of this elaborate crib written in 1787 by the count Joseph Gorani records that it included other references to the material culture of antiquity, in the form of 'amphorae, classical statues and Etruscan urns', as well as the ruins of a Roman aqueduct.[9]

The representation of antiquities in the Terres crib might be seen as continuing a trend that had begun in earnest three years earlier in 1782. This was the year in which the Neapolitan architect Gaetano Barba had been commissioned by the Confraternity of S. Giuseppe dei Falegnami to make a new setting for another group of older wooden figures—this time those sculpted by the sixteenth-century artist Giovanni da Nola (Fig. 10.11; see de Divitiis in Chapter 10 of this volume for a discussion of these figures in their original context of the church of S. Maria del Parto).[10] Again, Barba's updated scenography no longer survives, but contemporary descriptions indicate that it depicted the ruins of an ancient temple complete with ceiling coffers, Corinthian columns, and miniature representations of sculpted reliefs found in local excavations.[11] Historiographical studies of the *presepe* often repeat the statement that Giovanni da Nola was the first artist to introduce ruins into the *presepe*; for example, in an early study of the genre that was published in the *Atti dell'Accademia Pontaniana* in 1889, Francesco Proto (duke of Maddaloni) explained how Giovanni 'recoiled from representing the Saviour's birth in a crypt or stable, instead placing the manger and crib amongst the debris of a pagan temple'.[12] He continued: 'It is in this *presepe* of Merliano, then, that we find the origins of our own unique *presepi*. Many of the examples I've seen rise from the rubble of a pagan temple. I myself had one made this way, back when I built *presepi* before entering politics.'[13]

---

[9] Gorani (1793), cited in Mancini (1983), 23: 'Quello di Torres comprende anche urne, vasi etruschi e statue antiche.'

[10] Scalfaro (2005); Laschke and Deramaix (1992), 30.

[11] Borrelli (2001), 30.

[12] Proto (1889, cited in Mancini (1983), 62–70: 'I presepi casalinghi moltiplicaronsi dopo quello che adorna l'altare di S. Giuseppe dei Falegnami, opera bellissima del nostro gran Marliano. Il quale, schifando far nascere il Redentore in una cripta, in una stalla, mise la mangiatoia e la cuna fra le anticaglie di un tempio romano.' Mancini (1983), 66.

[13] 'Dei quali molti ho veduti, sorgenti dallo sfasciume di un tempio del gentilesimo. Io stesso ne avevo uno cosiffatto, quando, prima di dar nella politica, costruiva anch'io il presepe.' Mancini (1983), 66.

Fig. 14.2. The *presepe Cuciniello*.
Source: Naples, Museo Nazionale di San Martino. Reproduced courtesy of the Fototeca della
Soprintendenza per il PSAE e per il Polo Museale della Città di Napoli.

Proto's words here raise the possibility that contemporary and later
viewers erroneously identified Barba's eighteenth-century backdrop
as the work of Giovanni da Nola himself. They also suggest that ruins
were widespread in *presepi* of Proto's own time—a suggestion that
finds confirmation in a series of surviving nineteenth-century
examples. Ruined classical architecture is at the centre of what is
perhaps the most famous Neapolitan Nativity of all time—the *presepe
Cuciniello*—which can be seen on display today in the Museo
S. Martino (Fig. 14.2).[14] This stunning tableau was first assembled
in the kitchens of the Certosa di S. Martino on 28 December 1879 by
its donor, the Neapolitan playwright Michele Cuciniello, with the
help of the dramaturge Luigi Masi and the architect Fausto Nicolini.
It locates the Nativity against a background of classical ruins; pieces of
broken columns lie strewn on the floor while a miniature sculpted

---

[14] Stefanucci (1944), cited in Mancini (1983), esp. 294: 'Uno stormo d'angeli si
libra sulla rovina pagana della nascita.'

Fig. 14.3. *Presepe di sughero* (cork Nativity), exterior.

Source: Naples, Museo Nazionale di San Martino. Reproduced courtesy of the Fototeca della Soprintendenza per il PSAE e per il Polo Museale della Città di Napoli.

bas-relief decorates the archway. The Museo S. Martino also houses a particularly intriguing example of a nineteenth-century *presepe* with ruins: the so-called *presepe di sughero* ('cork Nativity'), which was designed and executed by an engineer in the service of Ferdinand II named Lorenzo Taglioni (Figs. 14.3 and 14.4). This *presepe*—currently in storage awaiting restoration—consists of more than 200 figures dressed in contemporary local costumes; it is encased in a calibrated mechanism almost 2 metres long which, when closed, takes the form of the temple of Neptune at the nearby site of Paestum.[15] It is unusual in many respects—for one thing, the temple model rests on a faux-marble half-column with a hidden music box that plays a lullaby. And while in all the other *presepi* discussed in this chapter the ruins are one of numerous miniature elements set within a

[15] Creazzo (2005), 22–3, 34 n. 8; Palladino (2002), 162–5. When closed, the model measures 198 cm in width, 56 cm in height, and 105 cm in depth (without the column). The same Paestum temple along with other ruins of Doric architecture was represented in a drawing for a *presepe* background also now in the Museo S. Martino (inv. no. 20527). See Borrelli (2001), 31.

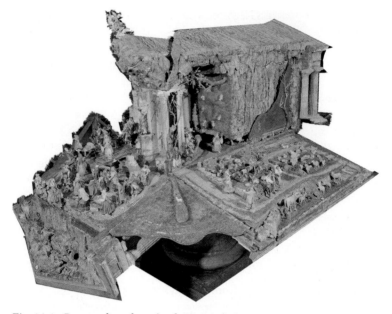

Fig. 14.4. *Presepe di sughero* (cork Nativity), interior.

Source: Naples, Museo Nazionale di San Martino. Reproduced courtesy of the Fototeca della Soprintendenza per il PSAE e per il Polo Museale della Città di Napoli.

complex landscape, the *presepe di sughero* inverts this relationship so that the classical architecture dominates the scene, becoming the frame for the entire *presepe* and all its inhabitants.

The selection of sources discussed so far gives some useful historical background to ruins in the contemporary *presepe*, allowing us to identify ways in which the older tradition is both continued and transformed in the modern examples. Today, the home of the *presepe napoletano* is the street of S. Gregorio Armeno, which winds its way from the church of the same name past the remains of the Roman market underneath the church of S. Lorenzo Maggiore towards the isolated Roman column that stands at the corner of Vico Figurari.[16]

---

[16] The site of the church of S. Gregorio Armeno may have been occupied in antiquity by a temple to the goddess Ceres, who was the recipient of small votive statuettes produced in this area. In 1234, there was an influx of Franciscan monks, who built a small church on the site that later became the church of S. Lorenzo Maggiore. St Francis is commonly cited as the originator of the Nativity tradition (he built one of the earliest recorded examples in town of Greccio in Lazio in 1223), and

The shops of Via S. Gregorio Armeno and the neighbouring Via S. Biagio dei Librai sell an impressive and ever-changing array of different figures destined for *presepi*, which are normally made from terracotta but sometimes from other materials such as plaster and plastic. While the range of *presepe* ornaments is vast and eclectic, certain categories of figurine and accessory appear in most of the different shops: these include the principal protagonists of the Nativity story, other stock figures such as the street sellers with a range of traditional produce (watermelons, fish, chestnuts, and so forth), and the models of ancient ruins that are the focus of this chapter. The modern ruin models come in different formats. Some are incorporated into larger models that provide a static background against which collections of figurines can be arranged, while others are sold as individual miniature components that can be taken home and added to existing panoramas. Others still appear in smaller scenes featuring the Holy Family that are sold ready-assembled inside glass boxes or domes (*scarabbatole*). In all cases, the most common type of ruin is the classical column, which is often shown surmounted by a Corinthian capital. The columns are represented either singly (as in Fig. 14.5), or in groups of three or four (as in Fig. 14.6). In the latter case they are generally surmounted by an ornate entablature—an image loosely reminiscent of the iconic group of three columns belonging to the ruined temple of Castor and Pollux in the Roman Forum.[17] Another popular category of ruin is the broken arch, which is commonly shown as made of decaying brick; as Alessandra Griffo has pointed out, these arches visually echo the remains of the city's aqueducts, like the one that brought the water of the Serino to Naples and Baiae (see de Divitiis, Chapter 10 of this volume).[18]

The central role of classical ruins in the contemporary *presepe* was brilliantly demonstrated by a figure that was on sale in S. Gregorio in

some have argued that it may have been the combination of this Franciscan tradition—mediated by the monks of the Order—with the ancient manufacture of small votive figurines, which led to the development of the *presepe* industry in the area of S. Gregorio. On St Francis and the Nativity see Beretta (2003).

[17] A long-standing source of inspiration for artists portraying ruins. Examples include Claude Lorrain's painting of the Roman Forum, 1633–4, illustrated at Zucker (1968), 52–3 and Pierre Lemaire's *Ancient Corner of the Forum*, illustrated at Zucker (1968), 54–5.

[18] Griffo (1996), 28–9.

Fig. 14.5. View of *presepe* merchandise on sale in Via S. Gregorio Armeno, including figurines of Pulcinella and S. Gennaro.

Source: Photograph: Jessica Hughes.

the winter of 2011 (Fig. 14.7). This model belongs to a category of motorized ceramic figurines that can be attached to a power supply and animated via an internal mechanism. They are set within small tableaux representing shops or work areas, and are normally articulated at the waist or shoulders, thus allowing their upper bodies and arms to move rhythmically backwards and forwards. Most of the activities and professions that are represented in these animated models also feature in the traditional Neapolitan *presepi*: so we find men shearing sheep, making copper pans, cutting hair, chopping logs, and making bread and pizza, while women are depicted washing,

Fig. 14.6. View of *presepe* merchandise on sale in Via S. Gregorio Armeno, including figurines of Totò and Eduardo De Filippo, the singers Adriano Celentano and Vasco Rossi, the footballer Edinson Cavani, and Marilyn Monroe.

Source: Photograph: Jessica Hughes.

ironing clothes, and slicing watermelons. This particular model was made in the workshop of C. Fusco (Via S. Gregorio Armeno 7); it represents a craftsman seated within a rustic alcove, behind a table on which rest a terracotta vase, sculptor's tools, and some half-finished models of classical columns. When the model is plugged into an electrical supply, the sculptor's right arm moves up and down to raise and lower the paintbrush in his hand; it thus constitutes a clever, self-reflexive representation in which a *presepe* maker (*figuraro* or *plasticatore*) is shown fabricating a series of new (but artificially antiquated) columns destined for inclusion within an imaginary 'meta-*presepe*' on an even smaller scale than the crib that the *figuraro* himself is destined to occupy.[19]

---

[19] C. Fusco, Via S. Gregorio Armeno, 7, <http://www.artedelpastore.it> [accessed 24 March 2014].

Fig. 14.7. Mechanized figurine of a *figuraro* (*presepe* maker), bought in S. Gregorio Armeno, Christmas 2011.
Source: Photograph: Benedetto De Martino.

MEANINGS AND FUNCTIONS OF RUINS IN THE *PRESEPE NAPOLETANO*

Why did classical ruins become—and remain—such a central and enduring component of the *presepe napoletano*? Clearly, on one level their introduction and subsequent development reflects a much broader contemporary interest in the material culture of classical antiquity, which followed the rediscovery of archaeological sites such as Pompeii and Herculaneum.[20] As Annalisa Marzano has already discussed in Chapter 13 in this volume, these rediscoveries exercised a powerful influence over all genres and aspects of eighteenth-century artistic and architectural production.[21] The ruins in the *presepe* clearly need to be considered alongside other classicizing objects of this period, and indeed there are often connections to be made between these different forms of material culture: the *presepe di sughero*, for instance, responds to a vibrant eighteenth-century tradition of representing the Paestum temples in different media, while the landscapes of many other *presepe* frequently bear similarities to paintings, engravings, and theatrical backdrops in the popular eighteenth-century genres of *rovinismo* and *capriccio*.[22]

However, while the contemporary passion for antiquity may have provided one obvious impetus for the development of *presepe* ruins over the course of the second half of the eighteenth century, it certainly cannot be seen as the sole motivating factor. Each of the strands of classical reception in this period had its own internal history of development, as well as its own specific sets of meanings: within the context of Christian material religion, classical ruins had already been appropriated for centuries as a means of indicating the triumph of Christianity over the ruins of paganism. Fig. 14.8 shows one early example—a painting in tempera dating to *c*.1400, which represents a tale that appeared in the late medieval collection of hagiographies known as *The Golden Legend*.[23] This tale told of the destruction (forewarned by an oracle of Apollo) of the Roman temple of Peace on Christmas day; as Salvatore Settis has noted in relation to the same painting, the narrative 'presented the ruins of ancient Rome and its idols and temples as a direct consequence of the Incarnation

[20] On the reception of Pompeii from its rediscovery to the present see Cremante et al. (2008); Hales and Paul (2011); Mattusch (2013), with further references. Other examples of eighteenth-century receptions of antiquity in Naples are discussed in the collection of essays edited by Ceserani and Milanese (2007).

[21] Mattusch (2013) illustrates many examples: see esp. the chapter on 'Flying Maenads and Cupids: Pompeii, Herculaneum and Eighteenth-Century Decorative Arts' by Nancy H. Ramage (pp. 161–70).

[22] On the eighteenth-century rediscovery of and passion for Paestum, see Ceserani (2012), who also discusses Piranesi's highly influential engravings of ruins. On *rovinismo* in theatre scenographies see Mancini and Simonelli (1992).

[23] Verdier (1982).

Fig. 14.8. *The Vision of the Emperor Augustus and the Ruins of the Temple of Peace, c.*1400, tempera.

Source: Stuttgart, Staatsgalerie. © Foto Staatsgalerie Stuttgart.

of Christ'.[24] In the painting, most of the visual field is occupied by a gigantic vision of Madonna and Child suspended in the sky; at the bottom left of the painting, the emperor Augustus (in red) falls to his knees, while on the right a group of Roman nobles watch in consternation as cracks appear in the walls of their precious temple. Other

[24] Settis (2011), 723.

fifteenth-century examples of ruins in Nativity scenes include Botti-celli's several versions of the *Adoration of the Magi* (1478–83), Ghirlandaio's *Adoration of the Shepherds* in the Sassetti chapel in the church of the S. Trinità in Florence (1485), and the *Adoration of the Shepherds* painted by Francesco di Giorgio Martini in 1493 for the church of S. Domenico in Siena; later Neapolitan examples include paintings by Francesco Solimena (1657–1747) and Filippo Falciatore (1718–68).[25] Ruins and fragmentary sculptures were also used to illustrate Christian victory over paganism in other Christian contexts (besides representations of the Nativity).[26] Fulvio Lenzo has already described in Chapter 12 of this volume how, in the sixteenth and seventeenth centuries, the architecture and sculptures from the ancient temple of the Dioscuri were presented by the Theatines as symbols of Christian triumph, while in earlier periods the gap in this church's pediment had been seen as physical proof of legends about St Peter's visit to the city, when he made the pagan images of Castor and Pollux fall to the ground.[27] We might also recall that the ceiling of S. Paolo Maggiore featured a painting by Massimo Stanzione in which the collapsed ancient temple of Castor and Pollux was repre-sented in the form of three truncated classical columns (Fig. 12.3)—an image that finds strong visual parallels in the ruins in the *presepe*. This example of the church of S. Paolo intimates how the classical cityscape of Naples might have interacted with the models of ruins in the *presepe* to confirm and adumbrate their primary symbolic mean-ing, guiding the city's inhabitants and visitors to read these miniature fallen columns and arches as further illustrations of the triumph over the *falsis diis* of pagan antiquity.

The fact that the classical ruins in the *presepe* were indeed per-ceived to represent the victory of Christianity over paganism is confirmed in the account of Francesco Proto cited earlier in this chapter, in which he follows his description of the ruins used by the sixteenth-century artist Giovanni da Nola with the following assertion:

---

[25] Griffo (1996), 26–7 points out parallels between ruins in a painting by Falciatore and a *presepe* in a Neapolitan private collection. For further examples of Nativities with ruins see Makarius (2004), 28–41; Settis (2011), 723–6.

[26] See e.g. Buddensieg (1965) on the destruction of pagan idols by Gregory the Great.

[27] Gaetano of Thiene (1480–1547), one of the founders of the Theatine Order, was in fact an early promoter of the *presepe*: see Griffo (1996), 11.

Certainly, Giovanni wanted to demonstrate that the New Era rose from
the ruins of paganism. There's nothing more to say. All those great
artists of ours were philosophers—all more or less erudite in theology
and hagiography. Even if they weren't philosophers or theologians, they
aspired to be. What more do you want? In those days there wasn't the
same multiplicity of bad, mediocre, and good schools that *we* pay for—
but instead they studied! And, unlike in our own time, those who didn't
know something weren't completely deaf and stubborn, but knew that
there were others they could approach who *did* know, and who could
advise them.[28]

Proto's provocative commentary clearly aims to contrast the wisdom
of earlier artists with the relative ignorance of his own age, but later
discourses about the *presepe* continue to attribute the ruins with
precisely the same theological meaning. Today, the association of
the ruins with the fall of paganism is repeated in books and websites
dedicated to *presepi*, as well as circulating in oral tradition and
Internet discussions.[29] In fact, this widespread interest in, and agreement about, the symbolic content of the ruins may provide us with
another reason for their continued popularity. Recent years have
witnessed a growth of interest in the so-called *simbologia* of the
presepe—a hermeneutic approach that sees every individual element
of these scenes as containing a hidden meaning beyond its literal
appearance. This symbolic approach is used to structure Robert De
Simone's best-selling 1998 study *Il presepe popolare napoletano*, in

[28] 'Certo, Giovanni di Nola volle significare come sulle ruine del gentilesimo
sorgesse l'evo novello. Né ci è che dire. Tutti quei nostri grandi artisti eran più o
meno filosofi, tutti bene o male eruditi in teologia ed in agiografia. E se no, a filosofi e
teologi si ispiravano. Che volete? Non vi avea, di quei giorni, tutta questa moltiplicità
di scuole, sottosculoe e sorrascuole, che noi paghiamo; ma si studiava. Ed, a differenza
del tempo nostro, quelli che non sapevano, non eran poi così sori, da non addarsi, che
vi ha per il mondo chi sappia e chi possa largheggiar di consiglio con gli indotti.' Proto
(1889), cited in Mancini (1983), 62–70.
[29] A brief canvas of online groups of *presepi* enthusiasts on Facebook in November
2012 yielded the following comments about what the ruins stand for: 'Credo che i
ruderi rappresentino la caduta delle religioni politeiste'; 'Una allegoria non tanto
velata al crollo del paganesimo'; 'Sicuramente è da imputare al crollo del paganesimo
a favore del Cristianesimo e al relativo avvento del Signore; storicamente avvenuto
con la venuta di Costantino'. A more formal version of the survey was devised later
that month and advertised to a list for Classicists: here, answers included 'simbolo di
un vecchio e logoro paganesimo', 'Le rovine intendono dimostrare che la venuta di
Cristo determina la fine del paganesimo', and 'È un simbolismo l'avvento del "nuovo"
Regno che dovrà sorgere sulla "fine" di un'epoca dominata da false rappresentazioni
divine'.

which the author, a well-known Neapolitan ethnographer and music-
ologist, lists the various figures and elements of the *presepe* alongside
explications of their deeper symbolic meanings.[30] We learn, for
instance, that the image of the bridge refers to the passage from life
to death, while the image of water (contained within the *presepe* in
both rivers and tubs) symbolizes the rivers of the Underworld, the
wine (sold by traders and drunk in the taverns) stands for the
Eucharistic blood of Christ, and so forth. Particularly fascinating in
the present context is the claim that certain figures represent the
classical pagan gods in disguise: so the popular image of an old
woman giving corn to a hen is representative of Demeter (the hen
is Persephone), while the spinning women are the Fates, the hunter is
Apollo, and the old man and woman sitting by the fire represent
Saturn and Rea.[31] Space does not permit a full discussion of these
'hidden gods' in this chapter, but it is worth noting that the continued
presence of these classical deities in the *presepe* may problematize the
simple equation of the model ruins with the death of ancient paganism. More generally, we can see how this rich system of hidden
meanings—which contains frequent overlaps with another Neapolitan tradition, the oneiric *smorfia*—both absorbs and perpetuates the
older allegorical meaning of the ruins, which now become one of the
more transparent aspects of a broader, and increasingly esoteric,
system of symbolic representation.[32]

Further insights into the role played by the ruins can come from
looking at the *presepe*'s internal aesthetic of historical 'layering' and

---

[30] De Simone (1998); see also Widman (2004), who uses the *simbologia* to formu-
late a Jungian analysis of the *presepe*.

[31] De Simone (1998), 25: 'Procedendo per confronti e riscontri, la scena della
vecchia che dà il becchime a una gallina è rappresentativa di Demetra, mentre la
gallina è l'emblema della figlia Kore. Le donne, o le vecchie che filano, che tessano e
che lavorano la lana, alludono alle Parche. Il cacciatore rimanda ad Apollo con l'arco.
La scena di due vecchi (uomo e donna) seduti presso un braciere, rinvia alla coppia
Saturno-Rea. La figura del pecoraio che guida un gregge in cammino, simboleggia il
dio Ermes o Mercurio come conduttore di anime (nella stessa tradizione campana le
pecore sono raffigurazione emblematica dei defunti). La nobile donna, biana o negra,
seduta in portantina, al seguito dei Re Magi, è rappresentazione di Diana o anche di
Erodiade (il personaggio, nel presepe settecentesco, era detto "La Georgiana"). Il carro
del Cicco-Bacco era preceduto e seguito da un corteo di uomini vestiti con pellini
caprine, i quali con zampogne, tamburi e pifferi scandivano gli orgiastici ritmi
dionisiaci.'

[32] On the *smorfia* see De Sanctis Ricciardone (1987).

anachronism.[33] It is true that the attendance at Christ's birth by worshippers dressed in the costumes of later periods is a prominent feature of Nativity paintings from other parts of Europe; however, this aesthetic of temporal collapse was both emphasized and accentuated in the Neapolitan *presepe*—to such an extent that it became, for some observers, its most distinctive feature. When Joseph Gorani viewed the Nativity belonging to the Terres brothers, he expressed his shock at finding the birth of Christ represented alongside events and people rooted in much later periods of history: these included Capuchin monks, Jacobins, and nuns, and the archbishop of Naples depicted in the act of stopping an eruption of Vesuvius by displaying the blood of the city's patron saint, S. Gennaro. This relaxed attitude to chronology extended to the representation of the climate and landscape, too: for 'instead of offering to the viewer the season of winter and the harshness that accompanies it, one's eyes rest on a nature embellished with the charms of spring, and on the gifts of Ceres as well as those of Pomona'. Meanwhile, 'further off one sees mountains and plains covered with snow, frozen ponds and trees with bare branches, while right next to them are leafy trees with fruit ripe for the picking'.[34]

In many ways, the modern *presepi* appear even more insistently anachronistic and full of contrasts than their predecessors, thriving as they do on the stylistic and iconographic clashes between the older figurines (*pastori*) and the often garish portrait images of today's celebrities (Fig. 14.6). Virtually all the figures and accessories in the contemporary cribs belong to periods much later than the central scene of Jesus' birth (notable exceptions include models of Roman centurions, and wagons decorated in the style of Pompeian wall paintings). The Holy Family and core cast of traditional *pastori*— who are often dressed in mock eighteenth-century vestments—are joined by other more recent symbols of the city, including the 'sacred triad' of Neapolitan writer-actors Totò (1898–1967), Eduardo De Filippo (1900–84), and Massimo Troisi (1953–94). In addition to

[33] Niola (2005) contains a suggestive discussion of anachronism in the *presepe napoletano*.

[34] Gorani (1793), cited in Mancini (1983), 23: 'invece di offrire al riguardante la stagione dell'inverno e i rigori che l'accompagnano, gli occhi si posano sulla natura abbellita dalle attrattive della primavera, sui doni di Cerere e su quelli di Pomona ... Più lontano, montagne e pianure coperte di neve, stagni ghiacciati, alberi dai rami spogli metre appena a fianco vi sono alberi frondosi e frutti pronti per essere colti.'

these familiar figures of Neapolitan cultural memory, the workshops of S. Gregorio produce a constant stream of new *pastori* drawn from current events happening in Naples, elsewhere in Italy, and around the globe. By the festival of the Epiphany on 6 January 2013, for instance, the shops already included figurines of the eminent Nobel Prizewinning Italian scientist Rita Levi-Montalcini, who had died the week before, former president Silvio Berlusconi with his new (Neapolitan) girlfriend Francesca Pascale, and the visibly pregnant Duchess of Cambridge, whose condition had been announced only a few weeks earlier.

The anachronistic aesthetic of the *presepe napoletano* has been recognized by many different observers as one of the crib's central and definitive features—and while Joseph Gorani lamented how, within the Terres *presepe*, 'the objects represented did not bear any resemblance to the objects they were meant to represent', more recent commentators have interpreted this temporal and chronological *bricolage* as having a deliberate theological significance.[35] The Neapolitan theologian and ecclesiastic Bruno Forte, for instance, suggests the overarching message of the city's *presepi* is that 'Christ is not born "elsewhere" or "in a far-off time", but "here and now", in "his" land and amongst "his" people, an authentic and incredibly faithful "God-with-us"'.[36] Similarly, Marino Niola has explained how 'at heart, the anachronism of the *presepe* embodies an allusion to the fact that the Nativity is relived in every era— that the Good News continues to broadcast, but that it can only do so with new words, otherwise it risks becoming cold dogma, stiff "historification"'.[37]

It is in relation to this pervasive aesthetic of historical anachronism that the image of the classical ruin plays one of its most important roles, since the rich chronological layering of the *presepe* is both reflected in, and amplified by, the ruin's own complex temporal identity. As recent scholarly work on ruins in other contexts has

---

[35] 'Si percepisce che l'oggetto rappresentato non ha nessun rapporto con l'oggetto da rappresentare.' Gorani (1793), cited in Mancini (1983), 23.

[36] 'Cristo non nasce "altrove" o "in un tempo lontano", ma "qui ed ora", in questa "sua" terra e fra questa "sua" gente, autentico e fedelissimo "Dio-con-noi".' Forte (1999), 41, cited in Niola (2005), 71.

[37] 'In fondo l'anacronismo del presepe rappresenta un'allusione al fatto che la Natività è rivissuta in ogni epoca, che la Buona Novella continua a dirsi, ma non può che farlo con parole nuove, pena il diventare dogma algido per un verso, e "storificazzione" ingessato per l'altro.' Niola (2005), 69.

shown, such images of fragmented buildings can embody references to several different temporal moments, including the time of their original manufacture and the time of their destruction.[38] This destruction can, in turn, be conceived of as a single, synoptic act (as in Fig. 14.8), and/or as a longer process of decay, such as that we might see in the Vivant engraving (Fig. 14.1), where a crumbling column is covered in slow-growing lichen. In this way, the image of the classical ruin can be seen to both encapsulate and augment the complex multi-temporality of the *presepe*, not only by embodying a number of discrete historical moments, but also by simultaneously *uniting* these different historical moments through the evocation of an ongoing, linear process of ruination and decay. This same sense of time passing can be seen in other iconographic and performative components of the *presepe*, such as the use of electric light to mimic the (accelerated) passing of day and night, and the explicit evocation of human biological decay in the hyper-veristic faces and bodies of the *pastori*. These latter representations of the 'ruin of the body' serve to emphasize the ephemerality and unrepeatability of normal human existence—qualities that stand in stark contrast to the eternal, recursive nature of the birth of the Christian Saviour.[39]

Each of the factors discussed so far has engaged with the *presepe napoletano* as a genre, focusing on aspects of ruins that apply to a wide range of historic and contemporary examples. However, when we turn to focus on individual *presepi* on display in the city today, we often find the ancient ruins being appropriated in unique and unexpected ways, often appearing in the context of visual narratives motivated by a broader sociopolitical agenda. As we might expect, some of these uses hinge on the innate capacity of ruins to encapsulate narratives of decline, evoking dismay and nostalgia in their viewers. For example, in a scene on display outside one of the S. Gregorio workshops in December 2012, a large model of classical

---

[38] On the complex relationship of ruins to temporality see Lowe (2012); his article focuses on images of classical ruins in computer games, but several of his points also resonate with the ruins in the *presepi*: for instance, he points out that many games set in the past use 'already old' relics, which thereby function to create a 'double-layered' interaction with the ancient world. Lowe (2012), 63.

[39] The phrase 'ruin of the body' is borrowed from duBois (2011). For duBois, much of the poignancy of the ruins comes from the fact that 'the viewer also inhabits a ruin, a body that is doomed to decay and death, destruction that ends with bones and ashes'. duBois (2011), 668.

columns topped with a crumbling entablature was incorporated into an assembly of motifs that was very hard *not* to read as a pessimistic comment on the current 'state of the nation' (Fig. 14.6). The central position was given to the figures of Eduardo De Filippo and Totò, each holding one of his catchphrases on a placard. Eduardo's read 'Povera Italia!!!', Totò's 'E Io Pago!!!' ('And it's me who pays'). When viewed together with the background of disintegrating architecture, at the end of a year marked by economic problems and political scandals—as well as concerns about the region's archaeological heritage—these phrases acquired an altogether more poignant level of meaning.

One particularly rich example of a contemporary reception of classical ruins is represented in Fig. 14.9. This photograph reproduces a view of a *presepe* that was made in the Ferrigno workshop in 2009 (Via S. Gregorio Armeno 8), the same year in which the town of L'Aquila (the capital of the Abruzzo region of Italy) was struck by a catastrophic earthquake.[40] Three hundred of the city's inhabitants died in the disaster, and more than 65,000 were left homeless; countless historic buildings were also destroyed. The ensuing rescue operations were based in the barracks of the Guardia di Finanza (the special branch of the Italian police force which deals with economic affairs) in the nearby village of Coppito, and it was in the Guardia di Finanza headquarters that the *presepe per L'Aquila* was displayed before being sold in a special charity auction, the proceeds of which went to the victims of the earthquake.

The photograph reproduced at Fig. 14.9 depicts the *Presepe for L'Aquila* when it was still on display in the Ferrigno shop in Naples. Measuring approximately 2.5 metres in length, it portrays Mary, Joseph, Jesus, and the Three Kings set against a background of classicizing ruins. So far, so traditional—however, a closer look reveals that the scene of the divine birth has been cleverly reconfigured to include references to the earthquake and its aftermath. The Three Kings are dressed in eighteenth-century costumes, but they have the recognizable physiognomies of the political leaders who played a role in the rescue efforts: the then-president Silvio Berlusconi, Guido Bertolaso (head of Italy's civil protection department), and General Fabrizio Lisi (the head of Coppito's Guardia di Finanza).

---

[40] For the Ferrigno workshop see <http://www.arteferrigno.it> [last accessed 24 March 2014]; De Caro (2007), 14.

Fig. 14.9. The *presepe per L'Aquila*, 2009, Ferrigno workshop, Naples.
Source: Photograph reproduced with the kind permission of Marco Ferrigno.

The American president Barack Obama, whose offer of international aid was one of the few accepted by Berlusconi, also appeared as a shepherd tending his sheep. But the most striking aspects of the representation in the present context are the 'classical' ruins, which have been replaced here by models of L'Aquila's most iconic buildings in their post-earthquake state. The building at the centre of the *presepe* in front of which the Holy Family gathers represents the eighteenth-century church of S. Maria del Suffraggio—one of the most important churches in the city, and one of the most badly damaged in the disaster. The building on the left represents the Scuola della Guardia di Finanza in Coppito; finally, although the columns and architrave of the building on the right assimilate it visually to the classical ruins that would normally appear in a *presepe*, the inscription on the architrave clearly identifies this structure as the collapsed Palazzo del Governo.

The *presepe per L'Aquila* thus provides us with one of the most striking examples of how the classical ruins might be reconfigured by modern Neapolitan artists and incorporated into narratives that are resolutely contemporary. As in earlier examples, these ruins contribute to the sense of historical anachronism, albeit through the representation of neoclassical buildings which were until recently still functioning. At the same time, the identification of these ruins with real buildings—made explicit through the textual labels—also collapses *space* by creating a fantastic *capriccio* of recognizable buildings that stood miles apart in reality. Crucially, this depiction of an identifiable architectural context serves to relocate the Nativity from Bethlehem to L'Aquila, showing the Abruzzo city as the (true) birthplace of the Christian religion.[41] Here, the presence of the Holy Family in the disaster-struck town might be seen to provide a source of potential comfort to its citizens, by showing the divine birth and its saving power as physically present amongst them.[42] Moreover, as well as functioning to transport the Holy Family to L'Aquila, other elements within this *presepe* also suggest that the ruins themselves should be read as symbols of hope and redemption. This reading is most explicitly signalled by the Latin phrase above the door of the Scuola della Guardia di Finanza, which reads *Nec Recisa Recedit*—'No retreat, even when broken'. This phrase—in fact the Guardia's motto—was noted and discussed by Pope Benedict XVI during his visit to the city on 28 April 2009 when, standing outside the building, he suggested that '*Nec Recisa Recedit* seems to express well what the mayor defined as your firm intention to rebuild the city, with the constancy that characterizes the people of the Abruzzo region'.[43] The pope appears in the *presepe per L'Aquila*, his arms uplifted in a physical gesture of optimism and encouragement: this gesture thus mirrors the pervasive optimism of his speech, which closed with an

---

[41] This 'relocation effect' had been a feature of earlier examples too, not only through the inclusion of ruins but also through the representation of topographic features, including representations of the Bay of Naples and the image of a smoking Vesuvius (as seen, for example, in the background of the *presepe Cuciniello* depicted at Fig. 14.2).

[42] Local poet Filippo Crudele likened the homeless citizens of L'Aquila to the Holy Family on their search for a place to stay in Bethlehem: 'A Natale, come sarà | Il nostro Presepe? | A L'Aquila, come a Betlemme, | Tutti in cerca di una casa, | ma soltanto al Re dei Re, | il privilegio di una stalla' ('Come a Betlemme', Christmas 2009).

[43] '"*Nec recisa recedit*": il motto del Corpo della Guardia di Finanza, che possiamo ammirare sulla facciata della struttura, sembra bene esprimere quella che il Sindaco ha definito la ferma intenzione di ricostruire la città con la costanza caratteristica di voi abruzzesi . . . A questa condizione, L'Aquila, anche se ferita, potrà tornare a volare.' The full text of the speech is available on the Vatican website: <http://www.vatican.va/holy_father/benedict_xvi/speeches/2009/april/documents/hf_ben-xvi_spe_20090428_sisma-laquila_it.html> [accessed 23 January 2013].

expression of hope that the town of L'Aquila (lit. 'the eagle') would 'rise up and fly again'.

Although on one level, then, the depiction of recognizable ruins in this *presepe* appealed to the viewer's profound awareness of loss, it also functioned to enhance the *presepe*'s function as a symbol of hope, comfort, and redemption. This dual nature dovetails neatly with comments made by Page duBois, who has drawn attention to the fundamental ambiguity of ruins and their potential to 'evoke fears of decay and death, even as they promise survival and even immortality'.[44] The *presepe per L'Aquila* thus cleverly plays with the deep-rooted ambivalence of the image of the ruin, which is here used not only to evoke a sense of sadness and nostalgia at the destruction of familiar historic buildings, but also to write those buildings into a more positive narrative of rebirth and renewal. Essentially, this *presepe* appropriates and overturns the 'accepted' allegorical symbolism of the ruins, which—as we saw earlier—posits them as unproblematic symbols of the triumph of Christianity over paganism. The central ruined building represents a Catholic church rather than a classical monument; meanwhile, rather than indicating the complete replacement of one obsolete civilization by another (as the *simbologia* of the modern *presepe* would decree), the ruins in this example are transformed into a symbol of the survival and continuity of a single (Christian) civilization in the face of unavoidable natural disaster. The *presepe per L'Aquila* thus demonstrates the agency of modern *figurari* to appropriate the traditional imagery of ruins for new meanings, while reminding viewers of the richness and multivalency of the ruin as a symbol of Classical Presences.

---

[44] duBois (2011), 663.

Afterwords

15

Neapolis and the Future of Naples' Museums

Stefano De Caro

The museographical representation of ancient Neapolis has always posed certain conceptual and practical problems. Firstly, we need to acknowledge that even in antiquity the Greek and Roman city was a rather modest entity—a *mikrà polis* when seen against the wider background of the ancient world and even the Bay of Naples itself, despite the presence of the venerable poets Virgil and Statius. For this reason, the city has only a few grand Roman monuments, and even these have been subsumed by later layers, allowing only rare, accidental findings of fragments from the subsoil. In fact, as Benedetto Croce famously noted, the most conspicuous *monumentum* to survive is the urban layout itself—and this is not something that can be contained within a museum (or at least not according to the terms of traditional museology). The urban layout is also continously transforming, rather like a living organism, meaning that it is almost impossible to articulate the city's history in clearly distinct phases in which the Graeco-Roman evidence is completely separate from that of later eras.

The history of Neapolitan collecting has also impeded the formation of nuclei of urban antiquities. In the seventeenth and eighteenth centuries, the city's collections were overwhelmed by the influx of material from the nearby Phlegraean Fields, as well as from the neighbouring provinces whose aristocratic rulers had moved into the city. This was the period in which the new Bourbon dynasty installed itself in Naples, bringing with it the great Farnese collections of pictures, coins, and precious gems; soon after, the 'Herculanense Museum' was created at the Royal Palace of Portici as a corollary of the grand imperial enterprise of the Vesuvian excavations, thereby taking Naples in a new museological phase. The prestige of these projects eliminated any possibility of a museological project centred on ancient Naples; later, the amalgamation of the royal collections in the Real Museo Borbonico (which was further enriched by Farnese collections) further overshadowed the Neapolitan finds. Only a tiny fraction of this material—a few Greek inscriptions which bore witness to the city's long Hellenic past—was ever exhibited in the museum, even after the unification of Italy.

Towards the end of the nineteenth century, however, the urban redevelopment projects (the *Risanamento*) brought the city's attention to the material presence of its ancient past. Excavations conducted at this time brought to light a continuous stratigraphic sequence dating back to the period of foundation, as well as objects from every subsequent era. In retrospect, it is clear that this would have been the perfect opportunity to create a civic museum—a 'Museo della Città di Napoli'. It is true that an interesting collection of objects from the medieval and modern periods relating to the theme of the city (including panoramas, models, sculptures, architectural elements, inscriptions, and coats of arms recovered from the demolition works) were brought together to form a collection in the Certosa di S. Martino, and amongst these were a few pieces from the classical period. However, the more important ancient pieces were automatically sent to the National Archaeological Museum (the 'Museo Nazionale', as the old Museo Borbonico was renamed), even though they were clearly not going to be exhibited there, due to the lack of physical exhibition space within an institution of such enormous scope, and to the 'inferior' nature of the Neapolitan finds, which could hardly compete with the masses of precious artefacts already in the collections. Meanwhile, it is worth remembering that the Certosa di S. Martino museum and the Museo Nazionale were administered separately, with the former being under the jurisdiction of the Archaeological Superintendency for Paestum and the area of Salerno, while the latter was managed by the Antiquities Superintendency for Naples. Such an odd administrative division hardly facilitated a unitary vision of Neapolitan antiquities.

In the early twentieth century, then, the dominant image of Graeco-Roman Naples was that which had emerged from the archival and philological studies of Bartolomeo Capasso and the contributors to *Napoli Nobilissima* (an epigraphic, historical, numismatic, and topographical project that was nevertheless an academic enterprise rather than a museological one). Things seemed destined to remain that way, until a different and perhaps more favourable situation arose after the Second World War. The transfer of the art-historical collections from the Museo Archeologico Nazionale to the Palazzo di Capodimonte enabled the rehousing of antiquities in new, larger spaces, allowing for the traditional organization to be reinvented according to new criteria and cutting-edge museographical themes. This in turn led to the development of the so-called 'Museo Topografico', in which the displays were organized according to the various provenances of the objects, starting with sites within Campania. At the same time, academic research on ancient Neapolis was also making notable progress. The excavations by Gennaro Pesce in the necropolis of Castelcapuano, for instance, had yielded a great mass of material to add to the finds from the monumental necropoleis in the areas of Sanità and S. Teresa. Meanwhile, respected academics and public servants such as Mario Napoli and Werner Johannowsky were making important contributions to historical and topographical research, publishing a wealth of new material. Notable examples include the extraordinary and unexpected discovery of the Archaic and early Hellenistic necropolis of Pizzofalcone, the sanctuary of Demeter on the acropolis of S. Aniello a Caponapoli, and the ancient Greek tombs and the waste from the ceramic ovens found under the street of the Corso Umberto I (the so-called 'Rettifilo'). Spurred on by these discoveries, Soprintendente Enrica Pozzi gathered together a number of academics engaged in research on the ancient city, including Ettore Lepore, to work on an exhibition of *Napoli antica* which was to be held at the Museo Nazionale in 1985. This was a preliminary exploration of a possible permanent exhibition of Naples' ancient history, which was eventually inaugurated in 1999 in the west wing of the first floor of the museum; it took the form of a topographic journey which illustrated the development of Greek culture in the Gulf of Naples from the arrival of the Mycenaeans up until the Roman era.

Napoli antica was followed by several years of enthusiastic research in the field, encouraged by Mayor Antonio Bassolino and others from the Comune di Napoli (including Vezio De Lucia, whose urban development plans put archaeological research high on the agenda for the first time). Agreements with the Università L'Orientale di Napoli (Bruno d'Agostino, Emanuele Greco) and the French Centre J. Bérard allowed the Archaeological Superintendency (Daniele Giampaola) to gather support for a new Urban Archaeology Laboratory in Vicolo della Serpe, which brought together various partners involved in research on the city, as well as facilitating other projects such as the new digitalization of the plan of the historical centre of Naples, an offshoot of a larger photographic mapping project, the 'Orthophoto-plan di Napoli'. These new methodologies were used to confront new challenges of urban preservation and have since been used successfully by archaeologists during the construction of the new lines of the Naples underground Metro system. Meanwhile, the post-seismic restoration programme that followed the Irpinia earthquake of 1980–1 led to crucial restoration and conservation work being carried out on several key monuments in the historical centre of Naples, including the sites of S. Lorenzo Maggiore and S. Chiara. The museological displays at these sites were innovative insofar as they aimed to tell the whole story of a monument from antiquity to the present day, and treated archaeo-logical remains as equally important as textual sources.

This background helps us to understand the 'two-level' museum system currently operating in Naples. On the one hand, we have a central exhibition at the National Archaeological Museum, which represents the history of the city in relation to the rest of the Gulf and the wider ancient world; on the other hand, we have a network of archaeological sites, distributed throughout the city, which recount the process of urban development through examples which embroi-der their stories onto the frame of the urban layout—a sort of dispersed 'Museo della Città'. This dual system has the potential to be deeply interesting, since it is able to link the permanent museum exhibition with the many sites and smaller nuclei of antiquities distrib-uted throughout the city—from the Roman theatre to the catacombs, from Pausilypon to the Crypta Neapolitana, from the Greek quarry of Poggioreale to the new sites found during the construction of the Metro.

These Metro sites have presented extraordinary new opportunities for the distributed Neapolitan museology described above, on account of their exceptional dimensions and the insights they give into the archaeological stratigraphy and the orographic and hydro-graphic evolution of the territory (in particular of the coast in front of the city). A number of temporary exhibitions have begun to explore the intriguing possibilities offered by these sites. A preliminary exhib-ition of the results from the Metro excavations was held in the tunnel that linked the new station Museo to the National Archaeological

Museum, while an exhibition of the fragments of an honorary imperial arch found in the area of the ancient port was recently staged in the entrance hall of the same museum. In some cases, the location of new stations coincided with sites of particular archaeological interest; here, they could be made into exhibition spaces in which Metro users might encounter pivotal moments in the history of the city, as documented at a particular point in space. The excavation of Piazza Nicola Amore, for example, has uncovered the heart of the sanctuary of the Neapolitan Isolympic games with its temple and the inscribed marble catalogues of victors. The station's design includes an 'archaeological' layer which illustrates this episode of urban history by exhibiting the base of the temple and related objects. Even more interesting and ambitious is the station of Piazza Municipio, a central node of the city's transport system (it is the terminal point of the two Metro lines, and is connected to the port station of Molo Beverello). The idea of a museum exhibition in the restored Beverello tower of the Castelnuovo has already been raised in the past, after excavations inside the castle (which is also known as the Maschio Angioino) yielded exceptional results. These were followed by further rescue excavations in the area of the two new Metro stations, which brought to light the wooden jetties of the Graeco-Roman port together with the remains of boats, followed in close succession by the Angevin residential quarters next to the castle, the Roman imperial baths, and the piers of the Roman port. This station too, then, will be enriched by a 'museum sector', which will project along the outside of the castle on one side of the large piazza connecting the port and the station.

In truth, the Comune di Napoli's decision to change the function of certain important large spaces like the Sala dei Baroni in the Maschio Angioino from an administrative to a cultural one might well lead to an exhibition project far greater in scope than the (albeit very important) display of finds from the local Metro station. This building, which is so rich in history and symbolism, could even provide the perfect home for the 'Museo della Città di Napoli' which the collections of the Certosa di S. Martino museum currently represent only in part. Ideally, this new museum would go beyond a simple presentation of the archaeological data by bringing together different disciplines and types of source to recount the multi-millennial story of the city in greater detail than ever before. This idea sparked some interest when I originally proposed it; however, these are difficult times—difficult in economic terms, but also in the spiritual sense, since the enthusiasm that nourished the so-called 'Neapolitan Renaissance' of the 1990s has now waned. I confess, then, that the idea of this museum (which would, like the extraordinary Museum of London, tell the no-less extraordinary story of a city and community that for many centuries has been amongst the most dynamic of Europe) now seems to be an unrealizable dream. This is certainly not due to a lack of material—on the contrary, even the archaeological finds made during the excavations of the Metro cannot fit into the storerooms of the Museo Archeologico Nazionale, and are currently being stored in a railway deposit in Chiaiano (probably not the most suitable long-term home for these discoveries). In London, where for several years now the problem of urban archaeology has been approached on a scientific basis, the 'laboratory storerooms' of the Museum of London have played an active role in creating an exciting new exhibition centre in the city's Docklands. I do not know if this could be a possibility for Naples, too: certainly, the huge amount of material recovered from the Metro works and other urban sites over these last decades is truly extraordinary in terms of historical importance. The conservation and exhibition of these finds, like those that came to light during the works on the high-speed railway between Rome and Naples, will certainly take several years to organize. However, if things unfold as they ought to, the next decade will see the creation of numerous valuable opportunities to develop innovative museological projects, involving many academic and institutional partners. Unfortunately a new law (L. 106/2014) has now further complicated the situation, imposing the separation of the Archaeological Museum of Naples from the Superintendency that has always taken care of the excavations in the city. This change will certainly not make it easier to carry out the project of a Museum of Naples.

16

Parthenope on the Metro

or, Links with the Past, on the Journey into the Future

Luigi Spina

The metropolitan network of Naples will soon be finished, with all its stations working from Piazza Garibaldi to the highest and furthest points of the city. The diverse people and places of the Neapolitan territory will be connected at every moment of the day, in the latest manifestation of the contiguity and promiscuity that have character-ized the city throughout its long history. Creating these new spatial connections has taken several exhausting years; during this time, the digging machines have brushed against ancient layers, bringing to light some precious evidence of the past. They have raised—perhaps involuntarily—new questions for the engineers of urban transport, such as how to connect different time periods and how to locate oneself within time. Is it possible (without constructing an actual time machine) to foster an awareness of a past that we might visit more often, and that we might make more accessible and understandable? What type of cultural machinery might we devise to facilitate these links and help us value the diversity and variety of all these layers?

These are indeed difficult questions, and they can give rise to some different answers—answers that are not always reassuring, if we look at the history of recent years. But perhaps Parthenope herself might suggest a way of preserving and of making usable the ancient culture of Naples, while also preserving it for future generations.[1] According to the tale told by Lycophron in his *Alexandra* (ll. 717–25), the Siren Parthenope was one of the victims of the lethal cunning of Ulysses (as were the Trojans of Aeneas, who managed to disembark alive some kilometres further north, thereby beginning the history of Rome). Parthenope, like her Siren sisters, was almost certainly the daughter of the river Acheloos and one of the nine Muses; this divine origin may account for the Siren's ability to incarnate *both* the threatening, hidden dangers of a song which simultaneously fascinates and bewilders, which both distracts one from everyday life and consigns it to oblivion, *and* the wise and beneficent presence which can grant favourable conditions for a journey and inspire the foundation of a city in a suitable location, endowing it with her feasts and her rites.

In fact, the body of the Siren was itself dual-natured, the remnant of an ancient metamorphosis. The Sirens, Ovid tells us in his *Metamorphoses* (5.551–63), were young girls, playmates of Proserpina, the daughter of the goddess Ceres who was kidnapped by Pluto and taken to Tartarus to be his queen. The Sirens asked the gods to be transformed into birds so that they could search for their friend in the most remote parts of the world. In the earliest phase of the myth, then, they were half-woman, half-bird; then, over the course of the centuries and via routes that are not entirely clear, the Sirens' bird-half turned into a fish-half, and this remained the most familiar image of the Siren until our own times. The hybrid nature of the Siren's body refers to a duplicity, a complex nature that cannot be reduced to a reassuring uniformity. Neapolis, as Strabo underlined, was at the same time a Greek city and a Campanian one. For this reason, the ancient name of the city evoked the hybridity of the population that lived there, as well as the Siren who had chosen to die there. Modern Naples, too, seems to adapt itself to this deep meaning of the myth: is not the Naples of our own time a kaleidoscope of different worlds, social classes, tastes, and abilities, which are held together and represented as a single 'body'—a body that is recognizable by its fascinating 'monstrosity'? And is it not perhaps the case that this 'monstrosity' can explain the city's 'extremes', which range from the highest peaks

---

[1] For more on the myth of the sirens, Parthenope, and the 'nostalgia' for the antique, see Bettini and Spina (2007); Spina (2009), 23–7; Spina (2010a); Spina (2010b).

of genius to the abysses of *Gomorra*?[2] We need to acknowledge these clashes before we can understand whether or not it will be possible to connect in a meaningful way with the history of this dynamic (and often destructive) city.

In May 2013 Naples hosted the second round of the 'Olimpiadi del Classico', a contest organized by the Ministry of Education which constituted a sort of 'national final' for the winners of the various classical language competitions (*certamina*) that had taken place in schools and communities across Italy. Young students who were passionate about Graeco-Roman culture, but who were at the same time resolutely contemporary (with all the characteristics of the 'digital generation'), challenged, and were themselves challenged by, a city and its chaotic everyday routines. This too resonated with the notion of hybridity, for these young students tried once again to interpret the antique, to translate and understand the ideas and passions of women and men who had lived many centuries before them. I say 'once again' because this is what the students of Statius' father did in this same city; this is what Leopardi wrote about; this is what dozens and dozens of other students did, before they became teachers in our schools and universities. This, in the end, is the scope of the present book. So far, all these efforts have kept the study of ancient culture alive, but we have arrived at a turning point, at a crisis more extreme than those of other eras; even if, looking back, Classical Studies have shown a surprising capacity for self-renewal, and for fostering receptions and cultural memory in later periods.

The future of the study of Naples' ancient past is now entrusted to this same hybrid, in the hope that it will be capable of keeping alive the historical contexts that have produced such a valuable culture. This is the only way that we can avoid transforming antiquity into an empty 'classicism of manners', from which we can only reap nostalgia. The ruins of ancient culture reflect the true nature of Time. History has never been afraid of Time itself, but only of abandonment and rejection, which reveal a conscious, inexorable deafness, as well as the inability to imagine a future.

---

[2] I refer, of course, to the celebrated 2006 book by Roberto Saviano, the English title of which is *Gomorrah: Italy's Other Mafia*. The title *Gomorra* is a pun on *Camorra*, which is the name of the mafia-type crime syndicate originating in Naples and Campania.

But let us return to our Metro, whose route should now (with the help of the four old funicular railways) cover the entire urban space of Naples. The metaphor of the journey is, of course, one of the most frequently recurring since antiquity, but it took an extraordinary Argentinian writer, Julio Cortázar, to imagine *un viaje atemporal París–Marsella*—a journey of over a month which covered the unremarkable distance between two motorway toll-booths, without ever leaving the motorway or tasting the undocumented life of the service stations.[3] Here, we find a model for a journey made not only in space, but also in 'Neapolitan time'—a journey that is able to project itself into the future without losing the concrete dimension of the present. The new stations of the Metro, which are both functional and artistic, already offer a great deal of symbolism and meaning.[4] They do not deny the existence of the hybrid; rather, they represent the best part of its nature; they are subjected every day to vandalism and degradation, but, almost miraculously, they bear far fewer scars than even the most pessimistic would ever have imagined.

Along with the compulsion for rapidity and precision of connection, one needs to be capable of valorizing, with a certain determination, moments of pause, of slowing down; that is, to use the stations not simply as interchanges between the above and below of the city (or, better, as an underground connection between two of the city's 'aboves'), but rather as pathways between the past and the present, as the materialization of a dialogue between different entities in a language that is nevertheless still comprehensible. Travelling like this, the journey of Parthenope would truly be a journey *towards* the future *with* the past—not simply a nostalgic journey *towards* the past. Parthenope certainly needs to respond to the needs of the present, but she should also exploit the new hybrid that is made from combining the *above* and *below* of the city, which are almost equivalent to its *before* and *after*. She should try to keep these connections open and alive, refusing to sacrifice to speed (which makes everything uniform and almost invisible) the beauties of an ancient country that still promises new discoveries to those who know how to slow down at the right time.

[3] This is the subtitle of the book that Cortázar wrote with his wife, Carol Dunlop: *Los autonautas de la cosmopista* (1983).

[4] <http://www.danpiz.net/napoli/trasporti/MetroArte-Frames.htm>.

The future of the classical heritage of Parthenope, whose complex identity is visible to all, is therefore entrusted to the creation and consolidation of entities that are stable but still mobile—entities like the new Metro stations, which are used by people and are therefore alive. The stations—the stopping points of this journey—do not need to be created because they are already present in the urban landscape. Meanwhile, the people who are shaped, taught, and guided in the educational institutions, centres of research, libraries, theatres, and in the countless initiatives taking place in the piazzas and streets of Naples—*these* are the new protagonists, the actors who are capable of making Parthenope once more the Siren who attracts people with her charm and her ingrained wisdom. This volume testifies to the fact that the challenge is not a new one, although today it is arguably more difficult. To know that in the past others have succeeded in the face of similar challenges should help us, perhaps making future generations conscious of the fact that they need to confront problems and over-come them with determination, in order to make the 'above' and 'below', the 'before' and 'after' of this city come alive with equal passion.

Bibliography

Abbreviations

AÉ	*L'Année épigraphique*
AION	*Annali dell'Istituto universitario orientale di Napoli*
ASNa	Archivio di Stato di Napoli
BAV	Biblioteca Apostolica Vaticana
CIG	*Corpus Inscriptionum Graecarum*, Berlin (1828–77)
CIL	*Corpus Inscriptionum Latinarum*, Berlin (1863–)
DBI	*Dizionario Biografico degli Italiani*, available online at <http://www.treccani.it/biografie/>
FGrHist	*Die Fragmente der griechischen Historiker*, ed. F. Jacoby (Berlin 1923–58)
IG	*Inscriptiones Graecae* (Berlin, 1873–90)
IGR	*Inscriptiones Graecae ad res Romanas pertinentes* (Paris, 1911–27)
ILS	*Inscriptiones Latinae Selectae* (Berlin, 1892–1916)
IvO	*Die Inschriften von Olympia* (Berlin, 1896)
LIMC	*Lexicon iconographicum mythologiae classicae* (Zurich, Munich, and Düsseldorf, 1981–2009)
LTUR	*Lexicon topographicum urbis Romae* (Rome, 1993–2000)
Napoli antica (1985)	*Napoli antica: Catalogo della mostra 'Napoli antica' organizzata dalla Soprintendenza Archeologica per le Province di Napoli e Caserta (Museo Archeologico Nazionale, Napoli, 26 settembre 1985–15 aprile 1986)* (Naples, 1985)
Neapolis (1986)	*Neapolis: Atti del venticinquesimo congresso di studi sulla Magna Grecia, Taranto, 3–7 ottobre 1985* (Taranto, 1986)
SEG	*Supplementum epigraphicum Graecum* (Leiden, 1923–).

References

Abbamondi, A. (1906). *Le Selve di P. Papinio Stazio ed un commento inedito di Giano Aulo Parrasio (Contributo alla critica Staziana)*, Naples.

Abbamonte, G. (1997). 'Ricerche sul commento inedito di Perotti alle *Silvae* di Stazio', *Studi Umanistici Piceni* 17: 9–20.

Abbamonte, G. (2003). 'Esegesi umanistica alle *Silvae* di Stazio: Parrasio', *Euphrosyne* 31: 133–53.

Abbamonte, G. (2011). 'Considerazioni sulla presenza dei modelli classici nella narrazione storica di Bartolomeo Facio', *Reti Medievali* 12/1: 107–30.

Abbamonte, G. (2013). 'La ricezione della *Silva* di Stazio sulla villa sorrentina di Pollio Felice nei commentari umanistici', in P. Galand and S. Laigneau-Fontaine (eds.), *La Silve: Histoire d'une écriture libérée en Europe de l'antiquité au XVIIIe siècle*, Turnhout: 337–72.

Abbott, F. F., and Johnson, A. C. (1968). *Municipal Administration in the Roman Empire*, New York.

Accame, M. (2008). *Pomponio Leto: Vita e insegnamento*, Tivoli.

Ackerman, J. (1988 [1961]). *L'architettura di Michelangelo*, Turin.

Adam, J. (2003). *Bilingualism and the Latin Language*, Cambridge and New York.

Adamo Muscettola, S. (1976). 'Ritratti di filosofi da Baia', *Rendiconti della Accademia di Archeologia, Lettere e Belle Arti di Napoli: Società Nazionale di Scienze, Lettere ed Arti* 51: 31–8.

Adamo Muscettola, S. (1984). 'Napoli e l'immaginario antico tra '600 e '800', *Prospettiva: Rivista di storia dell'arte antica e moderna* 39: 2–10.

Adamo Muscettola, S. (1985). 'Il tempio dei Dioscuri', in *Napoli Antica* (1985): 196–208.

Adamo Muscettola, S. (1994). 'Napoli e le belle antechetate', in F. Zevi (ed.), *Neapolis*, Naples: 95–109.

Adamo Muscettola, S. (1996). 'Da cratere dionisiaco a fonte battesimale: Una eredità della *otiosa Neapolis* o di *Napoli desidiosa*?', in C. Montepaone (ed.), *L'incidenza dell'antico: Studi in memoria di Ettore Lepore*, iii, Naples: 569–85.

Adams, J. (2003). *Bilingualism and the Latin Language*, Cambridge and New York.

Adams, N. (1993). 'L'architettura militare di Francesco di Giorgio', in F. P. Fiore and M. Tafuri (eds.), *Francesco di Giorgio architetto*, Milan: 126–62.

Addesso, C. A. (2005). 'Un "sepolcro di candidissimi marmi, & intagli eccellentissimi": Sannazaro nelle "guide" di Napoli', *Studi Rinascimentali* 3: 171–200.

Addesso, C. A. (ed.) (2007). *Ioan Berardino Fuscano: Stanze sovra la bellezza di Napoli*, Naples.

Alberti, L. (1550). *Descrittione di tutta Italia*, Bologna.

Alchermes, J. (1994). '*Spolia* in Roman Cities of the Late Empire: Legislative Rationales and Architectural Reuse', *Dumbarton Oaks Papers* 48: 167–78.

Alcock, S. E. (2001). *Archaeologies of the Greek Past: Landscape, Monuments and Memory*, Cambridge.

Alcock, S. E., and van Dyke, R. (eds.) (2003). *The Archaeology of Memory*, Oxford.

Alessio, G. C. (1979). 'Brunetto Latini e Cicerone (e i dettatori)', *Italia medievale e umanistica* 22: 123–69.

Alessio, G. C. (1992). 'Le istituzioni scolastiche e l'insegnamento', in C. Leonardi and G. Orlandi (eds.), *Aspetti della letteratura latina nel secolo XIII*, Spoleto: 3–28.

Alessio, G. C., and Villa, C. (1990). 'Il nuovo fascino degli autori antichi tra i secoli XII e XIV', in G. Cavallo, P. Fedeli, and A. Giardina (eds.), *Lo spazio letterario di Roma antica*, iii. *La ricezione del testo*, Rome: 473–511.

Alfano, G. (2011). 'Le *aspre battaglie amorose*: Boccaccio e il poema (da Marte a Venere)', in G. Abbamonte, J. Barreto, T. D'Urso, A. Perriccioli Saggese, and F. Senatore (eds.), *La battaglia nel Rinascimento meridionale*, Rome: 29–42.

Alisio, G. (1964). 'La chiesa e il campanile della Pietrasanta', *Napoli Nobilissima*, NS 3: 226–36; 4: 42–52.

Alisio, G. (1969). 'Le correzioni del Carletti alla pianta del Duca di Noja', *Napoli Nobilissima*, NS 8: 223–6.

Alisio, G. (1980). *Napoli e il risanamento: Recupero di una struttura urbana*, Naples.

Alonso, A. M. (1988). 'The Effects of Truth: Re-Presentations of the Past and the Imagining of Community', *Journal of Historical Sociology* 1/1: 33–57.

Altamura, A. (1974). *Cronaca di Partenope*, Naples.

Amirante, F. (ed.) (1995). *Libri per vedere: Le guide storico-artistiche della città di Napoli: Fonti, testimonianze del gusto, immagini di una città*, Naples.

Amodio, M. (2005). 'La componente africana nella civiltà napoletana tardo-antica: Fonti letterarie ed evidenze archeologiche', *Atti della Pontificia Accademia Romana di Archeologia, Memorie* 8: 1–257.

Ancel, R. (1908). 'Le Vatican sous Paul IV: Contribution à l'histoire du Palais Pontifical', *Revue Bénédictine* 25: 48–71.

Anderson, H. (2009). *The Manuscripts of Statius: Reception: the Vitae and Accessus*, iii, Arlington, VA.

Andreu, F. (1945). 'La relazione di D. Erasmo Danese su S. Gaetano Thiene', *Regnum Dei*, 1: 8–17, 60–72.

Anguissola, A. (2004). 'Note alla legislazione su spoglio e reimpiego di materiali da costruzione ed arredi architettonici, I secolo a.C.–VI secolo d.C.', in W. Cupperi (ed.), *Senso delle rovine e riuso dell'antico: Annali della Scuola Normale Superiore di Pisa, Quaderni* 14: 13–29.

Argan, G. C., and Contardi, B. (2007 [1990]). *Michelangelo architetto*, Milan.

Arnaldi, F., Gualdo Rosa, L., and Monti Sabia, L. (eds.) (1964). *Poeti latini del Quattrocento*, Milan.

Arnaldi, G. (1982). 'Fondazione e rifondazioni dello studio di Napoli in età sveva', in *Università e società nei secoli XII–XVI*, Centro Italiano di Studi di Storia e d'Arte, Pistoia: 81–105.

Arnaldi, G. (2005). 'Studio di Napoli', in *Federico II: Enciclopedia fridericiana*, ii, Rome: 803–8.

Arthur, P. (ed.) (1994). *Il complesso archeologico di Carminiello ai Mannesi, Napoli (Scavi 1983–1984)*, Galatina.

Arthur, P. (2002). *Naples, from Roman Town to City State: An Archaeological Perspective*, London.

Artifoni, E. (1995). 'Gli uomini dell'assemblea: L'oratoria civile, i concionatori e i predicatori nella società comunale', in *La predicazione dei Frati dalla metà del '200 alla fine del '300*, Spoleto: 141–88.

Ashmore, W., and Knapp, A. B. (eds.) (1999). *Archaeologies of Landscape: Contemporary Perspectives*, Oxford.

Assman, A. (2008). 'Canon and Archive', in A. Erll and A. Nünning (eds.), *Cultural Memory Studies: An International and Interdisciplinary Handbook*, Berlin: 97–108.

Assmann, J. (2006). *Religion and Cultural Memory*, Stanford, CA.

Astarita, T. (ed.) (2013). *A Companion to Early Modern Naples*, Leiden.

Augustín, A. (1765–74). *Antonii Augustini Archiepiscopi Tarruconensis Opera omnia quae multa adhibita diligentia colligi potuerunt*, Lucae.

Baldassarre, I. (ed.) (1983). *Archeologia urbana e centro antico di Napoli: Documenti*, Naples.

Baldassarre, I. (1986). 'Osservazioni sull'urbanistica di Neapolis in età romana', in *Neapolis* (1986): 221–32.

Baldassarre, I., and Giampaola, D. (eds.) (2010). *Il teatro di Neapolis: Scavo e recupero urbano*, Naples.

Balty, J. C. (1981). 'Antiocheia', *LIMC* i/1: 840–51.

Barberini, M. G. (ed.) (2008). *Tracce di pietra: La collezione di marmi di Palazzo Venezia*, Rome.

Baronio, C. (1588–1607). *Annales ecclesiastici auctore Caesare Baronio Sorano congregationis oratorii presbytero: Nunc vero tituli sanctorum martyrum Nerei et Achillei S. R. E. cardinale bibliothecario apostolico*, Rome.

Barresi, P., and Pensabene, P. (2002). 'Materiali di reimpiego e progettazione nell'architettura delle chiese paleocristiane di Roma', in F. Guidobaldi and A. Guiglia Guidobaldi (eds.), *Ecclesiae urbis: Atti del congresso internazionale di studi sulle chiese di Roma (IV–X secolo)*, Rome: 799–842.

Bartlett, K. R. (1991). *The English in Italy, 1525–1558: A Study in Culture and Politics*, Geneva.

Bartlett, K. R. (1993). 'The Journey into Sicily of Thomas Hoby, 1550', in E. Kanceff and R. Rampone (eds.), *Viaggio nel sud. II. Il Profondo sud: Calabria e dintorni*, Geneva: 151–9.

Bartlett, K. R. (2006). 'Thomas Hoby, Translator, Traveler', in C. Di Biase (ed.), *Travel and Translation in the Early Modern Period*, Amsterdam and New York: 123–42.

Basile, L., and Morea, D. (1996). *Lazzari e scugnizzi*, Rome.

Basso, P. (1997). *Via per montes excisa*, Rome.

Battaglia, S. (1960). *La tradizione di Ovidio nel Medioevo*, Naples.

Battisti, E. (1963). 'Riforma e Controriforma', *Enciclopedia universale dell'arte* 11: 366–90.

Beacham, R. (2005). 'The Emperor as *Impresario*: Producing the Pageantry of Power', in K. Galinsky (ed.), *The Cambridge Companion to the Age of Augustus*, Cambridge: 151–74.

Bejor, G. (1979). 'L'edificio teatrale nell'urbanizzazione Augustea', *Athenaeum* 57: 126–38.

Beloch, K. J. (1989 [1890]). *Campanien: Geschichte und Topographie des antiken Neapel und seiner Umgebung*, Breslau.

Beloch, K. J. (1926). *Römische Geschichte bis zum Beginn der Punischen Kriege*, Berlin and Leipzig.

Bell, R. (2009). 'Revisiting the Pediment of the Palatine Metroön: A Vergilian Interpretation', *Papers of the British School at Rome* 77: 65–99.

Beneduce, G. (1931). *Origine e vicende storiche sulla chiesa di S. Maria Maggiore in Napoli*, Naples.

Benjamin, W. (2007). *Immagini di città*, ed. E. Ganni, with a preface by C. Magris, with a contribution by P. Szondi, Turin.

Bentley, J. H. (1987). *Politics and Culture in Renaissance Naples*, Princeton.

Bernabò Brea, L. (1935). 'Il tempio napoletano dei Dioscuri', *Bullettino della Commissione Archeologica Comunale di Roma* 6: 61–76.

Bernard, J. H., Bernardi, P., and Esposito, D. (2008). *Il reimpiego in architettura: Recupero, trasformazione, uso*, Rome.

Beretta, R. (2003). *San Francesco e la leggenda del Presepio*, Milan.

Besse, J. M. (2009). 'The Birth of the Modern Atlas: Rome, Lafreri, Ortelius,' in M. P. Donato and J. Kraye (eds.), *Conflicting Duties: Science, Medicine and Religion in Rome, 1550–1750*, London.

Bettini, M., and Spina, L. (2007). *Il mito delle sirene*, Turin.

Bianchi, F. (2010). 'Il tempio di Giove Statore e la scena del teatro di Marcello: Maestranze e modelli decorativi tra epoca tardo repubblicana e media età imperiale', *Atti dell'Accademia Nazionale dei Lincei: Rendiconti* 21: 285–321.

Bianchi Bandinelli, R. (1976). *Introduzione all'archeologia classica come storia dell'arte antica*, Bari.

Binns, J. W., and Banks, S. E. (eds.) (2002). *Gervase of Tilbury, Otia Imperialia: Recreation for an Emperor*, Oxford.

Black, R. (2001). *Humanism and Education in Medieval and Renaissance Italy*, Cambridge.

Blessich, A. (1896). 'La pianta di Napoli del duca di Noja: Storia della pianta', *Napoli Nobilissima* 5: 74–8.

Boatwright, M. T. (2000). *Hadrian and the Cities of the Roman Empire*, Princeton.

Böhmer, J. F. (1870). *Acta Imperii Selecta*, Innsbruck.

Böhmer, J. F., Ficker, J., and Winkelmann, E. (1881–1901). *Die Regesten des Kaiserreichs unter Philipp, Otto IV, Friedrich II, Heinrich (VII), Conrad IV, Heinrich Raspe, Wilhelm und Richard 1198–1272*, Innsbruck.

Bologna, F. (1989). '*Caesaris imperio regni custodia fio*: La porta di Capua e la *interpretatio imperialis* del classicismo', in M. Del Treppo (ed.), *Nel segno di Federico II: Unità politica e pluralità culturale del Mezzogiorno*, Naples: 159–89.

Bona Castellotti, M., and Giuliano, A. (eds.) (2008). Exempla: *La rinascita dell'antico nell'arte italiana: Da Federico II ad Andrea Pisano*, Ospedaletto.

Borca, F. (2003). *Luoghi, corpi, costumi: Determinismo ambientale ed etnografia antica*, Rome.

Borrelli, G. G. (1970). *Il presepe napoletano*, Rome.

Borrelli, G. G. (1991). *Scenografie e scene del presepe napoletano*, Naples.

Borrelli, G. G. (2001). *Personaggi e scenografie del presepe napoletano*, Naples.

Borrelli, M. (1967). *L'architetto Dionisio Nencioni di Bartolomeo (1559–1638)*, Naples.

Bowersock, G. W. (1965). *Augustus and the Greek World*, Oxford.

Braccesi, L. (2008). 'Fra archeologia e poesia nazionalistica, l'anomalia del "caso Pompei"', in R. Cremante, M. Harari, S. Rocchi, and E. Romano (eds.), *I misteri di Pompei: Antichità pompeiane nell'immaginario della modernità*, Pompei: 67–73.

Bradley, G. (2006). 'Colonization and Identity in Republican Italy', in G. Bradley and J.-P. Wilson (eds.), *Greek and Roman Colonization: Origins, Ideologies and Interactions*, Swansea: 161–87.

Bragantini, I. et al. (1991). *Ricerche archeologiche a Napoli: Lo scavo di Palazzo Corigliano I*, Naples.

Bragantini, I. (ed.) (2010). 'Lo scavo di Piazza Nicola Amore a Napoli: Le fasi edilizie e decorative del complesso monumentale', *Atti del X Congresso Internazionale dell'AIPMA*, Naples, ii. 607–22.

Brandenburg, H. (2004). *Le prime chiese di Roma, IV–VII secolo: L'inizio dell'architettura ecclesiastica occidentale*, Milan.

Breglia Pulci Doria, L. (1987). 'Le Sirene: Il canto, la morte, la polis', *AION* 9: 65–98.

Breglia Pulci Doria, L. (1996). *Studi su Eforo*, Naples.

Brilliant, R., and Kinney, D. (eds.) (2012). *Reuse Value: Spolia and Appropriation in Art and Architecture from Constantine to Sherrie Levine*, Burlington, VT.

Bruschi, A. (2008). 'Luciano di Laurana: Chi era costui? Laurana, fra Carnevale, Alberti a Urbino: Un tentativo di revisione', *Annali di Architettura* 20: 37–81.

Bruzelius, C. (1995). 'Queen Sancia of Mallorca and the Convent Church of Sta. Chiara in Naples', *Memoirs of the American Academy in Rome* 40: 69–100.

Bruzelius, C. (1999). '*Columnas Marmoreas et Lapides Antiquarum Ecclesiarum*: The Use of Spolia in the Churches of Charles II of Anjou', in A. Cadei (ed.), *Arte d'Occidente: Temi e metodi*, Rome: 187–95.

Bruzelius, C. (2004). *The Stones of Naples: Church Building in Angevin Italy, 1266–1343*, New Haven and London.

Bruzelius, C. (2005a). *Le pietre di Napoli: L'architettura religiosa nell'Italia angioina, 1266–1343*, Rome.

Bruzelius, C. (2005b). 'San Lorenzo Maggiore e lo studio francescano di Napoli: Qualche osservazione sul carattere e la cronologia della chiesa medievale', in S. Romano and N. Bock (eds.), *Le chiese di San Lorenzo e San Domenico*, Naples: 27–50.

Büchner, G., Morelli, D., and Nenci, G. (1952). 'Fonti per la storia di Napoli antica', *La Parola del Passato* 7: 370–419.

Buddensieg, T. (1965). 'Gregory the Great, the Destroyer of Pagan Idols: The History of a Medieval Legend Concerning the Decline of Ancient Art and Literature', *Journal of the Warburg and Courtauld Institutes* 28: 44–65.

Burger, F. (1907). *Francesco Laurana: Eine Studie zur italienischen Quattrocentoskulptur*, Strasbourg.

Burns, H. (1993). 'I disegni di Francesco di Giorgio agli Uffizi di Firenze', in F. P. Fiore and M. Tafuri (eds.), *Francesco di Giorgio architetto*, Milan: 330–57.

Cachey, T. J. (2002). *Petrarch's Guide to the Holy Land: Itinerary to the Sepulchre of Our Lord Jesus Christ*, Notre Dame, IL.

Caglioti, F. (2008). 'Fifteenth-Century Reliefs of Ancient Emperors and Empresses in Florence: Production and Collecting', in N. Penny and E. D. Schmidt (eds.), *Collecting Sculpture in Early Modern Europe*, New Haven, CT: 67–109.

Cahn, H. A. (1997). 'Oceanus', *LIMC* viii/1: 907–15.

Calaresu, M. (2013). 'Collecting Neapolitans: The Representation of Street Life in Late Eighteenth-Century Naples', in M. Calaresu and H. Hills (eds.), *New Approaches to Naples c.1500–c.1800: The Power of Place*, Farnham: 175–202.

Calaresu, M., and Hills, H. (eds.) (2013). *New Approaches to Naples c.1500–c.1800: The Power of Place*, Farnham.

Camargo, M. (1991). *Ars dictaminis, ars dictandi*, Turnhout.

Cameron, A. (1970). *Agathias*, Oxford.

Camodeca, G. (2001). 'Iscrizioni pubbliche nuove o riedite e monumenti di Cumae, 1. Foro e tempio di Apollo', *Annali di archeologia e storia antica* 8: 149–62.

Camodeca, G. (2007). '*Cura secunda* di un *decretum* decurionale puteolano in onore di un cavaliere di età traianeo-adrianea', *Mélanges de l'École française de Rome: Antiquité* 119: 351–62.

Camodeca, G. (2010). 'Le città della Campania nella documentazione epigrafica pubblica del tardo III–IV secolo', in G. Volpe and R. Giuliani (eds.), *Paesaggi e insediamenti urbani in Italia Meridionale fra Tardoantico e Altomedieovo*, Bari: 283–94.

Campana, A. (1964). 'Barbato da Sulmona', in *DBI*.

Campana, A. (1965). 'Basinio da Parma', in *DBI*.

Campana, A. (1973–4). 'Ciriaco d'Ancona e Lorenzo Valla sulla iscrizione greca del tempio dei Dioscuri a Napoli', *Archeologia classica* 15–16: 84–102.

Campanelli, M. (2001). *Polemiche e filologia ai primordi della stampa. Le* Observationes *di Domizio Calderini*, Rome.

Cantarella, G. M. (1993). 'Ripensare Falcando', *Studi medievali* 34: 823–40.

Cantarella, E., and Jacobelli, L. (2013). *Pompei è viva*, Milan.

Cantilena, R. (1985). 'La monetazione', in *Napoli antica* (1985): 352–67.

Capaccio, G. C. (1607). *Neapolitanae historiae*, Naples.

Capaccio, G. C. (1634). *Il forestiero: Dialoghi in X giornate*, Naples.

Capasso, B. (1881–92). *Monumenta ad Neapolitani ducatus historiam pertinentia quae partim nunc primum, partim iterum typis vulgantur*, Naples.

Capasso, B. (1892). 'Pianta della città di Napoli nel secolo XI', *Archivio Storico per le Province Napoletane* 17: 422–84.

Capasso, B. (1895). *Topografia della città di Napoli nell'XI secolo*, Naples.

Capasso, B. (1905). *Napoli greco-romana*, Naples.

Capasso, M. (1983). *Il sepolcro di Virgilio*, Naples.

Cappelli, G. (2007). *L'umanesimo italiano da Petrarca a Valla*, Rome.

Caputo, P. (2004). 'La grotta di Cocceio a Cuma: Nuovi dati da ricerche e saggi di scavo', in L. Quilici and S. Quilici Gigli (eds.), *Viabilità e insediamenti nell'Italia antica*, Rome: 309–30.

Carabelli, G. (1996). *Veneri e Priapi: Culti di fertilità e mitologie falliche tra Napoli e Londra nell'età dell'Illuminismo*, Bari (Eng. edn.: *In the Image of Priapus*, London).

Caracciolo, A. (1612). *De vita Pauli Quarti Pont. Max. Item Caietani Thienaei, Bonifacii a Colle, Pauli Consiliarii*, Coloniae Ubiorum.

Caracciolo, Aricò A. M. (2006). 'Maio, Giuniano', in *DBI*.

Carafa, P. (2008). *Culti e santuari della Campania antica*, Rome.

Carletti, N. (1776). *Topografia universale della città di Napoli in Campagna Felice e note enciclopediche storiografiche*, Naples.

Carrella, A. (ed.) (2000). *La chiesa di Santa Maria del Parto a Mergellina*, Naples.

Cascella, S. (2009). 'Uso del marmo nella decorazione architettonica del teatro romano di Sessa Aurunca (CE)', *Marmora: An International*

Journal for Archaeology, History and Archaeometry of Marbles and Stones 5: 23–34.

Càssola, F. (1986). 'Problemi di storia neapolitana', in *Neapolis* (1986): 37–82.

Castaldo, G. B. (1615). *Vita del santissimo pontefice Paolo quarto fondatore della religione de chierici regolari, e memorie d'altri cinquanta celebri Padri*, Rome.

Catello, E. (1991). *Il presepe napoletano del Settecento*, Milan.

Catudella, M. (ed.) (2006). *Petrarca e Napoli: Atti del Convegno, Napoli, 8–11 dicembre 2004*, Pisa and Rome.

Cavallaro, M. A. (1984). *Spese e spettacoli: Aspetti economici-strutturali degli spettacoli nella Roma giulio-claudia*, Bonn.

Cavallo, G. (1975). 'La trasmissione dei testi nell'area beneventano-cassinese', in *La cultura nell'Occidente latino dal VII all'XI secolo*, Spoleto: 357–414.

Cébeillac Gervasoni, M. (1998). *Les Magistrats des cités italiennes de la seconde guerre punique à Auguste: Le Latium et la Campanie*, Rome.

Ceci, G. (1893). 'Il palazzo dei Carafa di Maddaloni poi di Colubrano (I–II)', *Napoli Nobilissima* 2: 149–52, 168–70.

Celano, C. (1692). *Notizie del bello, dell'antico e del curioso della città di Napoli per gli signori forastieri, divise in dieci giornate*. Naples.

Cesarini, C. (2008). 'Frammenti musivi inediti da scavi nell'ambito della basilica paleocristiana di S. Restituta a Napoli', in C. Angelelli (ed.), *Atti del XIII Colloquio AISCOM*, Tivoli: 187–94.

Cesarini Martinelli, L. (ed.) (1978). *Angelo Poliziano: Commento inedito alle Selve di Stazio*, Florence.

Ceserani, G. (2012). *Italy's Lost Greece: Magna Graecia and the Making of Modern Archaeology*, Oxford.

Ceserani, G., and Milanese, A. (2007). 'Antiquarianism, Museums and Cultural Heritage. Collecting and Its Contexts in Eighteenth-Century Naples', *Journal of the History of Collections* 19/2: 249–59.

Ceva Grimaldi, F. (1857). *Memorie storiche della città di Napoli dal tempo della sua fondazione sino al presente*, Naples.

Chaney, E. (1998). *The Evolution of the Grand Tour*, London.

Chassignet, M. (2004). *L'Annalistique romaine*, iii. *L'Annalistique récente: L'Autobiographie politique (fragments)*, Paris.

Chastel, A. (1989). 'Les "Idoles" à la Renaissance', in S. D. Squarzina (ed.), *Roma, centro ideale della cultura dell'Antico nei secoli XV e XVI: Da Martino V al Sacco di Roma 1417–1527*, Milan: 468–76.

Chiarini, G. B. (ed.) (1856–60). *Carlo Celano, Notizie del bello, dell'antico, e del curioso della città di Napoli*, Naples.

Chierici, G. (1934). 'Contributo allo studio dell'archeologia paleocristiana nella Campania', *Atti del III Congresso internazionale di archeologia cristiana*, Rome: 203–16.

Chroniche de la inclyta città de Napole (1526). Chroniche de la inclyta città de Napole emendatissime: Con li bagni de Puzolo et Ischia. Novamente ristampate, stampate in la inclita città de Neapole, per m. Evangelista di Presenzani de Pavia, adi XXVII de Aprile 1526.

Ciapponi, L. (1961). 'Appunti per una biografia di Giovanni Giocondo da Verona', *Italia Medieovale e Umanistica* 4: 131–58.

Ciarallo, A. (2006). *Scienziati a Pompei tra Settecento e Ottocento*, Rome.

Cilento, N. (1980). 'La cultura e gli inizi dello studio', *Storia di Napoli* 6: 312–20.

Clark, A. C. (1899). 'The Literary Discoveries of Poggio', *Classical Review* 13: 119–30.

Coarelli, F. (1993). 'Castor et Pollux in Circo *(fasti)*; Aedes Castoris in Circo Flaminio (Vitr.)', in *LTUR* i. 245–6.

Cocchiara, G. (1954). *Storia del Folklore in Europa*, Turin.

Coffin, D. R. (1982). 'The *Lex Hortorum* and Access to Gardens of Latium during the Renaissance', *Journal of Garden History* 2: 201–23.

Colombo, A. (1884). 'Il palazzo e il giardino della Duchesca', *Archivio Storico per le Province Napoletane* 9: 563–4.

Colonna, F. (1892). *Napoli: Nuove scoperte di antichità entro l'abitato, Atti della R. Accademia dei Lincei: Memorie della Classe di scienze morali, storiche e filologiche (1892–1892)*, ser. 4, vol. 10.

Comparetti, D. (1941 [1895]). *Virgilio nel Medioevo*, Florence.

Connerton, P. (1989). *How Societies Remember*, Cambridge.

Connerton, P. (2008). 'Seven Types of Forgetting', *Memory Studies* 1/1: 59–71.

Coppini, D. (2013). 'Calderini, Poliziano e il *subitus calor* di Stazio,' in P. Galand and S. Laigneau-Fontaine (eds.), *La Silve: Histoire d'une écriture libérée en Europe de l'antiquité ai XVIIIe siècle*, Turnhout: 317–35.

Correra, R. (1905). 'Il Tempio dei Dioscuri', *Atti della Reale Accademia di Archeologia, Lettere e Belle Arti di Napoli* 23: 214–27.

Cosimi, E. (2008). '*Fons Augusteus*: Le mura d'arce di Sarno ed il doppio canale di Palma Campania', *Gradus* 3/1: 23–42.

Costabile, F. (1984). *Istituzioni e forme costituzionali nelle città del Bruzio in età romana*, Naples.

Costabile, F. (1995). 'Le statue frontonali del tempio Marasà a Locri Epizefiri', *Mitteilungen des Deutschen Archäologischen Instituts, Römische Abteilung* 102: 9–62.

Costo, T. (1595). *Ragionamenti intorno alla descrizione del Regno di Napoli, e all'Antichità di Pozzuolo di Scipione Mazzella, per li quali e con ragioni e con autorità verissime si mostra, non pur esser molti errori e mancamenti in quelle due opere ma che le medesime son tutte cose copiate puntualmente dagli scritti altrui*, Naples.

Courtney, E. (1990). *Papini Stati Silvae*, Oxford.

Crawford, M. H. (ed.) (1993). *Antonio Augustín Between Renaissance and Counter-Reformation*, London: 279–89.

Creazzo, I. (ed.) (2005). *Il Presepe: Le collezioni del museo di San Martino*, Naples.

Cremante, R., Harari, M., Rocchi, S., and Romano, E. (eds.) (2008). *I misteri di Pompei: Antichità pompeiane nell'immaginario della modernità*, Pompei.

Cristilli, A. (2004). 'Sculture napoletane al Museo Archeologico Nazionale di Napoli', *Rivista dell'Istituto Nazionale d'Archeologia e Storia dell'Arte* 58: 7–35.

Croce, B. (1892a). 'La tomba di Jacopo Sannazaro e la chiesa di Santa Maria del Parto', *Napoli Nobilissima* 1: 68–76.

Croce, B. (1892b). 'L'arco di Sant'Eligio ed una leggenda ad esso relativo', *Napoli Nobilissima* 1: 147–51.

Crowther, N. (1989). 'The Sebastan Games in Naples (IvOl. 56)', *Zeitschrift für Papyrologie und Epigraphik* 79: 100–2.

Cubitt, G. (2007). *History and Memory*, Manchester.

Cuozzo, E., and Martin, J. M. (1995). *Federico II: Le tre capitali del Regno di Sicilia: Palermo—Foggia—Napoli*, Naples.

Curcio, G., Navone, N., and Villari, S. (eds.) (2011). *Studi su Domenico Fontana*, Mendrisio.

van Dam, H. J. (1984). *P. Papinius Statius. Silvae Book II. A Commentary*, Leiden.

van Dam, H. J. (2010). 'Silvae', in B. Egger and C. Walde (eds.), *Der Neue Pauly*, suppl. vol. vii. *Die Rezeption der antiken Literatur*, Stuttgart and Weimar: 932–46.

D'Angelo E. (2003). *Storiografi e cronologi latini del Mezzogiorno normanno-svevo*, Naples.

D'Arms, J. H. (1970). *Romans on the Bay of Naples*. Cambridge.

D'Arms, J. H. (2003). *Romans on the Bay of Naples and Other Essays on Roman Campania*, edited by F. Zevi, Bari.

De Beer, E. S. (1942). 'François Schott's *Itinerario d'Italia*', *The Library: Transactions of the Bibliographical Society* 23: 57–83.

De Blaauw, S. (1991). 'Papst und Purpur: Porphyr in frühen Kirchenausstattungen in Rom', in E. Dassmann and K. Thraede (eds.), *Tesserae: Festschrift für Joseph Engemann*, Münster: 36–50.

De Blaauw, S. (2001). 'Architettura e arredo ecclesiastico a Roma (V–IX secolo)', in M. S. Arena, P. Delogu, L. Paroli, M. Ricci, L. Saguì, and L. Vendittelli (eds.), *Roma dall'antichità al medioevo*, Milan: 52–61.

De Blasi, N. (1986). *Guido delle Colonne: Libro de la destructione de Troya*, Rome.

De Caro, S. (1974). 'La necropoli di Pizzofalcone in Napoli', *Rendiconti della Accademia di Archeologia, Lettere e Belle Arti di Napoli* 49: 37–67.

De Caro, S. (2007). 'Aspetti storici e artistici del Presepe Napoletano', *Working Paper Series, Department of Economics 'S. Cognetti de Martiis'*, Turin [available online at <http://www.eblacenter.unito.it/WP/2007/3_WP_Ebla.pdf>].

De Caro, S., and Giampaola, D. (2008). 'La circolazione stradale a *Neapolis* e nel suo territorio', *Stadtverkehr in der antiken Welt, Palilia* 18: 107–24.

De Caro, S., and Spinosa, N. (eds.) (2003). *Lo sguardo del Nilo: Storia e recupero del 'Corpo di Napoli'*, Naples.

De Castris, P. L. (1986). *Arte di corte nella Napoli angioina*, Florence.

de Divitiis, B. (2007). *Architettura e committenza nella Napoli del Quattrocento*, Venice.

de Divitiis, B. (2010). 'New Evidence for Sculptures from Diomede Carafa's Collection of Antiquities', *Journal of the Warburg and Courtauld Institutes* 73: 335–53.

de Divitiis, B. (2011). 'I resoconti di guerra come fonte per la storia dell'architettura', in G. Abbamonte, J. Barreto, T. D'Urso, A. Perriccioli Saggese, and F. Senatore (eds.), *La battaglia nel Rinascimento meridionale: Moduli narrativi tra parole e immagini*, Rome: 321–34.

de Divitiis, B. (2012). 'Un caso di rinnovamento urbano nella Napoli aragonese: La regio Nilensis e il largo di San Domenico Maggiore', in P. Boucheron and M. Folin (eds.), *Grands Chantiers de la rénovation urbaine: Les Expériences italiennes dans leur contexte Européen (XVe–XVIe siècle)*, Rome: 99–122.

de Divitiis, B. (2013). 'Castel Nuovo and Castel Capuano in Naples: The Transformation of Two Medieval Castles into "*all'antica*" Residences for the Aragonese Royals', *Zeitschrift für Kunstgeschicte* 76: 441–74.

de Divitiis, B. (forthcoming, a). 'Fra Giocondo nel Regno di Napoli: Dallo studio antiquario al progetto all'antica', in P. Gros and P. N. Pagliara (eds.), *Fra Giocondo architetto, umanista e antiquario*, Venice.

de Divitiis, B. (forthcoming, b). 'Giuliano da Sangallo's 1488 Sojourn in the Kingdom of Naples: Architectures, Antiquities and Patrons'.

de Divitiis, B. (forthcoming, c). *Humanism and Antiquarian Culture in Renaissance Southern Italy: Ambrogio Leone's De Nola (Venice, 1514)*.

De Dominici, B. (1742–5). *Vite de' pittori, scultori ed architetti napoletani*, Naples.

de Franciscis, A. (1954). 'Le recenti scoperte in S. Chiara e la topografia di Napoli romana', *Archeologia classica* 6: 277–83.

de Frede, C. (1960). *I lettori di umanità nello studio di Napoli*, Naples.

Deichmann, F. W. (1975). *Die Spolien in der spätantiken Architektur*, Munich.

de Jorio, A. (1825). *Viaggio di Enea all'inferno, ed agli Elisii secondo Virgilio*, 2nd edn., Naples.

de Jorio, A. (1832). *La mimica degli antichi investigata nel gestire napoletano*, Naples.

de Jorio, A. (2000 [1832]). *Gesture in Naples and Gesture in Classical Antiquity: A Translation of Andrea de Jorio's* La mimica degli antichi investigata nel gestire napoletano, trans. A. Kendon, with introd. and notes, Bloomington, IN.

de Lachenal, L. (1995). *Spolia: Uso e reimpiego dell'antico dal III al XIV secolo*, Milan.

de Lachenal, L. (1999). 'Reimpiego dell'antico e ideologia politica fra Roma e l'Italia Meridionale in età Normanna: Alcune osservazioni', in B. M. Giannattasio (ed.), *Atti X Giornata Archeologica: Il passato riproposto: Continuità e recupero dall'antichità ad oggi*, Genova: 93–129.

de la Ville sur-Yllon, L. (1894). 'Il corpo di Napoli e la "capa" di Napoli', *Napoli Nobilissima*, 3: 23–6.

Delle Donne, F. (1999). 'Una disputa sulla nobiltà alla corte di Federico II di Svevia', *Medioevo Romanzo* 23: 3–20.

Delle Donne, F. (ed.) (2003). *Nicola da Rocca: Epistolae*, Florence.

Delle Donne, F. (2004). '*Cipriani martiris epistolare opus offero ad scribendum*: Un'attestazione della trasmissione e della ricezione dell'opera di Cipriano alla fine del XIII secolo', *Italia Medievale e Umanistica* 45: 115–36.

Delle Donne, F. (2005). *Il potere e la sua legittimazione: Letteratura encomiastica in onore di Federico II di Svevia*, Arce.

Delle Donne, F. (2007a). *Una silloge epistolare della seconda metà del XIII secolo*, Florence.

Delle Donne, F. (2007b). 'Un'inedita epistola sulla morte di Guglielmo de Luna, maestro presso lo Studium di Napoli, e le traduzioni prodotte alla corte di Manfredi di Svevia', *Recherches de Théologie et Philosophie Médiévales* 74: 225–45.

Delle Donne, F. (2007c). 'La cultura e gli insegnamenti retorici latini nell'Alta Terra di Lavoro', in F. Delle Donne (ed.), Suavis terra, inexpugnabile castrum: *L'Alta Terra di Lavoro dal dominio svevo alla conquista angioina*, Arce: 133–57.

Delle Donne, F. (2010a). Per scientiarum haustum et seminarium doctrinarum: *Storia dello* Studium *di Napoli in età sveva*, Bari.

Delle Donne, F. (2010b). 'La rappresentazione del potere e le sue liturgie: Le testimonianze letterarie', in P. Cordasco and F. Violante (eds.), *Un regno nell'impero: I caratteri originari del regno normanno nell'età sveva: Persistenze e differenze (1194–1266)*, Bari: 493–533.

Bibliography

Delle Donne, F. (2011a). 'Gli usi e i riusi della storia: Funzioni, struttura, parti, fasi compositive e datazione dell'*Historia* del cosiddetto Iamsilla', *Bullettino dell'Istituto storico italiano per il medio evo*, 113: 31–122.

Delle Donne, F. (ed.) (2011b). *Annales Cavenses*, Rome.

Delle Donne, F. (2012). *Federico II: La condanna della memoria: Metamorfosi di un mito*, Rome.

Delle Donne, F. (ed.) (2014). *Andreas Ungarus:* Descripcio victorie Beneventi, Rome.

Del Pesco, D. (2001). 'Oliviero Carafa e il Succorpo di San Gennaro nel Duomo di Napoli', in F. P. di Teodoro (ed.), *Donato Bramante: Ricerche, proposte, riletture*, Urbino: 143–205.

Del Tufo, G. B. (1609). *Historia della Religione de' Padri Chierici Regolari*, Rome.

Del Tufo, G. B. (1616). *Supplimento alla historia della Religione de padri cherici regolari raccolta ed esposta in luce da Monsignor Gio. Battista Carafa, vescovo dell'Acerra*, Rome.

De Maio, R. (1965). 'Michelangelo e Paolo IV', in *Reformata Reformanda: Festgabe für H. Jedin*, Münster: 635–56.

De Maio, R. (1981). *Michelangelo e la Controriforma*, Rome and Bari.

De Maio, R., Giulia, L., and Mazzacane, A. (eds.) (1982). *Baronio storico e la Controriforma, atti del convegno internazionale di studi (Sora 6–10 ottobre 1979)*, Sora.

De Maria, S. (1988). *Gli archi onorari di Roma e dell'Italia Romana*, Rome.

De Marinis, T. (1947–52). *La Biblioteca napoletana dei re d'Aragona*, Milan.

De Martino, F. (1952 [1979]). *Diritto e società nell'antica Roma*, Rome: 328–38.

Demma, F. (2007). *Monumenti pubblici di Puteoli: Per un'archeologia dell'architettura*, Rome.

D'Engenio, C. (1623). *Napoli Sacra*, Naples.

Deniaux, E. (1981). '*Civitate donati*: Naples, Héraclée, Côme', *Ktema* 6: 133–41.

Deniaux, E. (1993). *Clientèles et pouvoir à l'époque de Cicéron*, Rome.

D'Episcopo, F. (1985). 'Tideo Acciarino: tra Poliziano e Parrasio', *Studi Umanistici Piceni* 5: 35–9.

Deramaix, M., and Laschke, B. (1992). '*Maroni musa proximus ut tumulo*: L'Église et le tombeau de Jacques Sannazar', *Revue de l'art* 95: 25–39.

De Robertis, D. (1988). 'L'esperienza poetica del Quattrocento', in E. Cecchi and N. Sapegno (eds.), *Storia della letteratura italiana: Il Quattrocento e l'Ariosto*, Milan: 371–817.

de Rosa, C. (1841). *Notizie di alcuni Cavalieri del Sacro Ordine Gerosolimitano illustri per Lettere e Belle Arti*, Naples.

De Rosa, L. (2008). *Da Acelum a Volsinii: gli acquedotti romani in Italia: Committenza, finanziamento, gestione,* Tesi di Dottorato in Storia, Università di Napoli Federico II.

De Sanctis Ricciardone, P. (1987). 'La "smorfia" nell'Ottocento italiano: Tradizione scritta e tradizione orale', *La Ricerca Folklorica* 15: 27–32.

De Seta, C. (1982). *L'Italia nello specchio del* Grand Tour, in C. De Seta (ed.), *Storia d'Italia. Gli Annali. V. Il paesaggio,* Turin: 127–263.

De Simone, A. (1985). 'Il complesso monumentale di San Lorenzo Maggiore', in *Napoli antica* (1985): 185–9.

De Simone, R. (1982). *Il segno di Virgilio,* Pozzuoli.

De Simone, R. (1998). *Il presepe popolare Napoletano,* Turin.

De' Spagnolis, M. (1984). *Il tempio dei Dioscuri nel Circo Flaminio,* Rome.

De Stefano, A. (1950). *La cultura alla corte di Federico II imperatore,* Bologna.

De Stefano, A. (1952). *L'idea imperiale di Federico II,* Bologna.

De Stefano, P. (1560). *Descrittione de i luoghi sacri della città di Napoli,* Naples.

De Stefano, R. (1961). 'Napoli sotterranea', *Napoli Nobilissima,* NS 1: 101–12.

Dickerson, C. D., and de Cavi, S. (eds.) (2008). *A Nativity from Naples: Presepe Sculpture of the Eighteenth Century,* Fort Worth, TX.

Di Falco, B. (1548). *Descrittione de i luoghi antiqui di Napoli e del suo amenissimo distretto,* Naples.

Di Falco, B. (1589 [1548]). *Descrittione de i luoghi antiqui di Napoli e del suo amenissimo distretto,* Naples.

Di Nanni, D. (2007–8). 'I *Sebastà* di *Neapolis:* Il regolamento e il programma', *Ludica* 13–14: 7–22.

Di Stefano, R. (1964–5). 'La chiesa di S. Angelo a Nilo e il Seggio di Nido', *Napoli Nobilissima,* NS 4: 12–21.

Di Stefano, R., and Santoro, L. (1961–2). 'La cappella di S. Maria dei Pignatelli in Napoli', *Napoli Nobilissima,* NS 1: 187–92.

Di Stefano, R., and Strazzullo, F. (1972). 'Restauri e scoperte nella cattedrale di Napoli', *Napoli Nobilissima,* NS 10: 3–59.

Divenuto, F. (2009). '*Deos nemorum invocat in extruenda domo:* Iacopo Sannazaro e la sua casa a Mergellina', in P. Sabbatino (ed.), *Jacopo Sannazaro: La cultura napoletana nell'Europa del Rinascimento,* Florence: 237–60.

Dodero, E. (2007). 'Le antichità di palazzo Carafa-Colubrano: Prodromi alla storia della collezione', *Napoli Nobilissima,* NS 8: 119–40.

Donattini, M. (ed.) (2007). *L'Italia dell'Inquisitore: Storia e geografia dell'Italia del Cinquecento nella 'Descrittione' di Leandro Alberti,* Bologna.

D'Onofrio, M. (2003). *Rilavorazione dell'antico nel medioevo,* Rome.

D'Onofrio, A. M., and D'Agostino, B. (eds.) (1987). *Ricerche archeologiche a Napoli: Lo scavo in Largo S. Aniello (1982–1983),* Naples.

Dotti, U. (ed.) (1978). *Epistole di Francesco Petrarca*, Turin.

D'Ovidio, S. (2006). 'La Madonna di Piedigrotta tra storia e leggenda', *Rendiconti dell'Accademia di Archeologia, Lettere e Belle Arti di Napoli* 74: 47–91.

D'Ovidio, S. (2012). 'Boccaccio, Virgilio e la Madonna di Piedigrotta', in G. Alfano, T. D'Urso, and A. Perriccioli Saggese (eds.), *Boccaccio angioino: Materiali per la storia culturale di Napoli nel Trecento*, Brussels: 329–46.

D'Ovidio, S. (forthcoming, a). 'Devotion and Memory: Episcopal Portraits in the Catacombs of San Gennaro in Naples', in I. Foletti (ed.), *The Face of the Dead and the Early Christian World*, Rome: 69–90.

D'Ovidio, S. (forthcoming, b). 'The *Crypta Neapolitana*: Perceptions of a Roman Tunnel throughout History', in L. Kouneni (ed.), *The Legacy of Antiquity: New Perspectives in the Reception of the Classical World*, Cambridge.

D'Ovidio, S., and Rullo, A. (eds.) (2007). *Pietro de Stefano: Descrittione dei luoghi sacri di Napoli*, Naples.

Dougherty, C. (1993). *The Poetics of Colonization*, New York and Oxford.

Dougherty, C. (1998). 'It's Murder to Found a Colony', in C. Dougherty and L. Kurke (eds.), *Cultural Poetics in Archaic Greece: Cult, Performance, Politics*, New York and Oxford: 178–98.

Dreszen, A. (2004). 'Oliviero Carafa committente *all'antica* nel Succorpo del Duomo di Napoli', *Römische Historische Mitteilungen* 46: 165–200.

Dubois, L. (1994). 'Un nom de magistrat énigmatique: Le λαυκέλαρχος napolitain', *AION* (Sezione filologico-letteraria) 16: 155–62.

duBois, P. (2011). 'Sappho, Tithonos and the Ruin of the Body', in A. Kahane (ed.), *Antiquity and the Ruin: L'Antiquité et les ruines*. Special Issue, *European Review of History/Revue européenne d'histoire*, 18/5–6: 663–72.

von Duhn, F. (1910). *Der Dioskurentempel in Neapel*, Heidelberg.

Ebanista, C. (2009). 'L'atrio dell'*insula episcopalis* di Napoli: Problemi di architettura e topografia paleocristiana e altomedievale', in M. Rotili (ed.), *Tardo Antico e Alto Medioevo: Filologia, storia, archeologia, arte*, Naples: 307–75.

Ebanista, C. (2010). 'Il piccone del fossore: Un secolo di scavi nella catacomba di S. Gennaro a Napoli (1830–1930)', *Rivista di Archeologia cristiana* 86: 127–74.

Ebanista, C. (2011). 'Le chiese tardoantiche e altomedievali della Campania: Vecchi scavi, nuovi orientamenti', *Post Classical Archaeologies* 1: 383–418.

Ebanista, C. (2012). 'Rilievo grafico e topografia cimiteriale: Il caso della catacomba di s. Gennaro a Napoli', in R. Fiorillo and C. Lambert (eds.), *Medioevo letto, scavato, rivalutato: Scritti in onore di Paolo Peduto*, Borgo S. Lorenzo: 281–314.

Ebanista, C., and Amodio, M. (eds.) (2008). 'Aree funerarie e luoghi di culto *in rupe*: Le cavità artificiali campane tra tarda antichità e medioevo', *Opera Ipogea* 1–2: 117–44.

Elia, E. (1938). 'Un tratto dell'acquedotto detto "Claudio in territorio di Sarno"', *Campania romana: Studi e materiali*, Naples: 99–111.

Engenio Caracciolo, C. (1624). *Napoli Sacra*, Naples.

Ensoli, S., and La Rocca, E. (eds.) (2000). *Aurea Roma: Dalla città pagana alla città cristiana*, Rome.

Erim, K. T. (1984). 'Aphrodisias', in *LIMC* ii/1: 1–2.

Erll, A. (2011). *Memory in Culture*, trans. Sara B. Young, Basingstoke.

Erren, M. (ed.) (2003). *P. Vergilius Maro: Georgica*, Heidelberg.

Esch, A. (1969). 'Spolien: Zur Wiederverwendung antiker Baustücke und Skulpturen im mittelalterlichenItalien', *Archiv für Kulturgeschichte* 51: 1–64.

Esch, A. (1998). 'Reimpiego', *Enciclopedia dell'Arte Medievale* 9: 876–83.

Esch, A., and Frommel, C. L. (1995). *Arte, committenza ed economia a Roma e nelle corti del Rinascimento (1420–1530)*, Turin.

Fairclough, H. R., and Goold, G. P. (1999). *Virgil: Eclogues, Georgics, Aeneid I–VI*, with an English translation by H. R. Fairclough, rev. by G. P. Goold, Cambridge, MA and London.

Falconi, M. A. (1539). *Dell'incendio di Pozzuolo di Marco Antonio delli Falconi all'illustrissima signora marchesa della Padula nel 1538*, Naples.

von Falkenhausen, V. (1992). *La Campania tra Goti e Bizantini*, in G. Pugliese Carratelli (ed.), *Storia e civiltà della Campania: Il Medioevo*, Naples: 7–35.

Fasola, U. M. (1975). *Le Catacombe di S. Gennaro a Capodimonte*, Rome.

Fava, M., and Bresciano, G. (1911–12). *La stampa a Napoli nel V secolo*, Leipzig.

Federico, E. (2010). 'Seirenoussai o Seirenes: Una semplice *nuance*? Strabone, le Sirene, Li Galli', in F. Senatore and M. Russo (eds.), *Sorrento e la Penisola Sorrentina tra Italici, Etruschi e Greci nel contesto della Campania antica: Atti della giornata di studio in omaggio a Paola Zancani Montuoro (1901–1987), Sorrento, 19 maggio 2007*, Rome: 255–89.

Federico, E., and Miranda, E. (eds.) (1998). *Capri antica: Dalla preistoria alla fine dell'età romana*, Capri.

Fentress, J., and Wickham, C. (1992). *Social Memory*, Oxford.

Fera, V. (1995). 'Un laboratorio filologico di fine Quattrocento: La *Naturalis historia*', in O. Pecere and M. D. Reeve (eds.), *Formative Stages of Classical Traditions: Latin Texts from Antiquity to the Renaissance*, Spoleto: 435–66.

Fera, V. (2002). 'Pomponio Leto e le *Silvae* di Stazio', *Schede Umanistiche* 16: 71–83.

Ferone, C. (1988). 'Sull'iscrizione napoletana della fratria degli Artemisi: *A.E.* 1913, 134', *Monumenta Graeca et Romana* 13: 167–80.

Ferrea, L. (2002). *Gli dei di terracotta: La ricomposizione del frontone da via di San Gregorio,* Milan.

Ferreri, P. (2013). '*Disiecta membra*: Il riuso dell'antico nel complesso di San Gregorio Armeno', in N. Spinosa, A. Pinto, and A. Valerio (eds.), *San Gregorio Armeno: Storia, architettura, arte e tradizioni* Naples: 75–86.

Filangieri, G. (1883–91). *Documenti per la storia, le arti e le industrie delle province napoletane,* Naples.

Filangieri di Candida, R. (1926). 'Il Tempietto di Giovanni Pontano in Napoli', *Atti dell'Accademia Pontaniana* 56: 103–39.

Fino, L. (2008). *Il mito di Napoli tra vedute e scritti di viaggiatori dal XVII al XIX secolo,* Naples.

Fiorani, F. (2005). *The Marvel of Maps: Art, Cartography and Politics in Renaissance Italy.* New Haven and London.

Fiore, F. P., and Tafuri, M. (eds.) (1994). *Francesco di Giorgio architetto,* Milan.

Fiorese, F. (ed.) (2004). *Vita e morte di Ezzelino da Romano,* Milan.

Fischer, M. (1996). 'Marble, Urbanism, and Ideology in Roman Palestine: The Caesarea Example', in A. Raban and K. G. Holum (eds.), *Caesarea Maritima: A Retrospective after Two Millennia,* Leiden and New York: 251–61.

Fishwick, D. (1989). 'L. Munatius Hilarianus and the Inscription of the Artemisii', *Zeitschrift für Papyrologie und Epigraphik* 76: 175–83.

Fittipaldi, T. (1979). *Scultura e presepe nel Settecento a Napoli,* Rome.

Fittipaldi, T. (1995). *Il presepe napoletano del Settecento,* Naples.

Fittschen, K. (1999). *Prinzenbildnisse antoninischer Zeit,* Mainz.

Fontaine, M. M. (1998). 'Quelques traits du cicéronianisme lyonnais: Claude Guilliaud, Florenti Wilson, Bathélemy Aneau et Simon de Vallambert', in *Scritture dell'impegno dal Rinascimento all'età barocca, atti del convegno internazionale di studio (Gargnano, 11–13 ottobre 1994),* Fasano: 35–69.

Fontana, D. (1590). *Della trasportatione dell'obelisco vaticano et delle fabriche di Nostro Signore Papa Sisto V fatte dal Cavallier Domenico Fontana architetto di Sua Santità: Libro Primo,* Rome.

Fontana, V. (1988). *Fra' Giovanni Giocondo architetto 1433c–1515,* Vicenza.

Fontana, V. (1989). 'Giovanni Giocondo e Jacopo Sannazaro a Mola e a Gaeta', *Napoli Nobilissima,* ns 28: 111–12.

Formichetti, G. (1991). 'Di Falco, Benedetto', in *DBI.*

Forte, B. (1999). *Il racconto del presepe,* Naples.

Fowler, B. H. (1989). *The Hellenistic Aesthetic,* Madison, WI.

Franchesi, A. (2006). 'Una lettura antropologica del presepe: Allestimenti presepiali della provincia di Padova', *La Ricerca Folklorica* 53: 127–36.

Frederiksen, M. W. (1984). *Campania,* London.

Furstenberg-Levi, S. (2006). 'The Fifteenth Century Accademia Pontaniana: An Analysis of Its Institutional Elements', *History of Universities* 21/1: 33–70.

Fuscano, I. B. (1531). *Stanze sopra le bellezze di Napoli*, Rome.

Fusco, G. V. (1841). *Frammento inedito di uno scrittore napolitano del secolo XVI*, Naples.

Fusco, L., and Corti, G. (2006). *Lorenzo de' Medici, Collector and Antiquarian*, Cambridge.

Gabrici, E. (1951). 'Contributo archeologico alla topografia di Napoli e della Campania', *Monumenti Antichi dell'Accademia dei Lincei* 10: 5–152.

Gagliardi, G. (1888). *La basilica di S. Giovanni Maggiore in Napoli e la sua insigne collegiata*, Naples.

Gaglione, M. (1998). *Il campanile di Santa Chiara in Napoli*, Naples.

Gaiga, S. (2014). 'La *Descrittione di tutta Italia* e il *Theatrum Orbis Terrarum* di Abraham Ortelius', *Incontri: Rivista europea di studi italiani*, 29/1 [forthcoming].

Galasso, G. (1982). *L'altra Europa: Antropologia storica del Mezzogiorno d'Italia*, Milan.

Galasso, G. (1994). *Alla periferia dell'impero: Il regno di Napoli nell'Impero spagnolo, secoli XVI–XVII*, Turin.

Galasso, G. (1995). 'Il sistema imperiale spagnolo da Filippo II a Filippo IV', in P. Pissavino and G. Signorotto (eds.), *Lombardia Borromaica: Lombardia spagnola (1554–1659)*, i, Rome: 13–40.

Galasso, G. (1998). *Napoli capitale: Identità politica e identità cittadina: Studi e ricerche 1266–1860*, Naples.

Galinsky, K. (ed.) (2014). *Memoria Romana: Memory in Rome and Rome in Memory*, Ann Arbor, MI.

Gardner, J. (1989). 'Review of P. Leone de Castris, Arte di corte nella Napoli angioina', *Burlington Magazine* 131: 562–3.

Garin, E. (1966). 'La letteratura degli umanisti', in E. Cecchi and N. Sapegno (eds.), *Storia della letteratura italiana: Il Quattrocento e l'Ariosto*, Milan: 7–368.

Garufi, C. A. (ed.) (1937–8). *Riccardus de Sancto Germano: Chronica* (*Rerum Italicarum Scriptores*, ser. II, 7, 2), Bologna.

Gasparri, C. (1973). 'Lo stadio panatenaico: Documenti e testimonianze per una riconsiderazione dell'edificio di Erode Attico', *Annuario della Scuola archeologica di Atene e delle missioni italiane in Oriente* 52: 313–92.

Gauthier, R. A. (1982). 'Notes sur les débuts (1225–1240) du premier Averroïsme', *Revue des Sciences philosophiques et théologiques* 66: 321–74.

Gaye, J. W. (1839–1840). *Carteggio inedito d'artisti*, Florence.

Geer, R. M. (1935). 'The Greek games at Naples', *Transactions of the American Philological Association* 66: 208–21.

Germano, G. (2005). *Il De aspiratione di Giovanni Pontano e la cultura del suo tempo*, Naples.

Ghisellini, E. (2004). 'Un acrolito tardo-ellenistico inedito della collezione Spada: Annotazioni sulla statuaria di culto della Tarda Repubblica', *Atti della Pontificia accademia romana di archeologia: Rendiconti* 76: 449–523.

Giampaola, D. (2004). 'Dagli studi di Bartolommeo Capasso agli scavi della metropolitana: Ricerche sulle mura di Napoli e sull'evoluzione del paesaggio costiero', *Napoli Nobilissima* 5: 35–56.

Giampaola, D. (2010). 'Il paesaggio costiero di *Neapolis* tra Greci e Bizantini', in *Napoli, la città e il mare*, Naples: 17–26.

Giampaola, D. (2013). 'Dalle *insulae* di *Neapolis* all'isola conventuale', in N. Spinosa, A. Pinto, and A. Valerio (eds.), *San Gregorio Armeno: Storia, architettura, arte e tradizioni*, Naples: 87–102.

Giampaola, D., and d'Agostino, B. (2005). 'Osservazioni storiche e archeologiche sulla fondazione di *Neapolis*', in W. V. Harris and E. Lo Cascio (eds.), Noctes Campanae: *Studi di storia antica ed archeologia dell'Italia preromana e romana in memoria di Martin W. Frederiksen*, Naples: 49–80.

Giannone, P. (1823). *Istoria civile del Regno di Napoli*, i, Milan.

Gigante, M. (1990). 'I frammenti di Sirone', *Paideia* 45: 175–96

Gigante, M. (1991). 'Virgilio e i suoi amici tra Napoli e Ercolano', *Atti e Memorie dell'Accademia Virgiliana di Mantova*, NS 59: 87–125.

Gilson, É. (1965). *Le Thomisme*, Paris.

Gioia, M. (1825). 'Riflessioni in difesa degli Italiani su l'opera intitolata *L'Homme du Midi et l'homme du Nord ou l'influence du climat* del Sig. Di Bonstetten', *Annali Universali di Statistica* 5: 5–62.

Girone, M. (1994). 'Sui laucelarchi', *Miscellanea Greca e Romana* 18: 81–7.

Goethe, J. W. (1885). *Goethe's Travels in Italy, together with his second residence in Rome and Fragments on Italy, translated from the German*, London.

Gorani, J. (1793). *Mémoires, secrets et critiques des Cours, des Gourvernements, et des Moeurs des principaux États de l'Italie par J.G.*, i, Paris.

Govan, J. L. (2007). *Art of the Crèche: Nativities from Around the World*, London.

Grant, J. N. (2011). *Lilio Gregorio Giraldi*, Cambridge.

Greco, E. (1985a). 'Problemi urbanistici', in *Napoli antica* (1985): 132–9.

Greco, E. (1985b). '*Forum duplex*: Appunti per lo studio delle *agorai* di *Neapolis* in Campania', *Annali di archeologia e storia antica* 7: 125–35.

Greco, E. (1986). 'L'impianto urbano di *Neapolis*: Aspetti e problemi', in *Neapolis* (1986): 187–220.

Greco, E. (1987). 'Napoli', *Enciclopedia Virgiliana*, iii, Rome.

Greco, E. (1994). 'L'urbanistica antica: Continuità dell'antico', in F. Zevi (ed.), *Neapolis*, Naples: 35–53.

Greenhalgh, M. (2008). *Marble Past, Monumental Present: Building with Antiquities in the Mediaeval Mediterranean*, Leiden.

Grévin B. (2008). *Rhétorique du pouvoir médiéval: Les Lettres de Pierre de la Vigne et la formation du langage politique européen XIIIe–XIVe siècle*, Rome.

Griffin, N. E. (ed.) (1936). *Guido de Columnis: Historia destructionis Troiae,* Cambridge.

Griffo, A. (1996). *Il Presepe Napoletano: Personaggi e ambienti,* Rome.

Grillo, U. (1998). *Il Presepe Napoletano: Dalle origini a San Gregorio Armeno,* Naples.

Grippo, M., Toscano, T. R., and Toscano, G. (eds.) (1992). *Benedetto Di Falco: Descrittione dei luoghi antiqui di Napoli,* Naples.

Gruben, G. (2006). 'I capitelli del tempio di Hera a Samo', in F. Costabile (ed.), *Polis 2: Studi interdisciplinari sul mondo antico,* Rome: 7–16.

Guarducci, M. (1936). *L'istituzione della fratria nella Grecia antica e nelle colonie Greche d'Italia,* Memorie della classe di scienze morali, storiche e filologiche dell'Accademia dei Lincei 6.6.1.

Guida, P. (1969). 'Il restauro della chiesa e l'isolamento del campanile del complesso monumentale di S. Maria Maggiore alla Pietrasanta in Napoli: Evoluzioni, involuzioni ed iscrizioni del tempio', *Atti dell'Accademia Pontaniana* 18: 125–70.

Guidobaldi, A., and Pensabene, P. (2005–6). 'Il recupero dell'antico in età carolingia: La decorazione scultorea absidale delle chiese di Roma', *Atti della Pontificia Accademia Romana di Archeologia: Rendiconti* 78: 3–74.

Gury, F. (1986). 'Dioskouroi / Castores', *LIMC* iii.1.608–35.

Halbwachs, M. (1992). (trans. L. Coser), *On Collective Memory,* Chicago.

Hales, S., and Paul, J. (2011). *Pompeii in the Public Imagination from Its Rediscovery to Today,* Oxford.

Hampe, K. (1910). *Beiträge zur Geschichte der letzten Staufer: Ungedruckte Briefe aus der Sammlung des Magisters Heinrich von Isernia,* Leipzig.

Hampe, K. (1923). *Zur Gründungsgeschichte der Universität Neapel,* Heidelberg.

Hansen, M. F. (2003). *The Eloquence of Appropriation: Prolegomena to an Understanding of Spolia in Early Christian Rome,* Rome.

Hardie, A. (1983). *Statius and the Silvae: Poets, Patrons and Epideixis in the Graeco-Roman World,* Liverpool.

Harloe, K. (2013). *Winckelmann and the Invention of Antiquity: History and Aesthetics in the Age of Altertumswissenschaft,* Oxford.

Harri, L. (1989). 'Statuaria', in E. M. Steinby (ed.), *Lacus Iuturnae I,* Rome: 177–232.

Harris, J. R. (1903). *The Dioscuri in the Christian Legends,* Cambridge.

Harris, J. R. (1906). *The Cult of the Heavenly Twins,* Cambridge.

Harris, W. V. (1989). *Ancient Literacy,* Cambridge, MA.

Haskell, F. (1993). *History and Its Images: Art and the Interpretation of the Past,* New Haven and London.

Haskell, F., and Penny, N. (1981). *Taste and the Antique: The Lure of Classical Sculpture, 1500–1900,* New Haven, CT.

Häussler, R. (2002). 'Writing Latin—from Resistance to Assimilation: Language, Culture and Society in N. Italy and S. Gaul', in A. Cooley (ed.), *Becoming Roman, Writing Latin: Literacy and Epigraphy in the Roman West. Journal of Roman Archaeology*, Portsmouth: 61–7.

Hazard, P. (1953). *The European Mind: The Critical Years, 1680–1715*, New Haven, CT.

Heinrich, H. (2002). Subtilitas novarum scalpturarum: *Untersuchungen zur Ornamentik marmorner Bauglieder der späten Republik und frühen Kaiserzeit in Campanien*, Munich.

Helas, P. (2009). 'Der Triumph von Alfonso d'Aragona 1443 in Neapel: Zu den Darstellungen herrscherlicher Einzüge zwischen Mittelalter und Renaissance', in P. Johanek and A. Lampen (eds.), Adventus: *Studien zum herrscherlichen Einzug in die Stadt*, Cologne: 133–228.

Hendrix, H. (2013). *New Approaches to Naples c.1500–c.1800: The Power of Place*, Farnham: 81–102.

Hendrix, H. (2014). 'Plagio e commercio nelle guide tardo-cinquecentesche dedicate a Napoli e Pozzuoli', *Incontri: Rivista europea di studi italiani*, 29/1: 41–53.

Heringman, N. (2013). *Sciences of Antiquity: Romantic Antiquarianism, Natural History and Knowledge Work*, Oxford.

Hersey, G. L. (1969). *Alfonso II and the Artistic Renewal of Naples 1485–1495*, New Haven, CT.

Herz, A. (1988). 'Cardinal Cesare Baronio's Restoration of SS. Nereo ed Achilleo and S. Cesareo de' Appia', *Art Bulletin* 70: 590–620.

Heurgon, J. (1987). 'Les Deux Sibylles de Cumes', *Filologia e forme letterarie: Studi offerti a Francesco della Corte* 5, Urbino, 153–61.

Hofstetter, E. (1997). 'Seirenes', *LIMC* viii/1: 1093–1104.

Hommel, P. (1954). *Studien zu den römischen Figurengiebeln der Kaiserzeit*, Berlin.

Hopkins, K. (1991). 'Conquest by Book', in M. Beard (ed.), *Literacy in the Roman World. Journal of Roman Archaeology*, Portsmouth: 133–58.

Horsfall, N. (1991). 'Statistics of States of Mind?', in M. Beard (ed.), *Literacy in the Roman World. Journal of Roman Archaeology*, Portsmouth: 59–76.

Hübner, A. (1869). *Inscriptionum Hispaniae Latinae*, in *CIL* 2.

Hughes, J. (2014). 'Memory and the Roman Viewer: Looking at the Arch of Constantine', in K. Galinsky (ed.), *Memoria Romana: Memory in Rome and Rome in Memory*, Ann Arbor, MI: 103–16.

Huillard-Bréholles, J. L. A. (1865). *Vie et correspondance de Pierre de la Vigne*, Paris.

Hülsen, C. (1984 [1910]). *Il libro di Giuliano da Sangallo, codice Barberino Latino 4424*, Rome.

Iacono, A. (1999). *Le fonti del* Parthenopeus sive Amorum libri II *di Giovanni Pontano*, Naples.

Iacono, A. (2005). *Uno studente alla scuola del Pontano a Napoli: Le recollecte del MS. 1368 (T. 5. 5.) della Biblioteca Angelica di Roma*, Naples.

Iacono, A. (2009). 'La *Laudatio urbis Neapolis* nell'appendice archeologico-antiquaria del *De bello Neapolitano* di Giovanni Gioviano Pontano', *Bollettino di Studi Latini* 39: 562–86.

Iasiello, I. M. (2003). *Il collezionismo di antichità nella Napoli dei Viceré*, Naples.

Ideologie e pratiche del reimpiego (1999) = Ideologie e pratiche del reimpiego nell'Alto Medioevo, XLVI Settimana di Studi CISAM, Spoleto 1999.

Imhoof-Blumer, F. (1923). 'Fluß- und Meergotter auf griechischen und römischen Münzen', *Revue suisse de numismatique* 23: 173–421.

Irwin, D. (1997). *Neoclassicism*, London.

Isler, H. P. (1970). *Acheloos: Eine Monographie*, Bern.

Isler, H. P. (1981). 'Acheloos', *LIMC* i/1: 12–36.

Jauss, H. R. (1970–1). 'Literary History as a Challenge to Literary Theory', *New Literary History* 2: 19–37.

Jauss, H. R. (1982). *Toward an Aesthetic of Reception*, Eng. trans., Minneapolis.

Jauss, H. R. (1991). *Ästhetische Erfahrung und literarische Hermeneutik*, Frankfurt.

Jauss, H. R. (1994). *Wege des Verstehens*, Munich.

Jauss, H. R. (1998). *Die Theorie der Rezeption: Rückschau auf ihre unerkannte Vorgeschichte*, Constance.

Jauss, H. R. (1999). *Probleme des Verstehens*, Stuttgart.

Johannowsky, W. (1960). 'Problemi archeologici napoletani con particolare riferimento alle zone interessate dal Risanamento', in G. Russo (ed.) *La città di Napoli dalle origini al 1860*, Naples: 487–505.

Johannowsky, W. (1976). 'La situazione in Campania', in P. Zanker (ed.), *Hellenismus in MittelItalien*, Göttingen.

Johannowsky, W. (1985). 'I teatri', in *Napoli antica* (1985): 209–13.

Johannowsky, W. (2000). 'Appunti sui teatri di Pompei, Nuceria Alfaterna, Ercolano', *Rivista di Studi Pompeiani* 11: 17–32.

Johnson, R., Ousterhout, R. G., and Papalexandrou, A. (eds.) (2012). *Approaches to Byzantine Architecture and Its Decoration: Studies in Honor of Slobodan Ćurčić*, Aldershot.

Jones, A. H. M. (1940). *The Greek City: From Alexander to Justinian*, Oxford.

Jones, I. (1970). *Inigo Jones on Palladio: Being the Notes by Inigo Jones in the Copy of I Quattro Libri dell'Architettura di Andrea Palladio 1601 in the Library of Worcester College Oxford, reproduced by Courtesy of the Provost and Fellows*, Oxford.

Jory, E. J. (1970). 'Associations of Actors in Rome', *Hermes* 98/2: 224–53.

Jouffroy, H. (1986). *La Construction publique en Italie et dans L'Afrique romaine*, Strasbourg.

Kahane, A. (ed.) (2011). *Antiquity and the Ruin: L'Antiquité et les ruines*. Special Issue, *European Review of History/Revue europénne d'histoire*, 18: 5–6.

Kaibel, G. (1890). 'Inscriptiones Italiae et Siciliae', in *IG* 14, Berlin.

Kallendorf, H., and Kallendorf, C. (2000). 'Conversations with the Dead: Quevedo and Statius, Annotations and Imitation', *Journal of the Warburg and Courtauld Institutes* 63: 131–68.

Kantorowicz, E. H. (1957). *The King's Two Bodies*, Princeton.

Kaufmann, K. M. (1959). *The Baths of Pozzuoli*, Oxford.

Keller, F. E. (1973). 'Die Zeichnung Uff. 363A von Baldassarre Peruzzi und das Bad von Poggio Reale', *Architectura* 3/1: 22–35.

Kelly, S. (2011). *The Cronaca di Partenope: An Introduction to and Critical Edition of the First Vernacular History of Naples (c. 1350)*, Leiden-Boston.

Kendon, A. (2004). *Gesture: Visible Action as Utterance*, Cambridge.

Kidwell, C. (1991). *Pontano: Poet and Prime Minister*, London.

Kinney, D. (1995). 'Rape or Restitution of the Past? Interpreting Spolia', in S. C. Scott (ed.), *Papers in Art History from the Pennsylvania State University*, ix (Philadelphia): 53–67.

Kinney, D. (1997). 'Spolia, Damnatio *and* Renovatio Memoriae', *Memoirs of the American Academy in Rome* 42: 117–48.

Kölzer, T., Stahli, M., and Becht-Jördens, G. (eds.) (1994). Petrus de Ebulo, Liber ad honorem Augusti sive de rebus Siculis: *Eine Bilderchronik der Stauferzeit aus der Burgerbibliothek Bern*, Sigmaringen.

Koortbojian, M. (1993). 'Fra Giovanni Giocondo and His Epigraphic Methods: Notes on Biblioteca Marciana, MS Lat. XIV, 171', *Kölner Jahrbuch* 26: 49–55.

Kruft, H.-W. (1972). *Domenico Gagini und seine Werkstatt*, Munich.

Kruft, H.-W., and Malmanger, M. (1975). 'Der Triumphbogen Alfonsos in Neapel: Das Monument und seine politische Bedeutung', *Acta ad archaeologiam et artium historiam pertinentia Institutum Romanum Norvegiae* 6: 213–305.

Kyriaci Anconitani Itinerarium (1742). *Kyriaci Anconitani Itinerarium nunc primum ex ms. cod. in lucem erutum ex bibl. Illus. clarissimique baronis Philippi Stosch. editionem recensuit, animadversionibus, ac praefatione illustravit, nonnullisque eiusdem Kyriaci epistolis partim editis, partim ineditis locupletavit Laurentius Mehus, Florentiae, ex novo Typographio Joannis Pauli Giovanelli* (1742).

Kytzler, B. (1960). 'Beobachtungen zum Prooemium der *Thebais*', *Hermes* 88: 331–54.

Lacroix, L. (1953). 'Fleuves et nymphes eponymes sur les monnaies grecques', *Revue belge de numismatique et de sigillographie* 99: 5–21.

Lancaster, J. (2009). *In the Shadow of Vesuvius: A Cultural History of Naples*, London and New York.

Langhammer, W. (1973). *Die rechtliche und soziale Stellung der* Magistratus Municipales *und der* Decuriones, Wiesbaden.

Lanselle, M. (1933). 'Un puériculteur oublié: Simon de Vallambert', *Bulletin de la Societé française d'histoire de la médecine* 27: 243–51.

Lappenberg, M. (ed.) (1869). 'Arnoldus Lubecensis: *Chronica*', in *Monumenta Germaniae Historica (Scriptores, XXI)*, Hanover: 101–250.

La Rocca, E., and Parisi Presicce, C. (2010). *I giorni di Roma: L'età della conquista*, Milan.

Laschke, B., and Deramaix, M. (1992). '*Maroni musa proximus ut tumulus*: L'Église et la tombe de Jacques Sannazar', *Revue de l'Art* 95: 25–40.

Lasena, P. (1688). *Dell'antico ginnasio napoletano: Opera posthuma di Pietro Lasena dedicata al signor Giuseppe Valletta*, Naples.

Laureys, M. (2000). 'Theory and Practice of the Journey to Italy in the 16th Century: Stephanus Pighius' *Hercules Prodicius*', in D. Sacré and G. Tournoy (eds.), *Myricae: Essays on Neo-Latin literature in Memory of Jozef Ijsewijn*, Leuven: 269–301.

Lazzarini, L. (2006). '*Poikiloi lithoi, versiculores maculae*: I marmi colorati della Grecia antica', *Marmora 2*, suppl. 1, Pisa and Rome.

Lecora, I. (1999/2000). 'Da Roma a Napoli: Marmi e monumenti antichi della via Appia nei disegni del XVI secolo', diss. Università degli studi di Napoli Federico II.

Leiwo, M. (1989). 'Philostratus of Ascalon, His Bank, His Connections, and Naples in 130–90 B.C.', *Athenaeum* 77: 575–84.

Leiwo, M. (1994). *Neapolitana: A Study of Population and Language in Graeco-Roman Naples*, Helsinki.

Lemerle, F. (2000). 'Introduction, traduction et commentaire', in *Les Annotations de Guillaume Philandrier sur le De Architectura de Vitruve, livres 1 à 4, fac-similé de l'édition de 1552*, ed. Frédérique Lemerle, Paris.

Lenzo, F. (2005). 'Architettura di marmi: Vaccaro e Solimena in San Paolo Maggiore a Napoli', in B. Gravagnuolo and F. Adriani (eds.), *Domenico Antonio Vaccaro: Sintesi delle arti*, Naples: 265–76.

Lenzo, F. (2006a). 'Aggiornamento', in A. Blunt, *Architettura barocca e rococò a Napoli*, Milan: 270–329.

Lenzo, F. (2006b). 'Frammento e iscrizione del tempio dei Dioscuri', in F. P. Fiore (ed.), *Leon Battista Alberti architetto*, Milan: 325–6.

Lenzo, F. (2008). 'Roma 1545–1547: Ligorio, Palladio e l'epigrafia', in F. Barbieri (ed.), *Palladio 1508–2008: Il simposio del cinquecentenario*, Venice: 113–16.

Lenzo, F. (2011). *Architettura e antichità a Napoli dal XV al XVIII secolo: Le colonne del tempio dei Dioscuri e la chiesa di San Paolo Maggiore*, Rome.

Lenzo, F. (2012). 'Immaginare l'antico: Pirro Ligorio e il tempio dei Dioscuri di Napoli', in A. Brodini and G. Curcio (eds.), *Porre un limite all'infinito errore: Studi di storia dell'archtiettura dedicati a Christof Thoenes*, Rome: 91–100.

Lenzo, F. (2014). 'Public Display of Antiquities and Civic Identity in the Seggi of Southern Italy (14th–18th centuries)', *Journal of the History of Collections*, in press.

Lenzo, F. (forthcoming). 'The Four Etchings: Between Word and Image', in B. de Divitiis (ed.), *Humanism and Antiquarian Culture in Renaissance Southern Italy: Ambrogio Leone's* De Nola *(Venice, 1514)*.

Leon, C. (1971). *Die Bauornamentik des Traiansforum und ihre Stellung in der früh und mittelkaiserzeitlichen Architekturdekoration Roms*, Cologne.

Leone, A. (1514). *Ambrosii Leoni in libellos De Nola patria*, Venice.

Leone, A. (1525). *Ambrosii Leonis Nolani de nobilitate rerum dialogus*, Venice.

Lepore, E. (1967a). 'Napoli Greco-romana: La vita politica e sociale 1. *Neapolis* nel quinto secolo a.C.', *Storia di Napoli* 1: 139–92.

Lepore, E. (1967b). 'Napoli Greco-romana: La vita politica e sociale 2. La comunità cittadina del quarto secolo a.C. tra Sanniti e Romani', *Storia di Napoli* 1: 193–240.

Lepore, E. (1985). 'La città antica', in *Napoli antica* (1985): 115–22.

Lepore, E. (1990). 'Parallelismi, riflessi e incidenza degli avvenimenti del contesto Mediterraneo e l'Italia', *Crise et transformation des sociétés archaïques de l'Italie antique au Ve siècle av. J.C.*, Rome: 289–97.

Lettere, V. (1984). 'Costo, Tommaso', in *DBI*.

Lettieri, P. (1560 [1803]). 'Discorso dottissimo del Magnifico MS Pierro Antonio de Lecthiero cittadino et Tabulario Napolitano circa l'anticha pianta et ampliatione dela Città di Nap. et del itinerario del acqua che anticamente flueva et dentro et fora la pred. Città per aquedocti mirabili quale secondo per più raggioni ne dimostra, era il Sebbetho celebrato dagli antichi auttori [ms. 1560]', in L. Giustiniani, *Dizionario geografico ragionato del Regno di Napoli*, vi. 382–411.

Levi, A. (1926). 'Camere sepolcrali scoperte in Napoli durante i lavori della direttissima Roma–Napoli', *Monumenti Antichi dell'Accademia dei Lincei* 31: 378–402.

Liebenam, W. (1900). *Städteverwaltung im römischen Kaiserreiche*, Leipzig.

Lipps, J. (2011). *Die Basilica Aemilia am* Forum Romanum: *Der kaiserzeitliche Bau und seine Ornamentik*, Wiesbaden.

Liverani, P. (2004). 'Reimpiego senza ideologia: La lettura antica degli *spolia* dall'arco di Costantino all'età carolingia', *Mitteilungen des Deutschen Archäologischen Instituts, Römische Abteilung* 111: 383–433.

Liverani, P. (2006). 'L'architettura costantiniana, tra committenza imperiale e contributo delle élites locali', in A. Demandt and J. Engemann (eds.), *Konstantin der Grosse: Geschichte—Archäologie—Rezeption*, Trier: 235–44.

Liverani, P. (2011). 'Reading Spolia in Late Antiquity and Contemporary Perception', *Reuse Value* (2011): 33–52.

Lljenstolpe, P. (1997–8). 'The Roman Blattkelch Capital: Typology, Origin and Aspects of Emphyments', *Opuscula Romana* 22–3: 91–126.

Llombart, G. (1962). 'S. Paolo Maggiore de Nápoles: Una iglesia de la primera reforma católica', *Regnum Dei* 19: 173–95.

Lomas, K. (1993). *Rome and the Western Greeks, 350 BC–AD 200: Conquest and Acculturation in Southern Italy*, London and New York.

Lomas, K. (1995). 'Urban élites and Cultural Definition: Romanization in Southern Italy', in K. Lomas and T. J. Cornell (eds.), *Urban Society in Roman Italy*. London and New York: 113–26.

Lomas, K. (1997). '*Graeca urbs?* Ethnicity and Culture in Early Imperial Naples', *Accordia Research Papers* 7: 113–30.

Lomas, K. (2002). 'Euergetism and Urban Renewal in Italy, 90 B.C.–A.D. 100', in T. J. Cornell and K. Lomas (eds.), *Euergetism and Municipal Patronage in Ancient Italy*, London: 28–45.

Lomas, K. (2003a). 'Public Building, Urban Renewal and Euergetism in Early Imperial Italy', in K. Lomas and T. J. Cornell (eds.), *Bread and Circuses: Euergetism and Municipal Patronage in Roman Italy*, London and New York: 28–45.

Lomas, K. (2003b). 'Personal Identity and Romanisation: Greek Funerary Inscriptions from Southern Italy', in E. Herring and J. Wilkins (eds.), *Inhabiting Symbols: Symbol and Imagery in the ancient Mediterranean*, London: 193–207.

Lomas, K. (2013). 'Language and Iconography: The Identity of Sub-groups in Italian Funerary Monuments', *HEROM: Journal of Hellenistic and Roman Material Culture* 2: 97–121.

Lo Monaco, F. (ed.) (1990). *Francesco Petrarca: Itinerario in Terra Santa (1358)*, Bergamo.

Longobardo, F., and Zeli, F. (2010). 'Considerazioni sulla tipologia architettonica del monumento', in I. Baldassare (ed.), *Il teatro di Neapolis*, Naples: 35–46.

Lo Parco, F. (1899). *Aulo Giano Parrasio: Studio Biografico-critico*, Vasto.

Lo Parco, F. (1909). *Niccolò da Reggio grecista italiota del secolo XIV e l'interpretazione dell'epigrafe greca del tempio dei Dioscuri di Napoli ricordata dalla Cronaca di Partenope*, Naples.

Lo Parco, F. (1910). 'Niccolò da Reggio antesignano del risorgimento dell'antichità ellenica nel secolo XIV', *Atti dell'Accademia di Archeologia, Lettere e Belle Arti di Napoli* 2: 241–317.

Lo Parco, F. (1916). 'Tideo Acciarino Piceno, promotore del risveglio umanistico calabrese', *Giornale Storico della Letteratura Italiana* 68: 381–94.

Lowe, D. (2012). 'Always Already Ancient: Ruins in the Virtual World', in T. S. Thorsen (ed.), *Greek and Roman Games in the Computer Age*, Trondheim: 53–90.

Lucherini, V. (2005). 'L'invenzione di una tradizione storiografica: Le due cattedrali di Napoli', *Prospettiva: Rivista di storia dell'arte antica e moderna* 113–14: 2–31.

Lyne, R. O. A. M. (2007). *Collected Papers on Latin Poetry*, Oxford.

Maddoli, G. (2010). 'La παλαιὰ συμμαχία fra Atene e Leontini nel quadro della politica occidentale ateniese', *Klio* 92/1: 34–41.

Madonna, M. L. (ed.) (1992). *Sisto V, Atti del VI Corso Internazionale di Alta Cultura (Roma, 19–29 ottobre 1989)*, i. *Roma e il Lazio*, Rome.

Magli, P. (1986). 'De Iorio, Andrea (1769–1851)', in T. A. Sebeok (ed.), *Encyclopaedic Dictionary of Semiotics*, i. 177–9.

Maiuri, A. (1913). 'La nuova iscrizione della fratria Napoletana degli Artemisi', *Studi Romani* 1: 21–36.

Maiuri, A. (1951). 'Origine e decadenza di *Paestum*', *La Parola del Passato* 5: 284.

Maiuri, A. (1959). *I Campi Flegrei*, Rome.

Makarius, M. (2004). *Ruins*, Paris.

Mallgrave, H. F. (2005). *Modern Architectural Theory: A Historical Survey, 1673–1968*, Cambridge.

Manacorda, D. (1979). 'Le urne di Amalfi non sono amalfitane', *Archeologia Classica* 31: 318–37.

Mancini, F. (1983). *Il Presepe Napoletano*, Naples.

Mancini, F., and Simonelli, P. (1992). 'Il rovinismo nella scenografia del Settecento', in G. Petrochi (ed.), *Il teatro a Roma nel Settecento*, i, Rome: 153–60.

Manfredi, R. (2005). '*La più amena e dilettevole parte che abbia il mondo*: Napoli nei "ritratti" di città del Cinquecento', *Studi Rinascimentali* 3: 153–70.

Maresca, A. (1888). 'Su due colonne esistenti nella chiesa di Santa Chiara', *Arte e storia* 7: 115–16.

Martelli, M. (1995). *Angelo Poliziano: Storia e metastoria*, Lecce.

Masi, G. (1996). 'Scampoli di sartoria testuale: Benedetto di Falco, Giovan Battista Carafa, Pandolfo Collenuccio', in R. Gigliucci (ed.), *Furto e plagio nella letteratura del classicismo*, Rome: 301–22.

Mathea-Förtsch, M. (1999). *Römische Rankenpfeiler und -Pilaster: Schmuckstützen mit vegetabilem Dekor, vornehmlich aus Italien und den westlichen Provinzen*, Mainz.

Mattusch, C. C. (2013). *Rediscovering the Ancient World on the Bay of Naples, 1710–1890*, New Haven and London.

Maurizi, N. (1993–5). 'La presenza ateniese a Napoli', *Annali della Facoltà di Lettere e Filosofia di Perugia. 1: Studi Classici* 17: 287–309.

Mazzella, S. (1586). *Descrittione del Regno di Napoli*, Naples.

Mazzella, S. (1591). *Sito, ed antichità della città di Pozzuolo e del suo amenissimo distretto*, Naples.

Mazzella, S. (1601). *Descrittione del Regno di Napoli*, Naples.

Mazzella, S. (1606). *Sito, ed antichità della città di Pozzuolo e del suo amenissimo distretto*. Naples.

Mazzella, S. (1652). *The Kingdom of Naples* (Eng. trans. James Howell), London.

Mead, W. E. (1914). *The Grand Tour in the Eighteenth Century*, Boston.

Mele, A. (1985). 'La città greca', in *Napoli antica* (1985), 103–8.

Mele, A. (2007). 'Atene e la Magna Grecia', in E. Greco and M. Lombardo (eds.), *Atene e l'Occidente, I grandi temi: Atti del Convegno Internazionale (Atene, 25–27 maggio 2006)*, Athens: 239–68.

Mele, A. (2009). 'Tra sub-colonia ed *epoikia*: Il caso di *Neapolis*', in M. Lombardo and F. Frisone (eds.), *Colonie di colonie, Le fondazioni sub-coloniali greche tra colonizzazione e colonialismo: Atti del Convegno (Lecce, 22–24 giugno 2006)*, Galatina: 183–201.

Melisurgo, G. (1889). *Napoli sotterranea*, Naples.

Mercando, L. (1996). 'Pirro Ligorio e il Tempio napoletano dei Dioscuri', *Studi Miscellanei* 30: 393–8.

Mercantini, A. (2000). 'Giovanni da Castrociclo', *DBI*.

Mercati, G. (1925). *Per la cronologia della vita e degli scritti di Niccolò Perotti, arcivescovo di Siponto*, Vatican City.

Mercati, M. (1589). *De gli obelischi di Roma*, Rome.

Merkelbach, R. (1974). 'Zu der Festordnung für die Sebasta in Neapel', *Zeitschrift für Papyrologie und Epigraphik* 15: 192–3.

von Mercklin, E. (1962). *Antike Figuratkapitelle*, Berlin.

Mesolella, G. (2012). *La decorazione architettonica di* Minturnae, Formiae, Tarracina: *L'età Augustea e Giulio-Claudia*, Rome.

Middione, R. (1993). 'Vicende del Nilo dal Medioevo a oggi', in S. De Caro and N. Spinosa (eds.), *Lo sguardo del Nilo: Storia e recupero del 'Corpo di Napoli'*, Naples: 23–36.

Millar, F. (2002). *Rome, the Greek World, and the East*, i. *The Roman Republic and the Augustan Revolution*, Chapel Hill, NC and London, 292–313.

Miranda, E. (1982). 'I cataloghi dei *Sebastà* di Napoli: Proposte ed osservazioni', *Rendiconti dell'Accademia di Archeologia, Lettere e Belle Arti di Napoli*, ns 57: 165–81.

Miranda, E. (1985a). 'Testimonianze epigrafiche dalle necropoli', in *Napoli antica* (1985): 298–300.

Miranda, E. (1985b). 'Istituzioni, agoni e culti: Le magistrature, gli agoni, I culti greci', in *Napoli antica* (1985): 386–94.

Miranda, E. (1988a). 'Tito a Napoli', *Epigraphica* 50: 222–6.

Miranda, E. (1988b). 'Due nuove fratrie napoletane', *Miscellanea greca e romana* 13: 159–66.

Miranda, E. (1988–9). 'Un decreto consolatorio da *Neapolis*', *Puteoli* 12–13: 95–102.

Miranda, E. (1990). *Iscrizioni greche d'Italia: Napoli I*, Rome.

Miranda, E. (1995). *Iscrizioni greche d'Italia: Napoli II*, Rome.

Miranda, E. (1998). 'Sacerdozi a Napoli in età romana', in S. Adamo Muscettola and G. Greco (eds.), *Culti della Campania antica*, Rome: 231–8.

Miranda, E. (2007). '*Neapolis* e gli imperatori: Nuovi dati dai cataloghi dei
Sebastà', *Oebalus: studi sulla Campania nell'Antichità* 2: 203–15.

Miranda, E. (2010). 'Consoli ed altri elementi di datazione nei cataloghi
agonistici di *Neapolis*', in M. Silvestrini (ed.), *Le tribù romane: Atti della
XVIe Rencontre sur l'Épigraphie*, Bari: 417–22.

Miranda De Martino, E. *See* MIRANDA, E.

Mitchell, C., and Bodnar, E. W. (eds.) (1996). *Francesco Scalamonti, Vita viri
clarissimi et famosissimi Kyriaci Anconitani*, Philadelphia.

Moe, N. (2006). *The View from Vesuvius: Italian Culture and the Southern
Question*, Berkeley, Los Angeles, and London.

Momigliano, A. (1950). 'Ancient History and the Antiquarian', *Journal of the
Warburg and Courtauld Institutes* 13: 285–315.

Mommsen, Th. (1883). *Inscriptiones Bruttiorum, Lucaniae, Campaniae,
Siciliae, Sardiniae latinae*, in *CIL* 10.

Monti, G. M. (1923). *Ricerche su Paolo IV Carafa*, Benevento.

Monticello, T. (1830). *Memoria sulla origine delle acque del Sebeto*, Naples.

Monti Sabia, L. (1973). *Ioannis Ioviani Pontani Eclogae*, Naples.

Montuono, G. M. (2008). 'L'approvvigionamento idrico della città di Napoli:
L'acquedotto del Serino e il Formale Reale in un manoscritto della Biblioteca Nazionale di Madrid', in *Atti del 2° Convegno Nazionale di Storia
dell'Ingegneria*: 1029–50.

Moores, J. D. (1971). 'New Light on Diomede Carafa and His Perfect
Loyalty', *Italian Studies* 26: 1–23.

Morel, J.-P. (1981). *Céramique campanienne: Les Formes*, Rome.

Morel, J.-P. (1985). 'La ceramica campana A nell'economia della Campania',
in *Napoli antica* (1985): 372–8.

Morelli, D., and Nenci, G. (1952). 'Testi e documenti', *La Parola del Passato*
7: 370–413.

Morford, M. (1985). 'Nero: Literature and Arts', *Aufstieg und Niedergang der
römischen Welt* II.32.2: 2003–31.

Mormile, G. (1670). *Descrittione della citta di Napoli, e del suo amenissimo
distretto, e dell'antichita della citta di Pozzuolo: Con la narratione di tutti i
luoghi notabili, e degni di memoria di Cuma, di Baia, di Miseno, e degli
altri luoghi conuicini*, Naples.

Moss, C. (1988). 'Roman Marble Tables', PhD Dissertation, Princeton.

Müller, E. (1913). *Peter von Prezza, ein Publizist der Zeit des Interregnums*,
Heidelberg.

Murphy, J. J. (1971). *Medieval Rhetoric: A Selected Bibliography*, Toronto.

Murphy, J. J. (1974). *Rhetoric in the Middle Ages*, Berkeley and Los Angeles.

Musi, A. (ed.) (1994). *Nel sistema imperiale: L'Italia spagnola*, Naples.

Mustilli, D. (1952). 'Gli studi sulla topografia di Napoli greco-romana dal rinascimento al secolo XIX', *La Parola del Passato* 7: 427–40.

Mustilli, D. (1958). 'Ricordi di sculture greco-romane nel portale della Cappella Palatina in Castelnuovo a Napoli', in *Il mondo antico nel rinascimento, Atti del V Convegno internazionale di studi sul rinascimento*, Florence: 195–206.

Napoli, M. (1997² [1959]). *Napoli greco-romana*, Naples.

Napoli, M. (1967). 'Gli edifici del Foro', *Storia di Napoli* 1: 444–7.

Natali, G. (1917). 'L'idea del primato italiano prima di Vincenzo Gioberti', *Nuova Antologia* 140: 126–34.

Nauta, R. R. (2002). *Poetry for Patrons: Literary Communication in the Age of Domitian*, Leiden.

Nauta, R. R. (2008). 'Statius in the *Silvae*', in J. J. L. Smolenaars, H. J. van Dam, and R. R. Nauta (eds.), *The Poetry of Statius*, Leiden: 143–74.

Nava, M. L. (2006). 'La ricerca archeologica in Magna Grecia: La Campania', *Atti dei Convegni di Studio sulla Magna Grecia* 46: 207–370.

Nava, M. L., and Salvatore, M. R. (2009). 'Le Rassegne Archeologiche: La Campania', *Atti dei Convegni di Studio sulla Magna Grecia* 49: 695–814.

Nazzaro, A. V. (1989). *Quodvultdeus: Promesse e predizioni di Dio. Traduzione, introduzione e note*, Rome.

Negro, A. (1985). *Trevi II*, Rome.

Newmann, J. (1980). 'Inigo Jones e la sua copia de *I Quattro libri di Palladio*', *Bollettino CISA Andrea Palladio* 22/3: 41–62.

Nicolas of Iamsilla (1726). *Historia*, in L. A. Muratori (ed.) *Rerum Italicarum Scriptores, VIII*, Mediolani.

Nicolini, F. (1904). 'Napoli descritta da Bernardo Tasso', *Napoli Nobilissima* 13: 172–4.

Nicolini, F. (1925). *L'arte napoletana del Rinascimento e la lettera di Pietro Summonte a Marcantonio Michiel*, Naples.

Niese, H. (1912). 'Zur Geschichte des geistigen Lebens am Hofe Kaiser Friedrichs II', *Historische Zeitschrift* 108: 473–540.

Niola, M. (2005). *Il Presepe*, Naples.

Nordera Lunelli, R., and Dunston, A. J. (1984). 'Calderini, Domizio', in *Enciclopedia Virgiliana*, i, Rome.

Norman, D. (1986). 'The Succorpo in the Cathedral of Naples: *Empress of All Chapels*', *Zeitschrift für Kunstgeschichte* 49: 323–55.

Nuzzo, E. (2010). '*Subtilitas Phlegraea*: Nota sulla formazione del linguaggio architettonico a Cuma in età augustea', *Mélanges de l'École Française de Rome* 122/2: 377–98.

Oakley, S. P. (1998). *A Commentary on Livy Books VI–X*, ii, Oxford.

Ohlig, C. (2001). De Aquis Pompeiorum: *Herkunft, Zuleitung und Verteilung des Wassers*, Nijmegen.

Osbat, L. (1982). *La missione del Baronio a Napoli per un procedimento dinanzi il Tribunale dell'Inquisizione*, in R. De Maio, L. Giulia, and A. Mazzacane (eds.), *Baronio storico e la Controriforma, atti del convegno internazionale di studi (Sora 6–10 ottobre 1979)*, Sora: 183–95.

Ostrowski, J. A. (1991). *Personifications of Rivers in Greek and Roman Art*, Kraków.

Pade, M. (2014). 'P. *Papinius Statius poeta Neapolitanus* . . . La *Vita Statii* di Niccolò Perotti', *Studi Umanistici Piceni* 34: 9–17.

Pagliara, P. N. (1986). 'Vitruvio da testo a canone', in S. Settis (ed.), *Memoria dell'antico nell'arte italiana*, iii, Turin: 5–85.

Pagliara, P. N. (2001). 'Giovanni Giocondo da Verona (Fra Giocondo)', in *DBI*.

Palladino, I. (2002). *Von neapolitanischen Krippen in Kork*, Ostfildern.

Palladio, A. (1570). *I Quattro libri dell'Architettura*, Venice.

Palma, B. (1998). *Pirro Ligorio e le erme di Roma*, Rome.

Palmentieri, A. (2005). 'Un tondo strigilato in porfido della cattedrale di Salerno: Sull'origine della produzione dei sarcofagi imperiali', *Prospettiva: Rivista di storia dell'arte antica e moderna* 119–20: 70–88.

Palmentieri, A. (2010a). Civitates spoliatae: *Recupero e riuso dell'antico in Campania tra l'età post-classica e il medioevo (IV–XV sec.)*, PhD Dissertation Università degli Studi di Napoli Federico II, 2010, <http://www.fedoa.unina.it/8311/>.

Palmentieri, A. (2010b). 'Su una chiave d'arco figurata dell'anfiteatro campano: Note e discussioni', *Napoli nobilissima*, NS 1: 60–5.

Palmentieri, A. (2013). 'Testimonianze romane nel centro di Sant'Agata dei Goti e i loro reimpieghi', *Napoli nobilissima*, NS 1.

Palumbo, G. A. (2012). *La biblioteca di un grammatico*, Bari.

Pane, G., and Valerio, V. (eds.) (1987). *La città di Napoli tra vedutismo e cartografia: Piante e vedute dal XV al XIX secolo*, Naples.

Pane, R. (1949). *Napoli imprevista*, Turin.

Pane, R. (1975). *Il Rinascimento nell'Italia Meridionale*, Milan.

Pane, R. (2008). 'L'antico e le preesistenze tra Umanesimo e Rinascimento: Teorie, personalità ed interventi su architettura e città', in S. Casiello (ed.), *Verso una storia del restauro: Dall'età classica al primo Ottocento*, Florence: 61–138.

Panormita, A. (1589). *Antonii Panormitæ de dictis et factis Alphonsi regis Aragonum et Neapolis libri quatuor*, Rostoch.

Parke, H. W. (1988). *Sibyls and Sibylline Prophecy in Classical Antiquity*, London and New York.

Parlato, E. (1990). 'Cultura antiquaria e committenza di Oliviero Carafa: Un documento e un'ipotesi sulla villa del Quirinale', *Studi romani* 38: 269–80.

Paschini, P. (1926). *S. Gaetano Thiene, Gian Pietro Carafa e le origini dei chierici regolari teatini*, Rome.

Patrignani, G. A. (1721). *Il piccolo santuario di alcune immagini miraculose*, Faenza.

Pensabene, P. (1982). 'La decorazione architettonica di Cherchel, cornici, architravi, soffitti, basi e pilastri', *150-Jahr-Feier Deutsches Archäologisches Institut Rom*, Mainz: 116–69.

Pensabene, P. (1990). 'Contributo per una ricerca sul reimpiego e il recupero dell'Antico nel Medioevo: Il reimpiego nell'architettura normanna', *Rivista dell'Istituto nazionale d'archeologia e storia dell'arte* 13: 5–138.

Pensabene, P. (1998). 'Nota sul reimpiego e il recupero dell'antico in Puglia e Campania tra V e IX secolo', in M. Rotili (ed.), *Incontri di popoli e culture tra V e IX secolo*, Naples: 181–231.

Pensabene, P. (2003). 'Il reimpiego a Santa Maria in Domnica', in A. Englen and F. Astolfi (eds.), *Caelius, I. Santa Maria in Domnica, San Tommaso in formis e il clivus Scauri*, Rome: 166–95.

Pensabene, P. (2005). 'Marmi e committenza negli edifici per spettacolo in Campania', *Marmora: An International Journal for Archaeology, History and Archaeometry of Marbles and Stones* 1: 69–143.

Pensabene, P. (2007). Ostiensium marmorum decus et decor: *Studi architettonici, decorativi e archeometrici*, Rome.

Pensabene, P., and Trucchi, D. (2002). 'Materiali di reimpiego e progettazione nell'architettura delle chiese paleocristiane di Roma', in F. Guidobaldi and A. Guiglia Guidobaldi (eds.), *Ecclesiae Urbis*, Rome: 799–842.

Percopo, E. (1997 [1893–5]). *Nuovi documenti su gli scrittori e gli artisti dei tempi aragonesi*, ed. M. Del Treppo, Naples.

Percopo, E. (1894). 'Nuovi documenti su gli scrittori e gli artisti dei tempi aragonesi', *Archivio Storico per le Province Napoletane* 19: 584–91.

Percopo, E. (1921). 'Ville ed abitazioni di poeti in Napoli: I. La villa del Pontano ad Antignano', *Napoli Nobilissima* 2: 1–7.

Percopo, E. (1931). 'Vita di Jacopo Sannazaro', *Archivio Storico per le Province Napoletane*, ns 17: 87–198.

Persico, T. (1899). *Diomede Carafa: Uomo di stato e scrittore del secolo 15*, Naples.

Peterson, R. M. (1919). *The Cults of Campania*, Rome.

Petrella, G. (2004). *L'Officina del geografo: La 'Descrittione di tutta Italia' di Leandro Alberti e gli studi geografico-antiquari tra Quattro e Cinquecento*, Milan.

Petrucci, L. (1979). 'Le fonti della topografia delle terme flegree dal XII al XV secolo', *Archivio Storico per le Province Napoletane* 97: 99–129.

Philandrier, G. (1544). *Gulielmi Philandri Castilionii Galli Civis Ro: In decem libros M. Vitruvii Pollionis De architectura annotationes*, Rome.

Piazza, S. (2003). 'Le scelte architettoniche dei teatini a Palermo: Il cantiere della chiesa di San Giuseppe', *Regnum Dei* 49: 251–64.

Picone, R. (2008). 'Reimpiego, riuso, memoria dell'antico nel medioevo', in S. Casiello (ed.), *Verso una storia del restauro: Dall'età classica al primo Ottocento*, Florence: 31–60.

Piekarski, D. (2004). *Anonyme griechische Porträts des 4. Jhs. v. Chr.: Chronologie und Typologie*, Rahden.

Pighius, S. W. (1587). *Hercules Prodicius seu Principis iuventutis vita et peregrinatio*. Antwerp.

Pinna, M. (1988). *La teoria dei climi: Una falsa dottrina che non muta da Ippocrate a Hegel*, Rome.

Pinsent, J. (1969). 'The magistracy at Naples', *La Parola del Passato* 24: 368–72.

Pisani, S., and Siebenmorgen, K. (eds.) (2009). *Neapel: Sechs Jahrhunderte Kulturgeschichte*, Berlin.

Pittaluga, S. (ed.) (1986). 'Riccardo da Venosa: *De Paulino et Polla*', in F. Bertini (ed.), *Commedie latine del XII e XIII secolo*, v, Genoa: 106–227.

Polak, E. J. (1993). *Medieval and Renaissance Letter Treatises and Form Letters: A Census of Manuscripts Found in Eastern Europe and the Former U.S.S.R.*, Leiden.

Polito, M. (2000). 'I decreti degli Artemisi a Napoli e il rapporto phratria-oikos', in M. Mello (ed.), *Studi di storia e geostoria antica*, Naples: 205–26.

Pontano, I. (1498). *De magnificentia*, Naples.

Pontano, I. (1509). *Ioannis Ioviani Pontani De bello Neapolitano et De sermone*, Naples.

Pontano, I. (1538). *De aspiratione*, Basileae, per haeredes Andreae Cratandri.

Porzio, S. (1817). *I tre rarissimi opuscoli di Simone Porzio, di Girolamo Borgia e di Marcantonio delli Falconi: Scritti in occasione della celebre eruzione avvenuta in Pozzuoli nell'anno 1538: Colle memorie storiche de' suddetti autori raccolte da Lorenzo Giustiniani*, Naples.

Potenza, U. (1996). 'Gli acquedotti romani di Serino', in N. De Haan and G. C. M. Jansen (eds.), *Cura aquarum in Campania: Proceedings of the Ninth International Congress on the History of Water Management and Hydraulic Engineering in the Mediterranean Region*, Leiden: 93–100.

Potts, A. (1994). *Flesh and the Ideal: Winckelmann and the Origins of Art History*, New Haven, CT.

Powell, E. (ed.) (1902). 'Thomas Hoby: A Booke of the Travaile and lief of me Thomas Hoby', *Camden Miscellany*, x, London.

Pozzi, E. (1986). 'L'attività archeologica in Campania: Provincie di Napoli e Caserta' *Atti dei Convegni di Studio sulla Magna Grecia* 26: 565–70.

Pozzi, E. (1987). 'L'attività archeologica in Campania: Provincie di Napoli e Caserta', *Atti dei Convegni di Studio sulla Magna Grecia* 27: 699–746.

Pozzi, E. (1988). 'L'attivita archaeologico in Campania: Provincie di Napoli e Caserta', *Atti dei Convegni di Studio sulla Magna Grecia* 29: 447–520.

Praga, G. (1960). 'Acciarini, Tideo', in *DBI*.

Previtera, C. (ed.) (1943). *Giovanni Pontano: I dialoghi*, Florence.

Prosperi, A. (1969). *Tra Evangelismo e Controriforma: G. M. Giberti (1495-1543)*, Rome.

Prosperi, A. (ed.) (2003). *Leandro Alberti: Descrittione di tutta Italia (anastatic reproduction of the 1568 edition)*, Bergamo.

Proto, F. (1889). 'Il presepe: Prolusione letta all'Accademia nella tornata del 3 Gennaio 1889 dal socio duca di Maddaloni', *Atti dell'Accademia Pontiana, Napoli* 19: 55–78.

Pucci, G. (1993). *Il Passato Prossimo: La scienza dell'antichità alle origini della cultura moderna*, Rome.

Pugliese Carratelli, G. (1952a). 'Napoli Antica', *La Parola del Passato* 7: 243–68.

Pugliese Carratelli, G. (1952b). 'Sul culto delle sirene nel golfo di Napoli', *La Parola del Passato* 7: 420–6.

Putnam, M. C. J. (2009). *Jacopo Sannazaro: Latin Poetry*, Cambridge, MA.

Radogna, M. (1873). *Monografia di S. Giovanni a mare: Baliaggio del S. M. O. Gerosolimitano in Napoli*, Naples.

Ranisio, G. (2003). *La Città e il suo racconto: Percorsi napoletani tra immaginario e reale*, Rome.

Raviola, F. (1990). 'La tradizione letteraria su Parthenope', *Hesperìa: Studi sulla grecità di occidente* 1: 19–60.

Raviola, F. (1993). 'Tzetzes e la spedizione di Diotimo a Neapolis', *Hesperìa: Studi sulla grecità di occidente* 3: 67–83.

Raviola, F. (1995). *Napoli origini (Hesperìa: Studi sulla grecità di occidente 6)*, Rome.

Rawson, E. D. (1987). '*Discrimina ordinum*: The *Lex Iulia Theatralis*', *Papers of the British School at Rome* 55: 83–114.

Rea, G. (2013). 'Scavi archeologici e scoperte di antichità nella città di Napoli nella Historia Neapolitana di Fabio Giordano', PhD Dissertation, Università degli studi di Napoli Federico II.

Reeve, M. D. (1977). 'Statius' *Silvae* in the Fifteenth Century', *Classical Quarterly* 27: 202–25.

Reeve, M. D. (1983). 'Statius' *Silvae*', in L. D. Reynolds (ed.), *Texts and Transmission: A Survey of the Latin Classics*, Oxford: 397–9.

Reeve, M. D. (1991). 'The Circulation of Classical Works on Rhetoric from the 12th to the 14th Century', in C. Leonardi and E. Menestò (eds.), *Retorica e poetica tra i secoli XII e XIV*, Spoleto: 109–23.

Reynolds, J. (1982). *Aphrodisias and Rome (JRS Monographs.1)*, London.

Ricciardi, R. (1968). 'Angelo Poliziano, Giuniano Maio, Antonio Calcillo', *Rinascimento*, ser. 2, 8: 277–309.

Riccio, A. (2002). 'L'antico acquedotto della Bolla', in F. Starace (ed.), *L'acqua e l'architettura: Acquedotti e fontane nel regno di Napoli*, Lecce: 115–79.

Richardson, L. (1992). *A New Topographical Dictionary of Ancient Rome*, Baltimore and London.

Riché, P. (1966). *Educazione e cultura nell'occidente barbarico dal sesto all'ottavo secolo*, Rome.

Riché, P. (1979). *Écoles et enseignement dans le Haut Moyen Âge, de la fin du V siècle au milieu du XI siècle*, Paris.

Riché, P. (1989). 'Les Écoles en Italie avant les universités', in L. Gargan and O. Limone (eds.), *Luoghi e metodi di insegnamento nell'Italia medioevale (secoli XII–XIV)*, Galatina.

Ridgway, D. (1992). *The First Western Greeks*, Cambridge.

Ringwood Arnold, I. (1960). 'Agonistic Festivals in Italy and Sicily', *American Journal of Archaeology* 64: 245–51.

Rizzo, V. (1984a). 'Scultori della seconda metà del Seicento', in R. Pace (ed.), *Seicento Napoletano*, Naples: 363–408, 541–3.

Rizzo, V. (1984b). 'Maestri pipernieri, stuccatori e marmorari del Seicento napoletano da documenti inediti dell'Archivio Storico del Banco di Napoli', *Ricerche sul '600 napoletano*, Milan: 187–200.

Rizzo, V. (2001). *Lorenzo e Domenico Antonio Vaccaro: Apoteosi di un binomio*, Naples.

Robb, P. (2011). *Street Fight in Naples: A City's Unseen History*, London.

Robert, L. (1939). 'Inscriptions grecques d'Asie Mineure', in W. F. Calder and J. Keil (eds.), *Anatolian Studies Presented to William Hepburn Buckler*, Manchester: 230–48.

Robert, L. (1970). 'Deux concours grecs à Rome', *Comptes rendus/Académie des inscriptions et Belles-Lettres* 114/1: 6–27.

Rodney, R. D. (2006). *Giovanni Pontano: Baiae*, Cambridge, MA.

Romanelli, D. (1815–19). *Antica topografia istorica del Regno di Napoli*, Naples.

Romano, S., and Bock, N. (eds.) (2005). *Le chiese di San Lorenzo e San Domenico: Gli ordini mendicanti a Napoli*, Naples.

Romano, S., and Enckell, J. J. (eds.) (2007). *Roma e la riforma gregoriana: Tradizioni e innovazioni artistiche, XI–XII secolo*, Rome.

Roncella, B. (1996). 'Il complesso di san Lorenzo Maggiore: Indagini nella cd. area sveva', *Bollettino di Archeologia* 39–40: 111–16.

Rosati, G. (2008). 'Statius, Domitian and Acknowledging Paternity: Rituals of Succession in the Thebaid', in J. J. L. Smolenaars, H.-J. van Dam, and R. R. Nauta (eds.), *The Poetry of Statius*, Leiden: 175–94.

Rossano, P. (2001). 'Le esplorazioni settecentesche all'ombra del Vesuvio', in D. Camardo and A. Ferrara (eds.), *Stabiae: Dai Borbone alle ultime scoperte*, Castellamare di Stabia: 17–22.

Rostagni, A. (1952). 'La cultura letteraria di Napoli antica nelle sue fasi culminanti', *La Parola del Passato* 7: 344–57.

Rotolo, H. (2003). *Restauri antichi e nuovi nel palazzo di Antonello Petrucci in Napoli*, Naples.

Rowlands, M. (1993). 'The Role of Memory in the Transmission of Culture', *World Archaeology* 25/2: 141–51.

Ruggiero, A. (1997). *Ambrogio Leone: Nola*, Naples.

Ruggiero, M. (1885). *Storia degli scavi di Ercolano ricomposta su' documenti superstiti*, Naples.

Ruggiero, M. (1888). *Degli scavi di antichità nelle province di terraferma dell'antico Regno di Napoli dal 1743 al 1876*, Naples.

Ruggiero, M. (1988). *Il presepe italiano: Storia di un costume*, Turin.

Russo, V. (2002). *Sant'Agostino Maggiore: Storia e conservazione di un'architettura eremitana a Napoli*, Naples.

Rutter, N. K. (1979). *Campanian Coinages 475–380 BC*, Edinburgh.

Rutter, N. K. (1980). 'La monetazione di *Neapolis* fino al 380 a.C.', in *La monetazione di Neapolis nella Campania antica: Atti del VII Convegno del Centro Internazionale di Studi Numismatici, Napoli, 20–24 aprile 1980*, Naples: 67–89.

Sabatini, F. (1975). *Napoli angioina: Cultura e società*, Naples.

Sabbadini, R. (1914). *Le scoperte dei codici latini e greci ne' secoli XIV e XV*, Florence.

Sacco, L. (1640). *L'antichissima Sessa Pometia*, Naples.

Salvioli, G. (1898). *L'istruzione pubblica in Italia nei secoli VIII, IX e X*, Florence.

Sambon, A. (1903). *Les Monnaies antiques de l'Italie*, Paris.

Sanchez, G. (1833). *La Campania sotterranea e brevi notizie sugli edifici scavati entro roccia nelle Due Sicilie e in altre regioni: Le catacombe nel tempo del Cristianesimo e del Paganesimo*, Naples.

Sansovino, F. (1575). *Ritratto delle più nobili e famose città d'Italia*, Venice.

Santangelo, M. (2013). 'Preminenza aristocratica a Napoli nel tardo medioevo: i tocchi e il problema dell'origine dei sedili', *Archivio Storico Italiano* 636: 273–318.

Sanudo, M. (1873). *La spedizione di Carlo VIII in Italia*, Venice.

Sarnelli, P. (1685). *Guida de' forestieri curiosi di vedere e d'intendere le cose più notabili della Regal Città di Napoli e del suo amenissimo distretto*, Naples.

Sartori, F. (1953). *Problemi di storia costituzionale italiota*, Rome.

Savarese, S. (1986). *Francesco Grimaldi e l'architettura della Controriforma a Napoli*, Rome.

Savino, E. (2005). *Campania tardoantica (284–604 d.C.)*, Bari.

Savino, E. (2006-7). 'Le diocesi nella Campania tardoantica: Considerazioni su identità regionale e identità cristiana', in G. Luongo (ed.), *San Gennaro nel XVII centenario del martirio (305–2005)*, Naples: 65–84.

Sbordone, F. (1967a). 'La cultura 1: Uno sguardo alle origini', *Storia di Napoli* 1: 511–20.

Sbordone, F. (1967b). 'La cultura 5: Gli spettacoli di Napoli antica', *Storia di Napoli* 1: 561–70.

Scalfaro, R. (2005). *Presepe di Giovanni da Nola della chiesa di S. Maria del Parto, Mergellina–Napoli,* Naples.

Scavizzi, G. (1981). *Arte e architettura sacra,* Reggio Calabria.

Schaller, B. (1993). 'Der Traktat des Heinrich von Isernia *De coloribus rhetoricis*', *Deutsches Archiv für Erforschung des Mittelalters* 49: 113–54.

Schaller, H. M. (1956). 'Zur Entstehung der sogenannten Briefsammlung des Petrus de Vinea', *Deutsches Archiv für Erforschung des Mittelalters* 12: 114–59.

Schaller, H. M. (1957). 'Die Kanzlei Kaiser Friedrichs II. Ihr Personal und ihr Sprachstil', *Archiv für Diplomatik* 3: 207–86.

Schaller, H. M. (1974). 'Die Kaiseridee Friedrichs II', in J. Fleckenstein (ed.), *Probleme um Friedrich II,* Sigmaringen: 109–34.

Schaller, H. M. (1980). '*Ars dictaminis, Ars dictandi*', in *Lexikon des Mittelalters,* i, Munich and Zurich: 1034–5.

Schaller, H. M. (1986). 'L'epistolario di Pier della Vigna', in S. Gensini (ed.), *Politica e cultura nell'Italia di Federico II,* Pisa: 95–111.

Schaller, H. M. (1993). 'Enrico Da Isernia (Henricus de Isernia)', in *DBI.*

Scherillo, G. (1859). *Della venuta di S. Pietro apostolo nella città di Napoli,* Naples.

Schipa, M. (1892). 'Il campanile di Santa Maria Maggiore', *Napoli Nobilissima* 1: 25.

Schipa, M. (1908). *Contese sociali napoletane nel Medioevo,* Naples.

Schminckius, J. H. (ed.) (1745). *Petrus de Pretio: Adhortatio ad Henricum Landgravium Thuringiae,* Lugduni Batavorum.

Schnapp, A. (2000). 'Antiquarian Studies in Naples at the End of the Eighteenth Century: From Comparative Archaeology to Comparative Religion', in G. Imbruglia (ed.), *Naples in the Eighteenth Century: The Birth and Death of a Nation State,* Cambridge: 154–66.

Schofield, R. (2002). 'Review of *Giovanni Sale, Pauperismo architettonico e architettura gesuitica: Dalla chiesa ad aula al Gesù di Roma,* with introductory essay by S. Benedetti (Milan, 2000)', *Annali di architettura* 23: 299–301.

Schott, F. (1600). *Itinerarii Italiae rerumque Romanarum libri tres,* Antwerp.

Schrader, L. (1592). *Monumentorum Italiae, quae hoc nostro saeculo et a Christianis posita sunt, libri quattuor,* Helmstedt.

Schreiter, C. (1995). 'Römische Schmuckbasen', *Kölner Jahrbuch* 28: 161–347.

Schreurs, A. (2000). *Antikenbild und Kunstanschauungen des Pirro Ligorio (1513–1583),* Cologne.

Schreurs, A. (2006). 'Lo studio dell'antico a Napoli: Il tempio dei Dioscuri, disegnato da Pirro Ligorio', *Journal de la Renaissance* 4: 89–110.

Settis, S. (1977). 'I monumenti dell'antichità classica nella magna Grecia in età bizantina', *Atti del XVII Convegno di studi sulla Magna Grecia*, Naples: 91–116.

Settis, S. (1986). 'Continuità, distanza, conoscenza: Tre usi dell'antico', in S. Settis (ed.), *Memoria dell'antico nell'arte italiana 3*, Turin.

Settis, S. (2008). 'Collecting Ancient Sculpture: The Beginnings', in N. Penny and E. D. Schmidt (eds.), *Collecting Sculpture in Early Modern Europe*, New Haven, CT: 13–29.

Settis, S. (2011). 'Nécessité des ruines: Les Enjeux du classique', in A. Kahane (ed.), *Antiquity and the Ruin: L'Antiquité et les ruines*, Special Issue, *European Review of History: Revue européenne d'histoire* 18/5–6: 717–40.

Shackleton Bailey, D. R. (ed.) (2003). *Statius, Silvae*, Cambridge, MA and London.

Sherk, R. K. (1993). 'The Eponymous Officials of Greek Cities: V', *Zeitschrift für Papyrologie und Epigraphik* 96: 267–95.

Sherwin-White, A. N. (1973). *The Roman Citizenship*, Oxford.

Silos, G. (1650–66). *Historiarum clericorum regularium a congregatione condita*, 3 vols., Rome.

Simon, E. (1984). 'Apollon / Apollo', *LIMC* ii/1: 363–446.

Sironen, T. (1989). 'I Dioscuri nella letteratura romana', in M. Steinby (ed.), *Lacus Iuturnae I*, Rome: 92–109.

Sivo, V. (1989). 'Studi recenti sull'*ars dictaminis* mediolatina', *Quaderni Medievali* 28: 220–33.

Skinner, P. (1994). 'Urban Communities in Naples, 900–1050', *Papers of the British School at Rome* 62: 279–99.

Slater, W. J. (2008). 'Hadrian's Letters to the Athletes and Dionysiac Artists Concerning Arrangements for the "Circuit" of Games', *Journal of Roman Archaeology* 21: 610–20.

Solin, H. (2004). 'Sulla tradizione manoscritta dell'iscrizione greca del tempio dei Dioscuri a Napoli', in S. Cerasuolo (ed.), *Mathesis e mneme: Studi in memoria di Marcello Gigante*, Naples: i, 283–90.

Spawforth, A. J. S., and Walker, S. (1985). 'The World of the Panhellenion I', *Journal of Roman Studies* 75: 78–104.

Spina, L. (2007). 'Il mito delle sirene', in M. Bettini and L. Spina, *Il mito delle Sirene: Immagini e racconti dalla Grecia a oggi*, Turin: 25–261.

Spina, L. (2009). *Der Mythos der Sirene Parthenope*, in S. Pisani and K. Siebenmorgen (eds.), *Neapel: Sechs Jahrhunderte Kulturgeschichte*, Berlin: 23–7.

Spina, L. (2010a). *Tra nostalgia e rifiuti, dal nostro inviato a Pompei*, 'Dionysus ex Machina' 1, available online at <http://dionysusexmachina.it/?cmd=articolo&id=11> [last accessed 25 July 2013].

Spina, L. (2010b). 'Napoli', in M. Bettini, M. Boldrini, O. Calabrese, and G. Piccinini, *Miti di città*, Siena: 168–79.

Spinazzola, V. (1901). 'La iscrizione greca del tempio dei Dioscuri', *Archivio Storico per le Province Napoletane* 26: 315–22.

Squarciapino, M. (1941–2). 'La decorazione frontonale in Africa e in altre provincie dell'impero', *Atti della Pontificia Accademia Romana di Archeologia: Memorie* 18: 209–30.

Stärk, E. (1995). *Kampanien als geistige Landschaft: Interpretationen zum antiken Bild des Golfs von Neapel*, Munich.

Stefanucci, A. (1944). *Storia del presepio*, Rome.

Stok, F. (1993). 'Virgilio a Napoli', *Giornale Italiano di Filologia* 45: 231–9.

Strazullo, F. (ed.) (1988). *Giovanni Tarcagnota: La città di Napoli dopo la rivoluzione urbanistica di Pietro di Toledo*, Rome.

Summonte, G. A. (1601). *Historia della città e regna di Napoli*, Naples.

Summonte, G. A. (1640). *Dell'historia della città e del regno di Napoli 1601–1643*, Naples.

Šváb, M. (1978). 'Latinské předkarlovskè kroniky a listy Jindřicha z Isernie ve vztahu k antice', *Antika a česká kultura*, Prague: 33–50.

Swain, S. (1996). *Hellenism and Empire: Language, Classicism and Power in the Greek World, AD 50–250*, Oxford.

Swan, P. M. (2004). *The Augustan Succession: An Historical Commentary on Cassius Dio's Roman History, Books 55–56 (9 B.C.–A.D. 14)*, Oxford.

Szelest, H. (1972). 'Stacjuszowy opis Neapolu (*Silv.* III 5,81–85)', *Meander* 27: 49–54.

Taliercio, M. (1986). 'Il bronzo di *Neapolis*', in A. Stazio and V. Zagli (eds.), *La monetazione di Neapolis nella Campania antica*, Naples: 219–373.

Tallini, G. (2012). 'Giovanni Tarcagnota', <http://www.nuovorinascimento. org/cinquecento/bibliografie.html>.

Tarcagnota, G. (1566). *Del sito et lodi della città di Napoli*. Naples.

Tateo, F. (1999). *Giovanni Pontano. I libri delle virtù sociali*, Rome.

Taylor, R. (2004). 'Hadrian's *Serapeum* in Rome', *American Journal of Archaeology* 108: 223–66.

Taylor, R. (2009). 'River Raptures: Containment and Control of Water in Greek and Roman Constructions of Identity', in C. Kosso and A. Scott (eds.), *The Nature and Function of Water, Baths, and Hygiene from Antiquity through the Renaissance*, Amsterdam: 21–42.

Taylor, R. (forthcoming). 'The Cult of the Sirens and Greek Colonial Identity in Southern Italy', in C. Scheffer and B. Alroth (eds.), *Attitudes towards the Past in Antiquity*.

Taylor, R., and Alchermes, J. (forthcoming). *Naples: A Documentary History: Ancient Naples*, New York.

Thornton, P. (2000). *Authentic Decor: The Domestic Interior 1620–1920*, London.

Toledo, P. G. da (1539). *Ragionamento del terremoto, del Monte Nuovo, dell'aprimento di terra in Pozzuolo nell'anno 1538 e della significazione di essi*, Naples.

Tormo, E. (1940). *Os Desenhos das Antigualhas que vio Francisco D'Ollanda, pintor portugués (1539-1540)*, Madrid.

Torresi, B. (1989). 'Interventi tardocinquecenteschi in S. Silvestro a Montecavallo', in *L'architettura a Roma e in Italia (1580-1621), Atti del XXIII congresso di Storia dell'Architettura (Roma, 24-26 marzo 1988)*, i, Rome: 277-91, 526-8.

Torresi, B. (1994). 'Un'architettura scomparsa del primo Cinquecento romano: La facciata di S. Silvestro al Quirinale', *Palladio* 14: 167-80.

Toscano, T. R. (1991). 'Due schede per Benedetto di Falco', *Critica letteraria* 19/4: 725-59.

Toscano, T. R. (2008). 'Dalla Senna al Sebeto: Simon de Vallambert, medico umanista, "socio" dell'Accademia dei Sereni di Napoli (in margine a una inedita orazione accademica)', in M. Deramaix, P. Galand-Hally, G. Vagenheim, and J. Vignes (eds.), *Les Académies dans l'Europe humaniste: Idéaux et pratiques*, Paris: 197-208.

Trapp, J. B. (1984). 'The Grave of Vergil', *Journal of the Warburg and Courtauld Institutes*, 47: 1-31.

Trendelenburg, A. (1911). 'Der Dioskurentempel in Neapel', *Archäologischer Anzeiger* 54-7.

Tutini, C. (1644). *Dell'origine e fundatione de' seggi di Napoli*, Naples.

Turler, H. (1574). *De peregrinatione et agro Neapolitano libri II*, Strasbourg.

Turler, H. (1575). *The traueiler of Ierome Turler deuided into two bookes. The first conteining a notable discourse of the maner, and order of traueiling ouersea, or into straunge and forrein countreys. The second comprehending an excellent description of the most delicious realme of Naples in Italy. A woorke very pleasaunt for all persons to reade, and right profitable and necessarie vnto all such as are minded to traueyll*, London.

Ungaro, L. (2004). 'La decorazione architettonica del Foro di Augusto a Roma', in S. F. Ramello (ed.), *La decoración arquitectónica en las ciudades romanas de Occidente*, Murcia: 17-37.

Valenza Mele, N. (1991-2). 'Hera ed Apollo a Cuma e la mantica sibillina', *Rivista dell'Istituto di archeologia e storia d'arte* 14-15: 5-72.

Valenza Mele, N. (1993). 'Napoli', in G. Nenci and G. Vallet (eds.), *Bibliografia topografica della colonizzazione greca in Italia e nelle isole tirreniche*, xii. *Monte Sant'Angelo (1)—Orsomarso*. Pisa: 165-239.

Valeri, C. (2005). Marmora Phlegraea: *Sculture del Rione Terra di Pozzuoli*, Roma.

Valla, L. (1984). *Laurentii Valle Epistole*, ed. Ottavio Besomi et Mariangela Regoliosi, Patavii.

Vallet, G. (1967). 'La Cité et son territoire', *Atti del Convegno di Studi sulla Magna Grecia* 7: 67–142.

Vallet Mascoli, L. (ed.) (1984). *Ferdinand Delamonce: Le Voyage de Naple (1719) de Ferdinand Delamonce*, Naples.

Vasori, O. (1981). 'I monumenti antichi in Italia nei disegni degli Uffizi', *Xenia: Quaderni, 1*, Rome.

Vassallo Zirpoli, E. (2008). 'Trasformazioni e restauri di un'architettura stratificata: Il caso della cattedrale di Napoli', in S. Casiello (ed.), *Verso una storia del restauro: Dall'età classica al primo Ottocento*, Florence: 333–61.

Vecce, C. (1998). *Gli zibaldoni di Iacopo Sannazaro*, Messina.

Vecce, C. (ed.) (2013). *I. Sannazaro, Arcadia*, Rome.

Vecchio, L. (2005). 'La documentazione epigrafica', *Atti dei Convegni di Studio sulla Magna Grecia* 45: 365–422.

Venditti, A. (1966). *Un secolo di storiografia bizantina*, Naples.

Venditti, A. (1967). *Architettura bizantina nell'Italia Meridionale, Campania, Calabria e Lucania*, Naples.

Venditti, A. (1973). 'Problemi di lettura e di interpretazione dell'architettura paleocristiana a Napoli', *Napoli Nobilissima* 12: 177–88.

Ventura, P. (2008). 'Mazzella, Scipione', in *DBI*.

Verdier, P. (1982). 'La Naissance à Rome de la vision de l'Ara Coeli: Un aspect de l'utopie de la paix perpétuelle à travers un thème iconographique', *Mélanges de l'École Française de Rome: Moyen Âge et Temps Modernes* 94/1: 85–119.

Villa, C. (1997). 'Trittico per Federico II *immutator mundi*', *Aevum* 71: 331–57.

Villa, C. (1999). 'Federico II e la "biblioteca" classica dell'aula imperiale', in C. D. Fonseca and R. Crotti (eds.), *Federico II e la civiltà comunale nell'Italia del Nord*, Rome: 447–68.

Villa, C. (2001). *La cultura della Magna Curia e la sua diffusione nel Mediterraneo*, in P. Corrao, M. Gallina, and C. Villa (eds.), *L'Italia mediterranea e gli incontri di civiltà*, Rome and Bari: 171–220.

Violante, F. (2002). 'Federico II e la fondazione dello *Studium* napoletano', *Quaderni medievali* 54: 16–85.

Visceglia, M. A. (1999). *Identità sociali: La nobiltà napoletana nella prima età moderna*, Milan.

Vita, E. (1991). *Il presepio: Ascendenze pagane nel rito cristiano del Natale*, Ravenna.

Vitale, G. (1989). 'Il culto di S. Gennaro a Napoli in età aragonese: Una rilettura delle fonti', *Campania Sacra* 20: 239–67.

Vitale, G. (2003). *Élite Burocratica e famiglia: Dinamiche nobiliari e processi di costruzione statale nella Napoli angioino aragonese*, Naples.

Vitale, G. (2005). 'I bagni a Napoli nel Medioevo tra pratiche igienico-sanitarie, industria, luoghi di piacere', *Archivio Storico per le Province Napoletane* 123: 1–48.

Vitale, G. (2010). 'Vita di Seggio nella Napoli Aragonese', *Archivio Storico per le Province Napoletane* 128: 71–95.

Vitolo, G. (2006). 'Nel laboratorio della storia: I medici di Salerno, le terme di Baia-Pozzuoli e la leggenda virgiliana di Napoli', *Rassegna Storica Salernitana* 46: 43–73.

Vitale, G. (2011). *Tra Napoli e Salerno: La costruzione dell'identità cittadina nel Mezzogiorno medievale*, Salerno.

Vitolo, P. (2008). *La chiesa della Regina: L'Incoronata di Napoli, Giovanna I d'Angiò e Roberto di Oderisio*, Rome.

Vollkommer, R. (1992). 'Mithras', in *LIMC* v/1. 585–626.

Wallace-Hadrill, A. (2008). *Rome's Cultural Revolution*, Cambridge.

Walter, I. (1964). 'Barrili, Giovanni', in *DBI*.

Ward, A. M. (1988). *The Architecture of Ferdinando Sanfelice*, New York and London.

Ward, J. O. (1978). 'From Antiquity to the Renaissance: Glosses and Commentaries on Cicero's *Rhetorica*', in J. J. Murphy (ed.), *Medieval Eloquence: Studies in the Theory and Practice of Medieval Rhetoric*, Berkeley and Los Angeles: 25–67.

Warr, C., and Elliott, J. (eds.) (2010). *Art and Architecture in Naples 1266–1713*, Oxford.

Wegner, M. (1956). *Das römische Herrscherbild: Hadrian, Plotina, Marciana, Matidia, Sabina*, Berlin.

Wegner, M. (1958). *Spolien, Miszellen aus Italien, in Festschrift Martin Wackernagel zum 75 Geburtstag*, Cologne.

Wegner, M. (1966). *Das römische Herrscherbild. Die Flavier: Vespasian, Titus, Domitian, Nerva, Julia Titi, Domitilla, Domitia*, Berlin.

Weiland, L. (1893). *Constitutiones et acta publica imperatorum et regum*, Hanover.

Weiss, C. (1984). *Griechische Flußgottheiten in vorhellenistischer Zeit*, Würzburg.

Weiss, C. (1988). 'Fluvii', *LIMC* iv/1: 139–48.

Weiss, R. (1950). 'The Translators from the Greek of the Angevin Court of Naples', *Rinascimento* 1: 195–226.

Weiss, R. (1969). *The Renaissance Discovery of Classical Antiquity*, Oxford.

Widman, C. (2004). *La simbologia del presepe*, Rome.

Willemsen, C. A. (1953). *Kaiser Friedrichs II. Triumphtor zu Capua: Ein Denkmal Hohenstaufischer Kunst in Süditalien*, Wiesbaden.

Winkelmann, E. (1880). *Über die ersten Staats-universitäten*, Heidelberg.

Winn, C. H. (2005). 'Introduction', in S. de Vallambert, *Cinq livres, de la manière de nourrir et gouverner les enfans dès leur naissance* (*Paris 1565*), critical edn. by Colette H. Winn, Geneva: 1–73.

Wiseman, T. P. (1995). *Remus: A Roman Myth*, Cambridge.

Woolf, G. (1994). 'Becoming Roman, Staying Greek: Culture, Identity and the Civilising Process in the Roman East', *Proceedings of the Cambridge Philological Society* 40: 116–43.

Woolf, G. (1996). 'Monumental Writing and the Expansion of Roman Society in the Early Empire', *Journal of Roman Studies* 86: 22–39.

Woolf, S. J. (1979). *A History of Italy, 1700–1860: The Social Constraints of Political Change*, London.

Worstbrock, F. J. (1989). 'Die Anfänge der mittelalterlichen Ars dictandi', *Frühmittelalterliche Studien* 23: 1–42.

Worstbrock, F. J., Klaes, M., and Lutten, J. (1992). *Repertorium der Artes dictandi des Mittelalters. I. Von den Anfängen bis um 1200*, Munich.

Wurm, H. (1984). *Baldassarre Peruzzi Architekturzeichnungen: Tafelnband*, Tübingen.

Zanker, P. (1988). *The Power of Images in the Age of Augustus*, Ann Arbor, MI.

Zevi, F. (2003). 'Le rassegne archeologiche: La Campania', *Atti dei Convegni di Studio sulla Magna Grecia* 43: 853–924.

Zevi, F., and Cavalieri Manasse, G. (2005). 'Il tempio cosiddetto di Augusto a Pozzuoli', in X. Lafon and G. Sauron (eds.), *Théorie et pratique de l'architecture romaine, la norme et l'expérimentation: Études offertes à Pierre Gros*, Aix en Provence: 269–94.

Ziebarth, E. (1905). 'De antiquissimis inscriptionum syllogis', *Ephemeris Epigraphica* 9/2: 187–332.

Zinsmaier, P. (1983). *Die Regesten des Kaiserreichs unter Philipp, Otto IV, Friedrich II, Heinrich (VII), Conrad IV, Heinrich Raspe, Wilhelm und Richard 1198–1272: Nachträge und Ergänzungen*, Cologne and Vienna.

Ziolkowski, J. M., and Putnam, M. C. J. (eds.) (2008). *The Virgilian Tradition: The First Fifteen Hundred Years*, New Haven and London.

Zucker, P. (1968). *Fascination of Decay. Ruins: Relic—Symbol—Ornament*, Ridgewood, NJ.

Index

Accademia Pontaniana 171–3, 178–9, 186–7, 223, 236–7, 289
Accademia Vitruviana 250
Accademia Ercolanese 278
Acheloos 43, 318
Ager Campanus 61–2, 86, 194
Alberti, Leandro 236–9
Alberti, Leon Battista 261
Alfonso of Aragon ('the Magnanimous') 114, 171–2, 178, 195–7, 200, 207, 210, 212, 247–8
Alfonso II of Aragon 193, 197, 200–2
Antiochus of Syracuse 20, 113
Apollo 7, 32, 48–9, 52, 56, 59–62, 70, 124, 137, 147, 184, 225, 297, 301
Aqueducts
Bolla 9, 114, 195–205, 216
Serino 195–205, 210, 216, 293
Archias 77, 82, 92
Aristotle 155–7
Artemis 48, 60–2, 75–6
Athens 20, 23–5, 29–30, 60, 71, 78, 93, 97–8, 276, 282
Augustus 7–8, 23–4, 31–4, 46–7, 53, 55, 60, 62–3, 69–72, 76–80, 83, 87, 97, 103, 107, 126–7, 129–131, 134, 136–8, 140, 142, 146–7, 158, 171, 195, 198, 207, 210, 298

Beccadelli, Antonio ('il Panormita') 11, 171–2, 176, 179–80, 186, 222–3, 247
Belisarius 9, 110–15, 195
Bellavista 281
Benevento 50, 69, 116, 142, 146, 163, 213, 278
Berlusconi, Silvio 303, 306
Boethius 9, 106, 109
Bolla see Aqueducts
boule 62, 74, 94–95
Bourbon dynasty 3, 264, 269, 275, 279, 282, 311
Byzantium 11–12, 114, 278

Calabria 108, 193–4, 200–201, 210
Calderini, Domizio 177, 183–7

Capa di Napoli (sculpture) 122, 150–1
Capaccio, Giulio Cesare 240
Capasso, Bartolomeo 312
Cape Athenaion 29
Capua 24, 30–1, 59, 61–2, 67, 106–7, 143, 145–6, 148, 152, 168, 172
Caracalla 87, 131, 136
Caracciolo-Carafa, Bartolomeo 5
Carafa, Carlo 148
Carafa, Diomede 122, 147–9, 190–1
Carafa, Gian Pietro 13
Carafa, Oliviero 13, 213–14, 246
Cassiodorus 9, 107–10
Castellammare di Stabia 278
catacombs 12, 195, 213–14, 314
Celano, Carlo 41, 137, 200, 240
Certosa di S. Martino 290, 312, 315
Chalcidians 20, 23–4, 30, 35
Charles I of Anjou 153
Cicero 32, 90, 159, 164, 182, 237
Claudius (emperor) 77, 96, 100, 195, 198
Cocceius, Lucius Auctus (see Crypta Neapolitana) 34, 206, 209, 210
Constantine, emperor 123, 126, 254, 258
Corpo di Napoli (sculpture) 1–2, 122, 151
Cortàzar, Julio 320
Counter-Reformation, the 245, 256, 264
Cripta dei Vescovi 213–14, 219
Cronaca di Partenope 5, 149, 166, 211, 221, 246–7, 249, 251
Crypt of Sejanus ('Grotta di Seiano') 5, 34, 207, 210
Crypta Neapolitana 5, 193, 208–9, 215–16, 284, 314
Cuma (Cumae) 22–7, 29–30, 34–5, 47–8, 52, 58–9, 106, 135, 137–8, 206–7, 237, 267, 282
Cumaean sibyl 5, 52, 158

de Columnis, Guido 158–9
De Filippo, Edoardo 115, 295, 302, 305
de Jorio, Andrea 13–14, 266–83
De Simone, Roberto 117, 300
De Stefano, Pietro 232–3, 239–40, 256
Dicaearchia see Pozzuoli

di Giorgio, Francesco 199–202,
    205–6, 299
Dioscuri, temple of the 5, 7, 13, 39–63,
    67–70, 72, 122, 136–7, 150, 242–3,
    245–8, 250, 257, 261–2, 264–5, 299
Diotimos 7, 60, 76, 78

earthquakes 39, 69, 97, 99, 189–90, 242,
    262–3, 305–6, 314
ephebeia 20, 76, 79, 91–2, 102
Etruscans 23, 36, 64, 266–7, 277, 289

Facio, Bartolomeo 171, 178, 195, 196
Florence 177, 277, 299
florilegia 161–2, 164
Fontana, Domenico 260
Fuscano, Ioan Berardino 225–6

Gennaro, Saint 212–14, 216, 294, 302
Giocondo, Fra 190, 192–3, 199–202,
    205, 210, 245, 247
Giordano, Fabio 67, 129, 132, 140, 149
Giordano, Luca 287
Gomorra 319
Gothic War 9, 105–17, 121, 130

Herculaneum 2, 14, 142, 173, 268–9,
    271, 275, 277–8, 281, 285, 297
Hercules 130, 147, 174, 217
hybridity 15, 72, 318–19

Justinian 9, 110, 112, 136, 156

Lafréry, Antoine 234–5
lazzaroni 273
Leone, Ambrogio 148, 150, 194, 198–9,
    208–9, 212, 237
Lombard dynasty 116, 199, 201, 213,
    234, 279
Lucan 158, 182
Lucullus, villa of 5, 135, 237
Lutatius Catulus 25–6, 28, 30, 58–9
Lycophron 25, 48, 59–60, 78, 318

Maio, Giuniano 179–3, 185–7, 191
Manfred of Swabia 10, 153–7, 162,
    166–7
Mazzella, Scipione 220, 239–40
Medici, Lorenzo de 185, 192, 277
memory 3, 6–9, 15, 25, 64–7, 71–3,
    79–84, 100, 104–6, 114, 123, 137,
    143, 146, 150, 164, 168, 174–5,

177–8, 185, 188, 255, 258, 264,
    303, 319
Mergellina 215, 223, 225–7, 229, 234
Metro, the 15, 70–1, 98, 314–17, 319–21
Milan 116, 187
mirabilia 14, 210
Miseno 140, 195, 205
Mithras 193, 210
museums 7, 14, 131, 141, 267, 311–16
    See also National Archaeological
    Museum

Naples, topographical references
    Castles
    Castel Capuano 15, 193, 201, 210, 313
    Castel dell'Ovo 166
    Castel Nuovo 202, 247–8, 315
    Churches
    Chiesa del Gesù Nuovo 128, 286
    Chiesa del Salvatore 135
    Pietrasanta basilica 122–3, 132, 134
    S. Agostino alla Zecca 122, 142
    S. Aniello a Caponapoli 313
    S. Chiara 122, 142–3, 247, 314
    S. Eligio Maggiore 122, 146–8
    SS. Filippo e Giacomo 287
    S. Gaetano 263
    S. Gennaro extra Moenia 136,
        212–14, 216, 246
    S. Giorgio Maggiore 122–3,
        128–30, 255
    S. Giovanni a Carbonara 287
    S. Giovanni a Mare 138–40
    S. Giovanni in Fonte 124
    S. Giovanni Maggiore 122, 123,
        132, 144
    S. Gregorio Armeno 67
    S. Lorenzo Fuori le Mura 246
    S. Lorenzo Maggiore 55, 67–9, 122,
        140–2, 292, 314
    S. Maria della Rotonda 122–3, 126–7
    S. Maria delle Anime del Purgatorio
        ad Arco 128
    S. Maria dell'Itra 211, 284
    S. Maria del Parto 214–16, 224,
        234, 289
    S. Maria di Piedigrotta 241
    S. Maria Donnaregina Nuova 68, 71
    S. Maria Incoronata 142–4
    S. Paolo Maggiore 7, 13, 39–41, 43,
        67–9, 122, 136–7, 242–65, 286, 299
    See also Dioscuri, temple of

S. Restituta 122–4, 126–8, 130, 136, 141
Stefania basilica 122–3, 125, 127–8, 130, 142–3
Monumental Gates
Porta Capuana 201
Porta S. Sofia 195
Piazzas
Piazza del Gesù 190
Piazza Garibaldi 317
Piazza Giovanni Bovio 122, 136
Piazza Municipio 71, 143
Piazza Nicola Amore 68, 70, 79–80, 98, 101, 122, 315
Piazzetta Nilo 1, 2, 122
Streets
Corso Umberto I (the 'Rettifilo') 313
Via Anticaglia 121
Via dei Tribunali 67, 70, 121, 200
Via del Duomo 67
Via Foria 81, 287
Via Litoranea 136
Via Mezzocannone 126
Via Nilo 222
Via Paladino 194
Via Putoleana 207, 223
Via S. Biagio del Librai 121, 190
Via S. Gregorio Armeno 14–15, 67–8, 71, 284, 292–3, 296, 303–5
Via Toledo 234
Vico Figurari 292
Vicolo delle Serpe 314
Palazzi
Palazzo Carlo Carafa 122, 194
Palazzo Corigliano 67–8, 71
Palazzo dell'Arco 222, 231
Palazzo di Capodimonte 266, 313
Palazzo Diomede Carafa 122, 147, 149, 191
Palazzo Serra di Cassano 218
Villa Antiniana 223
see aqueducts, catacombs, Cripta dei Vescovi, Crypta Neapolitana, Crypt of Sejanus, Lucullus (villa of), Metro, Pappacoda chapel, Pizzofalcone, Platamone, Poggioreale, Posillipo, Pozzuoli, Succorpo of S. Gennaro
National Archaeological Museum 7, 131, 193, 312–16
nativity *see presepe*
Nicolini, Fausto 290

Nola (city) 35–6, 86, 106, 126, 135, 143, 148, 150, 194–5, 198, 204, 208–9, 212, 258
Nola, Giovanni da 215, 289–90, 299–300

oracles 49, 52, 60
Ortelius, Abraham 227, 238
Ovid 37, 159–60, 318

Paestum 137, 141–2, 291, 297, 312
Palaepolis 4, 27–8, 31, 115
Pappacoda chapel 122, 145–6
Paris 42, 46, 48, 155–7, 320
Parrhasius 186–8, 232
Parthenope (Siren) 9, 15, 20–21, 26, 30, 45–6, 56, 58–60, 67, 72, 77–8, 82, 97–8, 135, 147, 151, 184, 251, 258, 317–21
Parthenope (toponym) 5–8, 22–30, 37, 46–8, 52, 56, 58–60, 105, 108, 131, 150, 168, 175–6, 180–2, 246, 249, 317–21
Pelagon 40, 70, 251
Peter, Saint 243, 251–3, 259–60, 262, 287, 299
Petrarch 12, 143, 166, 204, 211, 218–19, 221–2, 238, 244–5
Phaleron 24–5
Philargyrius 58
Philodemus 37, 281–2
Philostratus the Elder 32–2
Phlegraean fields 10, 34–5, 130–1, 135, 139–40, 143, 205–7, 210, 311
phratries 8, 20, 61, 75–6, 79, 82, 91–2, 97, 102–3
Piedigrotta 219–20, 223, 225–6, 237, 251
Pighius, Stephanus Winandus 42, 28–9, 52, 217–18, 227–8, 236, 239–40, 250
Pithecussae (Ischia) 20, 23–4, 30
Pizzofalcone 6, 22, 45–6
plague 26, 59, 63, 109, 245, 281
Platamone (caves of) 210, 216
Poggioreale 201–2, 226, 314
Pollius Felix 182–3
Pompeii 2–3, 14, 51, 69, 135–6, 202, 204, 267–9, 275, 278–9, 285, 297, 302
Pontano, Giovanni 11, 114, 171–3, 178–80, 186, 190, 197–200, 202–11, 222–3, 225–6, 229, 231–2, 234, 236
porosity 34–5, 205–6, 214

Posillipo (Pausilypon) 5, 34, 36, 174,
    194, 207, 211, 219–221, 223, 225–7,
    229, 237, 314
Pozzuoli (Puteoli, Dicaearchia) 107,
    126, 130, 137, 139, 165–6, 174, 183,
    190, 192–3, 198, 205, 207, 209–10,
    220, 223, 226, 231, 237, 239, 267
presepe 14–15, 215–16, 234, 284–308
Procopius 9, 106–15
Proserpina 145, 318
Puteoli *see* Pozzuoli

Quodvultdeus 107

Ravenna 51, 108, 110, 112
Real Museo Borbonico 266–8, 312
Reformation, the 13, 245, 260
relics 212–14, 304
Rhegium 92
Risorgimento, the 274, 277–9
Robert of Anjou 166, 218, 221, 246
Rome 8–10, 21, 27–8, 31, 36, 41, 47, 50,
    54, 57, 59, 61–5, 69–71, 77, 82,
    86–9, 91, 94, 100–1, 104, 108, 110,
    112, 116, 123, 125–6, 128, 130–1,
    134, 137, 139–40, 147, 172, 174,
    177, 184, 186–7, 199, 234–5, 243–6,
    250–1, 254–5, 259–60, 265, 269,
    274, 277–80, 288, 297, 316, 318
Romulus Augustulus 9
ruins 5, 14, 39, 124, 126, 129, 137, 139,
    141, 143, 147, 150, 190, 200, 204,
    207, 210, 243, 259, 284–308, 319

Salerno 139, 141–3, 154, 167–8, 199, 312
Samnites 24, 27–8, 30–1, 36, 61, 86
Sanfelice, Ferdinando 264
Sangallo, Giuliano da 192, 205, 247
Sannazaro, Jacopo 11–12, 171–3, 178,
    186, 202–5, 210–11, 215, 223–9,
    231–4, 236–7, 240
Sansovino, Francesco 203, 238
Sarnelli, Pompeo 224, 240
Scipio Africanus 82, 192
Sebasta (Augustalia) games 7–8, 31, 33,
    60, 76, 78, 80, 85–6, 95–103, 130
Sebethos (Sebeto) river 7, 29, 36, 45–6,
    137, 195, 202, 204–5
Seggi 192, 230, 257–8, 264

Seneca 160, 163, 207
Serino *see* aqueducts
Sessa Aurunca 127, 140, 193
Sidonius Apollinaris 9, 106, 176
Sorrento 29, 140, 174, 182, 228, 258
spolia 4, 9–10, 121–51, 164, 222, 284
Statius 11, 24–5, 32, 37, 48, 52, 61, 77,
    81–2, 92, 97, 170–88, 204, 311, 319
Strabo 6, 8, 19–38, 48, 52, 58, 62, 64–5,
    67, 70, 72, 75–8, 81–3, 91–3, 98,
    100, 102, 182, 206–7, 209, 237, 318
Succorpo of S. Gennaro 213–14, 216,
    246, 260
Suetonius 32, 230
Summonte, Pietro 41–2, 45, 48–50, 147,
    190, 194, 197–8, 201, 249–51,
    257–60
Syracuse 24, 35, 108, 110, 212

Tacitus 32, 64–5
Tarcagnota, Giovanni 233–4, 239
Tarentum 32, 92
Tarsos, Tiberius Julius 5, 40, 69–70, 243,
    245, 251
Terence 270
Theatine Order 13, 242–65, 299
Thiene, Gaetano 244, 261, 299
Tiberius (emperor) 47, 54, 62–3
Totò 115, 295, 302, 305
Toulouse 171, 175–6
Troisi, Massimo 302
Tyfernus, Agustinus 210, 247–9, 255

Vatican, the 259, 307
Venice 187, 244, 250, 278
Verona 163, 190, 192, 199
Vespasian 147, 149, 191, 279
Vesuvius 35, 108, 115, 165, 198, 228,
    302, 307, 312
Virgil 3–5, 9–12, 26, 35–8, 48, 52, 58,
    105, 116–17, 152–5, 164–8, 171–88,
    202, 204, 210–11, 215–16, 218–21,
    223, 225–9, 232–4, 237–8, 240–1,
    282–4, 311
    tomb of 5, 12, 38, 165, 170, 210–11,
    215, 219, 221, 223, 229, 241

Winkelmann, Johann Joachim 14, 269,
    276–7